POWER AND PEACE

THE DIPLOMACY OF JOHN FOSTER DULLES

Frederick W. Marks III

PRAEGER

Westport, Connecticut
London

Library of Congress Cataloging-in-Publication Data

Marks, Frederick W.
    Power and peace : the diplomacy of John Foster Dulles / Frederick
W. Marks III.
        p.   cm.
    Includes bibliographical references and index.
    ISBN 0–275–94497–2 (alk. paper)
    1. United States—Foreign relations—1953–1961. 2. United States—
Foreign relations—Soviet Union. 3. Soviet Union—Foreign
relations—United States. 4. Dulles, John Foster, 1888–1959.
5. Cold War.   I. Title.
E835.M328   1993
327.73′009′045—dc20   92–42442

British Library Cataloguing in Publication Data is available.

Library of Congress Catalog Card Number: 92–42442
ISBN: 0–275–94497–2

First published in 1993

Praeger Publishers, 88 Post Road West, Westport, CT 06881
An imprint of Greenwood Publishing Group, Inc.

Printed in the United States of America

The paper used in this book complies with the
Permanent Paper Standard issued by the National
Information Standards Organization (Z39.48–1984).

10 9 8 7 6 5 4 3 2 1

Copyright Acknowledgments

Portions of certain chapters have been included by permission of the *Pacific
Historical Review, Diplomatic History,* and the *Tamkang Journal of American
Studies.* Permission to quote and cite from various collections was granted by the
Princeton University Libraries, the Dwight D. Eisenhower Library, the
University of Birmingham Library (for the Avon Papers), Columbia University
Library (for the Wellington Koo Papers), Columbia University Oral History
Research Office, and the Richard B. Russell Memorial Library at the University of
Georgia (for the Russell Papers).

Jacket photo courtesy of Princeton University Archives.

To Mary Anne

Contents

Photo essay follows chapter 4

Prologue

The date was 27 May 1959, the occasion unprecedented. Never before had the funeral of a former secretary of state or foreign minister been attended by such a vast assembly of statesmen and world leaders. Among those paying their respects were Chancellor Adenauer of Germany, Prime Minister Menzies of Australia, and King Baudoin of Belgium, along with the foreign ministers of some fourteen nations including Britain, France, Austria, the Netherlands, Belgium, Italy, Turkey, and Japan. Other dignitaries present included Madame Chiang Kai-shek and UN Secretary General Dag Hammarskjold.

One mourner, however, attracted special attention owing to the totally unexpected nature of his presence. This was Soviet Foreign Minister Andrei Gromyko. John Foster Dulles had been in the van of a world-wide coalition against communism. It was hardly to be expected, therefore, that Moscow would send a high-level representative to attend his obsequies. Yet, as the caisson, drawn by seven white horses, advanced through embassy row on its way to a high grassy knoll in Arlington National Cemetery, the flag of the Soviet mission flew at half-mast and Gromyko rode with others in a mile-long cortege led by two hundred limousines. During the final words of benediction, pronounced over the remains of the man regarded by virtually all listeners as a fallen hero, the Russian minister could be seen standing in solitary revery some distance off beneath a yellowwood tree.[1] Curiously, although Dulles and Gromyko represented nations at diametrically opposite ends of the political spectrum, they were much alike, each in his own way dour, plodding, relentless, and encyclopedic in the sweep of a disciplined mind, each also surprisingly good-humored, albeit reserved.

Not all who met Dulles appreciated his particular brand of Yankee austerity. Few, on the other hand, doubted his ability. As French foreign minister Couve de Murville observed, one might not subscribe to all his policies, but he was "infinitely competent." Well before he took office in 1953, *Pravda* and *Izvestia*, in the company of their satellite counterparts, began hurling abuse. Now, however, such voices were stilled and the Kremlin could manifest its traditional respect for strength. Radio Moscow hailed the former secretary as an "outstanding statesman." Gromyko chose similar words, and First Deputy Premier Anastas Mikoyan remembered the secretary as both "intelligent" and tough-minded while, at the same time, "prepared to change his position." "We like strong men," he added, as opposed to "uncertain ones."[2]

Doubtless, Gromyko could recall numerous instances over the years in which he and his countrymen had attempted to match wits with their principal adversary. Dulles had been among the first to rally support for postwar France and Eastern Europe as well as for South Korea and the Republic of China. In the face of violent Russian opposition, and against daunting odds, he had negotiated a peace treaty with Japan. Neither could Gromyko have forgotten his victorious campaign for German integration into NATO or his eleventh-hour triumph in securing the evacuation of Red Armies from Austria on American terms. Wherever the cause of communism or that of the Soviet Union had foundered, it seemed, there was the name of Dulles writ large, whether in Quemoy, Iran, Guatemala, or Lebanon. He had been the chief architect of ANZUS and SEATO, not to mention bilateral defense pacts linking the United States with the Philippines, South Korea, Taiwan, Turkey, Iran, and Pakistan. He had obtained agreements for military bases in Spain. In fact, almost every time that Soviet leaders had faced rock-like opposition since the end of the war, and particularly since the early 1950s, be it at the microphone or over a green baize table, there had stood the familiar figure with steel-rimmed glasses and aquiline nose, tall, gray, angular, and commanding.[3]

On this twenty-seventh day of May, as a hushed throng stood beside the Arlington gravesite chanting the Lord's Prayer, Gromyko might have reflected on the fact that Dulles continued to demonstrate his diplomatic prowess, even in the hour of death, for the last in a series of Soviet ultimatums had just expired without accomplishing its stated purpose. Dulles had withstood an enormous barrage of propaganda, and in the end, Nikita Khrushchev found it impossible to oust Western troops from Berlin. Then, too, had Gromyko been clairvoyant, he might have foreseen still another cold war victory for which Dulles was to be responsible and which some would regard as his finest hour when it occurred in 1960. This was the extension of the Japanese-American security treaty, accomplished in the face of every threat and blandishment that Moscow could muster. Few words could have been more appropriate, then, than those uttered at the conclusion of the service in Washington's National Cathedral: "Death, where is thy sting . . . grave, where is thy victory?"[4]

Introduction

The purpose of the following essay may be simply stated: it seeks to redress a long-standing imbalance in historical works dealing with the period under review. Dulles has never received as much as half the recognition he deserves for his role in obtaining the Austrian State Treaty or for creating Western European Union even though entire books have been written on these and related subjects. He has been condemned for his alleged effort to involve the United States militarily in Vietnam when in fact the story of Dien Bien Phu contravenes almost all of what passes for historical truth. Likewise in the case of the Suez crisis. Traditionally, it is the rigid side of the secretary that has been featured with little or no attention paid to his flexibility, not to mention his hidden instrumentality in the fostering of Soviet-American détente. In describing the overthrow of the Arbenz regime in Guatemala, much has been made of covert operations directed by the Central Intelligence Agency while the significance of other, more substantive, factors escapes notice. Meanwhile, key Guatemalan sources are either ignored or neglected and Dulles' reputation suffers accordingly. His best-known achievement in the Far East, the Southeast Asia Treaty Organization, comes in for a good deal of criticism without regard to portions of the contextual framework that cast it in a more positive light.[1]

The list could be lengthened. For some reason, Dulles' statecraft has never been treated on a comparative basis in terms of what his predecessors and successors achieved, or failed to achieve. We know little about his image in the eyes of colleagues and fellow diplomats. What I have attempted to do, therefore, in both the opening and closing chapters of *Power and Peace*, is to fill this void, at least partially, by placing the secretary where he is most comprehensible: among his peers.

Next, I have addressed the standard query of who was in charge of policy-making, Eisenhower or Dulles, by ascertaining who shaped decisions day by day and case by case, something critical, it seems to me, for understanding other parts of the record. Almost to a man, statesmen of the period perceived the secretary as preeminent; yet within fifteen years of his death, most commentators were boosting the president. Thus it happens that for every historian who has regarded Dulles as the prime mover there is another who would give the palm to Eisenhower. Both men were powerful personalities, each in his own right capable of managing foreign affairs; hence an important element of collaboration may be taken for granted. However, this begs the question of where, and on what issues, the principals differed and whose view prevailed in which crisis.[2]

Since Dulles' skill as a negotiator puts him in a class by himself, I have tried in chapter 3 to demonstrate how consistently he hewed to the maxim, "you give nothing to get nothing"—six words that encapsulate a world of diplomatic theory and practice. I then proceed to deal with a series of myths that have proven remarkably durable. It would be hard to find anyone, with the possible exception of Theodore Roosevelt, who has been as much caricatured and misunderstood by his own countrymen as Dulles. A fair amount of space is therefore devoted to the winnowing of fact from fiction. Chapter 5 undertakes to examine what Dulles thought of the Soviets and their experiment as compared with what he is generally assumed to have thought. His estimate of Russian goals, along with his perception of strengths and weaknesses on both sides of the Iron Curtain, reveals much about the nature of East-West rivalry just as, on a higher plane, it helps to illumine the dynamic of competition between superpowers of any age. Finally, a companion chapter explores the intellectual side of Dulles, an aspect of his personal makeup which remains surprisingly obscure considering its importance as the foundation upon which he based his policy. Dulles was above all a thinker as few in his position have ever been.[3]

Although a good deal of the factual data that I have presented is fresh, the purpose of this volume is not so much expository as it is analytical. The emphasis throughout has been on raising new questions and wherever possible, furnishing answers to older ones. I hasten to add that there is a good deal of research still to be done and a fair amount of of archival material yet to be opened to the public. *Power and Peace* will have served its purpose, though, if it offers new viewpoints and throws additional light on the events of a complicated period.

I should like to thank those who helped in a special way to make this book possible, among them Marion M. Stewart, archivist in the Manuscript Division of the Public Archives of Canada; Dr. B. S. Benedikz, head of Special Collections at the University of Birmingham, England; John W. Hanes, Jr., of Alexandria, Virginia; James H. Armstrong, Jr., general manager of the Augusta National Golf Club (for a rare opportunity to view the famous "Eisenhower Cabin"); William Joyce, head librarian at Princeton University, as well as Jean Holiday, Ben Primer, and Nancy Bressler at Mudd Manuscript Library (Princeton University); Richard Sommers and Daniel Nettling at the United States Military History Institute (Carlisle Barracks, Pennsylvania); and Kathie Nicastro, Dane Hartgrove, John E. Taylor, and Wil Mahoney at the National Archives. Many were more than generous in granting personal interviews and allowing me to draw upon their rich store of historical experience, among them Lord Home of the Hirsel, Sir William Hayter, Avery Dulles, S. J., Eleanor Lansing Dulles, Mr. and Mrs. William B. Macomber, Jr., and Professor John W. F. Dulles. I should like to extend additional thanks to Thomas B. Lee, director of the Graduate Institute of American Studies at Tamkang University for facilitating access to the files of the Historical Commission of the Kuomintang at Yangmingshan. Dacre P. Cole of the Academic Relations Division of Canada's Department of External Affairs shepherded me through an enormous mass of documentation when the files of his department were in transit. Sandra Veronica Jiménez, head librarian at the Centro de Investigaciones Regionales de Mesoamérica in Antigua, Guatemala, helped me locate key Guatemalan sources bearing on the Liberation movement of June 1954. I am likewise indebted to Virgilio Pacheco, commander of Castillo Armas' second volunteer regiment, for submitting to a lengthy interview in Esquipulas with the aid of a gifted interpreter, Gerardo Louis Simon Waguespack. Brother Robert Hébert of the Abadia de Jesucristo Crucificado in Esquipulas was kind enough to share his impressions of the Arbenz leadership while Bishop Rodolfo Quezada Toruño of Zacapa, Vitalino Gómez of Chiquimula, and Marvin Sosa of Zacapa all met with me on different occasions in Guatemala. Ann Hartness of the University of Texas expedited my use of the university's impressive Latin American newspaper collection. Nancy Bartlett of the Bentley Historical Library extended a helping hand during my work in the Vandenberg Papers. The staff of the Eisenhower Library in Abilene proved most helpful. Lady Avon granted access to the papers of Lord Avon (Anthony Eden), and a number of individuals went out of their way to assist me in my research at the University of Georgia, among them Orlean Castronis, Anne Billups, Sheryl B. Vogt, and James Cross, who came to work on his day off so that I could make maximum use of the Richard B. Russell Papers.

Among those who read the manuscript in its entirety, some held views of the period that differed substantially from my own, but all were willing to offer helpful suggestions. They include Bradford Perkins, Thomas R. Maddux, William Stueck, William Widenor, Gary Ostrower, Robert Maddox, Randall Woods, Michael Guhin, Avery Dulles, S. J., Eleanor Lansing Dulles, and Mr. and Mrs. William B. Macomber, Jr.

Last, but not least, I owe an enormous debt of gratitude to my wife, Sylvia, who not only shared in the work of a research trip to Guatemala, but also read successive drafts of the manuscript and encouraged me to persevere amid trials and difficulties. She knew how to clear the sky and make the sun shine.

POWER AND
PEACE

CHAPTER 1

Dulles in Context

How does one measure greatness in a secretary of state? If fresh initiatives and newly minted ideas were to be the criteria, few if any statesmen would be highly regarded, for in diplomacy, as in law or business, it is management that counts. Vision, ingenuity, and prudence are certainly key requisites, but novelty per se has little place in a field where the patterns are largely derivative. FDR's Good Neighbor Policy rested upon Republican antecedents, and to cite a more recent instance, President Nixon's opening to China was a natural extension of policies set in motion by Dulles.

The cold war was an unprecedented phenomenon for Americans, calling as it did for nothing less than a brand new concept of Washington's place in the world, indeed of the very nature of that world. Under Franklin Roosevelt, the United States had become the most powerful nation on earth, but only after a war costing fifty million lives and a total destruction of the balance of power in both East and West. Directly or indirectly, Uncle Sam dominated most of the globe by 1945, yet he found himself in the unenviable position of having to carry much of it on his Herculean back. The situation confronting Truman was therefore fraught with difficulty, and both he and his successor, Dwight Eisenhower, were faced with a pressing need for adaptation. Moscow and Peking made giant strides in economic and scientific achievement during the 1950s and for the first time since 1812, Americans had to contemplate the possibility of a war that could bring instant devastation to their homeland.

The diplomatic record compiled by Eisenhower and Dulles is well known. It includes a variety of military pacts aimed at restoring the balance of power in Europe and the Far East, along with the Formosa Resolution, the Eisenhower Doctrine, and the Caracas Declaration. Settlements were reached in such vital areas as Austria, Trieste, Cyprus, and the Saar. Thanks to the Wriston reforms, a system already in effect in other major nations facilitated lateral movement between the State Department's foreign and civil service. At the same time, a burst of diplomatic innovation enhanced America's rapport with its neighbors to the north and south. Dulles set a new standard for diplomatic recognition, one which differed from the de facto and de jure yardsticks associated with Jefferson and Wilson. Likewise, the St. Lawrence Seaway, which had defied the political legerdemain of FDR and Truman, became a reality. Truman, who sought a reputation for evenhandedness in the Middle East after his recognition of the state of Israel, had tried in vain to interest Arab leaders in American loans and arms. Here again, Dulles achieved a breakthrough, although with results that have continued to spark debate. Dulles' conception of the United States as a Pacific power was vindicated along with his hopes for the United Nations as a peace-keeping force.[1]

This is not to deny that communism made important inroads in Cuba and that the United States sustained setbacks in Laos and Iraq due, at least in part, to ambivalence and confusion. For every failure, however, there were gains. The International Agency for Peaceful Uses of Outer Space, the UN Atomic Energy Agency for civilian use of nuclear technology, and the first arms-testing moratorium were not major advances, but they were symbolic of a gradually emerging larger picture.

One of the most striking developments of the Eisenhower era was the greatly increased level of peacetime defense spending—approximately three times the outlay under Truman. It is interesting that only three other presidents in the nation's history have operated on the basis of a notably strong defense posture—Theodore Roosevelt, James Monroe, and George Washington—and all three were outstandingly successful in the field of foreign affairs. Eisenhower, who kept a low profile, was shrewd enough to sell his program under the rubric of a "New Look" and "more bang for the buck." Deliberately, he emphasized such elements in his arsenal as the Strategic Air Command with its fleet of B–52 bombers, in preference to more conventional systems geared to the waging of small-scale war. But the latter were by no means neglected. One of his minor coups was to go down in history as a president who reduced military spending by 10 percent, even though such reduction came as part of a normal postwar demobilization, and the capability of the nation to fight any kind of war, limited or unlimited, small or large, conventional or nuclear, was substantially greater in 1958 than it had been on the eve of the Korean conflict as evidenced in part by the extraordinary speed and power with which American marines landed in Lebanon.[2]

To return, though, to the question of greatness in a secretary of state, if one goes by the degree to which the national interest is served, in consonance with traditional ideals and values, it may be fairly said that Dulles maintained a high standard. To be sure, American policy benefited from a sustained interval of prosperity. The mild recessions that occurred did not put an end to high employment, low inflation (much reduced from previous levels), balanced budgets (despite a doubling of social security recipients), increased productivity, and healthy trade balances, along with a record decrease in taxes. Foreign commerce expanded from a volume of $23 billion in 1953 to over $31 billion in 1959, just as American oil production soared as a result of U.S. involvement in Iran and Suez. By 1957, U.S. firms were producing twice as much oil in the Middle East as their British counterparts and they controlled 60 percent of the reserves.[3]

Such opulence laid the groundwork for a sizable defense budget and enabled Congress to vote hefty increases in foreign aid, something which Dulles valued as highly as any fleet of aircraft carriers. Washington was able to effect a doubling of capital at the World Bank, along with a 50 percent increase in the International Monetary Fund. Meanwhile, the awarding of American aid took several new directions. Asia, rather than Europe, and developing, rather than developed, nations tended to be the beneficiaries. The emphasis also shifted from grants to loans and credits, the staple of the Soviet program, and aid commitments were designed to extend beyond the fiscal year so that the United States could compete more successfully with the Kremlin.[4]

Few secretaries of state have compiled a more handsome peace record. With all of his rumbling about "massive retaliation," Dulles did much to facilitate negotiated settlements in Korea and Vietnam. On 10 August 1954, for the first time in more than twenty years, there were no large-scale hostilities anywhere in the world. In addition, the Geneva summit of 1955 and Eisenhower's later meeting with Khrushchev at Camp David ushered in an unprecedented thaw in the cold war which, however fleeting, was nonetheless real. Contrary to the popular impression, Dulles aimed consistently at détente and went far to establish the foundation for future relations with Peking by granting several forms of low-profile recognition. At the same time, his firmness appears to have hastened the coming of the Sino-Soviet split, widely regarded as the premier geopolitical event of the postwar era. Then, too, he was probably the most powerful of all secretaries if one takes into account a combination of length of tenure, technical competence, international prestige, and domestic influence. The *Times* of London aptly dubbed him "the strongest man in the strongest country."[5]

Dulles was always something of an enigma to those who did not know him. As candid as a public figure can afford to be, he was often portrayed as calculating and devious. While conscious of the moral dimension, he could nonetheless be coldly clinical. Willing on occasion to resist powerful tides of opinion as he strove to bend public sentiment to his perception of the needs of the time, he was also reputed to have a set of finely tuned political antennae. He could be taciturn or prolix as the occasion demanded, and although few officials were more sensitive to verbal nuance, he wound up with a reputation for sloganism. Paradoxically, his friends were impressed by his simplicity even as his enemies called him simplistic, and although he exuded a quality of gruffness and struck those around him as absent-minded—to the point of being rude on occasion (he did not suffer fools gladly)—he could radiate considerable charm and display patience under pressure. Part of the reserve in his personal makeup reflected an outlook on life that can only be described as spiritual. It was, of course, hard for observers to believe that he took religion seriously, if for no other reason than because this is not a trait normally associated with the heads of state chancelleries. Yet he is the only church leader ever to become secretary of state and, as we shall observe, his faith as a Presbyterian was not, by any means, hollow.[6]

How is it possible to classify an individual who was at once so rigid and yet so pliable? Extremely earnest and highly persuasive in presenting his point of view, he was apt to dominate a group by the mere fact of his presence at the same time that his plain-spoken conviction laid him open to charges of smugness and intolerance. On the other hand, his son Avery became a Jesuit priest while his sister Eleanor married a Jew, and although he did not approve of either decision, he accepted what he could not change, expressing a belief in the efficacy of the Catholic Mass and participating in interfaith meetings. During the San Francisco Conference of 1945, he sponsored the statement by Protestants, Catholics, and Jews. He also worked closely with the National Conference of Christians and Jews. His father, a man of the cloth, had questioned the Virgin Birth and officiated at the marriage of a divorcée, something that shocked a good many contemporaries, while Dulles himself devoted considerable time during the 1920s to the legal defense of liberal ministers whose right to preach was being challenged by denominational authorities.[7]

Given the scale of the conundrum, one is not surprised to find evaluations ranging from Churchill's "dull and clumsy" to Adenauer's "the greatest man" he had ever known. Bidault's opinion, verging on the negative, must be weighed against more positive accounts rendered by de Gaulle. Naturally, like all statesmen, Dulles tended to draw praise or criticism depending upon the impact of his policies. Thus French Premier René Mayer, who perceived him as *"un grand ami de la France,"* was an admirer and Premier Kishi lauded him as "the man who best understood Japan." The Russians, on the other hand, who were afraid of him if Adenauer and Macmillan are to be credited, kept their thoughts to themselves.[8]

As a rule, controversial figures do not engender neutrality, and Dulles proved no exception. Golda Meir of Israel remembered him as "that cold, gray man" whereas Randolph Churchill insisted that he was "worth five of our so-called statesmen." It is virtually impossible to arrive at an accurate appraisal on the basis of contemporary evaluations. He was as likely as not to leave the impression of rigidity. However, this does not square with his lifelong fascination with the processes of change or with his deep-seated belief in the need for flexibility. Shadings, qualifications, and escape clauses abound in legal documents bearing his name. Significantly, too, he proved himself a master of the joint communiqué, a device commonly used by diplomats to paper over differences, reconcile opposing points of view, and utilize the English language as a form of camouflage.[9]

To pursue the theme of contradiction, Yoshida found him authoritarian and Cadogan of England disdained him early in his career as "the wooliest type of useless pontificating American." Yet Erich Mende, the anti-NATO German parliamentarian, commended him as a good listener and Pineau of France singled him out for his intellectual tolerance. One can go further. France's Bidault recalled a certain headstrong quality and Chamoun of Lebanon stated flatly that Dulles was too much of an idealist to be a good diplomat. Any number of observers vouched for his basic honesty, and he was widely known as a man of his word—Italian diplomat Pietro Quaroni went so far as to call him "the conscience of the West." But to read the memoirs of British Foreign Secretary Herbert Morrison or to scan the diary of French ambassador Hervé Alphand, is to discover an individual who is crafty, even shifty. William Hayter, British ambassador to the Soviet Union, could respect Dulles; however, he found him "impossible" to trust. Finally, while he has been faulted for bearing down too hard on colonialism—Bidault accused him of being "rabid" on the subject—he has also been criticized for precisely the opposite reason.[10]

Opinions rendered by the historical profession are equally hard to reconcile. In the eyes of not a few, he exacerbated the tensions inherent in Soviet-American competition. Others, however, have come to a different conclusion. According to C. M. Woodhouse, the likelihood of world war receded substantially under Dulles, almost to the vanishing point, by virtue of his definition of an acceptable status quo in places like Hungary, Korea, and Berlin. New Delhi and Peking came to a tacit understanding on Tibet in 1954, the United States and the Soviet Union drew lines of demarcation around their vital interests; and after each had tested the resolve of the other, it became evident that neither cared to risk war. Canadian Ambassador Arnold Heeney was among those who noted a lessening of international tension at the time of the Korean armistice, one which lasted until President Kennedy virtually gave up the idea of a modus vivendi with the USSR. Further complicating the historiographical picture, there is a division among writers over such questions as whether or not Dulles should have established SEATO and supported the Baghdad Pact to the extent that he did. In some quarters, he is viewed as a victim of "pactomania" while elsewhere it is thought that he did not go far enough. Waldomar Gallman, after serving as ambassador to Iraq, painted a somber picture of an administration reneging on its commitments to Baghdad and bearing a measure of responsibility for the massacre of the royal family in 1958.[11]

Seasoned observers such as Lord Home (British Commonwealth secretary under Eden and foreign secretary under Macmillan) have remarked that of all Dulles' contributions none was more welcome than his success in redressing the balance of power by means of bilateral and multilateral defense agreements. Three-quarters of the German populace was marshaled on the side of the West by 1955 and, within a year, the northern tier alliance of Turkey, Iran, and Pakistan had sealed off 2500 miles of Soviet border, blocking Communist expansion toward the Persian Gulf. It was also widely assumed at the time that the Caracas Declaration of 1954 and the overthrow of a Communist-dominated regime in Guatemala (for which Caracas provided moral support) were important victories.[12]

The historian is doubly handicapped by a number of gaping holes in the documentation. "Political summaries" filed by the British ambassador in Iran after June 1953 and which preceded the London-sponsored coup against Mossadegh were found to be missing at the Public Record Office. Confidential annexes to British cabinet minutes proved virtually nonexistent, again without explanation, not to mention the many cabinet "conclusions" which had been deleted or marked "closed until the year 2004." Gaps appeared in the Alphand diary, the Wellington Koo papers at Columbia University, and portions of the U.S. Foreign Relations series. Working at the Eisenhower Library at Abilene, Kansas, as well as at Princeton University, one became aware of the disappearance of telephone conversations for critical periods in connection with the mounting crisis in Indochina.[13]

There is, in addition, the coincidental fact that as a consequence of Dulles' untimely death he was unable to take his own part. When Anthony Eden published the first volume of his memoirs, Dulles took a beating while Eisenhower, who was still president at the time, escaped virtually unscathed. Had Dulles lived longer, it might have made a difference in history texts as well as accounts by contemporaries. Eisenhower, when discussing the fall of Dien Bien Phu in his memoirs, presents himself as a figure of statesmanlike caution, something which, as we shall see, is apt to be misleading, even if true. The president likewise takes credit for the decision to hold Quemoy in 1958, and he portrays his secretary as an enthusiastic partner in opposing the ill-planned allied invasion of Suez.[14] Again, as I shall endeavor to demonstrate, the record raises serious questions.

It is well to bear in mind that Ike was not only a master politician adept at covering his tracks and taking a bow for history; he was also president, with all the prestige and perquisites that accompany such an office. Dulles' friends edited a number of commemorative volumes, and several biographies appeared immediately before and after his death. Such literature was but a rivulet, however, by comparison with the great stream of tribute that flowed in Eisenhower's direction. The president himself published several works, including a massive two-volume edition of memoirs. Selections from his diary, along with that of his press secretary, went to the printer, and his brother, Milton, brought out additional works. Among the accounts that found their way into print under the name of the president's lieutenants were those of Sherman Adams, Robert Cutler, Arthur Larson, Admiral Radford, General Ridgway, and Henry Cabot Lodge. Although some who served under Dulles wrote memoirs as well, the impression they left was spotty because the secretary tended to operate behind the scenes. Then, too, where Ike left behind a splendid presidential library staffed by archivists dedicated to the promotion of Eisenhower scholarship, Dulles' friends established the John Foster Dulles Library of Diplomatic History at Princeton (along with a memorial program of scholarship), and there is no comparison between the size of the two research collections or the function of their staffs.[15]

Owing to another accident of history, most accounts written by German and French leaders, many of which give Dulles relatively high grades, have not been translated into English. It is thus the ultracritical British interpretation that has come to be standard fare in America.[16]

One final barrier to an accurate appraisal of Dulles lies in the nature of his work and the style that he brought to it. His straightforward public statements were totally at variance with the wealth of distinctions and qualifications that regularly informed his private thought. When he spoke, he did so with an eye to Congress, and so his words were geared to the shaping of public opinion rather than to an expression of the inner man. Occasionally, too, he spoke as the mouthpiece of America's allies as, for instance, during his press conference of January 1958 when he came out in favor of continued nuclear testing and argued that the United States depended to a greater degree than the Soviet Union on a wide range of sophisticated weapons. According to Dulles, it needed "clean" tactical weapons to fight on the soil of its allies as well as long-range missiles to strike Soviet cities which, unlike many American urban centers, were not vulnerable to seaboard attack. What is interesting is how few were aware at the time that the secretary was personally willing to forego such testing in order to woo world opinion and arrive at a stable long-range peace. He spent untold amounts of time trying to win over the Atomic Energy Commission, the Defense Department, and the president himself. Meanwhile, leaders in Britain and France who were confidentially opposed to a test ban could pay lip service to arms control, secure in the knowledge that Washington would persevere in its opposition.[17]

In dealing with the Soviet Union, Dulles knew that successful bargaining could occur only with an aroused public behind him. Congress had to be willing, if called upon, to support an ambitious foreign aid program along with massive defense expenditures and a bold policy on the ground. In other words, only by ringing all the changes on Communist tactics and steeling domestic opinion to intransigence could he negotiate from a position of strength (and flexibility). Of course, when he overstated his case for effect, and especially when this involved speaking in moral terms and framing his message in the type of colorful, oversimplified prose calculated to move the average man, it frightened his aides who, quite correctly, sensed an opening for the opposition. Reinhold Niebuhr and George Kennan accused him of exaggeration in the use of terms such as "good" and "evil" while another writer scored him for "a remarkable capacity for convincing himself that whatever he did was morally justified." Few, if any, observers were able to penetrate to the inner recesses of his intellect by reading what he wrote to relatives or trusted confidants in an unguarded moment. Thus it is that he remains to this day what he was for the better part of a decade: something of a straw man.[18]

Many of Dulles' critics did not perceive communism as an unqualified threat to American institutions, certainly not to the degree that he did. Some rejected the notion of the world as ipso facto dangerous; others tended to regard institutional religion as more of a menace than atheism. Such groups would have been inconsistent had they not concluded that the United States should scale down its defense budget and take far less alarm at the advance of Communist-controlled movements around the world.

Another assumption frequently made was that if the United States were to shuck off its role as an opponent of Soviet aggrandizement, other nations would step into the breach. George Kennan, one of the better known exponents of this school of thought, favored a neutral Germany even though this meant that the great preponderance of Germans, along with their considerable industrial capacity, would be lost to the West. Kennan pressed not only for Red China's unconditional admission to the United Nations, but also for unilateral restraint in the testing of atomic weapons and the abandonment of Quemoy. He would have refrained from installing nuclear weapons systems in Europe; his program of arms control called for trust in Soviet promises; and he was more optimistic than most that a satisfactory inspection system could he worked out in the short run. Not surprisingly, he questioned Dulles' approach to the liberation of Communist satellites, objecting to what he regarded as an overtone of violence. A stable Europe, in Kennan's opinion, did not require the presence of American and British forces nor did the balance of power depend upon defense pacts.[19]

Needless to say, such views were never mainstream, even within the Democratic party, and not long after Dean Acheson became secretary of state, Kennan resigned as head of policy-planning.

For those seriously interested in understanding what made Dulles tick, there is no better place to begin than with the unique set of circumstances that set him on the road to Washington. As a youngster, he came to know two secretaries of state, one of them his grandfather John Watson Foster, who served under President Harrison and eventually became the dean of American diplomats; the other, his uncle Robert Lansing, who would be chosen for the top cabinet post by President Wilson. Extensive travel and language study afforded additional breadth of background, and he was fortunate while at Princeton to be selected as a French-speaking translator for the Chinese delegation to the Second Hague Peace Conference.

After graduating from college with highest honors, he enrolled for a year at the Sorbonne, followed by six weeks in Madrid, where he boarded with a family that spoke only Spanish. Bright enough to complete three years of law school in two at George Washington University, he broke all records with his grade point average. He then began as an attorney with Sullivan and Cromwell, agreeing to represent the State Department, as well as his own firm, on diplomatic missions to Central America and the Caribbean. During World War I, as assistant to the chairman of the War Trade Board, he negotiated to acquire foreign steamships for the war effort and, in so doing, devised a legal argument for appropriating eighty-seven Dutch vessels without compromising Dutch neutrality. After writing Wilson's statement on the subject, drafting the president's reply to a Dutch protest, and acting as liaison between the Trade Board and the chiefs of staff, he became legal adviser to the American delegation on the Paris Reparations Commission. Delegation chairman Bernard Baruch referred to him as "indispensable," and when Baruch left Paris, he put his able protégé in charge. Dulles then formulated the American plan for reparations, defended it in debate, and participated in the drafting of relevant sections of the treaty. Finally, at Wilson's urgent request, he remained in Paris to function as economic and financial adviser for the negotiation of treaties with Austria and Belgium.[20]

Within two decades, he had reached the pinnacle of his profession, but hardly a moment passed when he was not thinking or writing about diplomacy. He became a founding member of the Council on Foreign Relations, indeed an article that appeared under his name in the first issue of its prestigious journal, *Foreign Affairs*, was read and underlined by Lenin. By 1924, he was serving as counselor to many foreign nations and overseas firms, as well as foreign policy adviser to the Democratic presidential nominee, and some years later, as a member of the Federal Council of Churches, he began devoting an extraordinary amount of time to church-related activities focused on the study of war and peace. In 1941, he scored the Atlantic Charter for not proposing a successor to the League, and the pamphlet, "Six Pillars of Peace," for which he was largely responsible and which was circulated by the Federal Council, inaugurated a four-year campaign to mobilize support for a United Nations. In addition to holding seminars at his home in Cold Spring Harbor, he chaired national study conferences involving hundreds of delegates just as he traversed the country conducting "missions" on world order. Following the earlier Dumbarton Oaks Conference in Washington, he capped his effort by charging the administration with ignoring the rights of smaller nations.[21]

Such activity was not confined to barnstorming for an organization to replace the League of Nations, even though Dulles did as much as anyone to challenge FDR's scheme for a world run by Four Policemen. By the time he became secretary of state, his corpus of writing on world affairs included two books, twenty-two pamphlets, sixty-two position papers, ninety-five articles, and eight review articles. He had issued twelve press releases, held thirteen press conferences, granted twenty-nine interviews, and delivered 197 speeches. Among his radio interviews were eight for ABC, nine for NBC, and eleven for CBS. In addition, he had been interviewed by newspapers ranging from *La Prensa* of Buenos Aires to *Kathemeri* of Athens. He had addressed Britain's House of Commons, spoken over the BBC, and lectured at the Sorbonne. Other speaking engagements took him to Toronto, Manila, Seoul, Tokyo, Sydney, and Canberra. Republican leaders Dewey and Vandenberg retained him as a diplomatic adviser, as did four Democratic secretaries of state: Hull, Byrnes, Marshall, and Acheson.[22]

This, in itself, would have been more than enough to qualify him for the part he was to play in Eisenhower's cabinet, but his experience was not confined to what he wrote and said. It included participation in ten major international conferences, attendance at numerous sessions of the Council of Foreign Ministers, and leadership of the American delegation to the United Nations. Nor is this yet the full story. Personally responsible for many clauses in the UN charter, he obtained a decision to aid Korea under the "Uniting for Peace" resolution, and before this he had been a prime mover in the movement to gain international support for Israel. Prior to 1953, he had served an abbreviated term in the Senate, making a strong but unsuccessful bid for reelection. Besides heading the Carnegie Endowment for International Peace and the Rockefeller Foundation, he had testified at length before House and Senate foreign affairs committees and established himself as one of the architects of NATO. Dulles wore many hats. In conjunction with FDR, Hull, Vandenberg, and Dewey, he had been an originator and leading proponent of "bipartisanship," one of the hallmarks of postwar American foreign policy. At the same time, he pioneered in European integration and the internationalization of the Ruhr while figuring as a key personality in the founding of the World Council of Churches.[23]

In short, Dulles was something of a fixture on the national and international scene well before 1953, and it would be difficult to evaluate his record as secretary of state without first considering some of the achievements of the Truman administration under which he served in various capacities and upon which he was obliged to build.

As occupants of the Oval Office, Harry S. Truman and Dwight D. Eisenhower had much in common in terms of the task that lay before them. Both had to lead a nation woefully lacking in cosmopolitan instinct. As late as 1957, *Time* magazine was still pandering to the popular taste for ethnocentric journalism when it characterized Laotians as "unwarlike" and "hedonistic." In the same vein, Sam Rayburn, speaker of the House for most of the period

1940–60, liked to boast of never having set foot on foreign soil. Parochialism was as much a part of the times as the Communist bid for world power, and as much a connecting link between presidencies. Truman, as mentioned earlier, needed to recognize the situation for what it was and alter America's relationship with Russia from wartime ally to that of peacetime competitor. Events were moving rapidly. Whereas in 1939 there had been six or eight first-class powers ranged in relative balance, now there were only two, and it was up to the United States to shed the accumulated weight of over a century of self-imposed isolationism if it wished to prevent Moscow from becoming the arbiter of Europe and the Far East. To be sure, Truman did not have to deal with Soviet economic and scientific feats to the same extent as Eisenhower. Nevertheless, it was widely appreciated that Soviet armies had furnished the lion's share of the victory against Nazi Germany, and this was challenge enough.[24]

With this in mind, it may be fairly said that the haberdasher from Missouri left behind a remarkable legacy. His Marshall Plan, along with the Point Four Program and special aid packages to Greece and Turkey, established a precedent for the use of American power to halt the spread of communism. The Rio Pact, another milestone, cemented a hemispheric agreement on joint defense just as it helped to multilateralize the Monroe Doctrine and served as model for the North Atlantic Treaty Organization. NATO itself laid the groundwork for a new European balance of power, although it did not progress much beyond the planning stage until Dulles and Eisenhower opened the way to German membership. The Truman Doctrine, still another major departure, proved something of a mixed blessing despite its obvious merits for, on the one hand, it broadened the concept of America's overseas mission and conditioned Americans to accept the idea of global responsibility by pledging support for "free peoples" resisting "attempted subjugation by armed minorities or by outside pressures." On the other hand, it was couched in terms of freedom, rather than the balance of power, and as such it lacked ballast. Within a few years, John F. Kennedy would promise to "pay any price, bear any burden, meet any hardship, support any friend, oppose any foe to assure the survival and the success of liberty."[25]

A century and a half earlier, John Quincy Adams had described the policy of his native land rather differently: "Wherever the standard of freedom and independence has been or shall be unfurled, there will her heart, her benedictions, and her prayers be. But she goes not abroad in search of monsters to destroy. She is the well-wisher to the freedom and independence of all. She is the champion and vindicator only of her own." At some point along the line, the thought of Adams intersects with that of Kennedy, and it is here that the national interest lies. But Truman, perhaps because he sought to wean Americans from a long-standing aloofness, did little to clarify matters in this regard. Doubtless, too, as a dynamic leader, he knew that the best way, sometimes the only way, to move a nation is by invoking the moral

imperative. Senator Vandenberg told him frankly that if he wanted to intervene in remote regions he would have to "scare hell" out of the American
people, and this is precisely what he and his successors did. Unfortunately,
language that blurs important distinctions can also blur a nation's sense of
perspective. Civil liberties for the people of Greece was not the paramount
issue for Washington; yet the impression that it was would remain deeply
etched on the minds of the nation's lawmakers. The stage was thus set for
political dissemblers such as Castro of Cuba and Khomeini of Iran to garner
American support merely by promising greater freedom and trading on the
image of their rivals as "repressive."[26]

It is curious that Dulles should be the one normally associated with the
term "brinkmanship" when in fact Soviet-American cooperation ground to
a halt years before he took office. Truman went to the brink over situations
in Trieste, Greece, Turkey, and Iran, not to mention Berlin where an airlift
kept Americans on the edge of their seats for nearly a year. In 1949, the
Palais Rose Conference failed to produce so much as an agenda for a four-
power meeting. Truman was also the first to go beyond the brink—in Korea.
Clearly, references to "brinkmanship" apply more to the level of rhetorical
flourish than they do to substance. Equally curious is the standard notion
of Eisenhower as father of the "domino theory" when it can be shown that
such phraseology was pressed into service earlier to justify the Truman
Doctrine.[27]

"Rollback" is another slogan that has come to be linked exclusively with
the name Dulles, and again without justification. Truman, it is true, spoke
in rather modest terms when he vowed to "contain" the Soviet Union. But
rhetoric is one thing, reality another. A top-secret NSC memorandum dated
13 December 1949 defined American policy toward Communist satellites as
one of undermining Soviet control, and in 1951 an NSC subcommittee was
established to take the offensive in psychological warfare. In addition to
committing substantial sums to the support of French forces fighting communism in Indochina, Truman was the first president to approve CIA blueprints for the overthrow of Guatemala's Arbenz. Such plans, when they came
to light, were quickly shelved in order to placate an irate secretary of state
who was kept totally in the dark. Nevertheless, when Guatemala refused to
sign the Rio Pact, Truman imposed an arms embargo, and after Somoza of
Nicaragua launched "Operation Fortune" to bring Arbenz down, the White
House gave positive encouragement and material aid through the CIA. A
United Fruit Company vessel carried American arms to Guatemalan exiles
while Trujillo of the Dominican Republic and Pérez Jiménez of Venezuela
furnished cash. It was also under Truman that émigrés were landed by sea
and air in such places as Lithuania, Poland, and Ukraine. Additional landings
were attempted in Albania, again without success, but this did not deter
CIA operatives from extending the field of covert action. Few stones were
left unturned. George Kennan, diplomatic adviser to Truman and father of

the containment theory, was on the mark in 1954 when he said, "We are all in favor of 'liberation.'" Liberation and containment were two sides of the same coin.[28]

What happened is that Republicans, thirsty for power, decided to base their 1952 campaign on the allegation that Truman had been soft on communism. Americans, they declared, should attempt to roll communism back instead of seeking merely to contain it. It was a typical campaign year oversimplification, and when Dulles arrived at State, his Democratic friends were quick to reciprocate, drawing some rather neat political cartoons of their own. Among the targets were such phrases as "massive retaliation," "agonizing reappraisal," and "rollback."

It should be added that containment, as a term to describe America's stance vis-à-vis communism, was not the only portion of the Truman legacy regarded by Republicans as burdensome. The war in Korea had been unauthorized by Congress and, along with the secrecy associated with presidential commitments at Teheran, Yalta, and Potsdam, it triggered demands for the curbing of executive prerogative. Truman had no sooner denied entering into clandestine agreements at Potsdam than the media uncovered evidence of his promise to seek a new status for the Dardanelles. Declared the *Washington Post* in May 1953: "The American people are averse to any further exhibitions of personal diplomacy." Little did Dulles know when he backed the Bricker Amendment, which in its later version would have required congressional action on executive agreements and a majority vote in both houses on treaties, that it would hang like an albatross around his neck until its defeat in 1954 by the margin of a single vote. Another aspect of the Korean intervention which remained to haunt Dulles was its overwhelmingly American coloration. Ninety percent of the funding and manpower for UN operations on the ground came from the United States, and cries of "never again" reverberated through the halls of Congress.[29]

Republicans tended to take such matters lightly, though they did make an issue of Truman's refusal to maintain American armed forces at what they deemed a proper level of preparedness. Along the same line, they concentrated on his refusal to furnish South Korea with the type of weapons needed to deter attacks from the north, coupled with his failure to clarify America's commitment to South Korean independence. Seoul could not obtain a single tank, bomber, heavy vessel, or artillery piece capable of stopping heavy armor. At the same time, a casual Acheson described South Korea as beyond the U.S. "defense perimeter." If, therefore, Dulles appeared to go to the opposite extreme in his negotiation of bilateral defense pacts and multilateral groupings, it was because he wanted to avoid further misunderstanding as a cause of war.[30]

Still another sore point with Republicans, as with the public generally, was American policy toward Chiang Kai-shek since many were of the opinion that Roosevelt and Truman had betrayed a loyal ally. The point can be argued. What is certain is that Dulles was the first secretary of state to begin his term of office with a hostile China at his back and a majority in Congress anxious over Chiang's fate and determined to renew Washington's commitment to the Nationalist government. Where Truman had refused to send Chiang jet planes and destroyers, the Republican-controlled Congress of 1953–54 did a complete about-face.[31]

Truman's intent with regard to China had been to "let the dust settle." Accordingly, the United States stood passively by while Nationalist troops staged their courageous defense of Quemoy, an island just off the Mainland and Chiang's most valuable defense bastion. Ten thousand defenders turned back some twenty thousand Red Chinese and took seven thousand prisoners. Meanwhile, Peking insulted American diplomats and summoned J. Leighton Stuart, Truman's last ambassador, to appear before a people's court on charges of maltreating one of his servants. It arrested American consuls, seized American buildings, and refused to deliver mail to the United States embassy. Thus it was that in February 1950, when Mao signed a thirty-year military alliance with the Soviet Union, Truman found himself in diplomatic limbo, at odds with both Mao and Chiang. Nor was Peking yet satisfied. After calling upon the people of Southeast Asia to overthrow their colonial governments, it invaded Tibet and proceeded to bomb its monasteries, liquidating opponents by the thousands. Then, having entrenched itself in Tibet, it sanctioned the Korean War. Among the British, more than a few felt that their country had erred grievously in recognizing the Communist regime. In addition to Peking's policy of uncompensated expropriation and stubborn refusal to establish diplomatic relations on the ambassadorial level, it was not until the Geneva Conference of 1954 that Chou En-lai agreed to grant British ambassador-designate Sir Humphrey Trevelyan the status of chargé.[32]

With Britain's experience a byword among diplomats, forty nations continued to back American opposition to recognition, and the Senate voted unanimously against admitting Red China to the United Nations. In the spring of 1953, Senator Joseph McCarthy of Wisconsin spoke for the news media, as well as his constituents, when he called for a boycott by the United States and its allies of all trade with Peking. Indeed, so prevalent had pro-Nationalist sentiment become that Eisenhower's decision to settle for a negotiated peace in Korea was greeted with dissatisfaction not only by the Hearst and McCormick papers but also by the editors of the *New York Times*, who regretted that an aggressor had been merely stopped and not punished. Only within such a context is it possible to understand how much Dulles risked and how close he came to alienating the conservative wing of his party when he allowed a Red Chinese delegation to be seated at the 1954 Geneva Conference.[33]

One final liability stemming from the Truman years was a belief in certain quarters that federal agencies, in particular the Department of State, had

because communism and capitalism were irreconcil-
sian revolution would never be secure until its creed
r nations.[41] Now, his successors possessed a powerful
hasten the process. No longer could the United States
version merely by offering aid since such funds could
ome cases exceeded, by Soviet offers, notably in the
oviets were shrewd. Instead of grants, they extended
the while concentrating on a select list of countries,
India, Afghanistan, Indonesia, and Yugoslavia. Nor did
arms. Nikita Khrushchev never had to face the threat
to when he and his friends in the Politburo decided
ional interest to allow greater access to home markets.
the Kremlin extended $100 million in credits to Af-
on rubles flowed to the United Nations for an expanded
assistance even as Moscow offered to build a mammoth
Broadcasting to Africa began on a large scale. Arms were
, and $1.5 billion was pumped into China. India received
Five Year Plan, and when Khrushchev and Bulganin
nd Rangoon, they arrived with promises of supplemen-
particular, was so pleased with what it received that it
drawal of the American aid mission. By August 1956,
ans were at work in over a dozen countries in Asia and
ussian leaders announced that they would supply Egypt
tory for research in the peaceful uses of atomic energy,
eign minister tempted Syria and Lebanon with similar

registered equally impressive gains in steel output, ag-
on, military power, and foreign aid programs. During the
Peking channeled an estimated $1 billion to North Korea
mbodia obtained an aid package totaling $22 million, and
Ceylon was awarded $16 million for the rehabilitation of
In 1958, Red China sent seventy technicians and ap-
illion to Yemen. Meanwhile, during the period 1952–57,
ional product grew at the rate of 8 percent annually, far
other Asian country with the exception of Japan, and it
's third largest army and fourth largest airforce. This, too,
the Department of State.[43]
ors were in the cards, so to speak, when Dulles took office,
rm a part of the background against which his strong points
uccesses and failures, must be measured. Before examining
pth, however, it is important that we pause briefly and
ionship with President Eisenhower, for, as will be seen in
, he did not get on particularly well with the president
year; indeed the two men continued to disagree on major,

been infiltrated by Communist spies and sympathizers. In the mind of many, this helped to explain Roosevelt's betrayal of Chiang at Yalta, along with Truman's denial of aid to the Nationalist leader when he was locked in a life and death struggle with Communist rivals. "Communism, Korea, and Corruption," workhorse slogan of the 1952 Republican campaign, derived much of its appeal from the fact that in a comparatively short space of time, from 1945 to 1950, communism as a system emanating from Moscow had advanced from control of 3 percent of the world's population to a figure of 33 percent, a tenfold increase. At the same time, FDR's assistant secretary of the treasury, Harry Dexter White, whom Truman appointed head of the International Monetary Fund, died of a heart attack when faced with the need to defend himself against accusations of association with a Russian spy ring. White had been influential in shaping American policy toward China, and the charges of treason proferred against him in 1947 were substantiated to the satisfaction of not a few, including Eisenhower.[34]

Smarting from imputations of disloyalty at Foggy Bottom and in response to the action taken by a House subcommittee formed to investigate State Department personnel, Truman quietly dismissed over a hundred persons, with more to follow. In addition, he established a special Loyalty Review Board to overrule State where necessary, and on the strength of evidence gathered after an anonymous letter reached Senator Hickenlooper, he fired a number of officials charged with homosexuality. Coming, as this did, on the heels of an earlier resignation by Under Secretary of State Sumner Welles, it created a sensation (Welles had been threatened with a Senate probe on similar grounds under FDR). At about the same time, Alger Hiss, who assisted Roosevelt at Yalta, was brought to trial on charges of disloyalty and convicted of perjury in a dramatic confrontation with former Communist Whittaker Chambers. Truman called the case a "red herring." But it was far from that.[35]

All at once, Americans were presented with a spectacle of individuals associated with top-secret projects in the field of national defense being hauled into court. Two of them, Julius and Ethel Rosenberg, were convicted on charges of treason in 1951 following a similar conviction of Klaus Fuchs who had worked at the Los Alamos laboratory. Congress, in a state of alarm, passed the McCarran Internal Security Act over Truman's veto; the House Committee on Un-American Activities went into high gear; and Senator McCarthy began to demonstrate marked zeal in an ongoing effort to root out disloyal elements. Some observers, outraged at the harm visited on innocent victims by what appeared to be a latter-day inquisition, called for an end to "witch-hunting," while others, more disturbed by apparent laxity on the part of the chief executive, demanded greater vigilance. The nation was divided. Secretary of State Acheson, highly respected overseas, fell into disfavor at home and became the favorite whipping boy of Congress. Reputed not only for his mental toughness but also for occasional touches of Olympian scorn when it came to reporters and the rank and file of the State Department, he had to face charges of malfeasance after Chiang was forced to retreat from the Mainland. With McCarthy demanding his dismissal, Acheson's relationship with the press, never warm, turned to ice. This, too, was part and parcel of the atmosphere confronting Dulles in 1953. The State Department had fallen under a cloud. Morale was low.[36]

To recapitulate, there were many serious issues facing the nation in 1953, of which the situation at State was only one. Could a means be found to end the wars in Korea and Indochina? Would NATO emerge from its embryonic form and gain stature? Could Germany be brought into the Western defense community? These were hard questions. Acheson had more or less given up on the European Defense Community, warning Ike before the latter took office that EDC was in deep trouble. Adenauer's motion to submit the plan for debate had been defeated in the Reichstag, while in France it was being used by partisans as a vehicle to topple the party of Robert Schuman. This was a far cry from the optimism voiced at its signing in June 1952 when ratification was expected within six months, and there was always the danger that Germany, viewing rapprochement with Russia as the only route to reunification and the sole guarantee of Berlin's security, would sever its ties with the West. Moscow still hoped to bring all of Germany into its orbit and force the United States out of Europe.[37]

Elsewhere, prospects were much the same. In Latin America, communism had come within a hair's breadth of victory (in Costa Rica) and its supporters were busily pressing their suit on every front. Adolf Berle, leader of New York's Liberal party and one of the country's leading experts on Central America, concluded that Guatemala was also on the verge of a Communist takeover. Eisenhower, he insisted, should finish the job Truman had started prior to his volte-face. When the ninth regular conference of American states met in Bogotá in 1948 and its assembly learned that there would be no Marshall Plan for Latin America, the news had touched off three days of rioting punctuated by rifle shots in the vicinity of the house where Secretary Marshall was staying. Left-wing rebels seized all eight of the city's radio stations, several persons were killed, and sporadic violence persisted for days after the army moved in to restore order. Averell Harriman risked his life to attend a luncheon given by Colombia's president where, as it turned out, he and his interpreter, Vernon Walters, were the only guests who dared show themselves. Well could Dulles allude, as he did in his confirmation hearings of 1953, to a "rising tide of anti-Americanism in Latin America." It was an ugly scene.[38]

Nor was such sentiment confined to the Western Hemisphere. In Japan, MacArthur's occupation had begun to pall. Riots erupted in 1952 that were more violent and dangerous than those that would force the cancellation of Eisenhower's visit eight years later. On "Bloody May Day" 1952, American military vehicles were overturned and 1400 persons were injured, including

several Ameri
Arab world by
policy with bro
Henderson, wh
decision to bac
American leade
"I saw what we
months." In con
the formation of
success, so that
tation. To compli
war over a disput
had withdrawn or
Communist-led T
munist leaders w
strongly opposed.
tripartite initiative
unsigned after man
any new administra

One final word.
Peking and Moscow
growth. Much of th
aid programs of unp
breakthroughs in ato
decade in which Rus
siles with all that this
exploding an atomic
later, Soviet producti
annually, twice that o
instituted sophisticate
good use of the scienti
with a high salary and
finest radar for the tr
production of H-bombs
in the world was locate
the Volga. Incredible a
become the first nation
man-made earth satellit
first to circle the moon.
embarrassing failure of t
Soviets to build heavy b
have foretold that by 195
of the United States in tot
roughly equal in strength

Lenin had held that
ably opposed the Rus
was embraced by othe
weapon with which to
counter overseas sub
be matched, and in s
case of Egypt. The S
credits and loans, all
mainly Egypt, Syria,
they hesitate to ship
of a congressional v
that it was in the nat

During the 1950s
ghanistan. Four mill
program of technical
steel mill for India. I
shipped to the Arabs
$378 million for its
visited New Delhi a
tary aid. Burma, in
requested the with
Soviet bloc technic
the Middle East. R
with its first labora
and the Soviet for
prospects.[42]

Mainland China
ricultural productio
interval 1954–57,
alone. In 1956, Ca
the following year
its rubber culture
proximately $20 m
Peking's gross na
in advance of any
boasted the worl
was of concern to

All of these fact
and all of them fo
and weaknesses,
the record in de
consider his rela
the next chapte
during his initia

as well as minor, points throughout their term of office. What is extraordinary is that they managed to work together as harmoniously as they did. After a stormy shake-down cruise, they became so adept at reconciling differences that, even to this day, the most astute observers of the Eisenhower presidency still find it difficult to say who was at the helm of American foreign policy from 1953 to 1959.

CHAPTER 2

The New Team

It is almost a truism that Dwight D. Eisenhower and John Foster Dulles worked well in tandem, much the way President Monroe and Secretary of State John Quincy Adams did over a hundred years earlier during the golden age of American diplomacy. Dulles, like Adams, possessed a powerful intellect; and Eisenhower, like Monroe, came to the White House with a strong cosmopolitan background. Ike had spent thirteen years of his life overseas in contact with nearly every head of state in Western Europe. He was on friendly terms with Churchill, Eden, and Macmillan. He could speak with firsthand knowledge of Stalin. It was no simple task to play middleman between such antagonists as FDR and de Gaulle, yet he had gone beyond this to win favors from Admiral Darlan and Generals Giraud and Juin. During the war he had commanded French as well as Commonwealth units. English, Highlanders, Canadians, Australians, New Zealanders, Indians, South Africans, Poles, and Czechs all fought together under his supervision. As part of the wartime experience, he had bargained face-to-face with Italy's Marshal Badoglio before going on to serve as the first American military governor of postwar Germany. Operating in the North African theater, he had adapted to Moslem customs; and as army chief of staff under Truman, he played a key role in France's eventual decision to join the North Atlantic Treaty Organization.[1]

Had he done nothing more than direct the Western alliance militarily and steer NATO through its formative years, his qualifications for the presidency would have been exceptional. Yet there was more to the man than this. Wherever he went, people liked him for his sincerity, ebullience, and warmth coupled with a talent for grasping disparate points of view. Where the Russians were concerned, he was impressed by the caliber of their artists.

He could credit them with sincerity in espousing communism as a way of life; he also appreciated their love of laughter. It never struck him as peculiar that Soviet leaders should interpret America's passion for individual liberty as a form of immaturity inviting exploitation of the masses. He did not agree; but he understood. It was wrong, he believed, to "assume that our standard of values is shared by all other humans in the world. We are not sufficiently informed." In the same way, he came to love and admire the French people. Although he never learned to speak their language fluently, he could understand it fairly well and was capable of defending the most perverse qualities of the Gallic temperament. Once, overhearing a jibe at de Gaulle's hauteur, he remarked that when the chips were down, the Frenchman would be proud and stubborn "on our side." Characteristically, his answer to talk about "pulling French chestnuts from the fire" was to turn the tables. Do not try this argument, he warned, on any Frenchman old enough to remember how the United States sat on the sidelines through most of World War I while French boys gave their lives for the common cause.[2]

To be sure, Ike was not altogether immune from the American proclivity to prescribe narrow-gauged home-style remedies. He appeared to regard political instability as an automatic function of poverty, just as he thought nothing of advocating radical approaches to population control for devoutly Moslem, Hindu, and Catholic countries. Social reform and free elections were viewed as a kind of universal panacea, and he could be quick at times to deride unfamiliar customs such as Islamic purdah and fasting in Ramadan. To the degree that he found it hard to fathom the reserve with which Khrushchev pondered America's superhighways and teeming traffic, he was perhaps less broad than Dulles. But the difference between the principals is easily exaggerated.[3]

Eisenhower emerged from World War II with expertise in many areas: intelligence systems, secrecy, calculated risk-taking, censorship, and press conferences. Never before, perhaps, had a single individual won the trust and confidence of so many competing national interests. If the BBC was inclined to favor its own and to give Americans credit for such dubious achievements as the bombing of Rome, if certain GIs behaved as if their country were the savior of the world, or if the French proved touchy and difficult owing to the weight of the German occupation, Eisenhower was generally the man on the spot, managing in some way to find a solution to each individual problem as it arose. In time, he persuaded the British to submit their grievances directly to him, as supreme allied commander, rather than to the war office in London, and this in itself was a signal accomplishment. When de Gaulle refused to fly to France for a role in the occupation unless he could travel on a French plane, Ike had an American aircraft painted over in the tricolor. In the same way, on entering Paris, he went out of his way to pay the first courtesy call on de Gaulle rather than standing on ceremony. Quick to recognize that the British depended more on censorship than their American counterparts because they had to rely more on deception, as opposed to brute force, he was described by Selwyn Lloyd, foreign secretary under Harold Macmillan, as a "master of diplomacy." Needless to say, he derived additional benefit from a term as president of Columbia University, along with a wealth of experience dealing with congressional committees as head of the army. When, therefore, one tries to ascertain who set the course of American foreign policy, Eisenhower or Dulles, one must not forget that the president was a force unto himself, a person of finely honed political skills and definite ideas about what needed to be done.[4]

That such a commanding figure should impress his fellow countrymen as essentially an easy-going outdoorsman with a passion for golf is more a tribute to his political acumen than a reflection of reality. In fact, he could penetrate to the heart of almost any problem and, after listening to different views, go on to render a concise and accurate summation. After earning outstanding grades in high school and devouring practically every history book in sight, he scored first among those in his group who took the exam for Annapolis and second in the competition for West Point. His class standing at the Point was on the low side, but he placed first, once again, at the army's elite general staff and command school at Fort Leavenworth. Having served as a long-time speech writer for General MacArthur, he was proficient in the use of English and apparently able to dictate his best-selling *Crusade in Europe* in a record seven weeks. Withal, it was a side of his makeup that he strove to soft-pedal in deference to the traditional American preference for leaders who are "just plain folks." Furthermore, because he was naturally modest and inclined to garble his syntax, because he deliberately downplayed the martial aspect of his character and training, an image of mediocrity was not hard to come by. In accord with the antimilitarist strain in American history, he made frequent reference to the dangers of nuclear annihilation, warning against the so-called military-industrial complex and taking a surprisingly soft line on Korea and Suez.[5]

Dulles was probably more adept than Eisenhower at handling ideas, as opposed to people, but he was far from clumsy at the latter. There is, in fact, another side to the secretary that remains as well-shrouded as Eisenhower's intellect: namely, his capacity to enjoy the things of the world. A partial catalogue of Dulles' hobbies would include ping pong, golf, hiking, skiing, and swimming. To this should be added hunting, fishing, bridge, backgammon, and fine cuisine, along with languages, travel, tree surgery, bird-watching, and sailing. As a college student, he joined the chess team, competed ferociously on the tennis court, and captured the junior prize in debating. Little would one have guessed from his dour demeanor how much dating, dancing, and theater-going he had done in his younger days. He had a penchant for mischief-making too. It is recorded that he threw spit balls in grade school, climbed the drain pipes of Princeton's Nassau Hall, and participated in a student riot at the Sorbonne. Later in life, he memorized baseball averages and read detective stories. He also indulged in practical jokes and acquired a taste for whiskey, brandy, and caviar accompanied by cigars, pipes, and cigarettes. All along, he reveled in humor, often at his own expense. History bears witness to the success with which he suppressed these more human traits to play the part of an attorney who must appear at all times grave and magisterial.[6]

Further highlighting the similarity between president and secretary are the many political views they held in common, including the notion that Soviet communism posed a world-wide threat to freedom and democracy. Long after Dulles' death, Eisenhower warned the American people that the Communist menace was "diabolical," "atheistic," "insidious," and of "indefinite duration." He accepted Soviet-American rivalry as a given and, like his secretary, stressed the danger posed by a steady decline in American morality. Along with Dulles, he championed preparedness within the framework of a healthy economy as the best guarantee against war while favoring a European balance of power inclusive of Spain. Both men agreed on the likelihood of another war in the absence of prudent management and both were convinced that American weakness had been a factor in the outbreak of hostilities in 1914, 1939, and again in 1950. Power, Eisenhower held, was absolutely essential for the maintenance of credibility and the defense of the national honor as nothing else would hold the USSR in check or cement the loyalty of one's allies. Ike and Dulles were also as one in believing that atheistic materialism aimed at nothing less than "domination of the world." By and large, they judged democracy, as a form of government, to be superior, though not necessarily exportable. There were degrees of totalitarian rule, and in many cases the only alternative they could see to a right-wing dictatorship was an even more repressive regime on the left. Finally, they placed little stock in Soviet promises, regarded Soviet propaganda as relentless, and viewed the American press as inclined to arrogance and irresponsibility.[7]

It is often assumed that Dulles was the more religious of the two men, and this may be so. Yet both came from pious homes where first-hand acquaintance with the Bible was something taken for granted. To the end of their lives, they would be concerned with religion and what they took to be its natural offspring, morality. Ike, in particular, peppered his conversation with expressions such as "this world and then the fireworks" and "X hates Y more than the devil hates holy water." Well before he met Dulles, he had called democracy "essentially a religious concept" and termed "moral probity" the "pillar of the West." After holding a special religious service on the occasion of his 1952 victory at the polls, he introduced the practice of cabinet prayer and modified the pledge of allegiance to include the phrase "under God." This was a president who encouraged his secretary of state to appear on a "Back to God" radio program, and just as his memoirs include frequent Bible references, his speeches are positively laced with words like

God, good and evil, right and wrong. His first inaugural address alludes repeatedly to the forces of darkness and light, faith and freedom, along with God's guidance. He and Dulles were alike in holding that man is a creature with an immortal soul, and both cherished the ideal of a devout America walking humbly before its God.[8]

Even more erroneous, though, than the notion of Dulles as lone moralizer is the idea that he outdid Eisenhower in hawkishness. The acid test of Ike's disposition came after Dulles' death during the Kennedy presidency when he urged the sending of American troops to Laos with or without allied support. In addition to sharing General Clay's preference for a military response to the building of the Berlin Wall, he advised Presidents Kennedy and Johnson to follow through at the Bay of Pigs and in Vietnam regardless of cost. One of the issues which sets Dulles most clearly apart from Ike during the initial months of 1953 was his opposition to contingency plans for the use of nuclear weapons. In the eyes of the president, such weapons were not much different morally from any other type of armament and he felt that the West had to exploit its lead in technology if it was to hold its own against superior troop strength. Dulles simply could not agree to this, and his dissent foreshadows the strategy he would employ a year later during the Dien Bien Phu crisis, arguing that the United States should not act without the approval of its allies (something he knew to be highly unlikely). Although he eventually acquiesced in Eisenhower's position on nuclear armament, he never discarded a sentiment with deep roots in his Presbyterian past. In 1945, prior to the bombing of Hiroshima and Nagasaki, he had joined with Bishop Oxnam in calling for a warning to the enemy. Tokyo, he thought, should be informed of its impending fate and given time to reflect while Americans should be encouraged to ponder the consequences of their proposed course of action. Later, he was among the first public figures to advocate the international control of atomic energy, a conviction to which he clung tenaciously despite lukewarmness on the part of Eisenhower. The reason he usually gave for opposing the development and deployment of nuclear weapons was world opinion, but his stand was also conditioned by religious scruple. Treasury Secretary George Humphrey could recall cabinet discussions in which Dulles had spoken of atomic warfare as something almost sacrilegious.[9]

For a variety of reasons, this one included, Dulles and Eisenhower did not form a close partnership until late 1953 or early 1954. Apart from the comparatively minor, but nonetheless symbolic, misstep taken by Ike when he announced his choice of ambassador to the Court of St. James's without consulting Dulles (or even the British), there was the larger question of whether or not to arrange an early summit meeting between leaders of East and West. Eisenhower, announcing in February that he was prepared to go half-way to Moscow to meet with Stalin, encouraged Churchill to do the same. Dulles, on the other hand, wanted to use the summit as a bargaining chip in dealing with the prestige-starved Soviets. He also hoped to shield the Western alliance from division based on disagreement over the status of Berlin and Germany. In the end, after much pulling and hauling, Eisenhower deferred to his secretary. But the NATO Council, which seemed at first to go along with Dulles, soon backtracked. Europeans began to accuse the administration of rigidity, and so Eisenhower prevailed upon Dulles to support a tripartite meeting of Western heads of government at Bermuda. Later, at a "little Bermuda" held in Washington, agreement was reached on a four-power conference of foreign ministers to include the Soviet Union.[10]

Disagreement over the question of whether or not to take part in an early summit was exacerbated by Churchill who, fancying himself in the role of pacificator, liked to hark back to his record of wartime collaboration with Roosevelt and Stalin. As an elder statesman getting on in years, his political future seemed almost to hinge on the success of such an endeavor. Meanwhile, Eden, who might have acted as a restraining force, was undergoing a series of abdominal operations, leaving the prime minister to manage foreign affairs as well as the office of prime minister. The result was to shunt Dulles to one side of the Anglo-American circuit. Prior to the election of 1952, Eden had come out openly against Dulles' candidacy for the post of secretary of state, and although Eisenhower went his own way on the matter, he invited Eden to a private meeting at which he appeared to apologize for having appointed Dulles, hinting that the arrangement would not last.[11]

Chief among the remaining differences between president and secretary was the issue of war and peace in Korea. Dulles believed that too much of a willingness to compromise with Peking might undermine the Western position elsewhere, and needlessly so, for the United States was well enough ahead in the arms race to give the Red Chinese a good "licking." He was further convinced that a reversal of the stalemate in Korea, while not without risk, would set a good precedent. Although he did not favor a policy of driving the enemy all the way to the Yalu River for fear of provoking Russian forces stationed at Vladivostok, he did speak of drawing the line at Korea's "narrow waist." Thus, from the very outset, he hewed to a policy of "rollback" which he continued to champion in National Security Council meetings during March and April. The other side of the coin is that he shied away from the use of nuclear weapons, preferring instead to deploy the armies of Nationalist China if necessary (on this point he was overruled by Eisenhower). As regards the peripheral question of Rhee's unwillingness to accept the terms of the armistice and his unilateral release of prisoners, Ike was inclined to severity while Dulles adopted a less rigid attitude, enlisting congressional support and eventually prevailing upon the White House to refrain from precipitate action.[12]

Shifting, for a moment, to other areas of the world, Eisenhower viewed the British dilemma at Suez more sympathetically than Dulles. And once again, where Ike was prone to follow Churchill's lead, his secretary viewed

American support for a settlement on British terms as too valuable not to bargain for something in return. Conversely, if Dulles appeared to be more unswervingly anticolonial than the president, it was because he sought an increase in purchase power when dealing with London and Paris. What was said on Monday could be left unsaid on Tuesday—at a price. This was the same secretary who presented President Naguib of Egypt with a matched pair of silver-plated revolvers. The intensity of anticolonial rhetoric emanating from the American embassy in Cairo prompted Eisenhower to tell Dulles to his face at a National Security Council meeting that he was being too hard on Whitehall. Dulles, still feeling the effect of Ike's unilateral decision to send a friendly message to the Russian people on the death of Stalin, was also on the defensive politically after *Time* reported that he had "delighted Premier Saeb Salaam of Lebanon . . . [by] stoutly denying that the U.S. Middle East policy is Zionist-dictated . . . [and confiding that] the Jews as a whole had voted against him in the 1949 New York senatorial race (which he lost) and generally against Ike in 1952."[13]

Dulles recouped his reputation somewhat in June when the president confirmed his primacy over other cabinet members in the field of foreign policy. Still, there remained the problem of rapport. He appeared more willing than Eisenhower to do battle with McCarthy, telling reporters in June that he disagreed with the president, as well as with the Senate Foreign Relations Committee, on the need for an FBI investigation preliminary to a Senate vote on nominations. Furthermore, if he was less anxious than the president to nominate Bohlen for the Moscow mission, he was also less anxious to purge suspected members of the State Department. By this time, he had opposed a presidential initiative on defense cuts, saying that he did not believe in economy of this kind during a war. He was even somewhat antagonistic to Eisenhower's "New Look" policy, inveighing against defense cutbacks that would limit America's power to wage conventional war. It is ironic that history has linked him with the doctrine of "massive retaliation," with its implied willingness to resort to atomic warfare in situations that would normally call for a measured response, for with the possible exception of a campaign memorandum dated May 1952, which need not be taken at face value, he was speaking for Eisenhower rather than himself. Generally, he took exception to Eisenhower's talk of allowing allied forces to supplant America's naval presence in the Mediterranean just as he confronted the White House when it came to reducing conventional forces in Europe.[14]

When reports reached Eisenhower in July that Dulles seemed dubious as to the merits of the Reciprocal Trade Act, the president exploded, "I'll promise you we'll have a new secretary of state if that is so." Rumors began to circulate of an impending resignation, and Ike issued no denial. Instead, he suggested that Dulles tone down his rhetoric, in particular those portions of his speeches portraying Russia as the embodiment of all evil. Significantly, he offered his secretary the post of chief justice, and when, toward the end of the year, he journeyed to Canada, he did so without Dulles, bringing a substitute in the person of Henry Cabot Lodge, one of the Secretary's archrivals. Again he hinted at the possibility of a new head for State. Throughout the period, he remained firm in his preference for an early summit conference with the Russians, reflecting the natural preference of a politician for policies with public appeal. Included under this head would be Soviet-American cultural exchange, which he and his brother Milton espoused, but which Dulles regarded as an opening for Russian espionage. The secretary was not only more opposed than the president to a demilitarized European buffer zone involving mutual pullbacks of Soviet and American forces; he was also more definite in his conviction that firmness on Quemoy offered the best guarantee of a split in the Moscow-Peking axis.[15]

This is not necessarily to suggest that one man was always more hard-line on political questions than the other. It was Dulles, rather than his boss, who expressed a willingness to negotiate directly with representatives of Red China. There was also greater openness on his part to the possibility of recognizing Peking and voting for its admission to the United Nations. Rarely did such flexibility reach the public eye, but it figured behind the scenes as a regular part of Dulles' modus operandi. During a typical conversation with Ike in 1954, he argued for a two-China policy, with Peking to occupy Taiwan's seat in the Security Council and both Taipei and its counterpart on the Mainland to be seated in the General Assembly. Interestingly enough, Eisenhower made no reply. Similar pragmatism can be seen in Dulles' greater readiness to deal with East German authorities during the Berlin crisis of 1958. Or, to cite still another example, it was Eisenhower who initially refused to allow the relatives of American prisoners, along with representatives of the press, to go to Mainland China. As per custom, Dulles presented the president's views as his own, and he was taken at his word.[16]

Eisenhower tended to be more aggressive when it came to the tactical use of military force. On one occasion, after Peking shot down an American patrol plane, Admiral Burke dispatched units of the Seventh Fleet all the way up to China's three-mile limit with carrier jets screaming overhead. After several days, Dulles, suggested that it might be time to end the demonstration. However, the president ordered Burke to proceed. Similarly, during the overthrow of Guatemala's Arbenz, Eisenhower insisted on the interception of neutral shipping over objections from the State Department. In discussions bearing upon the Lebanon crisis of 1958, Dulles may have been on the side of intervention by the time it occurred, but he was lukewarm at best when the idea of marine landings was first broached by the president in April. He feared world opinion, along with Soviet involvement and possible damage to the oil pipelines. And later, when a full-blown crisis erupted (in July), it was Eisenhower who dominated the decision-making machinery and brushed aside Dulles' suggestion for a warning to Lebanon, accompanied by an offer to meet with the Soviets. Ike was not reckless. Neither was he imprudent. However, it seems fair to say that much of the restraining power came from Dulles who, incidentally, appeared more anxious than his chief to tighten American control over ROC military operations.[17]

In addition to the Lebanon crisis of 1957–58, there are at least two other cases illustrative of the cleavage between White House and State, and together they are worth exploring in some detail. The first of these is Suez. As mentioned in chapter 1, the president portrayed his secretary as in full agreement with him on the proper course regarding Nasser's seizure of the canal. But this was something less than the full truth. Dulles may have sounded as angry as Eisenhower with Britain's resort to arms (in concert with France and Israel), perhaps angrier. His vigorous leadership at the United Nations, based on a lifelong advocacy of organized resistance to the unbridled use of force, made a lasting impression. Still, the main body of evidence indicates that Ike was leading with Dulles' chin. For every official who names the secretary as the driving force behind American policy in this instance, one can cite a dozen others who point to the president, among them Eden, Lloyd, Hayter, and Couve de Murville. On the aftermath of the crisis, Dulles himself implied on several occasions, and to several individuals, including Pineau, Lloyd, and Harold Caccia (British ambassador to the United States), that he would have been delighted to see London and Paris thumb their noses at Washington and follow through militarily. Just before the invasion, he hinted in a press briefing that he was personally on the side of the allies but that American policy was being made by the White House rather than the State Department.[18]

One is tempted to conclude on the basis of what Dulles said in late August that he subscribed wholeheartedly to Eisenhower's logic. What he thought in private, however, may be gleaned from at least three sources: his conversations with Eisenhower during the first half of August, remarks he made to congressional leaders on 12 August, and the way he tried to delay Eisenhower's appeal to the United Nations. On 2 September, Ike came out strongly against the use of force, cabling Eden, "I am afraid, Anthony, that from this point onward our views . . . diverge. I must tell you frankly that American public opinion flatly rejects the thought of using force." It was at about this juncture that Dulles began to change his tune. However much he may have sympathized with Eden's resort to force, he adhered to the presidential position and as usual spoke his lines so convincingly that few failed to take his public utterances at face value.[19]

Within a few months of the denouement—by March of 1957 in fact—it was already clear to British leaders that the president, and the president alone, had been the architect of American policy. Eisenhower, not Dulles, insisted on undercutting Britain's gold and petroleum reserves. From the Oval Office came the orders to the Sixth Fleet which hamstrung British naval operations. American warships not only entered the battle zone without informing London of their whereabouts. They also shielded Egyptian destroyers from rocket attack just as they interfered with allied radar in their flights over Cyprus and buzzed allied ships. Admiral Burke, who had been instructed by Ike not to take any guff from anyone, later recalled that he honestly could not say at the time who the real enemy was. Eisenhower had been brutal, phoning Eden at the moment of decision and holding forth in stentorian tones.[20]

As a candidate running for reelection on a peace platform, the president obviously wanted to distance himself from anything resembling aggression on the part of the colonial powers. Consequently, although he agreed, by implication, to tolerate an invasion if it could be postponed until after the election, he would have none of it prior to 4 November, and he evidently expected his wishes to be heeded. American power relative to its allies was at an all-time high, and he spoke as a former supreme Allied commander with an eye to the Tripartite Pact of 1950, which bound Britain and France to refrain from the bilateral use of force. All of which helps to explain his reference to the allied invasion as a double cross. So furious was he that he considered the possibility of an outright blockade to halt further military action.[21]

He would have had fewer grounds for consternation had the operation been properly managed from a tactical point of view and had it not presented such an inviting target to the Soviets. In the event, Soviet leaders found themselves heavily engaged in putting down a revolt of their own in Hungary and they issued no threats until after hostilities had dragged on inconclusively for nine days. By this time, Washington had shown its hand. Still, the bear was always an unknown quantity, and throughout the crisis there was always the danger of miscalculation.[22]

Few undertakings in British history have been so thoroughly mismanaged. Eden's decision to order two postponements as a result of American pressure touched off a mutiny among British reservists who had been called up for immediate action. In addition, it led to a run on the pound sterling, presenting a golden opportunity for the opposition to organize in Parliament. Labor MPs took full advantage to show movie clips of civilians allegedly wounded in the bombing. In August, the government made plans for a landing at Alexandria on 15 September, preceded by two days of preparatory bombing. But on 4 September, after Dulles appealed for consideration of a Canal Users Association (SCUA), Eden shifted the date to 8 October and substituted Port Said for Alexandria, thereby removing Cairo from the direct line of attack. Soon after, on 1 October, he made a second change, once more as a result of American pressure and in accord now with his decision to go to the United Nations. And, as if this were not enough to generate confusion, he fixed still another date on 18 October, this time for the first week of November. The trouble was that, fearing a long list of casualties, he insisted on six days of preliminary aerial bombardment, instead of two. Moreover, because he refused to launch his troop ships until after the Israeli strike to avoid any appearance of collusion, the ships did not weigh anchor until 1 November and thus failed to arrive at their destination until the tenth of the month, nearly two weeks after the outbreak of war. On 3 November, the day British soldiers were due to attack, their commanders on Cyprus were still awaiting word from London as to the time and place of landing![23]

Shilly shallying to the very end, the prime minister scuttled a bombing run over Cairo airport lest he appear to be impeding the American evacuation, and on 2 November he ordered all bombing halted pending the dropping of leaflets with a humanitarian warning. So far as can be ascertained, the effect of his aeropsychological warfare campaign was worse than nil, for by hitting only military targets, it tended to inure the local populace to wartime conditions. Nasser's block ships were supposed to be sunk before they could be towed into place to obstruct the canal, but again nothing happened. Finally, when British troops were about to disembark, Eden instructed his naval commanders to avoid blitzing the beaches with guns larger than 4.5 inches. His officers, nonplussed and sensing disaster if they complied, went ahead anyway, and when he finally ordered an end to all bombardment, his instructions were again ignored.[24]

American military officials, having assumed that British and French troops would control the canal by 30 October, were thoroughly disgusted. In Eisenhower's opinion, the whole affair should have been over within twenty-four hours, in which case he would have accepted it.[25]

Dulles tried at various times to prevail upon Ike to be more conciliatory, but to no avail. Among other things, he suggested that American troops might be readied for deployment alongside allied units in order to bolster the Western negotiating position. He also told Eisenhower that White House support for Nasser at a time when Britain and France were engaged in sensitive talks was counterproductive. If the president had accepted the advice of his secretary, American oil tankers would also have been removed from mothball storage. Dulles, in expressing sympathy for the allied cause in a meeting with legislative leaders, may have hoped to outflank the White House politically, as he had done two years before during the crisis at Dien Bien Phu; but when he suggested a special session of Congress to request emergency assistance for London and Paris, Ike would not authorize it. All such chafing accomplished was to inject an additional note of ambivalence into American policy which, together with Eden's weakness, helped to bring on the very debacle it sought to avert.[26]

Lord Home has termed it a "sad lapse" in American diplomacy, as indeed it was. On the one hand, allied leaders were warned not to count on Washington, even for moral support. Beginning on 31 July, when Eisenhower advised Eden against the use of force, until 27 October, when he issued the same warning to Israeli premier David Ben Gurion, he promised only one thing, that he would "take care of the bear," and this he did in sternly worded messages addressed to Moscow on 31 July and 1 November. On the other hand, Dulles interlarded a generally negative line with copious words of encouragement, both before and after Nasser invaded. As late as 6 October, he declared that "no nation shall be required to live under a sword of Damocles," referring presumably to England. Three weeks later, speaking in the same vein, he pronounced the situation at Suez "intolerable." He spoke with similar bifurcation when he told the French ambassador that Washington would "stand aside" in the event of an allied invasion. All of this, one notes, at a time when journalists were reporting a willingness on his part to plead Nasser's case before the United Nations.[27]

A second weakness on the American side became apparent during the talks with Nasser. When Dulles and Eisenhower vowed that the United States would not stand for a show of force, they violated one of the cardinal rules of negotiation, which is to keep one's opponent guessing. While the phrasing of the American statements differed, the effect in every instance was to undermine allied bargaining power. Dulles, on 28 August, declared that Suez was "not a matter which is primarily of U.S. concern." Two days later, Eisenhower announced that "we are committed to a peaceful settlement of this dispute, nothing else" (he repeated himself on 5 September). Thereafter, within the course of eight days, Dulles let it be known that "we do not intend to shoot our way through." And on 2 October, he told reporters, "I know of no teeth" (referring to the possibility of sanctions under SCUA).[28]

Rhetoric notwithstanding, European leaders might have guessed that Eisenhower was not altogether opposed to military action if it could be executed with éclat and without the appearance of American involvement during an election campaign. Following the first London Conference, Dulles informed Lloyd that Washington did not wish to know of British troop movements. Popular uprisings in Poland and Hungary on 19 and 23 October militated against explicit support for a policy of force, particularly when Moscow appeared at first to react passively in its own sphere of influence. But as late as 3 November, Robert Amory, deputy director of the CIA, shouted over the phone to British officials, "Comply with the god-damn cease-fire or go ahead with the god-damn invasion. Either way, we'll back'em up if they do it fast. What we can't stand is their goddamn hesitation waltz while Hungary is burning!"[29]

This, in a nutshell, was the long and short of it. Eisenhower and Eden danced a "hesitation waltz" in 1956, although Ike's version was straightforward by comparison with the reverse tango he and Dulles danced two years earlier in Indochina. Which brings us to the second of the two major case studies in which president and secretary of state differed over diplomatic strategy and tactics.

Vietnam, like the Middle East crisis of 1956, belies all the received wisdom. Contrary to virtually every account, Dulles proves to be the prime mover on the American side, but this time in *opposition* to an interventionist course. Unlike Suez, Dien Bien Phu is extremely complex as a study in divided leadership. Consequently, while it comes first in chronological order, we have deferred the discussion so that it may be carried over into chapter 3. First though, a word on the historical context.

France's position in Southeast Asia had been undermined not only by Japanese hammering during World War II but also by FDR's refusal to succor colonial forces resisting a takeover by Communist-backed guerrillas. Indochina was therefore a troubled region. Truman, who broke with the policy of his predecessor, began to underwrite an ever larger share of the French war effort. However, by 1954, with 10 percent of its entire army in Vietnam and the toll of its military personnel rising exponentially, Paris was exhausted and determined, in the absence of some kind of dramatic turn-about on the battlefield, to arrive at a negotiated settlement. So it was that the Quai d'Orsay began to bargain with the United States for additional military assistance and then, after the fall of Dien Bien Phu, for political support in the Geneva talks which began on 26 April, looking to a compromise settlement based on recognition of Communist gains in the field.

Several points are worthy of mention at the outset. First, it was understood that French leaders would press for ratification of the European Defense Community (EDC) as a quid pro quo for American aid. Second, EDC was Dulles' highest diplomatic priority because it promised to enlist the lion's share of German manpower on the side of the West while eliminating the possibility of war among its signatories.[30] Third, there was a difference in outlook between Eisenhower and Dulles, though not the one generally assumed. Ike, who sympathized with France's effort to extricate itself from an increasingly hopeless situation, believed that the United States had enough of a stake in the resources and strategic position of Indochina to justify a policy of military aid with few, if any, strings attached. He was willing, therefore, to provide tactical air support in an emergency even if it had to be disguised, just as he was prepared to send ground forces as a last resort, with or without ratification of EDC. Dulles, by contrast, was more reserved. He, too, sympathized with the French, but he felt, perhaps more strongly than Ike, that military involvement could escalate and that U.S. armed forces should not be "fighting on the Asian mainland." Especially did he wish to bargain for cooperation on EDC, even to the point of risking short-term defeat on the battlefield. In addition, he hoped that French desperation could be utilized to commit Paris and London to a Far Eastern defense pact which would transcend the immediate issue and spread a mantle of protection over the entire area.[31]

If the secretary was to realize his principal aims, however, France had to be convinced that America was ready and willing to commence strategic bombing, because it was no more anxious than Britain to endorse the idea of SEATO in advance of the Geneva Conference, and EDC was coming under heavy fire at home. This meant, on the one hand, that domestic pressure for bombing, whether from the White House or Capitol Hill, had to be held in check. Otherwise, American support would be regarded as automatic and France could anticipate satisfaction without having to yield anything in return. On the other hand, such pressure was of the essence and, as such, could not be totally eliminated. To put it another way, Eisenhower's ardor had to be cooled without being frozen. It was a case of keeping all of one's options open and engaging in a delicate balancing act.

Given the complexity of the situation, Dulles' strategy had to be multifaceted. To contain Eisenhower's enthusiasm for military involvement, he insisted on "united action," in particular the backing of Britain, which he knew would be difficult, if not impossible, to obtain. Meanwhile, he managed to cage congressional hawks by concentrating on the bête noire of European colonialism. France, after refusing to grant full independence to the Associated States, would not allow Washington a major role in the training of Vietnamese troops, and this afforded a certain purchase power with American senators. The fact was that if Premier Laniel was reluctant to stake his prestige on an all-out drive for EDC, he was equally unwilling to be maneuvered into a position where he would lose control of Indochina. France's economic and moral influence was already threatened by the presence of American merchants, and Laniel was not anxious to involve large numbers of American and British troops under the rubric of "united action." United action might be used at Geneva as a bargaining chip, but it was not something French officials were prepared to welcome.[32]

The beauty of Dulles' position was that if France decided to go ahead with EDC, as promised, he could always deemphasize the colonial issue; Congress would then authorize intervention, and the requirements for British support could be waived by acting in concert with other nations, perhaps New Zealand, Thailand, or Australia. Of course, in the act of juggling all these factors, Dulles created an appearance of immense confusion. As acute an analyst as Sir Roger Makins, the British ambassador, characterized the political scene in Washington during the spring of 1954 as one "giant mist," and to this day, scholars and pundits alike believe that it was either the White House or Capitol Hill (or a combination of the two) that kept the United States out of an Asian land war. At certain times, the administration seemed to be edging toward military involvement; at other times not. Dulles was by turns rigid and flexible, the only constant being an apparent willingness on the part of Congress to approve whatever line of action he might recommend. Knowledgable observers agreed that public opinion remained fluid through April, May, and June and that congressional support was always on tap.[33]

One does not have far to go to observe the difference between Dulles and Eisenhower. In December 1953, at a National Security Council meeting, the president remarked that the future of Indochina seemed doubtful and, as in other cases of a "leaky dike," it might be best to put in a finger rather than let it be washed away. The "finger" he had in mind was a carrier-launched bombing raid with the insignia of the American planes removed. He may have been simply "thinking out loud" at this point. Two weeks later, at another NSC meeting, he weighed in with Treasury Secretary George Humphrey against the use of American ground troops; but he stated that he was not opposed to the use of American pilots. By February, he was sufficiently concerned about the direction of the war to suggest that Dulles find a new ambassador for Indochina, "somebody a little on the Machiavellian side." Hagerty noted in his diary that Ike, highly agitated and ready to run considerable risks, was adamant that "we must not lose Asia." As late as 1 April, he told newsmen that the United States might have to send its bombers after all, although, "of course, if we did it, we'd have to deny it forever." His remark appears cryptic until one recalls that Paris had not yet requested American military intervention as it was to do within a matter of days. He may have been implying that the United States was prepared to act without official French concurrence. In any case, this was not the cooing of a dove.[34]

Dulles, on the other hand, expressed himself in late March as dubious about a carrier attack, telling Admiral Radford, chairman of the Joint Chiefs of Staff, that the United States could not afford to be too intimately involved with France. On the contrary, to avoid association with an imperial power in decline, it might have to reconsider its entire commitment as any other course would invite the loss of Africa and Asia to communism. At the very least, Dulles remarked, Washington should not intervene until Paris agreed to genuine independence for its Associated States along with an American role in the training of indigenous troops. Speaking with Congressman Walter Judd on 29 March, he said he was less optimistic than Eisenhower on Dien Bien Phu's chances for survival. Likewise, in conversation with Ambassador Makins and Senator Wiley, he described France as acting hysterically and implied that Paris was running through American money as if it were an "unlimited bank account." He was not at all happy with French policy, he added, and Washington should not act alone. Senator Alexander Smith was informed that the United States did not want to get bogged down in the quagmire of an Asian land war. In the meantime, Under Secretary Bedell Smith heard Dulles outline still other reasons for a policy of restraint: American security was not directly threatened; intervention might not save Dien Bien Phu; the French government might be overthrown and if so, Washington would be left "holding the bag"; unilateral action would undermine American rapport with Britain; and finally, it would undercut American bargaining power by satisfying France without realizing anything commensurate in return. By this time, he was beginning to speak of the fall of Dien Bien Phu as "inevitable."[35]

As French troops found themselves besieged and Paris looked more and more to Washington for relief, Eisenhower warmed to the idea of a strike by American bombers and, in the hope that Dulles might be able to talk Congress into some kind of blanket endorsement, he instructed him to "develop" the "thinking of Congressional leaders." Little did he know that this was just what the secretary had been doing all along, though not necessarily in ways he would have approved. At a National Security Council meeting on 9 April, the president continued to sound hawkish, pointing out that the United States had to draw the line somewhere. In reply, Dulles stressed the danger of Red Chinese intervention if the United States should succeed in mounting effective resistance to the Vietminh. Congressional leaders, he pointed out, were on record as opposed to unilateral action; Britain would have to be a party; and France would have to grant independence and guarantee its staying power.[36]

The president's support for American troop involvement waned gradually as his secretary insisted on political preconditions which, as noted above, were virtually certain of rejection. But there was one moment during the crisis when the principals in the drama found themselves at high noon, so to speak, and it occurred on 2 April, the day before Dulles was scheduled to appear before a congressional leadership conference in the company of Admiral Radford. By this time, Premier Laniel was in the process of formally requesting American military support to relieve Dien Bien Phu and the evidence indicates that Eisenhower was disposed to give it. Nevertheless, Dulles proceeded to tell him, in Radford's presence, that he could not, and would not, press for intervention unless it were carried out as part of "united action"—that is, in concert with America's allies, including Britain. Nor would he stand for any divergence between his own position in this regard and that of the admiral, a superhawk by reputation. Radford, who seemed to shift gears on the spot, proceeded the following day to *discourage* the use of American airpower, telling congressional leaders that Dien Bien Phu could no longer be saved. He seems to have gone so far as to suggest that an air strike might ultimately necessitate the introduction of American ground forces by involving the United States directly in the war. As expected, the leadership of the House and Senate called for "united action" to include Great Britain, and Dulles was able to report to Eisenhower, only a few hours later, that although there were still serious problems, the meeting had gone "pretty well." It had indeed, as far as he was concerned. Significantly, he added that congressional sentiment reflected public opinion as a whole, something which may or may not have been the case.[37]

Plainly, Dulles did not go to Capitol Hill, as has long been assumed, to win congressional backing for aerial bombardment, but rather to put a damper on imminent action. Only with this in mind can one imagine why he would countermand the interventionist line on subsequent trips to Europe. While in London in mid-April, he showed unusual deference to Eden's point of view, which was one of icy reserve, and on arrival home he could inform reporters that he felt "very satisfied" with the outcome of his overseas mission when in fact Eden had only agreed to consider the possibility of forming a Southeast Asian treaty organization. Toward the end of the month, on a second flight abroad, he brought Radford along, and the admiral told his British hosts at Chequers that he no longer thought Dien Bien Phu could be relieved from the air. So cagey was the secretary at camouflaging his views on both sides of the Atlantic that Eden, as of 16 May, was not yet sure where the United States stood.[38]

The difference between Eisenhower and Dulles may be gathered from a variety of sources and situations. Somewhat earlier, in late March, France sent General Ely to sound the administration on prospects for American action in an emergency, and the general had dealt mainly with a friendly Radford, who gave the impression, quite naturally, of representing the views of his chief. Ely, however, was also granted the rare privilege of a personal interview with the president himself, and this confirmed him in his impression that Radford had been instructed to offer every form of support short of ground forces. That Eisenhower delegated considerable power to the admiral may be inferred from the presence of Radford's signature on a *note verbale* agreeing that Washington would react in the event that Peking were to strike on the ground or in the air.[39] Dulles, on the other hand, remained consistently noncommittal during Ely's visit, ticking off all the concessions that France would have to make before intervention of any kind could be seriously contemplated. When the secretary declined even to vouch for Radford's promise of support in case of an incursion by the Red Chinese, the admiral hastened to assure Ely that Dulles was not speaking for the administration. Ely had every right, therefore, to assume that Eisenhower would approve American bombing missions if and when requested. The planes were, after all, fueled and ready to go. At the same time, Dulles could maintain that no commitment had been made since he, as secretary of state, outranked the chairman of the Joint Chiefs, and neither he nor anyone else at State had given French officials the slightest reason to be optimistic.[40]

Even after Dulles appeared before congressional leaders and succeeded in putting a damper on interventionist sentiment, Eisenhower refused to be daunted, telling his secretary that while Radford's pledges may have been given confidentially, they had nonetheless been given. Whereupon Dulles rejoined that he knew of no such pledges; all he knew was that he had made clear to General Ely that political matters took precedence and that Radford had come to view an air strike as politically and legally impossible. Although the president offered no further resistance at this stage, except to ask Dulles to see if anything else could be done for Paris, he kept on pressing his case indirectly, unveiling the "domino theory" and applauding a trial balloon in which Vice President Nixon hinted that ground forces might eventually have to be sent. Dulles, for his part, countered by qualifying the domino theory and telling Senator Smith that Nixon's words had been unfortunate.[41]

Up to several days before the launching of a secret air strike, tentatively scheduled for 28 April, Ike was prepared to go personally to Congress to obtain authorization in the form of a joint resolution, even as he stood ready to interpret the slightest murmur on Britain's part as a sign of moral support. Neither did he hestitate to offer American protection for Hong Kong in return for British cooperation during France's hour of need. Needless to say, Churchill and Eden remained unmoved. With little desire to play savior to their nemesis across the Channel, they refused to give even provisional approval to American plans, knowing that this might enable the White House to woo Congress under false pretenses.[42]

The results are well known. Dien Bien Phu fell to the Vietminh on 7 May. Laniel's government then collapsed and a new cabinet assembled under the leadership of Pierre Mendès-France, who was pledged to negotiate an end to the war within four weeks or resign.

To be sure, Dulles occasionally spoke like a hawk. He was always, to some extent, the mouthpiece of the White House. Moreover, because EDC was the apple of his eye, along with SEATO to a lesser degree, he could not afford to let go completely of the inducement represented by a possible increase in aid to Vietnam. As late as mid-May, he was still careful to keep alive the possibility of full-scale ground intervention. No useful purpose could be served by shutting the door entirely, for what other assurance was Washington prepared to give in return for something it regarded as truly important?[43]

Among French leaders, Pineau, Bidault, and Ely were generally clear on the relationship between Dulles and Eisenhower. But Ely, for some reason, along with General Navarre, erred in depicting Dulles as a person bent upon swaying Congress toward intervention, and it is this "Ely-Navarre thesis" that caught the imagination of Americans when presented in article form by the journalist Chalmers Roberts. Roberts' piece shaped a mindset which Dulles was never able to shake, try as he might; indeed, it has been ensconced in the historiography of the period ever since. Among American commentators, only James Reston has proven consistently accurate in this regard. Even someone as close to the events of 1954 as Richard Nixon, who began by correctly identifying Ike as on the hawkish side, eventually wound up adopting the Ely-Navarre thesis. And not surprisingly. One of the main sources of confusion is Eisenhower's memoirs, for while the president admits that he never ruled out the sending of American troops and while he recalls Dulles as attaching stiff conditions, he also adds, somewhat disingenuously, "I had no intention of using United States forces in any limited action when the force employed would probably not be effective." On 13 January 1960, he strayed even farther from the truth when he stated that "there was never any plan developed to put into execution in Indochina."[44]

A number of American officials, among them Lodge, Nixon, Macomber, and Bowie, have observed that beneath Eisenhower's genial, easy-going exterior lay a hard substratum, and the notion is well developed by Fred I. Greenstein in a volume entitled *The Hidden-Hand Presidency*. Here was an hombre who made more decisions than one would imagine. If he was not always in control (Dulles was the one with the hidden hand at Dien Bien Phu), neither was he a rubber stamp. Moreover, he could, and occasionally did, overrule his secretary, as in the Suez crisis and on the matter of dumping American cotton surpluses. He also reviewed most of Dulles' speeches, altering passages here and there to soften the tone, simplify the message, or guard against oversimplification. At the same time, it is well to remember that it was Dulles who shaped the configuration of state policy and did the most to sell it. As Reston has suggested, he was the "informing mind" of American diplomacy. Very few who were close enough to the State Department and White House to speak authoritatively would have questioned this. Not without reason did Clare Boothe Luce describe Dulles as the most commanding secretary in American history. His dominance may be seen not only in connection with larger issues such as Dien Bien Phu and Quemoy, but also when it comes to relatively small matters such as the origination of an occasional catch phrase (e.g., "waging peace"). Needless to say, he was also the controlling factor in a host of middle-range questions, as for example whether or not to provide Iran with assurances of military backing and how advisable it would be to dispense with congressional authorization for the landings in Lebanon.[45]

Foreign commentators have been known to overstate the case for Dulles. Khrushchev once referred to Eisenhower as a mere "water boy," while Churchill, in a moment of pique, called the president a "ventriloquist's doll." But nearly all influential leaders with reason to know agreed that Dulles was the driving force behind most key decisions. Pineau, mirroring the opinion of the Quai d'Orsay, used the term "sole master" in reference to the secretary's position. Canadian ambassador Heeney called Dulles "preeminent," and Prime Minister Macmillan described Eisenhower as under Dulles' influence except on "very rare occasions of supreme importance." British ambassador Roger Makins described the secretary as "an awkward old buster" with "pachydermatous qualities," but he saw him as "in many ways a more forceful and positive character than the President," and with views that were "quite likely to be controlling."[46]

Even though Dulles was aware of the danger inherent in seeming to overshadow the White House, he had a way of speaking in the first person singular, as when he told reporters that "the Soviets respect me because they know I'll fight." At another of his news conferences, he remarked, "I don't proceed on the theory that the only areas that get detached from their present orbit are free world countries." This was not unusual, nor was he out of character when he confided to French Premier Mendès-France that if Diem fell from power, he (Dulles) would probably pull out of Vietnam.[47]

The wonder is that such an individual ever managed to survive in a world of presidential politics. Eisenhower was big enough, certainly, to surround himself with men of substance, but one can only conclude that Dulles was sufficiently cognizant of the danger of forfeiting Ike's confidence to act accordingly. His uncle, Robert Lansing, had lost favor with President Wilson by taking an independent tack, and he must have been familiar with the story of Seward and Byrnes. To avoid a similar fate, he phoned Eisenhower as many as eight times a day and made it a practice to stop off several times a week on his way home for private chats in the family quarters of the White House. On overseas trips, he dispatched reports with the regularity of a clock. Almost never did he deliver a speech or hold a press conference without first clearing his remarks with the president, and he rarely made a recommendation on the highest level unless it was fairly certain of acceptance. Equally to the point, he was vigilant in seeing to it that foreign leaders were required to go through the State Department on their way to the White House. At home, there were any number of would-be secretaries waiting in the wings for the slightest sign of a slip or fall, and as time passed, he found that he had to strike from his path one rival after another. Lodge, Stassen, Nixon, and Gruenther all tended to encroach at one point or another, not to mention C. D. Jackson, W. H. Jackson, Milton Eisenhower, and Nelson Rockefeller. In the end, only the president's brother posed a serious challenge, and then only in one area, the Western Hemisphere.[48]

Macmillan misrepresented Dulles in his memoirs when he quoted him as saying that when executive decisions were "tough" they were made by State, and when they were "idealistic" they were made by the president but "written by the Secretary of State." It is extremely unlikely that such things were ever said, or even hinted at. Sherman Adams, who noted that the secretary tended to be "secretive," reserved, and "withdrawn," was engaging in euphemism. An absolute stickler for presidential prestige, Dulles would take almost any amount of heat to shield his chief from criticism. Ike himself acknowledged that "no subordinate was ever more assiduous in establishing the President's authority . . . he [Dulles] used to give me little lectures on that." If Eisenhower achieved a landslide victory in 1956 and if, throughout his tenure, Congress upheld executive prerogative with the same kind of confidence that the Constitutional Convention of 1787 reposed in George Washington, it was due, in no small part, to Dulles' willingness to bear the brunt of political criticism. Had the relationship between White House and State Department been lacking in this or any other essential, Ike would not have referred to his secretary on several occasions as the "greatest" of all time, nor would his eyes have misted over when he announced Dulles' resignation in 1959.[49]

Ike's encomium, it should be noted, was based in large measure on Dulles' deftness in handling public opinion. Meeting more often with reporters to discuss matters of substance than almost any other secretary before or since— at least once a week while in Washington—he was also the first to go completely on record and to have his news conferences published in their entirety on a regular basis. By his own account, he approached the press with trepidation. But he prepared his statements with meticulous care and was ready to match wits with all comers. As one who knew how to "make" news, he rarely held forth without tossing out some kind of scintilating tidbit to appease a hungry audience. At the same time, he had an uncanny ability to avoid sensitive or delicate topics without appearing to do so. With all of his dodging, he was capable of admitting, from time to time, that he did not know something; and the impression he normally gave was of a person yearning to impart vital information on virtually every subject. By some act of legerdemain, he could explain what he was doing, and at considerable length, without divulging secrets. Where his predecessor, Dean Acheson, had been likely to respond under pressure with a "no comment," Dulles never did. He rarely ducked a question if he could address it, which was most of the time, even though he might be outfoxed or forced into a corner. Once, when a reporter who seemed to have him on the run was interrupted by another correspondent, Dulles rebuked the intruder with the air of one who disdained a handicap and wanted the jousting to proceed at full tilt with no quarter given or accepted.[50]

Along with his expertise in handling loaded questions went a knowledge of how and when to release information in the form of a leak. He had a corresponding sense for how much should be for the record, as opposed to "background." Moreover, he was always capable of taking the offensive with a well-aimed riposte. Asked about French criticism of the United States for arming Germany in the face of Russian disarmament proposals, he replied that it was a tribute to America that her allies felt free to criticize. Generally, he answered questions with such thoroughness that he could jest in the rare case of deliberate evasion. In fact, the ensuing game of cat and mouse often provoked laughter. A transcript of one conference held on 25 March 1958 indicates that he convulsed his audience no less than six times. Occasionally, too, he would join in the fun and let out a huge roar of delight, especially if he could see himself as the butt of someone else's humor.[51]

As a Wall Street Republican in the midst of Democratic reporters, he could easily have had a bad press. What is more, he was a lawyer with well-established church connections and one who was not bashful about injecting a spiritual element into the most mundane discussions. He was also inclined to be professorial in manner, holding reporters to a refined standard of verbal accuracy and lecturing them on distinctions that they either missed or would have preferred to ignore. Vintage Dulles was the answer he gave when a reporter asked, "When do you expect to be back in Washington [from Berlin]?" Replied the secretary, "If you had asked me when I *hope* to be back in Washington I could answer your question better." At the same time, he had great depth of experience, combined with mental agility, and although inclined to brusqueness, he generally came across in public as patient, courteous, clear, and accommodating.[52]

In short, Dulles' adversarial relationship with the media has been exag-

gerated. He is reputed in many quarters to have been devious and unforth-
coming. Yet virtually every journalist who ever reflected on the subject has
emphasized the respect that he enjoyed. Arthur Krock, dean of *New York
Times* columnists, was not the only one who thought that Dulles was well
regarded by the press of his time. Certainly, his news conferences, far better
attended than Acheson's, were packed to the walls, and he was *Time*'s "Man
of the Year" in 1954, as well as the favorite in a UP poll of over a thousand
client radio stations. The *New York Times*, after initially unfavorable comment, echoed his line on issues ranging from peaceful coexistence to summit
conferences; leading periodicals such as *Time*, *Life*, and the *New York Herald
Tribune* were consistently sympathetic on virtually all the major topics of
the day; and he could count on editorials appearing under the name of Roscoe
Drummond, David Lawrence, and Marguerite Higgins. At a National Press
Club conference in January 1958, he received a "certificate of appreciation"
along with repeated rounds of applause and a standing ovation (not given
lightly in those days), while CBS News had a special understanding whereby,
when he was incommunicado on Duck Island and out of telephone contact,
they would signal the need for a speedy return to Washington by announcing
that some piece of foreign news was certain to be "of interest to Secretary
Dulles."[53]

Naturally, there were the usual problems that plague any new administration. Efforts had to be made to counteract inaccuracy and false attribution,
and the press animus of the Acheson years had to be overcome. Dulles'
reputation among a number of intellectuals and journalists plummeted when
the government outlined what it described as an "even-handed" policy as
between Israel and its Arab neighbors. Israel insisted on diverting the waters
of the Jordan River, and Washington threatened to eliminate tax deductions
for contributions to the United Jewish Appeal. The tax-free status accorded
Zionist organizations was also declared in jeopardy. Tel Aviv had no choice
but to retreat, and later, in July, when Israel announced plans to transfer
its capital to Jerusalem, Dulles again barred the way. Finally, after Israeli
troops launched a stinging retaliatory raid on Qibya in October, Dulles
announced that the United States would withhold $60 million in aid. The
wounds eventually healed after an initial period of testing, but four years
later, the secretary found himself back on square one in the aftermath of
the Suez crisis. Walter Lippmann remained unremittingly critical, as did
the *New York Post* and the *St. Louis Post-Dispatch*.[54]

All things considered, though, Dulles did remarkably well. Reporters
appreciated his openness, while he, in turn, brought them into the State
Department on a basis of trust and confidence as never before, prevailing
on desk and division chiefs, as well as ambassadors, to grant interviews.
After securing more comfortable quarters for the press (on Virginia Avenue),
he invented the "backgrounder," an informal meal attended by a select group
of correspondents and bureau chiefs to whom he would speak for an hour

or two before answering questions with followups. Held initially at a hotel, then at the homes of reporters, and eventually at Dulles' own address, the invitations were extended to between ten and twenty persons at intervals of about two to three months. Exceedingly popular, one observer believed that they were enough in themselves to account for Dulles' success, and as time passed their number increased. Like Eisenhower, Dulles employed a professional speech analyst to help him with diction and delivery, and in 1957, when the Suez crisis intensified, he enlisted the services of an aide whose sole function was to dine with members of the press, present Dulles' line, and arrange tête-a-têtes with the secretary where they would do the most good. All of this added to the positive effect of a long-term campaign for media cooperation.[55]

A second set of individuals with whom Dulles got along rather well were the politicians. A record was set for the number and intimacy of functions held for the leaders of both parties as the secretary appeared before congressional committees six to twelve times a month and attended scores of White House briefings designed to influence opinion on the Hill. When funding was required for aid programs, as it was once a year, he would testify in person before three different committees from each chamber of Congress: armed services, appropriations, and foreign policy. Thirty-nine congressional appearances in one year alone (1953) constituted a virtuoso performance by almost any standard. But there was more to the tactic than frequency. His response to almost any request for consultation was prompt and overwhelming. He would tell his guests so much that they grew tired of listening. Far more popular than Acheson with the House Foreign Affairs Committee, he also made it a practice to meet with the Senate Foreign Relations Committee before and after international conferences, and during a crisis such as occurred in Lebanon in 1958, he would assign a special State Department official to brief senators and congressman daily.[56]

Few opportunities were overlooked as Dulles made it a point to open each congressional session with a world briefing. He also entertained special interest delegations led by luminaries such as Jacob Javits and Emmanuel Celler, and in every case he impressed his audience with his tact and good sense. This should not be surprising, as it was a repeat performance of the success he had with Congress in 1950–51 during his negotiation of the Japanese Peace Treaty. But surprising or not, he gradually came to possess a power all his own. Where previous administrations were unable to obtain approval of the St. Lawrence Seaway, he and Ike managed to do so, and although it seemed all but impossible to block passage of the popular Bricker Amendment, he found a way.[57]

Politics usually involves some kind of sacrifice, often enough the granting of a favor. James P. Richards of South Carolina, congressman for over twenty years and Democratic chairman of the House Foreign Affairs Committee, found that Dulles was delighted to stay with him as an overnight guest and

accept an honorary degree from the University of South Carolina. Walter
George of Georgia, who became chairman of the Senate Foreign Relations
Committee after the Democratic victory in 1954, made another discovery:
the secretary enjoyed breakfasting with him once a week on his way to work.
George was among those who supported the Formosa Resolution in 1955,
and later, when he and Richards retired, they represented the administration
on important overseas missions, helping to pave the way for enabling legislation in Congress. To cite two other examples, Representative Gerry Vorys
of Ohio was given advance copies of speeches and invited to dine with Dulles
at the State Department, and the secretary would occasionally host an informal dinner at his home, as he did for the Democratic contingent of the
Senate Appropriations Committee.[58]

Often, when Dulles was not working on some key person or group, Ike
was. The fact that the president took a cottage at the Augusta National Golf
Club and flew south for well-publicized vacations, that he befriended Georgia's influential senator, Richard Russell, by having him to the White House
for private breakfasts as often as could be arranged, and the fact that he
hosted more luncheons and meetings for members of Congress than any
other president on record—all of this mattered. By coincidence, Eisenhower
happened to have been born in Speaker Sam Rayburn's congressional district
and the latter was never allowed to forget it. Rayburn used to say with a
chuckle that he was Ike's vicarious congressman.[59]

For this reason, as much as any other, political leaders proved to be
unusually cooperative. Congressman McCormack of Massachusetts was one
of many who got behind the secretary to support the policies of the administration, some of which won unanimous approval. Among them were German rearmament, denial of UN membership to Peking, renewal of the Trade
Agreements Act in 1955, the Inter-American Highway Program, the Philippine Trade Act, and the amendment to the Foreign Service Act. Nearly
unanimous in their margin of approval were SEATO, the defense pact with
Taiwan, treaties granting sovereignty to Germany and admitting Bonn to
NATO, the Formosa Resolution, and a resolution denouncing Guatemala's
appeal to the UN Security Council. Although the House and Senate remained Democratic after 1954, only two of Eisenhower's 169 vetoes were
overridden. But sweetest of all, perhaps, since it was so unexpected, was
congressional renewal of the Reciprocal Trade Agreements Act in 1958 by
large majorities.[60]

This is not to suggest that Dulles bought the cooperation of Congress or
the press. He and Eisenhower had to earn it, and one of the ways they did
so was by shunning most forms of partisanship. Until 1952, no one knew
whether Ike would run as a Democrat or Republican, and when, at the time
of Dulles' death in 1959, the flag of the nation's capitol was lowered to half-
mast by order of Congress, such action was prompted, at least in part, by
the spirit of bipartisanship with which the secretary had long been associated.

Originated by FDR and continued under Truman when the latter lost control of Congress in 1946, bipartisanship became something of a fixture after Republicans suffered a similar loss in 1954. But apart from practical considerations, it is clear that Dulles, as one of its principal exponents, regarded it from the beginning as integral to the success of the democratic experiment, for only if American policy could command a broad two-party consensus, he maintained, would there be sufficient continuity between successive administrations to inspire confidence overseas.[61]

Action spoke louder than words. One of the first things the Secretary did in 1953 was to bank the fire of Republican campaign rhetoric by maneuvering to prevent a formal repudiation of Roosevelt's secret agreements with Moscow. Urging the need for unanimity and altering the wording of the proposed resolution in such a way as to convert an attack on FDR and the Democrats into an attack on the Soviet Union for not living up to its promises, he discouraged enough hard-line proponents of the measure to effectively kill it. A second measure was to brief congressional leaders of both political parties. He took other steps as well, hanging a portrait of Cordell Hull in his office and alluding to FDR on the tenth anniversary of his death as one of the nation's "very great" presidents. Leading Democrats were represented at the Caracas Conference, as well as at the first SEATO conference for the signing of the Manila Pact. They were also appointed to the nation's UN delegation. Dulles likewise went out of his way, after the signing of the Austrian treaty, to cable a message of thanks to Truman and Acheson for all they had done to lay the groundwork. It is interesting that once in office he never publicly blamed the opposition for anything, and through all of the campaign charges of 1956, he remained absolutely mum.[62]

Among Democratic office holders who stayed on or were named to responsible posts under Dulles were Walter Bedell Smith, Truman's ambassador to the Soviet Union and head of the CIA; Gordon Gray, Truman's secretary of the army; Loy Henderson, Truman's director of Middle Eastern Affairs; Vernon Walters, Harriman's interpreter; Andrew Berding, co-author of Hull's memoirs. In addition, there were Charles Bohlen, Robert Cutler, Henry A. Byroade, James P. Richards, Walter F. George, and John M. Allison, not to mention Walter Robertson, Robert R. Bowie, Robert Anderson, John E. Peurifoy, and David K. E. Bruce—all lifelong Democrats. Small wonder that Truman saw fit to back Dulles on Asia and the Middle East. Eisenhower had, of course, been FDR's leading general in the field before serving as Truman's chairman of the Joint Chiefs of Staff, while Dulles, who had been a Wilsonian in his younger days as well as a supporter of John W. Davis during the 1920s, remained on close personal terms with a number of Democrats, including Dean Rusk.[63]

Still another area in which the secretary showed marked ability was in his molding of grass roots opinion, a talent not unrelated to his rapport with Congress and the press. Woodrow Wilson, who regarded education of the

public as one of the supremely important political functions, must have
breathed some of this conviction into Dulles when the latter attended his
classes at Princeton. In any event, Wilson's protegé found a good many ways
of putting his professor's teaching into practice. Within days of taking office,
he invited television crews to film an extempore speech outlining America's
foreign policy goals. Thereafter, he spoke on radio and TV after every overseas trip, just as he addressed such groups as the American Bar Association,
the American Legion, the American Federation of Labor, and university
faculties across the country. In 1953, his first year at State, he spoke at
Princeton, Boston, St. Louis, Denver, Syracuse, and Cleveland.[64]

In sum, Dulles was a valuable player, offensively as well as defensively,
with a large number of assists to his name. That he was also a lawyer with
a penchant for obtaining the best possible terms from friend and foe alike
will be the subject of analysis in chapter 3. Suffice it to say that, all things
considered, he was the complete secretary.

CHAPTER 3

The Art of Negotiation

With all of his gifts for managing Congress, the press, and public opinion, Dulles would still have fallen short as secretary had he not been a high-powered negotiator. Indeed, of all his skills, this is probably where he excelled the most, owing to his background in international law. Once Soviet leaders knew that they could not manipulate American public opinion from behind the scenes, they had to confront the secretary head-on, and when they did, they encountered an individual who based his public life on the motto, "you give nothing to get nothing." In other words, one does not trade American "performance" for Communist "promise." Typically, he withheld support for Peking's admission to the United Nations because he viewed it as a bargaining counter in the Korean armistice talks. In the same manner, he rejected Moscow's bid for a summit when Kremlin leaders offered nothing more in return than a promise of cooperation.[1]

With each nation, the secretary utilized his leverage to the utmost. Egyptian officials found that they could obtain American arms and financing for the Aswan Dam provided they joined a pro-Western defense organization and mended relations with Israel. Adenauer could secure the remission of sentences for German war crimes and the relaxation of American occupation controls, but again for a price including curtailment of East-West trade, increased support for Allied troops, and a Saar settlement satisfactory to the French, something Paris was demanding as a quid pro quo for EDC and Western European Union (WEU).[2]

Where Downing Street was concerned, Dulles swapped economic concessions for British acquiescence in his treatment of Peking. Similarly, American expertise in nuclear technology was offered to Whitehall as a means of ensuring its cooperation in the Middle East, along with its support for the

British prime minister to leave his country than for a president since the former could rely on a king or queen to perform ceremonial duties. His participation, moreover, did not automatically convey the highest distinction on those present nor did it expose his country to the same loss of prestige.

Dulles, it should be noted, could be just as calculating and tight-fisted where America's allies were concerned as when he was dealing with adversaries. When Eisenhower proposed to return the American-held Amami Islands to Japan because they had little value as defense outposts, Dulles suggested that such a move "should be timed to extract the utmost advantage." In the same way, in line with his belief that South Korea should have borne a heavier share of the fighting from 1950 to 1952, he refused to negotiate a defense treaty with Seoul until Syngman Rhee offered pledges of restraint vis-à-vis North Korea, along with increased funding for the United States Eighth Army's power and dock facilities.[10]

The same technique is evident elsewhere. Mendès-France requested the secretary's presence at Geneva where the future of Indochina was being decided in 1954, but Dulles let it be known that he would appear only if France took action on EDC and agreed to avoid a Far Eastern Munich. Caring nothing for outward appearances when there was something of real value at stake, he declined to endorse the Geneva settlement because he felt there was more to be gained by disapproval than approval. This is the same Dulles who insisted that the United States had no business underwriting the security and economic well-being of Western Europe unless Europeans themselves stepped up their commitment to NATO and agreed to German rearmament. Some historians have assumed that he was bluffing when he spoke of an "agonizing reappraisal" (of American policy) should Germany be denied a place in the scheme of Western defense. But this is not so. Churchill and Eden, along with leaders on the Continent, took him quite seriously, as well they might. The idea of a "peripheral" defense of Europe, long on the drawing boards of the Defense Department, was a definite option in the mind of the president, as well as the Joint Chiefs of Staff. American troops could be withdrawn from France, and possibly England, to relocate in such places as Norway, Denmark, Spain, Turkey, Morocco, and Iceland, with less emphasis on ground forces and more on the capacity for massive retaliation. And lest anyone doubt his sincerity, Ike recalled four divisions from Korea while obtaining additional bases in Spain and Morocco (passage of WEU obviated the need for any further action along this line).[11]

The phrase "agonizing reappraisal" has also been portrayed by historians as a gaffe, and again the evidence indicates otherwise. Dulles' phrase appears not only in his opening statement at a press conference of 14 December 1953 but also in his response to questions. Interestingly enough, he used it earlier in addressing the NATO council; it was on his lips a week later in an appearance before the National Press Club; and it figured in one of his books. He continued to lead American opinion toward withdrawal from Europe after 1954 and in fact was still making noises to this effect in the fall of 1954.

That he used the phrase to good effect is equally clear. The idea of linking continued aid to Europe with Germany's admission to the Western defense system had won the overwhelming support of Congress. After the fall of Premier Laniel, Senate Majority Leader Knowland sponsored a resolution authorizing Eisenhower to take any and all steps necessary to restore German sovereignty, and his motion passed by the resounding margin of 88–0. Similar unanimity in the House (the Richards Amendment) mandated drastic reductions in aid to any ally that opposed German rearmament. On 28 August, the day Mendès-France submitted EDC to the Chamber of Deputies, Senator Alexander Wiley, chairman of the Senate Foreign Relations Committee, in anticipation of an adverse vote by the Deputies, proposed German inclusion in NATO with or without the approval of Paris. On the Democratic side, Senator Kefauver, a contender for his party's presidential nomination, seconded the idea; and several weeks later, as Dulles wound up two days of urgent pleading in England with little to show for it, Senator Knowland renewed his appeal for disengagement. Dulles' hand could scarcely have been stronger, and most commentators, including David K. E. Bruce and Winston Churchill, along with French officials and a number of French periodicals normally anti-American, applauded his tactics. Mendès-France, far from resenting outside interference or interpreting Dulles' phrase as a gaffe, made it clear that Paris was counting on blunt warnings from Washington, as well as London, to sway the Deputies.[12] One cannot assume that warnings which proved futile in the short run were necessarily inopportune. EDC was evidently beyond redemption.

Throughout the period, allied nations were apt to do a certain amount of leaching off the United States in the name of collective security, and the secretary was quick to reply with what later came to be known as the Nixon Doctrine. What this amounted to in practice was a concerted effort to purchase more security at less cost by shifting an increasing share of the burden to America's partners. Overseas ground forces, which could be maintained at a fraction of the cost of American troops, were expected to bear the brunt of the fighting wherever it might occur while the United States furnished a strategic shield against Moscow and Peking. If, for any reason, a foreign country gave evidence of being unable or unwilling to wage war on its own behalf Washington would not undertake to make up the difference. Essentially, therefore, it was a matter of tailoring ends to means. In Eisenhower's words, America could not go on forever being "an Atlas . . . supporting the rest of the world."[13]

As a fiscal conservative with an eye to the main chance, Dulles barred access to NATO's resources for the development of France's North African possessions just as he declined to commit large numbers of troops to SEATO and refused to allocate funds to the alliance per se, only to individual members on a recripocal basis. Eventually, too, he worked out trade arrangements with Japan which proved highly beneficial to other regions of Southeast Asia. President Magsaysay of the Philippines pared down one of his aid requests from $300 million to $125 million when Dulles waited until midnight of his last day in town to agree to fund an atomic reactor center. Another aid recipient, Brazil, was induced to buttress Washington's position on Communist subversion. Needless to say, the United States was not the only country that excelled at the game of quid pro quo. When Whitehall solicited American support for Egypt's Aswan Dam, it hinted at cooperation on trade sanctions against the Soviet Union, and when Churchill offered to back Dulles on the Far East it was plainly in return for American assistance in the Middle East. In this way, the future of China's seat at the United Nations and France's chances for victory in Indochina, not to mention the fate of SEATO, all hinged to some extent on Washington's stance with respect to Suez and the Baghdad Pact. Few of the world's statesmen, however, were better at such a game than Dulles.[14]

Two other features of the secretary's style, both of them classic, are worth noting. First, he strove to bargain from a position of strength. Second, he was prepared to risk failure at the end of a long and arduous negotiation if he felt confident of holding a winning hand. Working in unison, such tactics could produce spectacular results as in the case of the Austrian State Treaty.

Early in 1954, at the Berlin Conference of foreign ministers, Dulles offered the Soviets an Austrian settlement featuring substantial concessions on oil and Danube River transport if Moscow would agree to the permanent removal of all its troops from Austria. When the Russians declined and outlined terms less inviting than any of their previous offers, he decided to concentrate on German rearmament while making Austrian independence a sine qua non for both disarmament talks and a summit meeting. Several months elapsed, but during the late fall, as French approval of WEU seemed increasingly likely, the Soviet position began to soften. There was still a chance that Russian indulgence of Austria might sell the German people on neutrality and thus prevent three-quarters of them from enlisting in the Western camp. Conversely, Communist speeches and publications voiced the concern that a majority of Austrians (residents of the French, British, and American occupation zones) might merge with an independent West Germany. This latter-day prospect of *Anschluss*, real or imagined, found its way into the text of the Austrian State Treaty in the form of an express prohibition—but at a price, as we shall see. Time was on the side of Washington.[15]

Tactically speaking, it is clear that Dulles' dogged insistence on postponing the four-power summit until German rearmament and Austrian freedom were assured had a threefold effect. First, it safeguarded WEU from Soviet efforts to sow seeds of disunity. Second, inasmuch as it helped secure German entry into WEU, it all but forced Moscow to sign a satisfactory Austrian treaty. Third, since France longed for a summit almost as much as Russia at this stage, Dulles' stonewalling helped to induce French action on WEU. By refusing to hold a three- or four-power conference, even on the ministerial level, and in the face of heavy Soviet, French, and British pressure, the secretary conserved his strength until the very end when ratification of WEU seemed all but certain. Paris tried to turn the tables, demanding that he issue invitations to a summit prior to ratification, but he was able to make a graceful feint in this direction without yielding on substance. Britain, he agreed, might go ahead and issue invitations, but not for the summit, only for talks to *conclude arrangements* for such a summit, and by the time the invitations to an actual summit went out, Moscow had made sweeping concessions with regard to both Austria and Yugoslavia.[16]

Throughout the winter and spring of 1955, a time of severe testing, there was only one leader in the West who dared to execute a strategy of delay and insist upon better terms for Austria. Accused by the Soviet Union of being more Austrian than the Austrians, Dulles strained America's ties with her allies and more than once had to face the prospect of total failure. Late in the game, French and British leaders were willing to accept provisions which, in Dulles' view, threatened to demoralize Vienna and pave the way for communism. They also deemed it unwise for Dulles to insist on the withdrawal of every last Soviet soldier as the price of a treaty. Dulles alone was thus responsible for this concession, as well as for Austria's freedom to field an army and maintain its own military bases. For the first time since World War II, the Soviets felt obliged to yield substantial amounts of territory, something Dulles regarded as a positive precedent for Hungary and Romania. Some have speculated that the secretary's role may have been minor inasmuch as the Kremlin had domestic reasons for wanting better East-West relations and Malenkov and his successors were more liberal than Stalin. But such an explanation ignores the fact that Moscow capitulated under the lash of American firmness and the duress of time pressure generated by Dulles.[17]

A few dates will serve to illustrate the course of Soviet retreat, along with the centrality of Dulles' role. In April 1955, with French approval of the German treaties virtually certain, Moscow agreed to the permanent removal of all Soviet forces from Austria as well as local control of oil and river transport. Dulles beat back British and Soviet demands for a preliminary conference on the ambassadorial level long enough to apply maximum pressure so that when such a conference finally met in Vienna from 2–13 May, the Soviets approved an Austrian army of unlimited size in addition to Austrian jurisdiction over all Eastern European émigrés within its borders. However, on the day that Dulles was due in Vienna for the actual signing of the treaty, he heard that Moscow had gone back on its pledges regarding oil, river transport, and the permanence of Soviet troop removal. Immediately, he cancelled his flight and suspended all further plans until he was able to receive confirmation of the original terms of the agreement. He then made the trip to Vienna only to discover on arrival that another agreement was in jeopardy owing to a second Soviet reversal, this time regarding émigrés. Grim but poker-faced, he announced that he was prepared to scrap the entire package, along with the summit, and, for added emphasis, he ordered his plane readied for the trip home. Once again, the Soviet position crumbled with Molotov going a step further and actually granting a last-minute Austrian appeal for removal of the war-guilt clause. Dulles added a touch of velvet by acquiescing in an unfavorable wording on Article 35 regarding economic terms and accepting Molotov's promise that Austria would be permitted to interpret the article liberally. Adenauer had done the same thing in essence when Moscow agreed to release German POWs. He wanted the promise in writing but he accepted an oral stipulation, and the Kremlin delivered. In both cases, there was little to lose on the side of the West as it was in Russia's interest to follow through, but Western profession of trust added to the luster of Soviet statecraft and represented a minor form of concession.[18]

So it was that signatures were affixed to a treaty containing all the key points for which Dulles had contended over a period of years. He issued the long-awaited invitations for a four-power summit and when asked to comment on the significance of the treaty and his role in it, he remarked casually that Moscow had been guided by its respect for world opinion. What he himself had done to engender such respect would remain undisclosed.

Five hundred thousand Viennese, a third of the entire metropolitan population, turned out to celebrate their national liberation; and later, after all foreign troops had taken their leave, the Vienna State Opera opened its doors for the first time since the end of the war for a stirring rendition of Beethoven's *Fidelio*, the story of a faithful and daring wife, Leonora, who rescues her husband from prison. Nothing could have been more appropriate than the choice of opera unless possibly the presence of an American secretary of state in the audience.[19]

On balance, it cannot be said that Dulles' hard-nosed, low-profile approach always redounded to his popularity, but it did count in the winning of Austrian independence along with the attainment of two other major goals: German participation in the defense of the West and a security pact for Southeast Asia. Both are worth examining as examples of Dulles in action on familiar terrain where his special talent as a negotiator was given maximum play, and we shall take them in order, beginning with the idea of a European Defense Community (EDC).

The secretary was not, of course, the originator of EDC. French strategists, unwilling to rehabilitate a former enemy, had insisted that German troops be integrated into a "European" command composed of hybrid units. In this way, there would be no German army or corps as such because there could be no national unit larger than a division. What Paris was saying in effect was that it would sooner dispense with its army than risk a resurgence of the peril that had led to national humiliation in 1870, 1914, and 1939. This was the so-called Pleven Plan, named after its sponsor, the French defense minister of 1950, who envisaged a European Defense Community made up of France, Germany, Italy, the Netherlands, Belgium, and Luxembourg. EDC was to form the hard core for a greater NATO, and Eisenhower, acting on behalf of Truman in the role of supreme commander, lined up the necessary signatures after a six-month exercise in persuasion. Adenauer, Acheson, Dulles, and many others staked their political fortunes on Pleven's handiwork nothwithstanding odds estimated at no better than 60 percent because they felt this was the only way France would ever bring itself to accept German rearmament; also because Adenauer's future, and hence the future of German ties with NATO, seemed to depend on upholding Western commitments. Dulles was especially enamored of the supranational character of EDC with its potential to eliminate the possibility of war among its members.[20]

Churchill felt differently. Decidedly unimpressed with EDC, he would neither endorse the "sludgy amalgam," as he called it, nor offer the minimal military support needed to ensure ratification by Paris. Traditionally, the British viewed Franco-German tension as the key to their favored position as holders of the European balance of power, and true to form they wanted Germany free to rearm with few restrictions. As for the danger of Adenauer losing his grip and the Social Democrats striking a deal with their Communist neighbors, Churchill remained skeptical.[21]

As it developed, the French themselves began to have second thoughts. Generals like de Gaulle, Weygand, and Juin were wedded to the idea of a separate French army, and as the Geneva accords on Indochina had yet to release substantial numbers of French troops to serve at home or in North Africa, Paris was not about to be dwarfed by a resurgent Bonn. But what the French did, rather than disown their brainchild, was to hold out the prospect for ratification if certain conditions could be met, among them satisfactory terms on the Saar, the shielding of French colonial interests from verbal abuse, and an extension of NATO's commitment to the defense of the Continent from twenty to fifty years. London and Washington would have to agree additionally to retain a specified number of troops on the Continent; France expected to be included as an equal partner with Britain and the United States in the making of Western policy; and just as important, Eisenhower would be required to furnish more aid to French units fighting with their backs to the wall in Vietnam. This was asking quite a lot, and the French knew it. What is remarkable is that they came as close as they did to achieving all that they desired.[22]

During 1953 and early 1954, British leaders were induced by a variety of means to agree to guarantee their military presence on the Continent for a fixed term. They promised to consult with EDC before withdrawing and to contribute an armored division to the Supreme Allied Command in Europe (SACEUR), along with some Royal Air Force units. By March 1954, they had also offered to integrate their forces into a supranational command. None of this compares with what London would offer in September under the terms of Western European Union—four divisions and a tactical air force. Still, it indicates how fluid the British position had become under Dulles' prodding.[23] All along, Dulles appeared willing to step up American aid to Indochina, and when Laniel resorted to delaying tactics, so did Dulles. If the premier felt betrayed at the time of Dien Bien Phu, so did the secretary. It was, after all, in return for a pledge of French cooperation on EDC that Dulles had agreed to the Berlin Conference on January 1954, thereby bolstering Bidault's electoral prospects. He had gone out of his way to sing the foreign minister's praises, and it was in return for renewed promises of French cooperation on EDC that he had begun to refrain from anti-imperialist rhetoric while agreeing at Berlin to include Peking in a five-power conference with all the danger this posed to his standing at home.[24]

Owing to the use of clever conjuring tactics on the part of Dulles, the outlook for American intervention waxed and waned in accordance with the outlook for French approval of EDC. Washington had persuaded London at the Bermuda Conference in December 1953 to do all it could to secure French approval of EDC. Dulles had even spelled out his strategy of "linkage." Adenauer judged the odds to be little better than even with the outcome seeming to hinge on what could be accomplished by the use of carrot and stick. On 23 February, Dulles warned Bidault of "grave" repercussions if final movement on ratification were delayed beyond the Easter holidays. Doubtless, he foresaw that once the Geneva Conference opened on 26 April, Russian input would be likely to impair EDC's chances. Thus, as Dien Bien Phu was about to come under heightened attack in March, he offered to pledge the stationing of American troops in Europe for twenty years. Little happened at the other end. Bidault welcomed the proposal but warned against too much pressure for a definite timetable on EDC. Soon after, the secretary learned of French plans to postpone debate until 1 May. While this was not the end of the line, it was a bitter pill to swallow, coming, as it did, just as Whitehall was on the verge of making valuable concessions. Dulles had also prevailed upon Adenauer to accept the Van Der Goes report on the Saar. Paris, however, refused to be satisfied. With the granting of each new favor, a pretext was found for further delay, in this instance the alleged need for an economic union with the Saar whereby Germany would be assured of little more than limited trade privileges.[25]

During the first week of April there came another ray of hope when Luxembourg became the fourth country to approve EDC, following the Netherlands, Belgium, and Germany. At about this time, too, it was bruited that American bombers might be assigned for duty aboard French carriers, and the British ambassador detected a campaign afoot in Washington to prepare public opinion for possible intervention. Paris, sensing an opening, made its first formal request for American bombing. Eisenhower, in short order, introduced his domino theory; and a week later, on 14 April, French leaders were told that unless they made a definite commitment to EDC, "very grave consequences would ensue": Washington and London would negotiate independently with Bonn. The next day Laniel set a specific date to request the opening of debate in the National Assembly (18 May). Here, at last, was a tangible sign of progress followed almost immediately by Washington's promise of an increased troop commitment to Europe. Nixon suggested to newsmen that American troops might have to be sent to Indochina, with or without British backing, and contingency plans for mobilization and military operations were prepared. Dulles, as noted earlier, poured cold water on Nixon's suggestion, labeling it "unlikely," but he was careful to keep the idea alive. British observers believed that such a move might well win a sufficient number of votes in Congress. Laniel agreed to a new formula for the independence of the Associated States, but nothing further, and there was no word from Washington. In an obscure diary entry, Ambassador Alphand stated that France rejected an offer of American troops which would presumably have been accompanied by bombing, yet there is nothing in Alphand's account to indicate the terms of the bargain or why the negotiations broke down. Most likely, the ambassador himself did not know. [26]

Laniel simply could not and would not go forward with EDC in the manner or with the speed demanded by Dulles, and the Socialist party's repudiation of Mollet on 21 April, along with the unanticipated defection of Edgar Faure, cast another shadow over Laniel's ability to deliver. Dulles reacted to the latest setback by reiterating conditions for American aid which France had never been willing to meet. Even so, within days of the fall of Dien Bien Phu on 7 May, the United States and France were again negotiating for the introduction of American ground forces with the proviso that Laniel and his cabinet move ahead on EDC. Not until 9 June did the foreign affairs committee of the French National Assembly reject EDC decisively by a vote of 42–18. Laniel's government collapsed on 12 June, and Dulles reverted immediately to a rigidly negative stance, declaring that the United States would never fight for colonialism. Churchill and Eden were soon on their way to Washington for a series of talks which would lead in a matter of months to German membership in NATO.[27]

Still another sign of the central importance of EDC in Dulles' scheme is the fact that as long as there appeared to be any chance of its adoption, he catered to the French desire for tripartite meetings on world policy. Four such conferences were held in 1953, culminating in the three-power Bermuda summit of December. In mid-February 1954, there were three-power naval maneuvers in the South China Sea with tripartite consultation in full swing. But the instant French officials abandoned EDC, all such activity ceased, not to resume again until mid–1955 after WEU was safely in hand and Dulles had other objectives in view.[28]

When France finally made its decision on EDC in late August, it had as its premier someone who had been less than cooperative from the beginning and who, in the eyes of Dulles and others, had traded French rejection of EDC for Soviet good offices at Geneva. To some degree, at least, EDC does appear to have been a casualty of the war in Vietnam and France's need for a face-saving exit. Nevertheless, on the face of it, the vote of 30 August represented a stunning defeat for allied leaders, Dulles and Adenauer in particular, with their commitment to Germany as a sovereign power fully reconciled with France and French security under the terms of a supranational army. Happily, though, all was not lost. Eden toured European capitals in September and, during a conference held in London from 29 September to 3 October, he made his sensational offer to station four British divisions and a tactical air force on the Continent for as long as a majority of WEU members desired it. Western European Union (WEU), as the new arrangement came to be known, called for a full-fledged German army as part of NATO. Bonn's sovereignty would be limited only by the number of troops it could field (500,000), by the type of weapons it could produce, and by the stipulation that its officers could not form a general staff or assume command of NATO.[29]

It is curious that credit for the resuscitation of Western fortunes has generally gone to London, for if the British role appeared prominent, this is the way Dulles planned it. He deliberately concealed his own part as a means of gaining cooperation.

Such tactics were standard procedure. Just as he nudged France out in front during the Berlin Conference of 1954, he prevailed upon Eden in 1956 to go to Parliament and present the Canal Users Association as a creation of Downing Street when, in fact, its origin can be traced to Duck Island, Dulles' oft frequented vacation retreat. During the same Suez crisis, although the plan for a United Nations emergency force to serve as a buffer between Egypt and Israel originated in the State Department, Dulles stepped aside and invited Canada's Lester Pearson to introduce it as his own. These are but a few of the many instances that can be adduced. The so-called Eden Plan for Germany, unveiled at Berlin in January 1954 (free elections and reunification on German terms), was originally drafted by Dulles, just as the plan for German reunification presented by French foreign minister Pinay at Geneva in 1955 was again Dulles' brainchild. Even if he and Eisenhower had not played enough bridge to be well versed in the art of finesse, they believed it important for the United States to display modesty, and neither of them took excessive pride in authorship.[30]

That Dulles, rather than Eden, would spearhead a campaign for restoration of German sovereignty became evident as soon as Laniel resigned in June 1954 and prospects for EDC faded. The British may have been first to envision a fall-back position along the lines of Western European Union, which was essentially an expanded version of the 1948 Brussels Treaty— Eden claimed to have conceived it in his "bath" and his biographer has traced it to Richard Steele in the Foreign Office. What is certain is that late in the summer, it was Dulles, rather than Eden, who proposed a canvas of European capitals. The secretary snubbed Mendès-France on his own trans-Atlantic tour in order to facilitate Anglo-French negotiation, and, in return for British concessions, he was happy to accept Eden's proposal that WEU be given its official send-off from London. Disappointed, later on, that the British position did not evolve more rapidly and convinced that Eden's tour of the Continent had produced little in the way of agreement, he prevailed upon the foreign secretary to postpone the London Conference until additional groundwork could be laid. As he put it, there was no point in convening a major conclave with "so little preparation." Determined to assure such preparation, he remarked on his way to London that he had "set in motion some preliminary planning to try to smoke out Mendès-France and concert UK-US thinking," as indeed he had.[31]

When the conference opened on the 28th, he continued to avoid a visible role, letting others introduce crucial resolutions and playing generous tribute to Eden. But it is clear that when Eden's European tour failed to produce anything tangible, Dulles threatened London, as well as Paris, with unilateral German rearmament and a German-American alliance. Just before the opening of the London talks, he told Eden in no uncertain language that unless Britain was sufficiently forthcoming, Washington would review its entire defense posture, including its ties with England. Only weeks before the London Conference, Eden had referred to Mendès-France's request for a long-term specific commitment as "shop-soiled" and "totally unacceptable." Eden's last-minute concession to continental defense, something the French had sought for decades, must therefore be viewed as a response to some rather intense pressure emanating from Washington in conjunction with Dulles' offer to match Britain's commitment of troops to the Continent, for only after the United States decided to extend its NATO commitment and sustain its military presence in Europe over an acceptable length of time did Whitehall click into action. Granted, the American promise was never as explicit or legally binding as Mendès-France wished, but Dulles did satisfy France's main requirements, and there can be no doubt that the British offer was predicated upon American assurances. This is indicated not only by the WEU talks themselves, but also by the transcript of tentative agreements reached on EDC at the time of the Bermuda Conference in December 1953, along with Churchill's offers of March 1954.[32]

Dulles, not Eden, negotiated the plan for technical integration of German forces into NATO just as he inspired enough confidence in Adenauer to win support for a German national army. Intricate and sensitive arrangements had to be approved by Bonn, as well as Paris, and in view of German revulsion at anything which smacked of militarism so soon after the war, it required a signal effort. Beyond this, Dulles resolved a Franco-German dispute on arms control, engineered a compromise on the stationing of NATO troops in the Federal Republic, and brokered the final solution to the Saar region controversy. By satisfying Bonn that the United States would liberalize its occupation policy, he was able to pry loose some last-minute concessions regarded by France as imperative. At the same time, he managed a discreet U.S. guarantee of these agreements without opening a Pandora's box in Congress.[33]

The Paris meetings of 20–23 October 1954, which were held to formalize plans and confirm promises made during the previous month in London, involved a four-power conference which met three times, a nine-power conference which held three sessions, and a NATO ministerial conclave that convened once. In each case, Dulles exerted great influence, though not necessarily from center stage. Earlier in the month, he had brought Adenauer and Mendès-France together for talks on the Saar. Now, after introducing them a second time and leaving them to their own devices, he remained on call in his hotel room throughout the night in case he should be summoned for further assistance. By the time he retired the next morning, a major hurdle in negotiations on the Saar had been cleared and American occupation policy would begin to change. Again, it was Dulles, not Eden, who forced France's hand, bringing to bear moral suasion and ordering the withholding of American aid on a gradual, step-by-step basis rather than abruptly.[34]

More than anyone else, it was Dulles who kept NATO alive during 1953 and 1954, persuading it to adopt tactical nuclear weaponry and fending off Soviet efforts to sow the seeds of dissension. No sooner had Moscow proposed a four-power meeting, alternating honeyed promises with dire threats calculated to influence France's vote on EDC and WEU, than the secretary went to work, applying his balm. If he was not in Paris shoring up the confidence of NATO partners and chronicling the history of Soviet bluff, he was in London urging the British to withhold certain concessions until the moment of maximum impact. Through all vicissitudes he never tired of counseling resistance to Soviet blandishments which followed one after another. Time and again throughout the debate on EDC and WEU, Moscow held out the possibility of German reunification based on so-called "free elections." Neither was it bashful about applying for membership in NATO and offering to sign a security treaty of undefined scope. On 13 November, amid signs of progress on WEU, the United States and twenty-three European nations received Moscow's invitation to attend a European security conference tentatively scheduled for the 29th. This was actually the second of two well-planned moves on the part of the Communists, for on 3 September, just as WEU was about to come under serious consideration, Red China threw down the gauntlet on Quemoy. Indicative of the origin and purpose of the challenge was its disappearance on 22 May 1955, almost immediately after Germany's admission to NATO. In the meantime, during the critical period from September to May, Dulles went out of his way to placate British and French officials who conjured up the specter of World War III every time they saw a map of the Formosa Strait. With this in mind, he arranged to defend Chiang's offshore islands with conventional weaponry; he injected a note of ambiguity into the American commitment; and, as we shall see, he worked under British auspices to secure a cease-fire in the Formosa Strait contingent upon the withdrawal of Nationalist troops.[35]

But apart from all of the above and, one might add, his felicitous timing of concessions to Paris—he withheld final Anglo-American commitments on troop deployment until February 1955 when they were most needed—he promoted the cause of WEU by indulging French sensitivity on the colonial issue and acting with notable restraint both before and after key votes in the Chamber of Deputies. A year earlier, when Allied leaders gathered at Bermuda, the British had wanted to treat French procrastination with greater severity than Dulles thought advisable, and on this point he remained consistent. When France rejected EDC, Eisenhower's response proved surprisingly mild. Whitehall recommended an Anglo-American ultimatum during the eleventh hour of French deliberation late in December, but Dulles preferred a less forthright approach, rejecting at least three separate British proposals along this line. Although the first vote on WEU (24 December) proved to be negative (by a margin of 281–257), Washington's cheerful, upbeat attitude never varied. Eden issued a harsh warning, but Dulles kept a low profile, with Eisenhower telling reporters that he simply could not believe this was the final verdict of the great French people and their Chamber of Deputies. To avoid wounding French honor, the secretary also averted an abrupt cut-off of American aid under the Richards Amendment, and four days later, the Deputies reversed themselves, voting 289–251 in favor of German entry into NATO (within two days the Chamber made it official by approving WEU 287–260).[36]

Throughout, Dulles exhibited his customary flair for the use of diplomatic emolients. When it appeared that Paris would insist on an unacceptable European armaments pool, he devised a workable alternative and presented it as a "modification" of the French plan. Mendès-France balked at American control over the distribution of military aid, and again the secretary made concessions that assuaged French pride without removing Washington from the driver's seat. It was Dulles who suggested a scrapping of verbatim minutes when the conference got down to serious business (to put the delegates more at ease); Dulles also cancelled a radio broadcast on his return from London because he did not want to upstage Mendès-France's address to the Deputies. Likewise, if WEU did not suffer, as EDC had, from early ratification by Washington, it was because the secretary insisted on awaiting French action to deemphasize the American origin of the plan.[37]

As anticipated, WEU won approval in France's upper chamber in late March. On 3 May, the last obstacle to a Franco-German agreement on the

Saar region disappeared. Paris proceeded to deposit its ratification, and Moscow suffered its greatest of all cold war diplomatic defeats. It was only a matter of days to the signing of the Austrian State Treaty, and although some historians might prefer to call it the "Death of Stalin Treaty" (just as they tend to regard Western European Union as the "Eden Treaty"), a more appropriate title in both cases would be the "Dulles Treaty," for it was Dulles who acted throughout as guiding spirit and prime mover. As indicated earlier, one of the principal elements of leverage in obtaining concessions that were a sine qua non for WEU, as well as for the Austrian treaty, was American willingness to participate in a four-power summit. British, French, and Russian leaders were all intensely anxious for it as a means of boosting their political stock at home—so much so that they were willing to yield a certain amount of diplomatic ground, and it was Dulles who withstood the combined pressure of Eisenhower, Churchill, Laniel, and Bulganin for an automatic meeting in 1953. Here, as elsewhere, the individual that emerges from the record is a figure of considerable force and subtlety, altogether unlike the churlish, war-mongering caricature of textbook fame.

Much of the high-level diplomatic give and take involved in the struggle for WEU is contained in the concept of linkage, a term which gained a certain notoriety some years later when President Nixon journeyed to Moscow and negotiated a series of interlocking agreements in the same of détente. To many in the 1970s, such a notion must have appeared novel, but not to one who had acquired the bulk of his expertise under Dulles. Almost surely, Nixon recalled the tactic in connection with EDC, as well as the siege of Dien Bien Phu and WEU. If not, he would doubtless have remembered it as part of the series of events culminating in the Southeast Asia Treaty Organization (SEATO).

SEATO did not spring full-blown into existence simply at the command of the United States. We have seen how Dulles, prior to the Geneva Conference of 1954 and during its initial stages when Eisenhower was bent upon saving Dien Bien Phu, angled for something more valuable from a long-range point of view: British support for an Asian treaty organization. Such an arrangement promised to strengthen France's hand at Geneva while checking Communist expansion elsewhere in the region, and it was with this in view that Dulles flew to England on 12 April. By the time he left London a day or two later, he was able to tell the press, "I feel very satisfied with the outcome." Whitehall had agreed to commence talks aimed at the establishment of a Far Eastern defense pact. To the secretary's distress, however, London went back on what appeared to be an iron-clad commitment, pleading its need to consult Commonwealth partners and, in effect, postponing agreement on SEATO until after Paris settled with Ho and Mao.[38]

All he wanted, Dulles told Eden on 2 May, was moral support, something to undergird the French bargaining position. But British leaders, and to some extent the French as well, were reluctant to formulate plans for a treaty organization before the actual signing of a peace agreement, believing, unlike the secretary, that to do so might lead to greater intransigence on the part of Moscow and Peking. This, at least, was their argument. They were also concerned that the underwriting of a new defense pact, before the fall of Dien Bien Phu or before the conclusion of negotiations at Geneva, might furnish Eisenhower with enough political clout to intervene militarily, which could lead to further escalation.[39]

It was at this stage that Dulles decided to lay down his highest trump. Knowing how eager the British were for American aid in the settlement of their dispute with Egypt and that without it they were as hopelessly mired in Suez as the French were in Indochina, he held out the prospect of good offices, hinting that if Britain did not lend a hand in the Far East, American assistance to Cairo, including the delivery of military equipment, would increase. If, on the other hand, Whitehall chose to cooperate, the United States would be instrumental in facilitating the withdrawal of U.K. forces from Suez. As a bonus, Washington would undertake to guarantee the security of Hong Kong. It was a case of the carrot and stick, with more of the latter than met the eye. Dulles threatened to serve Peking with an ultimatum demanding the immediate cessation of all aid to Ho, something calculated to give Whitehall an acute case of the jitters. In addition, at a NATO council meeting held in Paris 21–24 April, and again at Geneva the following week, Radford and Dulles confided to the British that even if Dien Bien Phu appeared lost, Washington might decide to bomb regions to the north. This, of course, raised the unpleasant prospect of air strikes against Chinese airfields and supply depots, leaving London with only one option if it wished to obviate the need for drastic action: it would have to declare its intent to join in a Far East security pact.[40]

Meanwhile, in talks with French leaders, Dulles took a somewhat different tack. There was no talk of surrendering Dien Bien Phu; hopes for an American bombing mission were kept alive; and Paris was offered two or three atomic bombs. The sticking point was that in return for a carrier attack tentatively scheduled for 28 April, the French were expected to approve EDC and secure British acceptance of an Asian defense pact. Laniel, irked by Dulles' subordination of the crisis at Dien Bien Phu to other priorities, temporized by urging British adherence to an Asian treaty even as he deferred action on EDC. British strategy is also worth noting. Churchill accepted a link between Suez and the Far East, indeed insisted on it. But he sought to postpone execution of his side of the agreement long enough to keep the dogs of war at bay. Ultimately, France turned down Eisenhower's offer of atomic bombs as unduly hazardous and Britain continued to avoid any move that might afford the president an opportunity for offensive operations.[41]

The surrender of the garrison at Dien Bien Phu on 7 May embittered French leaders, souring them permanently on EDC. However, it did not extinguish hope for what later came to be known as SEATO. One can argue that Dulles' strategy backfired inasmuch as Britain delayed its acceptance of SEATO, France rejected EDC, and the United States wound up doing a job in Vietnam which might have been accomplished sooner and more easily if Dulles had not erected so many barriers. Bidault, for one, pinned the blame squarely on the American secretary of state. Perhaps. But the thesis raises some interesting questions. Assuming the secretary had been prepared to run the risk of all-out war, how willing would England have been to enter the fray? The CIA estimated that Peking "would take whatever military action" was deemed necessary to sustain the Vietminh including the use of "Chinese Communist forces in Indochina." Other questions come to mind. What, one wonders, would have become of the Western alliance? What of Germany? If the French had not been able to recall their troops in 1954, would they have acquiesced in German rearmament? And had the United States been drawn into an Asian land war, how willing would an exhausted France have been to carry on while yielding operational control to Washington? British observers did not expect the Vietnamese to fight any more effectively under American leadership than they had under the French. Dulles did what he could to maximize the chances for EDC, but with Paris lukewarm and London opposed, the cause appears to have been well-nigh hopeless. Remarkably, SEATO materialized within a few months; EDC's demise set the stage for another approach to German rearmament; and, as a result of American firmness during the Geneva talks, Communist forces gained little in conference that was not already theirs on the battlefield.[42]

The story of the Geneva settlement and its relationship with SEATO is an interesting one. With Gallic panache, Mendès-France, who succeeded Laniel on 12 June as the youngest premier in French history, promised to conclude negotiations for a cease-fire within four weeks or resign. In this way, he virtually guaranteed for himself the weakest of all bargaining positions. Although, as the leader of a party whose views on EDC were distinctly unsympathetic, he could offer EDC's defeat in return for Russian aid at the bargaining table, he needed more than this. Assistance from Washington was absolutely necessary if his fondest hopes were to be realized, and fortunately for his government, such assistance was forthcoming. When Churchill and Eden arrived in Washington, they found Dulles willing to tailor an Egyptian aid program to British needs, but for a price. On 28 June, Eden agreed to a communiqué pledging cooperation on an Asian defense pact regardless of the outcome at Geneva. A major diplomatic deal had been struck. SEATO came into being on 8 September, and the Anglo-Egyptian treaty, announced 28 July, was signed on 19 October. There were some hitches in implementation. Although the name SEATO originated with Churchill, London refused its whole-hearted cooperation until Washington extended itself unconditionally in the Middle East. Nonetheless, it was the expression of British *intent* that counted as far as Dulles and Mendès-France were concerned, and this was assured by July 1954.[43]

Equally significant, there was never any doubt about Eisenhower's willingness to fight. Dulles informed the Senate Foreign Relations Committee on 4 June that Washington might have to act without London, so "grave" was the situation on the ground and so "fraught with danger not only to the immediate area but to the security of the United States and its allies in the Pacific." This was not the first time the administration had suggested possible action along this line to political leaders. As early as May, Dulles had entertained the idea of intervening with Australia, New Zealand, Thailand, and the Philippines. Moreover, it was only one of many ways in which Dulles attempted to lay the necessary groundwork. When Paris sent an urgent message on 27 June imploring him to take a serious view of things if the Geneva talks broke down, he could give a credible answer because he had just told legislators that the United States would have to draw the line in Asia and resist Communist aggression, overt or covert. What was needed he suggested, was a series of outposts manned not by American troops but by indigenous forces backed by an American willingness to match Soviet aid dollar for dollar and gun for gun. By this time, Senate Majority Leader Knowland was on record as having said that America might have to fight if it wanted to avoid losing the entire region to communism.[44]

One notes that the jogging of the European political process was accompanied by a parallel flexing of American military muscle. Additional aircraft carriers were dispatched to the South China Sea. The First and Seventh Fleets were stationed together off the coast of Vietnam. Five-power military staff talks got under way in Washington, and consideration was given to the possibility of a massive air strike, along with the landing of up to six divisions. Curiously, Eden accused Washington of stalling military talks even though it was the British who had balked at meeting openly on a five-power basis and were arguing instead for secret bilateral discussions of restricted scope.[45]

Here, as in the case of Korea and the Austrian State Treaty, the secretary tended to take a harder line in dealing with communism than his British counterpart. When Eden hesitated to include a number of anti-Communist clauses in the SEATO treaty, Dulles had them incorporated in an appendix—eighteen years later, Churchill was still complaining about Dulles' sharp practice! Likewise, during the Washington talks of 25–28 June 1954, when the British proposed an Anglo-Soviet summit, Dulles refused to countenance it. Where Eden favored an Anglo-American statement "trusting" that France would do all it could at Geneva to retain jurisdiction over the territory it controlled in Vietnam, Dulles argued that Britain and the United States should express "unwillingness" to accept anything less than the 18th parallel as a line of demarcation between the Communist and French zones. Characteristically, Dulles wanted to insist on French adoption of a seven-point list of goals formulated during Churchill's visit to Washington. Eden, on the other hand, was content to express a pious wish. The secretary was again alone in believing that France should demand more in return for the surrender of Haiphong and Hanoi, and where Eden was prepared to "welcome" the French negotiating position, Dulles would only agree to "take note" of it (the word "welcome" was in fact deleted from the joint communiqué). Although Eden professed to view Dulles' methods as exasperating, confusing, and unrealistic, he generally bowed to them once he found he could not make an end run around the secretary and appeal directly to Eisenhower.[46]

The climax of Dulles' effort to stiffen French resolve came on 13 July when he and Eden conferred with Mendès-France at the Hotel Matignon. Thus far, the Vietminh had proven steadfast in their refusal to settle for any boundary north of the 13th parallel, and a single week is all that remained prior to Mendès-France's self-imposed deadline mandating resignation in the absence of a settlement. True to form, Dulles voiced strenuous objection to a list of last-minute French concessions. He did not, he made clear, want a Communist country on the international control commission where it could exercise veto power, nor would he tolerate the neutralization of Laos and Cambodia, for this would amount to a second Yalta. With every hour that passed, Dulles bore down harder on Mendès-France to endorse the points previously outlined in Washington, among them effective international supervision, the withdrawal of all foreign troops from Laos and Cambodia, and the exclusion of any line south of the 17th parallel as a border between north and south. He argued, in addition, that South Vietnam, Laos, and Cambodia should have their own defense forces and foreign advisers. Finally, there must be free transit across the border between North and South Vietnam. Eventually, after extracting an American guarantee against further Communist aggression (which he had to qualify as subject to congressional approval), Mendès-France accepted every one of Dulles' points. In retrospect, he had little choice. His position at home was such that he could not afford to risk the loss of American moral support, in particular a high level of U.S. representation at the talks. Dulles, who attended the first week of the Geneva Conference in return for the exclusion of Peking's delegate as chairman, had withdrawn in protest against French waffling. But he agreed to send Under Secretary Smith as an observer provided France changed its tune.[47]

Thus it was that Smith's return to Geneva coincided with a renewed French demand for partition at the 18th parallel. With the handwriting plainly on the wall, Ho's delegates ceased insisting on the 13th parallel and declared their willingness to settle for the 16th. Mendès-France, without blinking, reiterated his determination to settle for the 18th, whereupon Ho offered the 17th, a proposition sweet enough to satisfy even John Foster Dulles. France's leader said that he regarded the breakthrough as a miracle attributable in large part to the American secretary of state. And with good reason. Dulles had been relentless and careful throughout to ensure that his words were perceived as proceeding from strength. On 19 July, it had become known that Eisenhower was reserving prime-time TV to take his case for full-scale intervention to the American people.[48] Concessions from the Vietminh followed immediately.

The final settlement came on 21 July, fifteen hours after Mendès-France had vowed to resign. France gave up the Red River Delta, but Ho Chi Minh ceded a fourth of the territory he controlled, and the list of provisions bore a striking resemblance to Dulles' seven points. France's ambassador to the United States indicated that his country's fate hinged on Russia's perception of American willingness to wage war, and it was an opinion shared by Bidault and Ely. [49]

The remainder of the story is well known. Hanoi violated the Geneva accords, affording Saigon a ready-made excuse to refuse participation in nation-wide elections scheduled for the end of two years. By fielding twenty divisions instead of seven, the maximum number allowed, by sealing off its border, and by refusing to withdraw its troops from Laos, it showed its contempt for paper promises. Whether the arrangements were adequate to allow the South Vietnamese, with American support, to establish a viable government is a moot point involving controversial decisions taken over an extended period by the heads of six American administrations. Armchair strategists speak of what was "inevitable," but historians know differently. Inevitability is a hard thing to prove. All one can say with any degree of certainty is that the Geneva agreements of July 1954 appear to have been the best obtainable under the circumstances short of all-out war. They also proved more durable in the short run than most observers, including Dulles, expected.[50]

The Indochina settlement was, of course, a triumph for the West only insofar as it avoided total defeat, or at least postponed it. But if Dulles had not negotiated from a position of military superiority, coupled with a demonstrated willingness to use it and a highly charged public at his back; if, in addition, he had not risked his popularity by barring high-level American representation at Geneva during the initial stages in accordance with the axiom of giving nothing to get nothing, a positive result of any kind would almost surely have eluded him.

Such was the stuff of power politics which, one hastens to add, was but a single element of Dulles' style. Equally important, particularly when it came to less dramatic scenarios, were several other elements, including what one historian has referred to as his skill in devising "placating modifications." We have already noted instances of this in connection with WEU and the Austrian State Treaty, but there are examples relating to his negotiation of the Japanese Peace Treaty that are revealing in a different way. Realizing, first of all, that Tokyo would shy away from any clause placing her national security explicitly in the hands of the United States, he drew up a separate security treaty at the "request" of an ostensibly sovereign Japan in the form of a "contract" implying equality. Tokyo also agreed "voluntarily" to accept American proposals for the preservation of certain fisheries. Secondly, when London objected to a provision naming Washington as protector of the Ryuku Islands, the offending clause was transferred from the peace accords to the security treaty, of which British officials could plead ignorance. Thirdly, when Philippine leaders let it be known that they felt entitled to more in the way of reparations than Dulles thought advisable, he encouraged them to send a delegation to Japan where they would "discover" Japan's inability to pay.[51]

Face-saving in the above sense, or the leaving of an "escape hatch" for friend and foe alike, was especially evident during the Lebanon crisis of 1958 when Dulles side-stepped a risky confrontation with Moscow by recourse to the United Nations before Soviet *amour propre* could become an issue. Almost as soon as the first American soldier set foot on foreign soil, Dulles invited Moscow to join in working out a mutually satisfactory timetable for withdrawal; an international emergency force was constituted for garrison duty; and when Khrushchev demanded a summit conference, the United States agreed to a top-level meeting at the Security Council. It is interesting, too, as an aside, that the UN route was used as a channel to ease earlier British and Israeli military withdrawals from Jordan and Suez respectively. An appeal to the World Court reduced Middle East tension by holding out the prospect of a decision on Israel's rights at Suez and Aqaba, and in the meantime, the Israelis were politely reminded that nothing would please the Arabs more than Israel's refusal to withdraw as this would mean a breach in relations between Washington and Tel Aviv.[52]

Timing was apt to be crucial. When Senator Richard Russell objected to American military intervention in Lebanon on the ground that Russian prestige was committed, Dulles replied that although this was not so, it soon would be if American marines did not move with dispatch. The strategy of delay could also be effective, as when Red China continued to hold Americans captive, insisting on a Communist trial and Communist justice. In this case, Dulles slowed the pace of negotiation so that Peking could announce at the time of the prisoners' release that they had served a portion of their sentences. Another graceful postponement occurred during the Berlin crisis of 1958–59 when Dulles assented in principle to an unwanted foreign ministers' conference while making certain that the conditions for American participation remained vague enough to necessitate a series of responses calculated to let the Soviets down slowly.[53]

It was undoubtedly with such tactics in mind that Senator Jacob Javits of New York could say of Dulles that he "engendered a respect for American sophistication" while Bidault of France would recall how extremely careful his American colleague had been never to "close the door to Molotov." Foreign Secretary Lloyd, on the occasion of Dulles' death, stressed that he was "not at all the rigid and inflexible man that some people thought him to be . . . [he was] ready to listen." And to quote another member of the British foreign office, one who kept a close watch on Washington during the first ten months of 1953, "Rigidity does not come naturally [to him]. . . . If he has a weakness it is rather the flexibility that comes from a desire to please and from his forensic training."[54]

What is remarkable is that this three-dimensional portrait of Dulles drawn by his peers bears so little resemblance to the one rendered by research historians. To this day, it is still difficult to draw a bead on Dulles due to the wide gap between appearance and reality that existed during his lifetime and that has continued to exist down through the years, giving rise to myriad misconceptions.

CHAPTER 4

The Man and the Myth

Arthur Krock of the *New York Times* once observed that he had never known anyone in public life so thoroughly misunderstood as John Foster Dulles. Judging from the sheer inconsistency of the criticism leveled against the secretary, Krock may have had a point. On the one hand, there were those who viewed him as simplistic, dangerously bellicose, and "obsessed" with the Communist menace. To members of this group he seemed the personification of the "cold warrior" and they derided him for his so-called legalistic-moralistic approach to world affairs. One scholar hypothesizes that he underwent a seachange in his thinking between the decade of the 1930s, when he appeared tolerant and open-minded, and the decade of the 1950s, when he engaged in a blind prosecution of the cold war. On the other hand, there were those who wished for greater firmness, Adenauer and Chiang Kai-shek, for example. The Thais regarded him as weak-kneed for refusing to grapple head-on with a Communist insurgency in Laos while still others accused him of left-wing sympathies. Alan Stang published a book which sought to prove that Dulles was secretly on the side of Moscow and, as such, responsible for the failure of the Hungarian revolution, the division of both Korea and Vietnam, Communist gains in Cuba, and the surrender of the Tachen Islands to Peking.[1]

Generalization is always difficult but never more so than when an individual presents so much in the way of paradox. It is easy to mistake a form of two-dimensional rhetoric for carelessness, forgetting that Dulles weighed his every word and phrase, committed remarkably few gaffes, and was capable of making his listeners scratch their heads when it suited his purpose. Asked on one occasion if it was not reckless to encourage revolution in Eastern Europe, he replied that he was merely "activating the latent difficulties." Granted, this is only one side of the story, but it is an important one.[2] It is also worth bearing in mind that while Dulles was apt to appear hidebound in adhering to a given course of action, appearances could be deceptive. Steadfast in principle but pragmatic in application, he stressed that "the capacity to change is an indispensable capacity. But equally indispensable is the capacity to hold fast to that which is good." Belgium's premier, Paul-Henri Spaak, felt that simplicity is what gave Dulles his power: he "knew what he wanted." In this sense, he could indeed be unyielding. Yet his views were subject to metamorphosis, whether in relation to the creation of a German army, the partition of Germany, a confederation of German states, or the internationalization of the Ruhr and Rhineland. Similarly, his position on the Soviet Union from March of 1945 through the early postwar period underwent significant shifts.[3]

"Never" and "forever," he maintained, "are words which should be eliminated from the vocabulary of statesmen." Accordingly, he argued for greater tolerance in the face of growing German and Japanese power during the 1930s just as he could be found among those who held that the United States had done well to recognize the Soviet Union in 1933. On the aftermath of the Second World War, he opposed Italy's recovery of her colonies, but only so long as he did not feel the pressure of domestic politics. In the same way, he did not trust Mendès-France at first; but once more, his opinion changed. One simply cannot classify Dulles by reference to the standard political lexicon. Alphand felt that nothing came closer to reflecting his personality than the style of his handwriting, with its incredible maze of crossing and counter-crossing curves and parabolas.[4]

One envoy objected to Dulles' "colossal vanity" and it has been suggested that he kept George Kennan off the reservation out of unalloyed personal dislike. In the absence of hardcore evidence, such accusations are, of course, speculative. They also lack confirmation on the basis of known patterns. Dulles took hours out of a busy schedule to chat with Hubert Humphrey, a senator who had called for his resignation; and when Loy Henderson was bold enough to tell him that his Suez scheme would not work, he expressed genuine gratitude. Nor are these isolated instances. John Allison, who publicly took issue with Dulles during the Truman years, became his ambassador to Japan. Closer to home, no country was more outspokenly critical of Dulles than Canada, certainly at first; yet Ambassador Heeney came to regard him as eminently fair. To Eisenhower, who knew him well, his greatest virtue was always his "good nature," defined as the ability to disagree and not bear ill will; and this is borne out by friends and enemies alike. Walter Lippmann, who had virtually nothing good to say about Dulles during his lifetime, later conceded that the secretary had tolerated dissent without rancor. James Reston, another of his media critics, noted in like vein that he was among the very few who did not mistake dissent for perversity.[5]

Without wishing to exaggerate the mellower side of Dulles, it may be fairly said that he was capable of admitting that he had been wrong. Despite an air of conscious rectitude verging on self-righteousness, he stunned Ambassador Alphand one day by confiding that Washington had erred in agitating for a rapid end to colonialism: "We have been too quick," he said "to relax our controls on all the people still submerged in the darkness of barbarism. Even with Morocco and Tunisia we should have waited. We have been wrong opening to them the doors of the UN without daring to say that they lacked the qualifications required under the charter." This is of a piece with what he told Foreign Minister Pineau regarding the Suez crisis of 1956: "We were wrong, you were right."[6]

There were few, if any, leaders at home or abroad with whom he did not get on personally. Speaking once of Secretary of State Cordell Hull, he remarked that Hull was stubborn; but, he added, "perhaps I seemed that way to him." He was on a good-humored, bantering basis with labor bosses, and if he occasionally disagreed with the service chiefs, he nevertheless presented a strong case for their point of view in cabinet meetings and sessions of the National Security Council. In fact, he liked nothing better than to play the devil's advocate. Not many overseas officials were more abhorrent to him than Nasser, yet he was perfectly prepared to cultivate Egyptian good will on the aftermath of the Suez crisis. There is also the time when he made a special call on Foreign Minister Fujiyama to protest Japanese criticism of the Lebanon landings. For emphasis, he jabbed a pencil into the table. Yet when Fujiyama stood his ground, Dulles seemed to value his associate all the more. Fujiyama later came to Washington seeking to renew the Japanese-American defense treaty on more favorable terms, and he found Dulles waiting for him at the airport, entirely open-minded and objective. No Anglophile, Dulles could still recognize the British as originators of the concept of UN trusteeship, and while he did not get along with Anthony Eden any better than Acheson had, his working relations were, for the most part, smooth. Much as he resented Eden's about-face on talks regarding a Far East defense pact, he was willing, as we have seen, to credit him with WEU and to admit two years later that Washington had undermined the British position at Suez. One of his closest advisers has gone on record as saying he thought the secretary actually liked Eden.[7]

That Dulles should have succeeded in concealing his opinion of Britain's foreign secretary is all the more extraordinary considering Eden's estimate of Dulles, which was never in doubt—he judged the American to be narrow, arrogant, and chauvinistic. Of course, the two men were extremely different, not only in their private lives but also in their ability to separate personal feeling from public policy. Moreover, the strain in their relationship antedates Eisenhower's term of office. During negotiations on the Japanese Peace Treaty, it was understood by Downing Street that Japan would remain technically free to recognize whichever China it wished. However, under the weight of the American occupation, "free choice" was a misnomer. Few doubted that Tokyo would recognize Taipei rather than Britain's choice, Peking; and British cabinet officials, fully aware of this, resisted "free choice" until forced to accept it at diplomatic gunpoint. The phrase was chosen with one purpose in mind: to save British face while safeguarding American interests. In effect, it was a gentlemen's agreement. Unfortunately, members of Congress proved to be as suspicious of the formula as anyone in Parliament, and so Dulles was obliged to obtain a letter of intent from the Japanese foreign minister. After showing it to the British ambassador, he asked that Eden be duly informed and went out of his way to mention it to Eden. Whereupon the latter responded vaguely, saying only that he would not press the British position. Later, however, when a hue and cry arose in England, the foreign secretary claimed that he had never seen the contents of the Yoshida letter (which was technically correct). Furthermore, Herbert Morrison, who had been foreign secretary at the time of the original agreement, accused Dulles of violating the understanding on free choice, all of which was patently unfair. Eden himself gave the lie to Morrison's charges when he outlined the essence of his position for members of the foreign office: Britain, he noted, did not want to be "regarded" as having acquiesced in American policy. It was a matter of appearances.[8]

Following the Suez debacle, and in connection with his decision to halt offensive operations, Eden denied in a letter to the American ambassador that Eisenhower ever lectured him over the phone—he had not spoken with the president, he insisted, until after his government agreed to a cease-fire. But this does not square with documentation supplied by Foreign Secretary Lloyd or with the diary kept by Eisenhower's personal secretary. Eden behaved the same way after Washington warned Paris of dire consequences in connection with a failure to ratify EDC. First, he (and Churchill) backed Dulles in his use of the phrase "agonizing reappraisal" to threaten disengagement. Later, though, after the phrase had become a target for critics, he gave the impression of having disapproved. This was the same Eden who, in the wake of the Anglo-French-Israeli attack on Egypt, lied flatly about "foreknowledge" and "collusion."[9] Dulles' standards were different.

One of the reasons for comparing the secretary with his opposite number in England is that it points up a quality of fairness which may have been instrumental in his ability to reach out to leaders representing many different points of view. France's Christian Pineau, who would have been a liberal Democrat had he cast his ballot in America, paid Dulles the ultimate compliment when he pointed out that he had a way of inspiring "friendship and confidence" even in those who did not share his ideas. It is true that Pineau also chided his American friend for assuming that what every country needed was a free market economy. But in this case, Dulles was probably speaking more as a salesman than as a philosopher. Washington, he knew, could not deal in absolutes, for as he put it, "nations which depend greatly upon us do not always follow what we believe to be the right course." As well as anyone, he realized that the world at large would not necessarily "conform to our ideas and wishes." As an archcritic of what he liked to call the "devil theory" of international relations, he was revolted by the chauvinistic interpretations of "dime-novel history."[10]

Reinhold Niebuhr took him to task for equating rigity in the cold war with morality and viewing flexibility on the part of the world's uncommitted as a form of expediency. In actuality, Dulles admitted a series of qualifiers depending on a nation's geographical location, relative size, and potential for leadership. There was a difference, he pointed out, between the status of Laos and that of Switzerland or Sweden. The word "neutralism" must not be confused with the word "neutrality" although the two were often used interchangeably (even by Dulles). "Neutrality," as he defined it, precluded military involvement. "Neutralism," on the other hand, tended to shun any preference for freedom over tyranny, religion over atheism. He liked to point out that Indian leaders who preached "neutrality" were often anti-Communist at home even as they feared Peking too much to support the Western diplomatic campaign against Moscow. On his first trip to the Subcontinent in 1953, Dulles showed himself to be keenly aware of the situation. And when Sukarno of Indonesia asked him how he could condemn neutralism when the United States professed neutrality on issues pitting Indonesia against the Netherlands, Pakistan against India, and Israel against the Arabs, the secretary drew a distinction between matters of profound moral import and those that were strictly political.[11]

Here, as elsewhere, one must observe what Dulles *did* in conjunction with what he *said*. Eastern Europe, in his view, was evolving gradually toward a situation like that of Finland, and with this end in view, he inaugurated an economic assistance program for Poland in the hope of weaning Warsaw away from Moscow. He would gladly have established top level diplomatic relations with Bulgaria and other Iron Curtain countries had Congress been willing. He also favored military as well as economic aid to such satellites in contrast with the view of the Defense Department, all at a time when Senate Majority Leader Knowland and publisher Henry Luce were adamantly opposed to foreign aid programs for India and Indonesia, not to mention Communist countries. Few secretaries have fought as hard or as long as Dulles did for aid to New Delhi and Belgrade. It therefore comes as no surprise that on both of his trips to India he hit it off with officials, as well as the press, rating the rare privilege of a low altitude flight over the Taj Mahal. Another measure of his success in wooing neutrals is the help Nehru rendered in arriving at a Suez settlement and securing the release of American prisoners held by China. Then, too, the Bandung Conference of neutrals which met in 1955 proved remarkably benign, refraining from any serious criticism of American policy on Matsu and Quemoy. At the same time, communism came under blistering attack by Iraqi and Ceylonese leaders who branded it a form of colonialism deadlier and more reprehensible than anything the West had produced.[12]

It was the neutralism of Laos, Cambodia, and Indonesia that struck Dulles as dangerous and his views were not exactly unfounded. Within a few years of his death, the people of these unfortunate countries suffered a death count in the millions from civil war. Within twenty years, Afghanistan, which Bulganin had lauded for its nonalignment, would have to reckon with over a million dead, countless wounded, and hundreds of thousands uprooted. India, interestingly enough, for all of its vaunted neutrality, spent between a third and a half of its annual budget on defense. Yet, in spite of this, Communist China did not hesitate to crush a Tibetan uprising in 1959. Nor did it have any scruple about invading India itself three years later. Nehru, with second thoughts about his foreign policy, fired his leftist defense minister, Krishna Menon, and died a sober, if not bitter and disillusioned, man.[13]

Another reason why Dulles declaimed against nonalignment and registered displeasure when individuals such as President Gronchi of Italy showed signs of wanting to play mediator between the United States and the Soviet Union was that there were some gigantic political prizes at stake. Britain, Norway, and the Netherlands were on the verge of furnishing launchpads for NATO missiles just as the leaders of Spain and Morocco were being asked to host U.S. Strategic Air Command bases. All parties could have avoided the risk of obliteration by Russian missiles had they cottoned to Soviet pleas for nonalignment. Where Germany was concerned, it was a matter of keeping three-quarters of the populace on the side of the West. Neutralist sentiment could have prevented Adenauer from passing a conscription law, as nearly happened in 1956, and in Dulles' view, Germany would not long remain neutral on account of its powerful military-industrial complex. Beyond this, neutralism, in the opinion of Dulles, presented an opening wedge for communism in Latin America, and if he was going to thwart Russian designs there, as well as in the Middle and Far East, by means of a northern tier alliance, SEATO, and pro-Western Japan, he could ill afford to appear complacent.[14]

After 1955, with Western European Union, SEATO, and the Caracas Declaration safely in hand, Washington could take a somewhat different line, as Moscow itself was beginning to do. The Kremlin had come a long way from its denunciation of Swiss neutrality during the First World War, a forerunner of Stalin's later refusal to ship arms to non-Communist states (among Dulles' personal possessions were several copies of a 1939 speech by Stalin pleading for collective security and labeling "immoral" any manifestation of neutralism in the struggle against Hitler). Some years later, Nikita Khrushchev would tongue-lash Tito, calling him a hypocrite who gave Moscow one cheek to kiss while giving the other to Washington. As late as 1959, the Soviet boss was still trying to lay down the law to Nasser, labeling nonalignment a myth, while Mao Tse-tung was calling neutralism a "word for deceiving people."[15]

There is a suppleness to Dulles' outlook, not only on the issue of neutralism, but on others as well, that serves to underscore a pronounced cosmopolitan bent. He was, for example, a champion of the democratic ideal, but this did not blind him to the fact that in certain regions of the world, the only alternative to right-wing dictatorship was chaos or communism. Nor did he believe it possible under all conditions for the United States to export its social and political system. "Freedom," he liked to say, "accepts diversity" and he took pride in being on good terms with leaders ranging from Tito to Franco. He also became the first secretary of state to have an official audience with the pope although, with characteristic adroitness, he managed to do so without appearing to make a formal request.[16]

Closely linked with the internationalist side of Dulles was a powerful strain of pragmatism. Because the dismantling of colonialism (on the part of countries other than the United States) was not nearly as vital to the national interest as certain other items on the agenda, he made a conscious decision at the outset to act accordingly, and after setting up a group including Dean Rusk to study the subject, he decided to subordinate the anticolonialist cause to other more important goals, in effect using it as a bargaining counter. Thus, he was willing to support far more in the way of compromise than one would imagine from the tone of his public utterances. Earlier, in 1949, he had seen no reason to withdraw American envoys from the Soviet satellite states, as their presence did not convey moral approval (though he ceased to expound such a view in the heat of the 1952 presidential campaign). Along the same lines, it was inevitable that Adenauer would perceive Dulles as overly optimistic about the chances for rapprochement with the USSR. The secretary endorsed economic and cultural ties between East and West Germany, and before his death he suggested that reunification might come about without free elections via confederation. When, in late 1958 and early 1959, he indicated that the West could recognize East German officials as Soviet agents, it proved too much even for Bonn's Social Democrats. Willy Brandt accused him of yielding to "salami" tactics and warned that the Western position could be eroded through a gradual process of piecemeal concession.[17]

Appearances to the contrary, Dulles was not an alarmist incapable of making distinctions and anticipating departures from the norm. Communists, he recognized, were one group, those influenced by communism another. While the leaders of Guatemala in 1954 and Syria after 1957 belonged, in his view, to the latter group, he regarded Syria as a borderline case. Similarly, the expansionism of Russia was one thing, that of "international communism" another. George Kennan, who was far from sympathetic with Republicans generally, suggested that Dulles would have been quick to note the rise of polycentrism. "In fact," recalled Kennan, "he probably did see it." As early as 1954, the secretary told Adenauer that Peking did not seem to him as much under Moscow's thumb as appearances would suggest, and a year later, he found Tito in agreement with him on the breakdown of the Communist monolith. To be sure, the Chinese were still operating under a Kremlin system supported to some degree by Russian rubles, and Peking was still a dangerous customer. But Dulles saw gradations. Gomulka, he felt, might turn out to be the Tito of Poland, and there was a difference between "orthodox" and unorthodox communism.[18]

In this respect, he was light years ahead of Congress. Hints from Foggy Bottom in late 1953 that the United States might recognize Red China and support its admission to the United Nations should Peking decide to distance itself from Moscow, caused an ominous stir on Capitol Hill. Although the secretary did his best to curb Russian and Chinese expansion, he had to tell the Senate Foreign Relations Committee that "setbacks to the cause of freedom might have to be accepted." Although the United States would fight for its ideals, it must expect partial and temporary defeat. When Communist party membership rose in India and Indonesia, he pointed out that many Asian Communists were Communist in name only. In Europe, it was much the same. "For a good many years in France and Italy," he recalled, "there were Communist parties which attracted quite a lot of votes. That wasn't because the people voting that way were Communists but because they found that a way of expressing a protest vote." Communist leaders in France and Italy might be hostile, but they were scarcely a carbon copy of their opposite numbers in Russia. They were neither a small and tightly knit group, nor were they highly trained and disciplined. It is significant, too, that when the Senate voted 85–0 to make membership in the Communist party a criminal offense, Dulles and other Republican leaders persuaded the House to pass a more moderate bill so that the final version provided penalties only for members of "Communist action" groups along with those who failed to register under the Subversive Activities Control Act.[19]

As far as the Russians themselves were concerned, Dulles felt that they would alternate between a conservative and liberal line without necessarily changing their underlying goals and convictions. From time to time, the wolf would go about in sheep's clothing; the outward appearance of the Soviet system, like the surface of a deep running stream, would seem "sometimes ruffled, sometimes smooth." On balance, though, he detected signs of mellowing and felt that pure communism would evolve into a modified form of socialism. As far as he could see, there was nothing in the Soviet system per se that barred a return to religious faith and certainly no necessity for Communists go to on believing in the justification of means by ends. Tito had renounced violent methods while styling himself a Communist; Bukharin had championed peaceful competition between dissimilar socioeconomic systems. If the latter paid dearly for his ideas, he had nonetheless held them, and it seemed to Dulles that the system could tolerate a fairly wide margin of freedom in the realm of thought and spiritual practice. Already, he could discern a certain movement toward Western ideas of law, individual security, and consumer preference. To be sure, the movement was slow and could not be taken as a harbinger of significant progress in the short run. The socio-economic structure of the Marxist state would not wither away all at once. But there would come a time when international adventurism would yield to a concern for natural well-being. With the "erosion of time and circumstance," and with the demands for freedom that were certain to arise from increasingly sophisticated industrial, military, and scientific sectors, there would undoubtedly be long-term evolution and quite possibly revolution. In this sense, Soviet leaders were very definitely beholden to public opinion, even if not to quite the same extent as their American confreres.[20]

Dulles was capable of recognizing that communism had done much to improve the lives of its people. Admittedly, this was not his usual line in public, but he did recognize the attractiveness of a guaranteed job, education, and leisure time, just as he admired the dynamism of the Soviet revolution. Never one to underestimate the ability of the Russians at science, engineering, or indeed at anything to which they set their minds, he foresaw their success in developing the atomic bomb and he shared the opinion of the Marquis de Custine, a contemporary of Tocqueville, who had observed that the Russians were clumsy and inept at everything except the conquest of the world (*inepte à tout excepté à la conquête du monde*). He took them seriously, and although he judged the United States and its way of life superior in the abstract, he also wondered if it might not find itself, like ancient Athens, at a disadvantage vis-à-vis a Spartan garrison state which rewarded discipline and ruthlessness.[21]

It goes without saying that this third dimension of Dulles' thought would have been lethal ammunition in the hands of his domestic foes had it come to light. It was one thing for him to remind his colleagues at State that Russian officials were simply looking out for the interests of their country; that their fears and suspicions should not be viewed as abnormal or sinister; and that if invited into the parlor, they might be better behaved. It was quite another thing for him to go public with such ideas. On one occasion, he planned to tell a group of midwestern 4-H clubs that although communism might be a cruel system in American eyes, it had produced higher living standards; but he thought better of it.[22]

This same element of flexibility, which is visible to some degree in all of Dulles' dealings, figures most prominently, perhaps, in the relationship he established with Communist China. For Peking, the pearl of great price was diplomatic recognition, and Dulles never ruled it out, basing his policy not upon traditional moral factors, or on the equally traditional ground of de facto control, but rather on the national interest. The only question in his mind was whether or not the United States would have more to gain than

bombing, mainly of supply depots and airfields regarded as a threat to Taiwan. Communist ships were also being seized and in some cases sunk. Although Chiang had promised informally not to mount a sizable campaign against the Mainland without consulting Washington, he sometimes operated independently, and when he did decide to consult, his American ally was often divided, with the State Department favoring one course of action and the armed forces another. Dulles proceeded with characteristic ingenuity to work out a face-saving mechanism whereby the two countries entered into a mutual defense pact without preconditions. At the same time, Eisenhower gained operational control through a separate exchange of notes between Dulles and Foreign Minister Yeh. This did not eliminate all difficulties immediately. Chiang continued to act independently. In one instance, his navy seized a Red Chinese tanker, the *Tuapse*, and Dulles urged Eisenhower to be more assertive in claiming his rights under the Dulles-Yeh agreement. But, for the most part, things were better and Washington continued to authorize military strikes and undercover operations against the Mainland. When Allen Dulles visited Taipei in October 1956, he proposed that the ROC parachute two Nationalist spies into each of Mao's counties.[28]

The only real problem stemmed from tactics that were far from straightforward on the American side. Chiang expected the guarantee of Quemoy and Matsu to be open and explicit whereas Dulles, for a variety of reasons, preferred to remain vague. In a meeting between American and Nationalist leaders on 19 January 1955, Dulles promised Yeh an announcement on the defense of the Quemoy area, but he did not say what kind of an announcement it would be, and when he told Yeh that he did not think Matsu should be included, the latter left the meeting visibly annoyed. Two days later, Dulles met once more with the Nationalist foreign minister, this time to include Matsu, but also to stipulate that his announcement would not refer to any of the islands by name because this would not be feasible "at the present time." Yeh was again deeply disturbed even though Dulles added that he would seek a congressional resolution giving the administration blanket authority. Chiang, who had been holding back on his evacuation of the Tachens, wanted the evacuation announcement to coincide with an unambiguous American statement on the Quemoy area, but Dulles insisted that since his first priority was passage of the Formosa Resolution he had to placate liberals who viewed the commitment as unsound and provocative. Thus, for the Nationalists it was one disappointment after another.[29]

On 25 January, the Formosa Resolution passed the House by a margin of 410–3, and within a few days, the Senate concurred 83–3. Dulles' wording, deliberately ambivalent, authorized the president to "employ the armed forces of the United States as he deems necessary for the specific purpose of securing and protecting Formosa and the Pescadores against armed attack, this authority to include the securing and protecting of such related positions and territories of that area now in friendly hands and the taking of such other measures as he judges to be required or appropriate in assuring the defense of Formosa and the Pescadores." Assistant Secretary Robertson told Wellington Koo, Chiang's ambassador, that specific reference to Matsu and Quemoy would have to wait. After hearing Dulles say the same thing on 28 January, Koo noted ruefully in his diary that the secretary had changed his mind. In fact, Dulles had not changed his mind nor had he broken his word from a technical standpoint. Chiang was nonetheless chagrined to find on the following day that the message delivered by Eisenhower after signing the Formosa Resolution still made no mention of Quemoy. He therefore filed another complaint and Ike responded by issuing a written promise that did finally refer specifically to Matsu and Quemoy, though the pledge was not for public consumption and was hedged about with escape clauses such as "at this time" and "in present circumstances." Two days later, on 2 February, the president's words were transmitted orally by Ambassador Rankin. Chiang, for his part, continued to maintain that Washington should honor the spirit of the commitment made by Dulles on 19 January. He continued to call for an open and explicit commitment just as he continued to postpone his evacuation of the Tachens as a form of leverage. Whereupon Eisenhower, refusing to give way, delivered a counterpunch: if Chiang did not proceed immediately with the Tachens operation, the United States would remove its five aircraft carriers and the islanders would have to fend for themselves against a superior force of Mainland Chinese.[30]

Soon after the evacuation began on 4 February, Peking, after being invited to attend United Nations sessions as a guest, rejected the plan for a cease-fire. But within a week, approximately twenty thousand civilians and ten thousand troops were removed to the safety of other outposts. Meanwhile, on 9 February, the Senate approved the treaty with Taiwan, stipulating that American participation in the defense of any territory other than Formosa and the Pescadores would require the advice and consent of the Senate. Dulles was now free to be more specific, and during a press backgrounder on 12 February, as well as in a New York address delivered on 16 February, he came very close to satisfying Chiang's requirements. The United States, he said, had "no commitment and no purpose to defend the coastal positions *as such*. Their basic purpose is to assure that Formosa and the Pescadores will not be forcibly seized" (emphasis added). For anyone familiar with the kind of distinctions that were the secretary's stock in trade, such language left little to be desired. Eisenhower, too, made himself clear at a White House stag dinner in March, one day after Dulles suggested that the Communist conquest of Quemoy would be but the prelude to an attack on Taiwan itself judging from Peking's language after its seizure of the Tachens. Although the administration would persist in denying that any "private assurances" had been given to Chiang, its commitment to Quemoy became increasingly clear as it helped to modernize Nationalist defenses.[31]

Whether one looks at the Formosa Resolution, the security treaty with

Taiwan, or Eisenhower's decision in 1954 not to have the Seventh Fleet make calls on Matsu and Quemoy, the policy was one of deliberate ambiguity with the name of the secretary written in bold letters across its face. Under Truman, when Dulles sought Senate approval of the North Atlantic Treaty Organization, he had equivocated on the question of how the nation would react if one of its allies came under attack. In this way, by softpedalling executive prerogative and leaving the door ajar for senatorial input, at least in theory, he was able to corral some important votes. Studied vagueness was also the way he had handled conflicting demands on the part of London, Tokyo, Taipei, and Washington during the drafting of the Japanese Peace Treaty, and the same tactic was integral to his handling of the White House, as well as France and England, throughout the Dien Bien Phu crisis.[32]

In reference to Quemoy, it would seem that Dulles had a fair number of reasons for not delivering all that Chiang desired. He wanted, first of all, to safeguard congressional support for the defense treaty and the Formosa Resolution by denying the opposition any serious grounds of contention. This is not to imply that Congress was kept in the dark as to the administration's basic intent. On the contrary, by the time a vote was taken, the tenor of the debate left no doubt as to Dulles' underlying purpose. Hence the rationale for later claims that the Formosa Resolution was a rock-solid guarantee of Matsu and Quemoy. At the same time, liberal reputations were not put directly on the line. Secondly, he wanted to be certain that the United States would not have to defend Matsu and Quemoy until ROC forces had done all they could on their own. Four years later, a thousand Nationalist troops were killed or wounded in two weeks of intense fighting before Washington offered to handle resupply operations. Doubtless, too, he wanted the Tachens evacuation to precede anything approximating a public pledge on Matsu and Quemoy. Of even greater moment in 1954 and early 1955 was the need to ensure British and French cooperation on Western European Union by holding out the possibility of obtaining a UN-sponsored cease-fire in the Formosa Strait. British leaders were violently opposed to any formal guarantee of Quemoy, and the prospect of a cease-fire sponsored by Downing Street virtually guaranteed their cooperation in the UN and elsewhere. It was only when the British cabinet felt satisfied, as it did by 24 January, that Washington had abandoned its "proposal to give a provisional guarantee to defend Quemoy" that it expressed its willingness to take the lead at Turtle Bay.[33]

As Dulles began to clarify his position on Matsu and Quemoy, especially for the benefit of Canadians, Australians, and New Zealanders, British leaders more or less acquiesced, though they refused to revive their campaign for a cease-fire. Meanwhile, Dulles kept up his courtship. With final approval of WEU due in the spring of 1955, he queried Churchill about the possibility of a trade-off involving British support for Taipei in return for a sacrifice of the offshore islands to Peking. Pressure, real or apparent, was also applied to Chiang to thin out his forces on Matsu and Quemoy, a first step presumably toward renunciation. It is significant, however, that once Dulles attained his principal goals, once WEU and the Austrian State Treaty were safely in hand, one heard little more about such schemes. Shelling from the Mainland ceased altogether, and on 22 May, newspapers reported an informal cease-fire reflecting Chou En-lai's statement at Bandung that "the Chinese people are willing to strive for the liberation of Taiwan by peaceful means as far as this is possible."[34]

Of course, the real test for Dulles' integrity came in 1958. By this time, Washington had suspended all ambassadorial talks with Peking. On 30 June, Mao issued an ultimatum giving the United States fifteen days to return to the bargaining table. Dulles replied calmly that he hoped such talks would resume, and with Warsaw as the venue, but not in an atmosphere of recrimination and threats. On 15 July, the PRC extended its deadline, then dropped it, and Dulles promptly agreed to resume talks on the ambassadorial level. However, on 15 July came the landing of American marines in Lebanon. All along, Eisenhower had been receiving reports of Communist preparation for a renewed offensive against Quemoy. Heavy bombardment began on 23 August accompanied by a naval blockade, and the target, just as in 1954, was Matsu, as well as Quemoy, even though the latter, owing to its close proximity to the Mainland, was by far the more vulnerable of the two islands.[35]

During the shelling, Moscow weighed in on the side of Peking by announcing that in an emergency it would honor its defense treaty with the Mainland, and for good measure Khrushchev sent Eisenhower a long, abusive letter which the president returned without comment. Ike, who had already ordered two carriers from the Sixth Fleet to join their sister ships of the Seventh Fleet, now dispatched additional units to within striking distance of the threatened islands. At the same time, contingency plans for the use of tactical nuclear weapons were made public, and Chiang's pilots shot down twenty-four Communist MIGs with the use of American-made Side-winder missiles. All at once, on 5 October, Khrushchev began to distance himself from Mao, declaring that Moscow had no intention of interfering in what was plainly a civil war. Dulles had called the Soviet bluff before, and he would do so again. But now, for the first time, seasoned observers could detect a deep fissure in the Sino-Soviet axis. Indeed, the entire geopolitical map was in the process of flipping upside down.[36]

On hindsight, the events of 1958 make eminently good sense. Yet at the time no one could be certain exactly what developments were in train, and Dulles had to weather a storm which buffeted the White House, the State Department, and Capitol Hill, along with the entire nation. The challenge was a particularly sharp one for the secretary given the fact that Ike evidently felt less strongly about the need for firmness and gave him little direct backing. Eisenhower's memoirs indicate more backbone on the part of the chief executive than actually existed. In truth, Ike was uncomfortable. Viewing the military situation as risky and provocative, if not untenable from a political point of view, he was anxious to see Chiang evacuate his front-line troops as the first stage of a total withdrawal from Quemoy in return for American aid in securing Taiwan. One source of his difference with Dulles may stem from the latter's skepticism when it came to Soviet protestations of support for Peking. But in any event, neither Chiang nor Dulles flinched, and herein lies the key to what transpired.[37]

Certain allied leaders who supported Dulles privately refused to do so in public, while others came out vehemently against him. Canadian officials, for example, lined up with the British in saying they would not fight for Matsu or Quemoy. Meanwhile, the secretary faced hostile majorities at home—in the media, Congress, and the public at large, as indicated by the volume and tone of incoming mail. In addition to career foreign service officers who presented an almost solid phalanx of opposition at State, there were individuals of prominence such as Dean Acheson and Reinhold Niebuhr. According to Admiral Stump, the only person on Dulles' immediate staff who agreed to join him in urging Eisenhower to defend administration policy on television (something the president eventually decided to do) was Assistant Secretary Robertson. Dulles had to take on the Joint Chiefs of Staff, the chairman of the Senate Foreign Relations Committee, and a host of journalists who would normally have been on his side. Senator Morse called for his impeachment and, in a highly unusual move, someone at the State Department, who must have been familiar with his personal mail, leaked the embarrassing news of its contents. In the end, he could take a certain amount of pride in knowing that he had withstood a veritable tidal wave of criticism. With *Sputnik* circling the earth and Soviet prestige at an all-time high, he rode out all elements of resistance, domestic as well as foreign, and Eisenhower made it clear, in a letter to Theodore Green, the new chairman of the Senate Foreign Relations Committee, that loyalty to one's allies and an honorable discharge of one's obligations came before peace, indeed was its only real guarantor.[38]

It would be one-sided, of course, to concentrate on Dulles' iron resolve without alluding again to the "escape hatch" that he fashioned for his adversaries. For every aircraft carrier ordered to the Formosa Strait, he held out at least one offer of compromise. At Warsaw, in angling for an agreement to neutralize the offshore islands, he offered a phased withdrawal from Matsu and Quemoy, hinting that a cease-fire agreement could lead to a four-power foreign ministers conference with one of the seats to go to Chou En-lai. Chiang, as an added bargain, was brought to renounce, in the most unequivocal language to date, any use of force as a means of returning to the Mainland. Later, when Peking announced that it would engage in bombardment on odd-numbered days only, Chiang thinned out his forces and ceased challenging Mao's claim to territorial waters extending twelve miles offshore. Americans could relax once more, and the ratio of disapproval registered by Dulles' incoming mail declined from 4–1 to 1–1. To be sure, he had risked a great deal, but what he risked is not what most commentators tend to assume. From intelligence reports based in part on U-2 observation, he knew that the Red Chinese were not prepared to follow up their shelling of the islands with an actual invasion. Furthermore, in spite of *Sputnik* and partisan charges of a dangerous discrepancy in the arms race, he was aware that the United States had never been farther ahead of the Soviet Union in military terms. He was also well posted on Sino-Soviet relations. The main challenge, then, was not so much Moscow or Peking, but rather the home front.[39]

That Dulles rarely conformed to stereotype and was less of a gambler than appearances would suggest highlights the strain of caution which, next to flexibility, is probably his least known trait. Despite his reputation for "brink-manship," it is control and restraint, rather than whimsy or bellicosity, that dictated the outcome of explosive situations from 1953 to 1959, though again one would never have guessed it from reading the Communist press or sampling the opinion of his critics at home. In late 1954, when Peking sentenced thirteen Americans to imprisonment on espionage charges widely regarded as specious, sentiment ran high for drastic action. Majority Leader Knowland, together with Senators Dodd of Connecticut and McCarthy of Wisconsin, called for a naval blockade of the Mainland. Senator Daniel of Texas suggested an ultimatum with an early expiration date. Dulles, however, was willing to wait. To reporters he said that "we must have the courage to be patient." Knowland was notified that "a blockade is an act of war." On another occasion, when Cuban guerrillas hijacked a busload of American bluejackets and spirited them away into the Sierra Madre Mountains, Admiral Arleigh Burke advised the secretary to dispatch a rescue platoon or, at the very least, to insist that Batista take swift action. Instead, Dulles temporized. Likewise, when Western access routes to Berlin were threatened in November 1958, the Joint Chiefs wanted to send in an armored division. French officials were equally anxious for a show of force. Dulles, on the other hand, preferred to bide his time, pleading the need to cultivate world opinion. The upshot is that although Eisenhower prepared the army and air force for any eventuality, all he actually did was send a small armed convoy with orders to probe but to retreat in the face of resistance and not to fire unless fired upon.[40]

Invariably, Dulles' first reaction to a volatile situation was to soothe the press. The new administration had no sooner taken office than it had to deal with speculation over contingency plans for ending the Korean War.

Eisenhower, who made low-key remarks to reporters and diverted their attention to domestic issues, did not even refer to Korea in the opening statement of his first press conference. In the same way, Dulles gave non-committal answers to questions and merely suggested that he was weighing an appeal to the United Nations for sanctions against North Korea. Asked about the possibility of a naval blockade, he replied blandly that this was one of several measures under review. According to the British ambassador, "the impression now studiously being given the public [by Dulles] is that the administration intends no hasty dramatic action . . . care is evidently being taken to avoid anything which might fan the flames . . . [for] there is a ground swell which could quickly be whipped up into a storm."[41]

Throughout the 1950s, there were periodic reports of the shooting down of allied aircraft by Soviet, Chinese, and North Korean forces. Occasionally, an incident would occur after an unreported American attack on Communist aircraft. At other times, an apparently unproven incident might be followed by American retaliation. Whatever the case, the administration generally adopted a conciliatory line in order to prevent an explosion of popular sentiment. First came the shooting down of two planes in East German air corridors and the harassing of a third. Washington remained impassive. In another instance, when Senator Knowland suggested a break in diplomatic relations with Moscow, Dulles decided to take his case to the United Nations. In October 1954, when the Soviet Union fired on an American reconnaissance plane off the coast of Japan, New York's *Daily News* joined Senator Knowland in calling for the severance of diplomatic relations; but Eisenhower, after describing the situation as "complicated" and "tricky" and outlining the Soviet point of view, did little more than extol the blessings of peace. Once, after an American military aircraft was downed, Eisenhower explained that the plane had strayed beyond Moscow's three-mile territorial limit and that Communist gunfire had probably been defensive. In this instance, it is possible that the Kremlin may have been retaliating for an incident involving the loss of two MIG-15s. Nevertheless, it was not long before a squadron of American saber jets destroyed three Soviet MIGs in the air. Soon after, there were reports of an attack on an American patrol plane. But this time, Moscow offered compensation, along with an apology, and Dulles was quick to suggest two possible scenarios: (1) the plane in question might have flown closer to the Russian border than usual; or (2) Russian radar might have been at fault.[42]

Similar caution is implicit in Dulles' conception of a proper balance between means and ends. On the one hand, the size of America and the extent of its natural resources dictated a sizable share of responsibility for international law and order. This called for defense forces powerful enough to carry out a peace-keeping mission and deter Communist aggression when it threatened the national interest. On the other hand, neither Dulles nor Eisenhower was an alarmist when it came to projections of Soviet might. Thus did the president dismiss the idea of a preventive attack on Peking, pointing out that it would be a long time before China could threaten the United States, by which time the configuration of world power might well have shifted. Dulles, always chary of intervention, regardless of when or where, rejected out of hand the assumption that whenever a problem arose anywhere in the world it was up to Uncle Sam to fix it. "We are not omnipotent," he insisted, "we are not 'Mr. Fixit.'" In the long run, he felt, the United States would not retain its influence abroad unless it kept its own house in order and set an example good enough to attract a following of loyal allies. Asked if he was prepared to use force to overthrow the government of Egypt should it drift into the Soviet orbit, his answer was a categorical no; and earlier, when Truman proposed the interdiction of Soviet arms shipments to the Middle East, he was again opposed.[43]

Dulles has been accused of egging on Hungary's freedom fighters to rise against Soviet armor on the assumption that America would come to their aid. To be sure, Radio Free Europe did engage in a certain amount of provocation. But this was not true of the official Voice of America, nor did such language come from the lips of the president or the secretary. The latter made it clear time and again that Washington was offering nothing but moral support. In his book *War or Peace* published in 1950, Dulles stated clearly that his policy of rollback was not an invitation to armed insurrection: "The people have no arms, and violent revolt would be futile," he wrote, for it would "precipitate massacre. We do not want to do to the captive peoples what the Soviet Union did to the Polish patriots in Warsaw under General Bor. They were incited by the Russians to revolt against the Germans, and the Soviet army stood nearby content to watch their extermination." Two years later, at Madison Square Garden in the heat of the presidential campaign, when he heard Eisenhower make a comment on Eastern Europe that might be misconstrued, he told Britain's delegate to the UN that Ike's reference to the "liberation" of satellite countries had not been "well phrased." According to Dulles, once Eisenhower took office, he would shun "any rash action in the direction of forcible liberation." On 21 October 1956, several days before the installation of Imre Nagy in Hungary, the secretary was interviewed on "Face the Nation," and again he recommended tactics of nonviolence, indicating that America would not meddle or use force. If Soviet forces were deployed, the United States would "watch closely," he stated, nothing more. On 30 October, at a press backgrounder, he repeated himself, while Eisenhower said the same thing the following day after there had been signs of violence (but before the bloody outbreak of 4 November). It is hard to imagine how a cautionary message could have been driven home with greater force or clarity.[44]

Two more illustrations of restraint on the part of the secretary will suffice, and both are traceable, at least in part, to Suez. During the fall of 1957, after Damascus was forced by the West to withdraw an armored regiment from Jordan, it looked as if Syria might be in line to become the next Soviet vassal state. Washington, reacting instantly, encouraged the Turks to mass troops along the Syrian frontier. Meanwhile, Teheran and Amman prepared to join Ankara in what appeared to be an impending invasion. All three were poised to strike, and if Dulles had wanted war, this would have been an ideal opportunity. Despite lukewarmness on the part of London and Riyadh (Syrian pipelines carried a third of Saudi oil to the Mediterranean), Israel was as eager as Turkey to go to extremes. Furthermore, Dulles did not believe Moscow was prepared as yet to fight in the Middle East and, as in other situations, he thought it important to respond vigorously. At the same time, he feared that if the United States initiated movement on the ground, it might touch off a "cycle of challenge and response." And needlessly, for there were other ways of preserving Syrian neutrality. American fighter aircraft were flown to Turkey. The flagship of the Sixth Fleet headed eastward. The Strategic Air Command was placed on alert, and Loy Henderson flew to Ankara for talks with the leaders of Turkey, Iran, and Jordan. In October, a border incident between Turkey and Syria triggered Soviet mobilization, placing a lighted match within inches of the tinderbox. Russian warships steamed into the Syrian port of Latakia, five thousand Egyptian troops were landed, and Dulles announced that if the Soviet Union invaded Turkey, Washington would not limit itself to defensive operations. This, however, is as far as things went. Syria took its grievances to the United Nations, the political situation in Damascus began to stabilize, and the crisis petered out.[45]

In his youth, Dulles had ventured out onto tree limbs in search of birds' nests, but only after testing the branches to see how much weight they would support. He had swum over two miles at a stretch, but always with a rowboat at his side. Over the years, his conservative instincts had served him well, and they continued to inform his outlook in 1958. For six weeks preceding Iraq's bloody left-wing coup in July, he refused to dispatch troops to Lebanon despite the urgent request of President Camille Chamoun. Chamoun claimed that his country was being infiltrated by Nasserite elements spilling over the border from Syria. Dulles, in reply, told him to take his case to the Arab League or the United Nations. The secretary declined to ship police weapons or tear gas to Beirut until it could be ascertained that Chamoun spoke for his entire government, until other Arab states agreed, and until Chamoun promised not to run for reelection on shaky constitutional grounds. Only when Washington received the chilling news from Baghdad of assassination and wholesale slaughter of the royal family did it agree to authorize American military action, twice threatened by this time and twice postponed. Even so, the order originated with Ike, not Dulles, and it occurred at the behest of Turkey, Pakistan, Iran, and Jordan. Although, by the time the marines arrived in Beirut, two American libraries had been put to the torch, United States troops refrained from occupying predominantly Moslem areas. They also allowed Lebanese forces to do most of the police work. As a result, they were well received locally and able to participate in joint patrols of Beirut.[46]

Once order had been restored to Beirut and Amman by American and

British troops respectively, Macmillan, in league with the leaders of Turkey, Saudi Arabia, and Jordan, wanted to roll on into Syria and Iraq. But once more, Dulles decided against precipitate action and, in line with the pattern of events since 1953, he showed what could be accomplished by the use of quiet diplomacy backed by force. Iraq did not go Communist, as feared. Instead, its leaders turned out to be independent nationalists, and the situation in the Middle East improved on almost every count. Later, Khrushchev would recall that although the secretary was a vicious "cur," he "knew how far he could push us, and he never pushed us too far."[47]

The other point worth making is that once the administration decided to move, it did so with lightning speed and awesome power. Revolution struck Baghdad on 14 July, and by the 15th, within twenty hours of Lebanon's call for assistance, 3600 fully equipped marines were on hand, backed by seventy warships, four hundred aircraft, artillery capable of firing atomic shells, and thousands of reserves. "When you commit the flag," declared Eisenhower, you "commit it to win." "If we ever have to resort to force," he added, "there's only one thing to do, clear up the problem completely." Dulles reflected in similar vein that if the United States had been forced to commit its prestige in Vietnam in 1954, it would not have rested content with anything less than total victory. Material strength and willpower, as well as caution, were essential ingredients in a modus operandi having peace as its goal. Dulles, it should be noted, had to face down a good deal of skepticism on Capitol Hill, along with adverse reaction at the United Nations at a time when Khrushchev was warning that the ships of the Sixth Fleet could be turned into "coffins" (Ike replied that he would not submit to "ballistic blackmail"). From General Nathan Twining, chairman of the Joint Chiefs, came still another argument against intervention: the United States might be in Lebanon for ten years or longer. Again, needless to say, such fear proved groundless. All American troops were on their way home by 25 October without taking a single Lebanese life or causing a single injury (one American was killed by accident).[48]

Eden, too, displayed a form of caution at the time of the Suez invasion. But it was caution of a different sort, unaccompanied by either power or resolution. Some have concluded that the prime minister simply lost his nerve, which may have been the case. What is beyond dispute is that his decision to suspend British operations antagonized not only Churchill but also the French who felt it a grave mistake to turn back once the fat was in the fire. Commanding generals on both sides regarded the operation as totally botched, an opinion shared by members of Eden's own party, including Alexander Cadogan and Lord Home. Ultimately, despite all the talk about runs on the British pound and oil shortages—problems that were not unreal—it came down to the personality of a single man and his philosophy of force. Long before Suez, Eden had been reputed for a soft inner core. The press, accustomed to using words like "dithering," "fidget," and "fusspot" in reference to him, claimed that he was "slow to make up his mind and quick to change it." In one of its issues, the *Daily Telegraph* noted that he often used a fist-in-palm gesture, but "the smack is seldom heard."[49]

Where Dulles was concerned, the smack was always heard, but he rarely reached the stage where he had to make a fist, for there was as much of the fox in him as there was the lion.

Before turning to other aspects of Dulles' performance, in particular his high profile role as "Red-baiter," there is one final subject worth investigation if we are to arrive at a balanced assessment of the man behind the myth. Time and again, historians have faulted Eisenhower's secretary for his supposed tolerance of "McCarthyism." Perhaps the two most common charges along this line are first, that he "knuckled under," and second, that, as a result of failing to take a firmer stand, he wreaked havoc on State Department morale.[50] Both accusations are without foundation.

To be sure, one of Dulles' first acts as secretary was to let it be known that nothing less than "positive loyalty" would be required of his subordinates.[51] R. W. Scott McLeod, a hard-liner and personal friend of McCarthy, was named chief security officer. In addition, John Paton Davies, John Carter Vincent, and others were forced to resign, in large measure because they had taken a positive view of Chinese communism.[52] Books written by left-wingers were removed from American overseas information libraries and eleven of them (out of two million) were burned.[53] Then, too, when McCarthy went over Dulles' head to negotiate with Greek shipowners in an effort to cut trade links with Communist China, Dulles made an ambiguous statement which seemed to compromise the administration's opposition to such interference.[54]

All of this is true. Still, it was Eisenhower, not Dulles, who called the political shots; and although Ike, like Truman, turned down congressional requests to examine executive files and refused to require federal officials to testify on Capitol Hill, it was his Executive Order #10450 on loyalty that set the standard for later action such as that taken against Davies and Vincent.[55] Equally to the point, McCarthy wielded such enormous clout that few thought it expedient, or even possible, to mount a frontal attack.[56] White House strategy was to ignore the senator when possible, and when not, to take the wind out of his sails through a series of calculated concessions, *reculer pour mieux sauter*.[57] Such tactics were not new. During the 1952 presidential campaign, Ike repudiated McCarthyite methods in Denver. But after being approached by McCarthy on the campaign trail, he decided to hedge. The result is that although Ike delivered a second blast against unscrupulous inquisitorial tactics in Green Bay, Wisconsin, McCarthy's home state, he scuttled a defense of General Marshall scheduled for delivery in Milwaukee.[58] In other words, he took on the opposition but without committing himself entirely in the expectation that McCarthy, if given enough rope, would hang himself, as proved to be the case.[59]

This is precisely the strategy one sees, and that one would expect to see, in Dulles' own modus operandi. On the one hand, the secretary bent a little. On the other, he angered McCarthy in a variety of ways. For example, he recommended Paul Nitze for the Defense Department planning staff (Nitze did not make it). He pressed for the confirmation of Charles Bohlen as ambassador to the Soviet Union, masterminding the strategy by which McCarthy received something of a political thrashing.[60] He also backed Harvard President James Conant for the post of high commissioner to Germany. Where Bohlen had offended anti-Communists by defending the Yalta accords, Conant had tried to shield his faculty against charges of Communist infiltration, and in both cases, the targets of McCarthy's ire won confirmation.[61] Nor is this all. The senator was not happy to have Walter Beddell Smith confirmed as Under Secretary of State, recalling that Smith had defended Davies.[62] Neither was he gratified when Davies and Vincent were permitted to resign on full pension with all charges of disloyalty waived.

Dulles also instituted a new review process under which State and Foreign Service officers could be let go without automatically being stigmatized as traitors or perverts. In practice, this meant that the range of offenses was broadened to include failure to measure up to department standards of analysis and reporting. Suspects were likewise allowed, for the first time, to cross-examine those who filed charges against them. On balance, it was a fairer system that the one employed by Truman and it allowed Dulles some leeway in dealing with cases such as Davies and Vincent which, for political reasons, may not have been adjudicable to everyone's satisfaction.[63] One might add parenthetically that the cost of the Bohlen victory was high, resulting, as one author has observed, in a "coalescence of factions within the Republican Party and with it a reassertion of the McCarthy balance." Taft warned that there must be "no more Bohlens."[64]

This is not to mention that Dulles allowed John Stewart Service, who had been dismissed by Truman on charges of disloyalty and without pension, to return to the department with accrued back pay after a successful appeal in the courts.[65]

More to the point is the fact that the secretary put an end to bookburning, which he had never sanctioned in the first place—Robert Johnson, chief of IIA (forerunner of USIA) had been recruited by Eisenhower to head up a semiautonomous agency. Once again, Dulles maneuvered on procedural grounds, this time altering the rules under which books could be removed so that the political leanings of an author were no longer decisive as a criterion.[66]

While it is true that an element of appeasement figures in the case of the Greek shipowners, Dulles made it clear that he would brook no further interference, and when McCarthy again intruded to demand an end to all allied trade with Peking, he was stopped dead in his tracks.[67] Perhaps it is significant, too, that of all Eisenhower's cabinet members, Dulles was not only the one most severely badgered by McCarthy; he is also the only one who stood up to the controversial lawmaker from year one, denouncing him at a news conference for unwarranted interference in American foreign policy.[68] His hands may have been somewhat tied by the White House, but he was far from a patsy, especially in view of his embarrassing connection with Alger Hiss—it was he who had recommended Hiss as president of the Carnegie Foundation in the face of warnings by Congressman Walter Judd that Hiss' FBI file contained incriminating data. Moreover, there were others in Congress besides Senator McCarthy who regarded Dulles as "soft" on communism.[69]

One can go further. The same political factor evident in Scott McLeod's appointment—McLeod having been an aide to the powerful Senator Styles Bridges whose cooperation Eisenhower badly needed—is apparent when one looks at the way in which other department heads reacted to harassment. Invariably, whether we are speaking of the IIA, the CIA, the army, or the Government Printing Office, the person in charge generally responded to a threatened probe by agreeing to meet with McCarthy, often in the company of Vice President Nixon, and the next step was concessions.[70] The pattern is too consistent to have any other name on it but that of Eisenhower. Ike needed a united GOP to enact legislative programs, and many felt that to alienate McCarthy was automatically to write off the help of the mighty conservative wing of the Republican party.[71] Besides, communism was an issue which the White House wanted to address for a variety of reasons, substantive as well as political. Had this not been so, Attorney General Herb Brownell would not have charged Truman with having promoted Harry Dexter White while in possession of data furnished by the FBI indicating that White had been a Soviet spy.[72]

And what of the charge that Dulles' supposedly weak-kneed response to McCarthy undermined State Department morale? Esprit de corps did seem to fall to a record low during the early 1950s. Still, this was not necessarily the fault of Dulles, or even of Eisenhower. Hiring freezes and sweeping layoffs will affect any organization—out of a staff of 42,000 at State, the secretary detached 16,000 by transfer to other agencies while terminating 5000.[73] In the second place, an overwhelming majority at State had never known anything but a Democratic administration. Certain changes were bound to come as something of a shock.[74] Thirdly, one cannot assume that morale had been particularly high during the period 1950–52. It was under Truman, after all, that communism had swept over Eastern Europe and China. It was in response to the administrative policies of Roosevelt and Truman that "McCarthyism" itself had originated, preceding the rise of the senator from Wisconsin by several years. Furthermore, it was Truman, not Eisenhower, who had been the first to set up loyalty and security review boards, the first to let hundreds of government officials go under political pressure.[75] According to Fred J. Cook's graphic account, *The Nightmare Decade*, Truman was the "real author" of "guilt by association" owing to his Executive Order #9835 which made individuals liable to dismissal on mere suspicion based on reports of informers who were not required to reveal their identity.[76]

It was not on Ike's watch that General Marshall felt impelled to leave public life nor was it a Republican attorney general who declared that Communists were "everywhere."[77] On 21 March 1947, Truman ordered all government employees, along with job applicants, to undergo loyalty investigations. Anyone belonging to, or sympathetically associated with, a subversive organization, as defined by a list from the attorney general's office, was subject to dismissal. Some were examined eight or nine times as the criteria for loyalty changed or new information appeared in a given file. In sum, as Roberta Feuerlicht suggests in her volume, *McCarthyism: The Hate That Haunts America*, it was Truman's program that "succeeded in initiating the climate of panic and unreason that is usually attributed to Joe McCarthy."[78]

Beyond this, there are no reliable figures to indicate that morale under Dulles was any lower than it had been under his predecessor.[79] On the contrary. Confidence at State seems to have begun to turn around by mid-decade coinciding with the respect that Dulles himself came to inspire in the mind of John Q. Public, as well as in Congress. At the same time, the secretary did what he could to put Foggy Bottom on a more professional basis. Political appointments on the ambassadorial and top departmental level declined dramatically to the point where all heads of mission in the Far East were drawn from the ranks of the career foreign service.[80] By comparison with the Acheson years, when there had been only three career assistant secretaries, Dulles ensured that all assistant secretaries responsible for geographical areas save one, as well as an under secretary and two deputy under secretaries, were career professionals.[81] Loy Henderson's opinion that morale at State was higher in 1959 than he had ever known it may or may not be admissable since Henderson was appointed deputy under secretary for administration in January 1955 and, as such, had an axe to grind.[82] Nevertheless, he was highly regarded by opposition leaders, and with so many new agencies bidding to encroach on State's prerogative, Dulles left behind a department very much in command and confident in the ability of its leadership.[83] By 1961, applications for the foreign service had picked up considerably.[84] If, therefore, one is going to speak of morale, one must differentiate between the department Dulles inherited and the one he turned over to his successor. Still another indicator of health at Foggy Bottom was mentioned earlier: the unanimity with which Dulles' subordinates testified that, contrary to stereotype, their chief consulted at all levels and was interested in soliciting a wide range of opinion on subjects across the board.[85]

At the White House (left to right): Dulles, Churchill, Eisenhower, and Eden. June, 1954. Photo courtesy of Princeton University Archives.

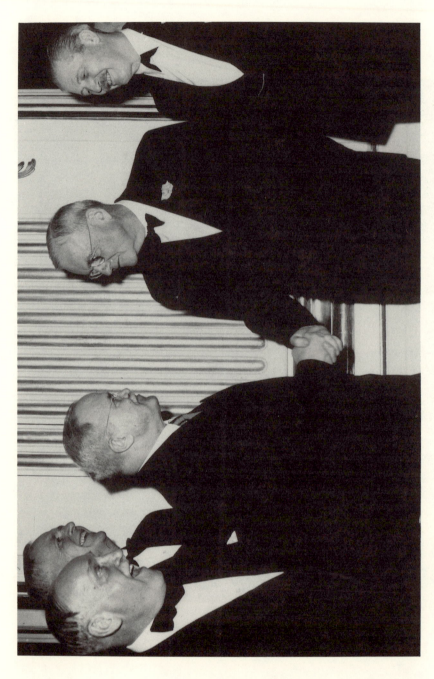

Dulles flanked by British Foreign Secretary Harold Macmillan and shaking hands with Soviet Foreign Minister V. M. Molotov at Geneva, 1955. Photo courtesy of Princeton University Archives.

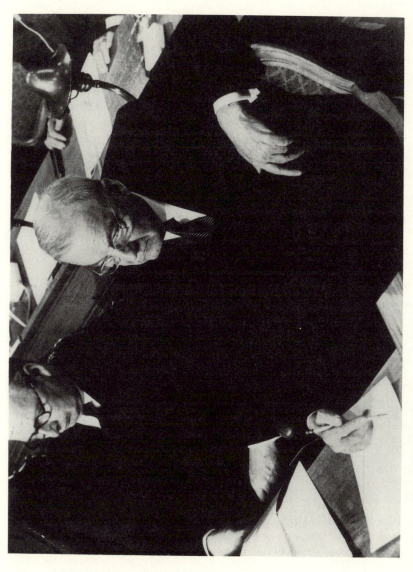

Dulles, pencil in hand, leading UN opposition to the Anglo-French-Israeli invasion of Suez in 1956 with British Foreign Secretary Selwyn Lloyd to his right. Several days later, Dulles was hospitalized for cancer. Photo courtesy of Princeton University Archives.

Dulles and Adenauer in 1954, kindred spirits. German rearmament within the Western defense system was the principal goal of American foreign policy. Photo courtesy of Princeton University Archives.

Dulles with Janet, his wife, best friend, and constant traveling companion, 1955.
Photo courtesy of Princeton University Archives.

Dulles in the foreground with French Foreign Minister Georges Bidault (center) and France's ambassador to the United States, Henri Bonnet, 1953. Photo courtesy of Princeton University Archives.

Dulles with Maurice Couve de Murville, French ambassador to the United States
(Bonnet's successor) and later French foreign minister. Photo courtesy of Princeton
University Archives.

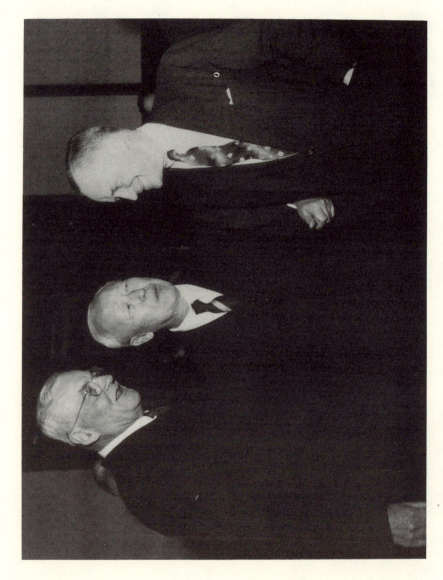

Dulles with Korean President Syngman Rhee along with U.S. Assistant Secretary of State Walter Robertson, 1956. Photo courtesy of Princeton University Archives.

CHAPTER 5

The Challenge of International Communism

After 1945, it seemed that virtually every diplomatic issue of any consequence turned on Washington's relationship with Moscow. Almost by definition, the prestige of one capital could not rise or fall without affecting the status of the other. Moscow, less well-connected but with more depth of experience in great-power rivalry, had succeeded in amalgamating over a hundred ethnic and linguistic groups under one flag to form a single nation. As such, it presented a fascinating study of world politics in microcosm and in this respect, as well as others, it was uniquely fitted to exploit the opportunities for global leadership which fell to it on the aftermath of World War II.[1]

Throughout the period following the First War, when Russia and the United States had clashed, Dulles usually figured in some unique way or expressed a view of the rivalry that proved prophetic. Under President Wilson, for example, he had served as secretary and treasurer of the Russian Bureau of the War Trade Board. In this position, he implemented his chief's design for intervention in the Soviet revolution, dispatching shiploads of aid to the White Russian challengers of Lenin and Trotsky. Soon thereafter he was championing a policy of conciliation toward Russia's traditional foes, Japan and Germany. We see him backing the Yalta agreements before their controversial provisions came to light, urging greater cooperation with the Soviet Union during the initial postwar euphoria, and assuming that the United States had to accept some kind of a Soviet sphere of influence in Eastern Europe and the Balkans. But such views, de rigueur at the time, say little about his ability to prognosticate, for in contrast with FDR, he anticipated the need to station observers in Eastern Europe to prevent a Communist takeover. Earlier than most, he shifted to a hard anti-Soviet line, backing Churchill, rather than Roosevelt, in the matter of rebuilding France and resisting Red advances in Greece. He was likewise among the first to see that Russian cooperation could not be obtained except on humiliating terms. As early as 1945, he sensed the need to remain firm, even if this placed the signing of the peace treaties in jeopardy. Six months before Washington, London, and Paris decided to consolidate their German occupation zones, he had suggested as much in a radio address.[2]

The part that he played extended beyond mere words. During the framing of the UN charter, he was instrumental in causing the Soviets to lose out on matters pertaining to regional association and the limiting of discussion. Working with Senator Vandenberg, he also defeated Moscow in its attempt to bluff at the eleventh hour, taking on Harold Stassen, the *New York Times*, and the State Department. But perhaps the most stunning of all Russian setbacks occurred at San Francisco in September 1951 when the Japanese Peace Treaty was signed, with Dulles as conference organizer. Included among his triumphs are the institution of a UN trusteeship council, the placing of the Japanese islands within its jurisdiction, and a UN Balkan Commission which secured the Greek border from Communist attempts to infiltrate men and materiel. He had been active in obtaining the withdrawal of American and Soviet forces from Korea; in the decision to hold Korean elections under UN auspices (elections which were never held); and in the creation of the so-called Little Assembly or Interim Committee, an official veto-proof body which continued to meet in 1948 and 1949 despite Soviet boycotts.[3]

It was Dulles again who urged that South Korea be given explicit assurances of American support in 1950, and with Truman's permission, he delivered such assurances in person before the Korean national assembly. Soon after, he was among the first to press for a rapid response to North Korean aggression, going so far as to urge the recall of General MacArthur for dereliction of duty because the general, disinclined initially to rush emergency assistance to Seoul, spoke of writing off the American commitment. Meanwhile, as a lonely Chiang strove to secure his position, first on the Mainland and later on Taiwan, Dulles stood nearly alone among Truman's advisers in championing a policy of American aid. Finding the president unwilling to listen, he warned Chiang frankly that he might have to sacrifice the lives of some of his soldiers as an earnest of his determination. This was the Dulles who forecast Communist inroads in Latin America and counseled Truman to appeal to the United Nations on behalf of freedom in Eastern Europe (Truman declined).[4]

Given his behind-the-scenes effectiveness in blocking Soviet expansion and exposing Communist aims, it should not be surprising that Bulganin and Khrushchev responded with ferocious attacks. He was accused of instigating the Korean War, and to prove it, photographs were circulated to members of the Security Council showing him standing on the 38th parallel hours before the fighting erupted. As early as the 1930s, *The Arsonists*, a Russian novel available in English translation, linked him with Hitler in a murder plot against FDR, and this was only the beginning. Soviet calumny mounted as his political star began to rise. By 1944, his detractors were likening him to Hitler and Franco; indeed the charges had become so scurrilous that he offered to resign from the Federal Council of Churches. When he published two articles in a 1946 issue of *Life* outlining a long-range plan for dealing with international communism, the *Red Reporter* called his work "the most skillful and dangerous . . . anti-Soviet propaganda in a long time." Two years later, while advising Secretary Marshall at a Moscow meeting of the Council of Foreign Ministers, a Soviet May Day parade featured him on a specially designed float chopping down the tree of peace. During the same period, Andrei Vishinsky, Soviet delegate to the United Nations, branded him a warmonger and suggested that he be put in chains. Although the Soviet press muffled its attacks after 1953, satellite voices continued to employ such epithets as "cannibal," "sinister," "snaky," "Hitlerite," "brutal," and "Fascist." *Praha* of Prague described him as a "fervent advocate of atomic war" and had him saying that "Americans are the supreme race called upon to rule the world." Meanwhile, the Chinese, not to be outdone, accused him of paving the way for Hitler by promoting the Dawes Plan. His appointment as secretary of state, they averred, was a payoff to Wall Street.[5]

Dulles, for his part, had read and reread such classics as *The Short History of the Communist Party* (its official Bible) and Stalin's *Problems of Leninism*, of which he had four copies—one in his office, one at his home, one on Duck Island, and one for traveling. As a subscriber to translations of the Russian press, he attempted to digest large quantities of Soviet literature, reports, and propaganda, searching for clues to the future of the Party, and by 1946 he was beginning to publish his conclusions. Two of his articles appeared in *Life* with a full-page ad in the *New York Times*. He would also participate over the next few years in eight major East-West conference sessions.[6]

There were very few tricks in the bag that he had not seen. On the night before the signing of the Austrian State Treaty, just as a meeting of foreign ministers was about to convene, American ambassador Llewellyn Thompson suggested that he find out what kind of ceremony it was going to be. Accordingly, he sounded the Russians and received assurances that they planned nothing but perfunctory toasts. When the time came, however, Molotov rose to deliver a speech in which he effectively claimed credit for the treaty. Sitting next to Dulles was Thompson who, with his knowledge of Russian, was able to relay the jist of Molotov's message, whereupon the secretary took the floor and proved himself more than equal to the occasion. Another time, when Jacob Malik, the Soviet delegate to the United Nations, came to Dulles' home on 91st Street for scotch and soda to discuss the Japanese peace treaty, the secretary assumed that Malik would keep his visit confidential. Much to his annoyance, however, news of it leaked, and when he invited Malik a second time, it was with the express understanding that there would be no publicity. To his astonishment, details of the discussion again found their way into the public prints. Worse still, although he went out of his way to solicit Malik's views on the treaty, Malik cried on reporters' shoulders that he had never been consulted. It was simply a different philosophy of life, a different view of truth, and an altogether different idea of the function of language, one with which he would become increasingly familiar.[7]

Characteristically, the Soviets engaged more often than Western leaders in such psychological warfare techniques as blowing hot and cold. Dulles called it "zigzag" while Eisenhower referred to it as the "wearisome policy of alternating sweet words with saber-rattling." The length of a cycle could range from years to only days or hours. But the basic pattern did not vary. In negotiations at the highest level, Russian officials tended to behave cordially at the outset. They would then shift gears to assume a posture of sullen confrontation. Finally, toward the end of a conference or negotiation, they would return full circle to their original warmth and cordiality. As Macmillan described the tactic, it consisted of three distinct phases: the honeymoon, the cold spell, and the final resurrection of courtesy.[8]

Because the secretary was a seasoned observer of Soviet aims and methodology by the time he reached State, he felt comfortable taking the lead at East-West conferences. Generally, he would begin with a well-sculpted statement laying out Allied policy and setting the tone for debate. He then proceeded to dissect Soviet rhetoric point by point, calling upon a sweeping command of precedent. Finally, after hours of thrust and counterthrust, he would deliver a hard-hitting peroration timed to hold conferees right up to the moment of adjournment. Sometimes, he was able to anticipate Soviet strategy by means of a Russian-speaking lip-reader who observed the Soviet delegation at close quarters and kept up a running commentary. In any case, he was among the very few who could match wits with Molotov, on occasion causing him to lose his temper.[9]

Typical is his reply to Molotov's preliminary statement at Berlin in January 1954: "It was . . . a matter of profound disappointment to hear the opening address of the Soviet Foreign Minister. It was not that he said anything new. I have heard the same speech many times before. What was saddening was . . . to accumulate and repeat the old false charges." When Molotov warned that the rearmament of West Germany would invite a Soviet bloc response, Dulles recalled the way in which Communist forces had attacked an unarmed South Korea. Later, when Molotov accused him of refusing to recognize the existence of a nation containing a billion persons (Red China), he was unfazed. No one denied that Peking existed, he rejoined, or that it had power; but it was "one thing to recognize evil as a fact," quite another "to take evil to one's breast and call it good." The government of Mao Tse-tung was still an international outlaw censured by the United Nations for its actions in Korea, Vietnam, Cambodia, and Laos.[10]

In answer to Molotov's imputation that the West seemed suspicious of the leaders of East Germany, Dulles shot back: "I admit to distrust of the German Democratic Republic." Ninety-eight percent of the East German people who were eligible to vote, he observed, had appeared at polling places following a warning that any who failed to appear would be treated as "enemies of the peace." Whole villages had been forcibly rounded up, and their people marched to the polls where they received a ballot that had been secretly printed and not made public until election day. "I have here a copy" of the ballot, said Dulles at Berlin, containing "a list of names. There is no way to indicate approval or disapproval. There is no way except to vote 'yes,' a privilege which, as I recall, Hitler conceded to his subjects. It is interesting that the list is headed by Mr. Ulbricht, a one-time Soviet citizen." The West, Dulles reminded his listeners, was not alone in its "distrust" of such an election. One million Germans had fled from the east, hardly a testimony of trust, while those who remained had sought and obtained five million food parcels from the West. Hardly a testimony of satisfaction. There were 250,000 armed police officers in East Germany, one for about every thirty-three citizens as compared with a ratio of 1–80 in West Germany. So much for "free elections."[11]

Depicting Molotov as pulling rabbits from his hat in an attempt to involve the "Big Five" in all kinds of issues reserved to the United Nations, he said he had taken occasion to "look over" the Charter of the United Nations. He had "seen" that Article 2 gave the General Assembly, not the Big Five, responsibility for introducing proposals on disarmament. He had likewise "seen" that Article 13 gave the General Assembly responsibility in another area which Molotov proposed to ignore. After ringing all the changes on Articles 14, 26, 33, 51, 61, 62, and 99, he concluded: "When I thus compared the United Nations Charter with Mr. Molotov's speech, I saw that in effect he proposed that the Council of the so-called 'five great powers' should supersede the United Nations."[12]

Verbal agility, combined with a familiarity with the finer points of international law, enabled Dulles to dismiss countless objections. Listen, as a case in point, to one of his ripostes at the fourth session of the Berlin Conference on 28 January: "Mr. Molotov attempted to meet my earlier statement . . . by pointing out that the Potsdam agreement created a Council of Foreign Ministers even after the United Nations Charter had been adopted. But this analogy is not applicable. The Council of Foreign Ministers established under the Potsdam agreement was established pursuant to the provisions of Article 107 of the Charter which expressly authorized the Allied powers to conclude the peace settlement. That was the limited purpose of the Potsdam Council. Mr. Molotov's present proposal for a council does not fall within the exception provided for by Article 107 of the Charter."[13]

As often as he could, Dulles would focus on Soviet techniques of "bloodless aggression" as they affected the Baltic states, Poland, Czechoslovakia, Hungary, Romania, and Bulgaria. He would then draw the obvious parallel with

Soviet plans for Germany: "Aggression, Soviet style, does not need the whistle of bombs or the whine of shells. It has been accomplished with words, and we heard those words yesterday." Mr. Molotov's "only reaction to my reminder of his historic speech in 1939 was a suggestion that I acquire a book published in Moscow in 1948 entitled 'The Falsifiers of History.' If the last ten days are any criterion I need not read the book. . . . If we were to eliminate what we Americans call double-talk and what a brilliant British diplomat referred to as Communist upside-down talk, what have we got left? We have a proposal to combine the undemocratically elected rulers of East Germany with what will remain after a Communist purge in West Germany to form a group to organize a Soviet type election for all Germany. . . . Really, Mr. Molotov, such a proposal was credible in 1945, became less credible shortly thereafter, became doubtful after your coup in Prague in 1948, and became downright incredible after the North Korean attack in 1950."

Rarely did he overlook an opportunity to discomfit his Soviet counterpart. After Molotov had promised peace in Korea and Indochina, an end to the armaments race, the abolition of atomic weapons, prosperity, and the elimination of tension everywhere, all to be made possible if Chou En-lai were invited to a foreign ministers' conference, the secretary wanted to know who this Chou En-lai was "whose addition to our circle" would "automatically satisfy the aspirations for peace and welfare that men have had throughout the ages" and "make possible all that has for so long seemed impossible." After repeatedly referring to Chou as "the fabulous Mr. Chou En-lai," Dulles observed that "Mr. Molotov has entertained us by an exhibition of his ability to make the preposterous seem plausible. However, we did not come here for entertainment. We came here in the hopes of doing some serious business. . . . I do not know what the Soviet Foreign Minister really thinks about us. Whatever his judgment is, he must know that he is not infallible. He has sometimes been wrong, and he might have been wrong when he accused us yesterday of being the enemies of peace. I recall that Mr. Molotov was wrong in October 1939 when he condemned France and Britain as being aggressors and praised Hitlerite Germany."[14]

One of his favorite techniques was to introduce a picturesque phrase and return to it again and again, as if to a codeword. He alluded, for instance, to the fact that the Soviet Union always managed to find some excuse for refusing to withdraw its occupation troops from Austria, even if it was merely the fact that someone had failed to settle his "bill for dried peas." Later in the conference, delegates were regaled with repeated reference to "dried peas" until it became a standing indictment of the hollowness of Soviet promises. Molotov grew accustomed to feeling the bite of American sarcasm and innuendo. "The Soviet Foreign Minister," Dulles would intone with mock seriousness, "seeks to justify requiring. . . Austria to accept for an indefinite period the presence of foreign troops, which he says are not occupation troops. But they are certainly occupying Austria. They do not stay suspended in the air somewhere; they are in Austria."[15]

Naturally, Dulles went about his needling with the air of a gentleman, dropping occasional compliments even as he punctured the myth surrounding Soviet catch words such as "free elections" and "peace." Thus did he advance toward his primary objective, which was to keep the Allies united on questions relating to German unification and the status of Red China. In the end, all of Molotov's efforts to split the West by holding out economic inducements and glittering political alternatives came to naught.

The Berlin Conference was Dulles' first great coup as secretary of state and, in a sense, the keystone for all that followed. At the Geneva summit of 1955, he fought a long, hard, and ultimately successful battle for inclusion of a written Soviet commitment to German reunification under free elections. The pledge was reduced to a dead letter at a subsequent foreign ministers' meeting when Soviet spokesmen insisted they would not stand for any turning away on the part of the German people from the social progress that had been made. Nonetheless, Dulles gained the upper hand by forcing Molotov to admit in the process that Moscow had no use for Western-style elections. This was something American officials had been trying for months to demonstrate to the world, and the secretary could not have been more pleased.[16]

Another reason why Dulles got results when he dealt with Kremlin leaders is related to his finely nuanced view of the Bolshevik experiment. He could admire the Russians for their proficiency at chess, a game he had learned to play as a youngster, just as he could respect them as individuals. In his opinion, Borodin was one of the ten most influential people of the twentieth century, Vishinsky the most powerful advocate he had ever known, and Khrushchev, while volatile and often dangerous owing to his fondness for drink, a man who did his homework. The Soviet boss, for his part, was pleasantly surprised to find, after all he had heard about Dulles, that here was a person with whom he could communicate, one who understood the Russian slant on things and got along well with Soviet diplomats, whether it was Shepilov who sold arms to Egypt, or Molotov with whom he did not mind sharing a sofa after dinner. Dulles also had high praise for his opposite number, and this spirit of amiability and mutual respect that characterized their relationship shone through at Geneva when Molotov was introduced to Under Secretary Bedell Smith. Smith was under strict orders not to let Soviet-American camaraderie show through, but it did.[17]

True to his reputation, Dulles took the Russians seriously when they spoke of world conquest; indeed he took pride in being able to quote relevant passages from their writings. But he was also convinced that true friendship could not exist anywhere on the international level, and if Russian leaders did not abide by the normal standards of behavior, they could be relied upon to look to their interests. They would be no more anxious than Americans to provoke a war. Similarly, they would have the same desire to curb arms spending as a means of unshackling their economy. They would also cooperate in establishing a new era in Soviet-American relations based on a tacit agreement respecting modes of competition—in other words, détente.[18]

As he saw it, there were three principal forces driving Soviet policy. The first of these was ideology, and this could change. Second came a deep-seated desire to expand the parameters of imperial control; and third on the list was a chronic insecurity complex, which might also change. Of the three, the most basic, as well as the most enduring, was the second; and, in the contest for survival, Kremlin operators were likely to be savage, unrestrained by any sense of tradition. Lacking respect for human life and unbeholden to public opinion in the short run, they could and would resort to every kind of violence and misrepresentation. The record showed that they would think nothing of fomenting civil strife overseas with an eye to paving the way for left-wing totalitarianism. In postwar France, they had organized street brawls and strikes, while in Czechoslovakia word was passed of an imminent invasion by the Red Army accompanied by a not too subtle hint that all who opposed Soviet policy would be liquidated. That few could overlook the proximity of Moscow, with its history of brutality, gave Communists a certain staying power combined with an appearance of invincibility—by 1959, it was reported that the Kremlin was assigning its disinformation campaign to a separate section of the KGB. Another consideration was that Soviet officials could cheat on arms agreements and sign treaties they intended to break because there was no free press to raise a cry. The failure of missile launchings could be suppressed and propaganda pitched to different audiences in different ways without having to face charges of inconsistency. Instead of fearing the media, party leaders would utilize it as a means of molding opinion. In addition, Soviet leaders, unlike American presidents who had to run for reelection every four years, expected to remain in power for the duration. They could therefore experiment with different tactics and gear their strategy to the long term. Austerity campaigns could be imposed upon the people and policies pursued that might be beneficial but not easily understood. The irony of it all is that Russian promises, however hollow, were often thought to be worth more in foreign eyes because they were not as likely to be nullified by media or legislative resistance.[19]

Due to the absence of an independent Soviet news service, bluff became the norm. Moscow, after refusing to attend a conference on German reunification until after the United States agreed to recognize Red China, thought better of it. In another instance, Kremlin leaders threatened Morocco with condign punishment should it agree to lease military bases and missile sites to Washington. Nor was Morocco alone. Norway, Denmark, Sweden, and the Netherlands, along with Britain, Iceland, Greece, and Spain were all subjected to a campaign of high-decibel rocket-rattling in a vain effort to head off German entry into the Western defense system.

Kremlin officials insisted that if such a plan were ever consummated, they would cease negotiation on German reunification and kill the Austrian State Treaty. Dulles, who could recall similar fire-breathing exercises in connection with the Marshall Plan, NATO, Turkey's membership in NATO, the formation of the Federal Republic of Germany, and Yugoslavia's break with Moscow, was not moved. Doubtless, he remembered that the Soviets had threatened Tokyo with a renewal of hostilities should it sign a separate peace. The point is this: had the secretary, indeed Western leadership in general, been a trifle less resolute, Kremlin strategists might well have accomplished their purpose.[20]

The Communist system suffered from obvious defects. At the same time, it enjoyed certain advantages in dealing with the West. It could utilize democratic openness to spread propaganda. It could organize front groups, lobby, and wherever possible, gain adherents to the Party line among members of Congress and the press. Peace offensives could be launched and insincere disarmament proposals floated with seeming ease and such devastating effect that Dulles wondered if Washington should not come forward with a few bogus propositions of its own. Again and again, Moscow succeeded in using public opinion to stampede Western parliaments into ill-advised action, just as it invoked pacifist sentiment, to undermine the unity of NATO and WEU. Furthermore, by the simple expedient of simulating a cordial atmosphere, it could lull Western constituencies into demanding major reductions in defense spending. Not for nothing did the Russians spend ten times as much as the Americans on propaganda.[21]

Dulles realized, of course, that the vaunted Soviet armor had its chinks. As he told the Senate Foreign Relations Committee, "despotisms are always weaker than they appear." If a particular ruler proved incompetent or irresolute, the state stood to be convulsed by a succession of attempted coups. But what impressed Dulles even more was the resilience of the Soviet system, its hardiness, and the ways in which it stood to gain from East-West cultural exchange. In the first place, it rarely, if ever, allowed genuine access to its people. Visitors from abroad addressed a hand-picked audience; their speeches and broadcasts were subject to party-line editorializing; and the scenarios within which they functioned were prearranged by the Kremlin with freedom of movement severely circumscribed. Presumably, too, there were some who would arrive in Moscow with a relatively open mind, inviting attempts at conversion. Those, on the other hand, who traveled to the United States from Russia would be carefully screened for ideological purity and political reliability with an eye to their value as propagandists and spies. Dulles was especially concerned lest Soviet-American exchange threaten the less stable nations of Latin America and the Far East where officials would be under pressure to embark upon similar experiments with less chance of resisting Communist subversion.[22]

For this reason, as well as a variety of others, the secretary never assumed that "free peoples" would automatically prevail over their adversaries, and neither did Eisenhower, who wondered aloud if the United States might not perish someday because it had to operate under the Marquis of Queensbury's rules with one hand tied behind its back. The pessimistic predictions of Tocqueville and Macaulay were more than once the topic of White House conversation. Would the system of constitutional checks and balances, by absorbing enormous amounts of a secretary's time in appearances before House and Senate committees, make it increasingly difficult for an executive to arrive at decisions and carry them out? How was one to sell democracy and free enterprise to leaders of less developed nations where oligarchic state socialism might be better adapted to their needs, as well as culturally more palatable?[23]

Dulles regarded the United States as fortunate in occupying a position of marked prominence when it came to the development of weapons systems, indeed it was a position that both he and Ike proposed to exploit. Addressing the Council on Foreign Relations early in the winter of 1954, he declared that in response to overt Communist aggression, America would depend "primarily upon a great capacity to retaliate, instantly, by means and at places of our choosing." The Korean War had ended, he opined, because Peking knew that Washington was prepared to expand the conflict "beyond the limits and methods which he [the enemy] had selected."[24]

Such a notion was not new. But the press soon gave it a new name, "massive retaliation." Eisenhower had outlined it a few days earlier before a group of congressional leaders and one finds the seed of it in Ike's first State of the Union Address. Dulles had said much the same thing in an article, as well as in speeches dating to 1950; and, if one wants to go back even farther, one can find mention of it in the original Senate debate on NATO.[25]

At the same time, even though the concept was familiar by the time Dulles made his celebrated presentation in 1954, it drew criticism in certain quarters because the secretary seemed to be saying that Washington would have automatic resort to its most lethal weapons the moment Moscow or Peking mounted any kind of military challenge, either directly or through proxy, anywhere in the world. Had such been the case, "massive retaliation" would have been either a giant bluff or a recipe for total war. At the very least, it would have strained the nation's credibility.[26]

In fact, the administration's proposed response to aggression was not intended to be automatic. Dulles, in his Council talk, noted that "local defense will always be important." Later on, he explained that the United States would consult its allies. Both president and secretary made it clear on any number of occasions that retaliatory action might take many forms short of an all-out nuclear strike against Moscow or Peking.[27] Dulles had said as much in May 1952 when he told Cyrus Sulzberger of the *New York Times* that instead of waging another ground campaign against Red China, the United States would be well advised to initiate naval and air action against the enemy's home ports and islands.[28] At about the same time, he pointed out that Moscow could be held in check by targeting ports and communication lines in Siberia. Four years later, when he referred in one of his papers to the possibility of using atomic weapons against China, the suggested target was Manchuria.[29] Eisenhower, in much the same way, defined possible action in defense of French Indochina in terms of an assault, not on Peking, but rather on Chinese coastal areas, airfields, and support facilities, along with the island of Hainan.[30] One also recalls the 1958 crisis over Matsu and Quemoy when American participation was limited to naval and air resupply operations coupled with action on the diplomatic front.

Why, then, did Dulles speak as he did? In the first place, he wanted to make it crystal clear that America would go to extremes rather than allow further erosion of the "free world" position. Moscow and Peking were put on notice, that they could not keep chipping away at American interests, could not engage the West in a series of piecemeal operations aimed at exhausting its patience and strength. As Dulles put it, "we don't want to be committed to a series of Koreas around the globe."[31] What if Peking should decide to wade into the Indochina war? Ike was unwilling to tolerate any repetition of Korean-style privileged sanctuaries here or elsewhere. Thus, an attack by the USSR on Turkey would not necessarily be dealt with on Turkish soil.[32] The aim here, as elsewhere, was to eliminate the kind of misunderstanding that had led to World War I, World War II, and the Korean War—the notion that Washington would not react in time, or with sufficient power, to become a major factor in hostilities. Potential adversaries had to know that America would not shrink from the first use of nuclear weapons in an area where it enjoyed high ratio superiority (6–1). According to Eisenhower, such weapons were the only viable expedient against a Soviet invasion of Europe.[33] In addition, overseas allies had to be reassured that in a clinch they could count on America's nuclear umbrella. Eisenhower was criticized by the British in 1957 for using the qualifier "with all appropriate force" because they felt it might tempt the Soviets.[34] Later in the decade, things were, of course, different. As Washington's lead in nuclear weapons started to dwindle, Western officials began to doubt that an American president would put his homeland at risk, and as a result, they were increasingly unwilling to permit the use of local military facilities. U.S. credibility, which had once required a clear-cut statement of willingness to wage nuclear war, now pre-supposed a realistic plan to stop Russian armor with nonstrategic theater weapons.[35]

Another advantage of the doctrine was that it served to drive home to Americans the notion that there must be no repetition of Korea. Thus, while Communist leaders were made to realize that in future contests they could not expect their choice of weapons and terrain, the administration was also building consensus and bolstering resolution on the home front.[36]

Still another element in the doctrine of "massive retaliation," and one spelled out on various occasions, was what James Reston referred to as "2X": if the Communists inflicted X amount of damage, they could expect to suffer "2X" in return. In other words, aggression in the future would not only be futile; it would boomerang.[37] "Greater sanctions" was the term Dulles employed in reference to Korea before taking office, and he thought along the same general line as secretary.[38]

But even if war on the Korean model had been viewed as feasible from a military-political standpoint, neither Eisenhower nor Dulles could very well have entertained the idea seriously when cuts in the defense budget stood so high on their list of priorities. Journalist Walter Lippmann, in his influential work, *The Cold War* (1947), had argued that America lacked the manpower and financial resources to contain Communist aggression if this meant allowing the enemy his choice of time, circumstance, terrain, and weapons. For the United States to attempt to prepare on every front for the mobilization of local, limited counterforce, as implied in George Kennan's theory of "containment," was, in Lippman's view, to be wedded to a hodge-podge of undependable allies.[39] Just so, "massive retaliation," which Dulles defined as "maximum deterrent at a bearable cost," and which Ike dubbed "more bang for the buck," answered the call of economic convenience, as well as defense.[40] It was also known as the "New Look," and Eisenhower showed his concern for a proper balance between means and ends by seating his treasury secretary on the National Security Council.[41] As Dulles explained over the airwaves, unless Uncle Sam was ready and willing to strike at the heart of aggression, he would go bankrupt, for Soviet and Chinese forces in combination numbered seven million and were poised to strike at dozens of points along the border.[42]

One might add parenthetically that the degree to which America's conventional capability, and therefore capacity for limited war, suffered erosion has been exaggerated. In the opinion of military authorities, Eisenhower maintained a higher level of preparedness for conventional, limited war than Truman had.[43] It is interesting to observe, too, that "New Look" thinking extended beyond Washington to such capitals as London and Moscow.[44] It was in the air.

One of the standard criticisms of "massive retaliation" (a phrase, incidentally, not found in Dulles' speech) is that it constituted a form of bluff. According to one recent account, Eisenhower "never considered the nuclear option viable."[45] There is a certain plausibility to the thesis because from time to time, Ike did seem to imply that initiation of nuclear warfare by the United States was unthinkable. On the other hand, most specialists in the field of nuclear history would disagree.[46] The president was doubtless at pains in certain instances to portray himself as a prudent and responsible military man. But for every such instance, one can cite numerous instances to the contrary.[47] Speaking seriously, for example, in National Security Council meetings of plans for the use of nuclear weapons, he pressed for such plans and insisted on regarding the atomic bomb as "simply another weapon in our arsenal."[48] On more than one occasion, speaking as commander-in-chief, he indicated a clear willingness to go nuclear.[49] He likewise required that planning in all branches of the armed services "reflect the possible use of nuclear weapons across a wide range of contingencies."[50]

The record shows Dulles announcing in no uncertain terms that Chinese aggression in Indochina would have "grave consequences which might not be confined to Indochina."[51] At the same time, the secretary promised U.S. allies *in private* that Washington would strike at Chinese targets if Peking resorted to overt aggression against French and Vietnamese forces.[52] This is consistent with the line he had taken before 1953. It jibes with Ike's recollection in his memoirs of a readiness to strike at "the head of the snake" during crises involving Indochina, Quemoy, and Berlin.[53] And it squares with what the president told congressional leaders in strict confidence: that if South Korea were to come under renewed attack by the North, American forces would "hit them with everything we got."[54] Ike, it should be noted, recommended a similar stance to Lyndon Johnson during the Vietnam War.[55] There is, finally, a manuscript in the Dulles papers dated 21 April 1956 stating that if North Korea were to attack a second time across its borders, the United States would see to it that Communist leaders suffered losses greater than anything they could possibly hope to gain.[56]

To recapitulate, the phrase "massive retaliation" was neither bluff nor provocation. Essentially, it was defensive in tone and purpose, the hope being that by mobilizing public support for a vigorous response to Communist aggression, such aggression would never occur, and hence there would be no need to respond. Foreign Minister Georges Bidault of France, who knew Dulles well, remarked in his memoirs that the secretary was given to describing his policy as one of "calculated risks" but that in practice this meant that he calculated a lot and risked nothing.[57]

In line with this, it is important to bear in mind that Dulles viewed physical power as only one of many determinants affecting a nation's overall influence. As a case in point, he spent considerable time pondering the question of how Washington could shed its image as a collaborator with Western colonialism. Stalin pinpointed Asia as the most fertile of all fields for Communist expansion and ultimately the road to victory over the West because a centuries-old colonial occupation had left deep scars, inviting communism to advance under the dual banner of nationalism and racial equality. Japan and the Persian Gulf were obviously high on Moscow's priority list, but Dulles expected the Kremlin to fish in troubled waters everywhere, stirring up hatred between Arab and Jew, Pakistani and Indian. Foreign aid was a specially powerful weapon in the hands of Moscow when geared to capitalize on local pride and sensitivity. The United States should therefore do more, in his view, to dissociate itself from France and England. Although, as we have seen, he made a conscious decision to subordinate anticolonialism to other more immediate causes such as EDC and WEU, he was far from indifferent because he realized that Moscow would continue to portray Washington as a villain in league with hated former overlords. Uncle Sam might denounce imperialism in the abstract, but he would end up being the proverbial mourner at the grave who lays a wreath while someone else collects the inheritance.[58]

Naturally, imperialism meant different things to different people. Latin America, a prime example, had thrown off an imperial yoke of long standing with the moral backing of the United States. But it had also been subjugated to a certain extent by the very power claiming to be its champion. Traditionally, and by virtue of geographical propinquity, the area south of the Rio Grande had always been an American sphere of influence—not a colony exactly, yet not altogether free. By the same token, Communist leaders had long sought a base of operations in the Western Hemisphere, one country, large or small, which they could call their own and from which they could launch military probes, conduct espionage, and broadcast propaganda linking the Colossus of the North with the region's political and economic ills. Dulles was struck by the fact that as early as the 1820s Russia had formed a European coalition dedicated to the destruction of democracy. Two-thirds of the Monroe Doctrine had in fact been aimed at countering what was basically an ideological threat "made in Moscow," and Russia had been warned not to extend its "political system" to "any portion" of the Americas. Now, nearly a century and a half later, it was still being warned. Dulles supported Truman's defense of "the first and most fundamental of our foreign policies," and during the 1950s, when the Kremlin announced that it would buy all of Cuba's sugar crop, even as it began shipping heavy weapons to Havana, Washington declared the doctrine to be "as valid today" as it was in 1823. Echoing Monroe's dictum, the State Department avowed that, "We owe it . . . to candor . . . to declare that we should consider any attempt on their [the European powers'] part to extend their system to any portion of this hemisphere as dangerous to our peace and safety." Dulles was imbued with something of the same spirit when he refused to countenance the delivery of Soviet bloc arms to Guatemala aboard the *Alfhem* in 1954.[59]

Since events in Guatemala, along with the American role in helping to shape them, are still controversial and since, in addition, they afford a rare glimpse of communism in retreat, the story is worth telling in some degree of detail. Nowhere else, certainly, has Dulles been more universally taken to task on moral grounds.

The case against American policy may be simply stated. The secretary was on record as saying that he believed "military force should not be used aggressively to achieve national goals," yet during his tenure at Foggy Bottom American planes and American advisers helped secure the overthrow of a popularly elected president, Jacobo Arbenz Guzmán. Arbenz, for his part, claimed to view American policy as the cat's paw of corporate greed and attributed a large share of his nation's problems to the United Fruit Company, maintaining that communism posed no threat to his people and that American aid to rebel leader Carlos Castillo Armas constituted unwarranted interference in the domestic affairs of another country. Essentially, he held that the revolutionary movement which overthrew him was "Made in the U.S.A." by the Central Intelligence Agency and that its base of support among the Guatemalan masses had been negligible. He also minimized the military strength of the opposition, making it appear as if the downfall of his government could be explained solely in terms of clever propaganda beamed from clandestine radio stations in conjunction with a campaign of aerial bombing, all of it orchestrated by Washington. This has been the position taken by his friends ever since, just as it has been featured in scholarly monographs.[60]

According to revisionist historians whose theory has won a large measure of acceptance, Castillo Armas crossed over from Honduras on 18 June 1954 with a "ragtag" band of two hundred men. He then occupied the Guatemalan town of Esquipulas which is a Catholic stronghold only six miles from the border, and there he sat while the CIA went to work, exaggerating the strength of the Liberation Army, crediting it with fictitious gains, bombing a wide variety of targets, and intimating the dread possibility of armed intervention by the United States. In short, Arbenz was "psyched out" by a CIA strategem; he lost his nerve and resigned without a fight.[61]

If all of this were true, it would indeed place Dulles in an awkward spot since he would appear to have been not only an imperialist but also the worst kind of manipulator. As will be seen, however, the picture is somewhat more complicated.

Castillo Armas' initial force was indeed small—approximately two hundred facing a government Goliath of about five thousand—but it was also highly trained and exceedingly well equipped. Included in its arsenal were twenty-two thousand rockets, forty-five thousand rifles, four hundred mortars and pieces of heavy artillery. Members of the party trained for between one and two years in Honduras, El Salvador, and other countries with the help of American military advisers so that this was no raggle-taggle band and its commander no common soldier. Castillo Armas graduated from the Escuela Politécnica, Guatemala's West Point, and attended the U.S. Army's elite staff and command school at Fort Leavenworth before returning home to run the Escuela and head up the Fourth Military District. Like Arbenz, he had been the leader of a previous coup attempt.[62]

Within a matter of days, the number of his troops had risen dramatically to between one and five thousand, depending on the account one reads and whether it includes all anti-Arbenz partisans or only enlisted combatants. Official records, which put the number conservatively at between one and two thousand, include only battle-trained troops. But it is clear that as Castillo Armas advanced, his ranks were swelled by a massive influx of ranchers, peasants, and other sympathizers who together posed a real threat to the regular army.[63]

Furthermore, instead of merely sitting in Esquipulas, a good-sized town by Guatemalan standards and the most revered religious shrine in all of Central America, the rebels invaded at three different locations on the perimeter to attack a series of choke points along the country's jugular vein, the rail artery running east-west from Puerto Barrios on the coast to the capital.[64]

Military progress was bound to be tortuously slow on account of the rugged terrain. Certain commentators seem surprised at how little mileage Castillo Armas made and how close to the border he remained. However, he was limited to a few primitive roads which snaked their way through hill country that was as easily defended by government forces as it was precipitous. Moreover, the two most highly prized military targets in Guatemala were within thirty miles of the border, the first of these, and by far the most important, being Zacapa because it controlled two major rail lines, the east-west route already mentioned and the nation's sole access route to El Salvador. It was the site, too, of the largest military base outside Guatemala City and the key to the capital itself since it handled most of its commerce. Next in importance, and close to Zacapa at about fifteen miles due south over the mountains, was Chiquimula, a provincial capital of 25,000 inhabitants which dominated the rail link with El Salvador. Secondary targets were Gualán and Puerto Barrios owing to their location on the eastern sector of the railroad and at its terminus. But it all came down to a question of who controlled Chiquimula and Zacapa.[65]

Castillo Armas pressed relentlessly on to capture Chiquimula in nine days of blood and iron. Nearby Vado Hondo, where Liberation units approaching from the south and east linked up, had been heavily fortified by government troops along with independent Communist groups. For Castillo Armas, its capture was imperative, and his soldiers gave their all. During seven hours of blistering attack and counterattack, insurgent columns numbering between five hundred and fifteen hundred converged to face heavy artillery, mortars, and machine gun nests. Arbenz, realizing the importance of Vado Hondo for the defense of Chiquimula, and indirectly Zacapa, reacted energetically, dispatching three hundred fresh troops to bolster it. Nevertheless, the rebel cause triumphed and Castillo Armas advanced in three columns against widely separated targets in Chiquimula proper. Defense forces estimated at between one and two thousand, and including fifty-five sharp shooters, deployed mortars and cannon, but in vain.[66]

Anticipating the surrender of Zacapa itself, antigovernment partisans rose in savage door-to-door fighting. Arbenz, taking personal charge of the army, dispatched an additional five hundred troops from the nation's capital to augment a force of between one and two thousand charged with putting down the uprising, while Castillo Armas' aircraft rained down dozens of hundred-pound bombs reducing the fort and military headquarters to a rubble. Some idea of the resultant damage may be gauged from the fact that within days of Arbenz's surrender, a Red Cross team and a private relief organization delivered over 106,000 pounds of emergency provisions. Moreover, even as Castillo Armas' forces were pounding Zacapa by air, he was preparing to finish the job by means of an assault mounted by an elite force of one thousand when news arrived of the surrender of the two-thousand man government garrison.[67] For all practical purposes, the war was over.

Clearly, the story of Arbenz's overthrow is multifaceted, though little of this is reflected in today's literature. It is surprising that more has not been done to investigate the role of the Catholic Church, along with that of university students. Both of these groups were adamantly anti-Arbenz by 1954, and both were highly influential.[68] Archbishop Mariano Rossell y Arellano warned as early as 1946 that communism was on the threshold of victory. Later, he risked his life to crisscross the country, alerting people to the rising danger and carrying in his hands a replica of the "Black Christ" of Esquipulas. Pastoral letters followed, including one dated 9 April 1954, urging the citizenry to rise as one against an unprecedented and mortal threat to their freedom and spiritual welfare. As for the students, revisionists stress the part they played in ousting Ubico, the old-fashioned dictator. But they say nothing about what these same students did to bring Arbenz and his predecessor Arévalo into disrepute.

The man who would probably have been elected in 1950 in Arbenz's stead, had he not been assassinated the year before, was the popular and anti-Communist army chief, Col. Francisco Javier Arana. His chauffeur escaped an automobile ambush to identify several of the assailants as Arbenz henchmen and the assassins' car as belonging to Mrs. Arbenz. But President Arévalo did virtually nothing to bring these men to justice. The nonpolitical association of university students, the AEU, was so incensed that it joined in street demonstrations that nearly brought down the government when police opened fire, killing a medical student. AEU also participated with university faculties in a series of strikes which crippled hospitals, schools, and courts where students held vital positions. Later, when the Guatemalan supreme court struck down the agrarian reform law and congress reacted by removing four out of five justices, the AEU demonstrated in front of the national palace where a copy of the constitution was burned. Leading newspapers such as *El Imparcial* and *La Prensa* applauded the students. By 1954, with Arbenz resorting to widespread arrests, beatings, water cures, and other forms of torture and intimidation, student sentiment again reached the boiling point. Two years earlier, when reports of such activity first began to be heard, the AEU had appealed to the supreme court for injunctions against the interior minister and chief of police. But this has been well nigh lost to posterity. Historians have gone into detail on Ubico's use of torture to subdue his political opponents prior to the revolution of 1944. Yet Arbenz's record, which may well have eclipsed that of Ubico in this respect, passes without notice even though there is as much evidence on the one side as there is on the other.[69]

Equally curious is the fact that more of an effort has not been made to document the many ways in which Arbenz botched the administration of agrarian reform. Decree 900 was vaguely worded as to which lands would be subject to expropriation; appeals could not be made to the judiciary, only to the reform tribunals, and although government officials sat as judges alongside spokesmen for the peasant and workers' classes, the former were instructed to side with the latter in any situation involving land or labor. In a nation accustomed to gradual reform and abundant red tape, the pace of change appeared almost illegitimate even as it led to organizational failures. Land that had been taken in one instance from a village of 2500 was distributed to sixty peasants. In other instances, the landowner found that instead of having to give up a self-contained package, he lost isolated strips leaving the remaining portions of his property disconnected. Dozens of private farms were seized illegally in the period December 1953 to April 1954. By one account, land was sometimes awarded to people with no interest or ability in farming who, in turn, sold it and squandered the proceeds; in other cases, the land was distributed disproportionately to Arbenz cronies. Meanwhile, the average man often found it hard to distinguish between land reform and plain theft. The extent of corruption in government circles became increasingly clear with the exposure of scandals in late 1953 and early 1954, and the general economic condition of the country continued to deteriorate.[70]

The role of neighboring countries in supplying Castillo Armas with arms and bankrolling his operation is still another story that has yet to receive the exposure it deserves considering the fact that much of the outside support received by rebel forces came from leaders of Central American, Caribbean, and Caribbean rim countries who feared communism as much as Washington did, perhaps more.[71]

Additional digging could be done to ascertain the facts of electoral fraud in the contests of 1950 and 1952. Arbenz is depicted by his friends as "popularly elected." But he defeated his leading opponent, Miguel Ydígoras Fuentes, only after the latter's meetings were closed down, ballot boxes were stuffed, and illiterate peasants were marched en masse to the polls to vote on orders. In 1952, the electoral returns were sufficiently even in spite of government rigging to constitute a virtual repudiation of Arbenz, certainly by Guatemalan standards. One hundred thirty thousand pro-Arbenz votes filled twenty-nine seats in Congress while the remaining 105,000 filled only three seats, and the election was followed by wholesale arrests and assassinations. One of the losers, Colonel Mendoza, was the same gentleman who fought side by side with Castillo Armas.[72]

Finally, a good deal more could be done to highlight the position of Communist leaders in Arbenz's Guatemala.[73] Although there were no Communists in the nation's cabinet, it was not a cabinet with real power such as belonged to the heads of key civilian groups and, above all, to Arbenz himself. The president, whose campaign was managed by José Manuel Fortuny, founder of the Guatemalan Communist party, had at his side an energetic and politically active wife who had become ardently and openly pro-Communist after studying in the United States. Moreover, the Communist party itself, using popular front techniques, had joined with the Labor party to fill fifty-one out of fifty-six seats in Congress. By April 1954, four out of ten party delegates who advised Arbenz on national policy were Communists, and while there were only four outright Communists in the legislature, they chaired the crucial committees. In addition, the nation's Federation of Labor was run by a Communist, Victor Manuel Gutiérrez, as was the National Orphanage. When Ubico resigned in 1944, Arévalo recruited the Communist Virginia Bravo Letelier who, along with Gutiérrez, formed the teachers' union. Thereafter, with the unions under Communist control, it became increasingly difficult to be elected or to teach school without adhering to the strict Party line. Bravo Letelier, who fled to East Berlin after the 1954 revolt to engage in Eastern European propaganda, served as secretary to Mrs. Arbenz, as did another Communist, Matilde Elena Lopez.[74]

Communists or Communist sympathizers soon took over the education ministry, the social security administration, and the agrarian reform program, not to mention the official press and radio, which followed Moscow's line on world events. By March 1954, the hammer and sickle had begun to appear in government offices, and newspaper correspondents representing Reuters and the *New York Times* had been expelled. Church leaders found death threats in their mail. Religious processions were banned. Scores of people simply disappeared. At the same time, Soviet bloc arms were beginning to pour into the country in quantities suggestive of an intent to supply guerrilla movements across the border, and documents were captured confirming Soviet plans for a takeover of the entire Central American region. Eighty thousand citizens signed a petition to compel Arbenz to enforce Article 32 of the constitution banning political parties with foreign ties (e.g., the Communist party) and the number "32" had begun to appear everywhere.[75]

This, too, represents an aspect of Arbenz's isolation and must be counted as a factor explaining the victory by two hundred over five thousand.[76] In short, there were many reasons why the Liberation Army emerged victorious, most of which have received short shrift. It is true that Castillo Armas obtained much from the United States in the way of shoes, food, arms,

planes, and military advice. Americans may have been involved in his reconnaissance and ground radio communications, and the United Fruit Company made a generous contribution. It is no secret, either, that mercenaries
were used, although not nearly as many as Arbenz apologists have claimed.
All of this must be weighed, however, against Soviet aid which was also a
factor. If there is any single fact that stands out clearly it is that the Liberation
movement drew its main strength from native financing and native
manpower.[77]

Much of the above material becomes clearer and assumes added significance when seen in light of another uprising that occurred during the same
period. The overthrow of Iran's Mossadegh bears a striking resemblance to
events in Guatemala, as once again, a leftist leader increasingly dependent
upon Communist support and unpopular with large segments of his people,
was ousted by American-backed insurgents.

When Premier Mohammad Mossadegh nationalized British oil properties
in 1951, the world's largest refinery at Abadan shut down and British employees returned home. At the same time, a Western boycott caused Iranian
oil production to plummet even as Saudi and Kuwaiti levels of production
rose exponentially. Mossadegh enjoyed a fairly broad base of support among
his people, but Shah Mohammad Reza Pahlavi was also popular in a peasant
nation deeply imbued with the monarchial principle and broadly committed
to traditional ways. The stage was thus set for conflict the moment Mossadegh
insisted on playing East against West, thereby situating himself in a position
of increasing dependence on the Left. In January 1953, Iran's parliament,
the Majlis, sustained Mossadegh's dictatorial powers for another year, and
he improved on the occasion to denounce the nation's sovereign as an agent
of "foreign interests"—at which point the Shah resigned for "reasons of
health." So great, however, was popular indignation, with mobs choking the
streets and rioting out of control, that within hours of the Shah's abdication
he was persuaded to resume his lawful place.[78]

Mossadegh, after promising freedom and extolling Western political systems, muzzled the press and arrested recalcitrant editors. After blocking a
quorum in the Majlis by ordering his supporters to absent themselves, he
suspended new elections. On another occasion, when the Shah refused to
dissolve the legislature, Mossadegh gained his objective unconstitutionally
by holding a mock referendum. He also dissolved the supreme court and
erected over a score of gallows on Sepah Square, where public enemies
were hung without trial. All along, by branding his opponents agents of
Great Britain, packing the courts, and transgressing the law, he was in effect
rendering the constitution a dead letter. Pro-Mossadegh thugs and hooligans
led by members of the Tudeh (Communist) party roamed freely in the streets
of Teheran even though the Tudeh organization had been outlawed for
attempting to take the Shah's life. They desecrated the mausoleum housing
the remains of the Shah's father; windows of shops whose owners were bold

enough to display a picture of the Shah were smashed; and Mossadegh's foreign minister, hurling opprobrious epithets at the ruling family, referred to the royal palace as a brothel.[79]

None of this improved the premier's standing in the eyes of the ordinary Iranian or, for that matter, other groups. Army officers, whose ranks had been thinned by the forced retirement of 1200 men within two years, led a mob to his house in early 1953, and he barely escaped with his life. He was disliked by businessmen generally, with the exception of exporters, because he frittered away the country's financial resources and brought on hard times. By 1953, his treasury lay empty, and civil service personnel fretted to see their salaries and positions threatened across the board. Then, too, in the Majlis, where a charismatic leader like Mossadegh might normally have expected to hold sway, members proved defiant. Priority legislation stalled, and it is to the legislative chamber that General Fazlollah Zahedi, Mossadegh's principal rival, came seeking asylum. Early in the spring of 1953, when Mossadegh requested laws which would have made him commander-in-chief of the Iranian army to replace the Shah, the Majlis refused. Later, on 19 June, he attempted to stage large-scale demonstrations in the capital only to fail signally. Although cars equipped with loud speakers made the rounds and Radio Teheran did its best to attract a crowd, only a few thousand showed up, mainly from the Tudeh party and assorted front organizations. That the government would countenance open participation by the outlawed Tudeh was itself significant. Another government rally the same day at Tabriz produced only four hundred supporters who were quickly dispersed by stone-throwing opponents. In a word, the long-range outlook for Mossadegh was not good. The American embassy predicted that the "downward trend" of his popularity would continue. And so it did.[80]

On 5 August, Mossadegh held a bogus plebiscite and with 99.4 percent of the vote forced the Majlis to declare its own dissolution. Only a small minority protested. Nevertheless, the Shah responded with alacrity, dismissing Mossadegh as he was constitutionally empowered to do, and naming General Zahedi to succeed him. Mossadegh arrested the messenger bearing the Shah's orders and refused to resign. But several days later, when the premier instructed army officers to restore order in public places, his troops charged Tudeh sections of the crowd, forcing them to praise the Shah. Large numbers of demonstrators then began to converge on Mossadegh's home, and soldiers who were sent to subdue the mob began to join it. This was the turning point.[81]

Washington's role was relatively minor. The CIA contributed an estimated $60,000, not a great deal when one considers that United Fruit gave this much to the Guatemalan Liberation movement in a country only a fraction of the size of Iran. All major operations, moreover, involving American agents were masterminded by London, just as it was the British who handled communications from their base on Cyprus.[82]

The fact of the matter is that the lion's share of the momentum behind Mossadegh's overthrow is traceable not to Washington, or even to London, but rather to Teheran. Kermit Roosevelt, who coordinated the American side of the operation, was correct in assuming that outside support for the Shah would be worse than useless in the absence of strong backing from the people and the army. By 1953, Mossadegh was clearly turning to the Kremlin for a solution to his economic difficulties as well as for a settlement of border disputes—so much so, that commentators representing a broad spectrum of opinion believed that the Shah, and the Shah alone, stood between Iran and a Communist takeover. One might expect such an assessment from Downing Street where Churchill had an axe to grind. But this was also the view of leaders in neighboring countries such as Turkey and Iraq. Officials in Baghdad regarded Mossadegh's regime as a threat to the entire Middle East. Even Zahedi's own critics were inclined to admit that the nation would probably have gone Communist had it not been for the daring of the royal family. Thereafter, popular affection for the Shah held firm until he began to embrace Western culture in a way incompatible with the religious and social mores of his countrymen. When Eisenhower visited Teheran in 1959, the public thoroughfares were lined with Persian carpets. Half a million people turned out to greet him, and as in the case of Guatemala five years earlier, one may assume that such jubilation was based not only on the prospect of American economic and military aid but also on popular perceptions of justice.[83]

Abstract concepts such as justice and freedom, particularly freedom of religion, can make a difference in the way American foreign policy is framed, as also in the way it is perceived by the people of other countries, and so it is to the intellectual underpinnings of American diplomacy, something absolutely central to the secretary's modus operandi, that we now turn for a brief *tour d'horizon*.

CHAPTER 6

The Mind of the Secretary

One of the more unusual features of the secretary's mind is the way in which it combined the spiritual with the practical. As a lawyer, he was bound to be matter-of-fact and down-to-earth. Still, Dulles was the son of a preacher. He had also majored in philosophy at Princeton and so could not help being attuned to a loftier set of values. Believing that the future of mankind depended on ideals and that those who possessed a "righteous faith" would prevail over those who did not, he felt it incumbent upon America, as leader of the free world, to draw upon its Judeo-Christian heritage for renewed vigor and inspiration.[1]

Imitating Wilson, whom he admired as the moral leader par excellence, he stressed that greatness in nations, as in people, depended upon "character." In Dulles' view, America had been a burnt-out civilization during the 1920s and 1930s in the way it shirked its duty to the rest of humanity. Although vibrant new faiths were born during the interwar period, they were not born in the United States. By 1943, with the Axis star beginning to wane, he feared the familiar syndrome of victory and moral fervor, followed by lassitude. Students, he observed, were no longer searching for truth and goodness because the foundations needed to sustain such a search were under attack at institutions of higher learning. As a result, cynicism had become the order of the day, and it was steadily sapping American patriotism. Heroes and villains, he maintained, had disappeared from the pages of history as scholars chose to interest themselves in the peccadilloes of the great.[2]

Dulles agreed with Theodore Roosevelt who held that the historian of highest rank must needs be a moralist. Consequently, what was required was a rebirth of the spirituality that had given rise to democracy, along with the immortal works of music, art, and literature—the standard that had fostered organized charity. He was further convinced that religion, as a foundation, had not only humanized Western man; it had also put imperialism on the road to ultimate extinction. Religious leaders, like all mortals, were prone to abuse their power on occasion, and he allowed that their zeal, when politicized, could lead to inquisition and war. At the same time, he could see that for sheer wanton cruelty and mass killing, no century surpassed the twentieth, with its lapses in religious faith. Traits such as magnanimity, as exemplified by Lincoln, along with the courtesy associated with medieval chivalry, were a function of the supernatural, he believed, and whenever faith fell off, morality could not be far behind, for "practice unsupported by belief" was a "wasting asset." One of his favorite quotations came from a first edition of Washington's Farewell Address: "Reason and experience both forbid us to expect that national morality can prevail in exclusion of religious principle."[3]

He was acutely aware that the Communist credo, "from each according to his ability, to each according to his need," had inspired an extraordinary willingness to sacrifice on the part of a significant number of the world's people. Not since the high tide of Islam in the fifteenth and sixteenth centuries had the threat to Western civilization been greater in his view. Americans were therefore faced with a grave challenge and they must either respond with all the resources at their command or sink. It was not enough merely to stockpile arms and pioneer in technology. The Achilles heel of the United States was its tendency since World War I to succumb to secular humanism, giving only nominal allegiance to the law embedded in man's conscience and discernible in the natural order. Russia's principal weakness, on the other hand, was that its system frustrated man's built-in "yearning" for basic freedoms. And chief among these, he believed, was freedom of religion, which was rooted not only in human nature but also in centuries of Slavic tradition.[4]

Change, for Dulles, was the law of life. The dynamic would always prevail over the static, just as running water would eventually wear away the hardest of rock. During the 1930s, the Axis had pressed its suit on the basis of injustices stemming from the Versailles Treaty, as well as a double standard implicit in the Western condemnation of Japanese imperialism. Although Article 19 of the League Charter was designed to facilitate timely adjustment within the framework of law, the status quo powers would have none of it, and Dulles prophesied at the time that change could be resisted only at the price of war. During the 1950s, he again identified certain winds of change stemming from injustice. This time, however, it was the Soviet Union that stood in the way.[5]

Not that natural law was the only reason for introducing moral considerations into public discourse. Most of the world's people were religious. This was particularly true in the Middle East and parts of the Orient where

Moslem, Hindu, and Buddhist leaders could be counted upon to oppose atheistic communism with a large measure of consistency. Pakistan's allegiance to SEATO and the Baghdad Pact, along with the attitude of figures like Bourgiba, Hussein, and Ibn Saud could not be explained solely in military-strategic terms. Eisenhower once claimed that "I never fail, in any communication with Arab leaders" to emphasize "the importance of the spiritual factor in our relationship . . . that belief in God should create between them and us" a "common purpose." To be sure, the tactic did not always work—Saud replied that communism was a long way off as compared with Israel—but Ike and Dulles agreed that the religious dimension should not be ignored.[6]

During the nineteenth century, Czar Alexander I had drawn up a document asserting that "the precepts of Justice, Christian Charity, and Peace . . . must have an immediate influence on the Councils of Princes and guide all their steps." It was signed in 1815 by the Austrian emperor and the king of Prussia, as well as by the czar, while other European sovereigns followed suit. To Metternich, the Holy Alliance, as it was called, seemed a "loud-sounding nothing," to Castlereigh so much "mysticism and nonsense." We have already noted President Monroe's response. Alliance arrangements fell into further disrepute after 1917 when historians began to equate them with political repression, and Dulles was the first to make clear that he held no brief for the czar's political style. It may be significant, however, that among the papers found in the secretary's possession on his death were four copies of the Holy Alliance declaration.[7]

By the 1950s, the notion of a political-religious entente had once again begun to make sense in certain quarters and Dulles was not alone in recognizing its value in purely practical terms. Adenauer, who founded his Christian Democratic Union to combat nationalism, materialism, and atheism, saw in Christianity one of several bases for the union of Europe. De Gaulle, for his part, insisted that if France did not find a new moral equilibrium and rid itself of religious apathy, it would soon be faced with intellectual anarchy and communism. *Life* magazine ran an article on the devil in early 1948 quoting not only Adenauer, de Gaulle, and C. S. Lewis, but also de Gasperi of Italy and Salazar of Portugal.[8]

As a student of history, Dulles could doubtless appreciate what might be accomplished by a people dedicated enough to live and die for their faith. One had only to recall the early growth of Christianity or the rise of Islam, with its lightning expansion from Mecca to the gates of Vienna. The Jews, too, had proven invincible whenever they had been loyal to their ancestral beliefs. Perhaps it was with this in mind that he liked to reiterate the biblical injunction: "Seek first the kingdom of God and all things will be added unto you."[9]

Mainly, though, when he referred to the utility of religion, he was thinking of an approach that cut across national boundaries. While a church-sponsored

Oxford conference on world peace succeeded in forging a consensus in 1937, an earlier League-sponsored meeting that convened in Paris with a similar agenda had fallen prey to nationalistic divisions, making it impossible to agree on even so innocuous a principle as freedom of access to the world's raw materials. Practicality for Dulles meant many things. Since churches were global in their organization, they had a better chance than other groups to avoid chauvinism. In addition, morality was a common language which people the world over could understand and with which they could feel comfortable. It moved them as nothing else could, and its absence would arouse suspicion. Doubtless, this is what Grandfather Foster had in mind when he suggested that the way to acquire influence was to sponsor great principles. A studious grandson later pointed out that this was how Woodrow Wilson had earned his reputation at home and abroad.[10]

In concrete terms, the biblical injunction, "be slow to anger and quick to forgive," served the cause of peace by underscoring the need for national forebearance. According to Dulles, if religious leaders during the 1930s had done more to jog the conscience of their flocks, there might never have been a war. Later, he acted on the basis of what he believed. Following the advice of his uncle, Robert Lansing, who had said that "a victor inspired by revenge sows the seeds of future hatreds," he campaigned after World War II to treat the vanquished nations with unprecedented leniency.[11]

Beyond this, a special-issue envelope with a four-cent stamp commemorating Dulles' work as secretary and bearing the familiar motto "peace with justice," had a twofold meaning: a righteous peace was the only peace worth having; it was also the only one that would last.

Closely related to justice was the virtue of honesty defined as loyalty to agreements and one's allies. This would contribute to peace by enhancing a nation's credibility and securing the status quo. Japan, in the first instance, was thought to need continual reassurance of American resolve in order to turn back challenges from the radical left. Implicit in the notion was also an unwillingness to trade honor for security, which, in turn, implied firmness under pressure. To be sure, Dulles eschewed passionate attachment to any foreign nation believing that the principle of interpersonal friendship could not be applied collectively. Nations allied with the United States might or might not share its political ideology. What was important was that such ties served the national interest; the moment they ceased to do so, they ceased to bind. At the same time, he believed that Washington should make commitments only if prepared to carry them out and only after factoring in the full range of risks. Lebanon's Malik used to say that in negotiating with Dulles, one had to read the fine print and be constantly on the lookout for escape clauses, but once the secretary made a commitment, it was solid. Among others who remembered Dulles as "a man of his word" were Foreign Minister Carlos Romulo of the Philippines, Japanese Premier Shigeru Yoshida, Japanese Foreign Minister Katsuo Okazaki, Chiang Kai-shek, and three

Korean prime ministers, Chung Il Kwon, Paik Too-chin, and Pyun Yung-tai.[12]

Dulles liked to contrast America's record of living up to its treaty engagements with the Soviet performance based on Lenin's witticism that "promises are like pie crusts: made to be broken." Molotov, he once remarked, was the cleverest diplomat of his generation. However, because his word could never be taken at face value, he did not fully merit the title statesman. No sooner had the ink dried on the Japanese surrender agreement than Kremlin leaders were seeking a way to violate it.[13]

One hastens to add that Dulles was far from transparent and there were times when he may have misspoken. Syngman Rhee claimed that the United States had assured him well in advance of the Geneva Conference that neither the Soviet Union nor India would be admitted to deliberations affecting the future of his country. As it developed, they were. Although the exact degree of Dulles' culpability in this case remains unclear, Rhee may well have had a point. In another instance, the secretary had no sooner told the king of Laos that SEATO would support a campaign to reclaim Communist-held areas in northern Laos than he found Britain and France unwilling to agree. To his chagrin, he had to restrict the commitment to cases of Red Chinese intervention. It was not a happy moment, for although he may not have gone back on an iron-clad commitment, he had been premature. There can be no denying, either, that the secretary often spoke elliptically and was capable of misleading by indirection. We have alluded to his expertise in the art of ambiguity where Quemoy was concerned, and there are other examples. This is a man who was highly skilled at drafting communiqués designed to paper over differences and accommodate diverse points of view. In the last analysis, however, it seems fair to say that he was about as reliable as an individual in his position could be given the vicissitudes of the democratic system, along with those of the international system.[14]

Withal, if there was a problem with Dulles' approach to religion as a basis for politics, it was not so much that he failed to practice what he preached as that Jesus of Nazareth was not a social reformer. He favored no special government and propounded no particular vision of world order. His admission that "my kingdom is not of this world" coupled with the famous description of Satan as "prince of this world" indicate that Christianity transcends differences on the economic and political level. One can be liberal or conservative, Communist or capitalist, and still be a follower of Jesus. Dulles seems to have been at least minimally aware of this, for he held that churchmen should confine themselves to the broader principles of spirituality and refrain from prescribing specific remedies for political disorder and social injustice (the principle of generality). Yet he could be contradictory. On the one hand, he opposed a resolution of the Federal Council of Churches to recognize Red China arguing that it violated the principle of generality. On the other hand, he advocated organized church efforts to ban atomic weaponry and establish the United Nations, issues on which good men could disagree. He often spoke as if he believed Almighty God to be on the side of the West, causing his son Avery, a Jesuit theologian, to warn against making a "cult" of democracy and rendering to Caesar the things that belong to God. Although he knew his Bible reasonably well and displayed a copy of the Christian New Testament in his offices at State and at the United Nations, his interpretations could be strained by orthodox standards. In defense of military preparedness and the capacity for massive retaliation, he once quoted Jesus as having said that "I come to bring not peace but a sword." It was this type of thing that prompted Israel's Abba Eban to describe Dulles' spirituality as "thin and achromatic."[15]

Clare Boothe Luce once remarked that Dulles could make any policy seem moral, and in a sense she was right. As chief counsel to the president, he could scarcely have been a stranger to casuistry; indeed he would have thanked Luce for the compliment. But to imply, as she did, that he was in some way hypocritical is to fly in the face of all that is known of his upbringing and lifelong commitment to organized religion.

Because his father had been a pastor, Sunday meant automatic attendance at four church services in addition to Monday evening sessions for the Dulles children and Wednesday prayer meetings. There were contests and games to see who could memorize the longest Bible passages and give the best hymn rendition. Both parents were bent upon seeing their eldest son enter the ministry, and young Dulles must have pleased them mightily when he committed to memory virtually the entire text of the Gospel of St. John (reciting it with a pet crow perched on his shoulder). Summertime meant a three-mile walk to church accompanied by the singing of traditional hymns, including his favorite, "Work for the Night is Coming." He had to stay alert, too, when he entered the family pew, for he was expected to take careful notes on each of his father's sermons so that when questioned at the dinner table he could give an intelligent accounting. If his impressions were fuzzy or vague, the father would assume full responsibility and query the family on ways to make himself better understood.[16]

It must be understood that as an adult, Dulles was not religious to the point of regular church attendance, any more than he adhered to a steady regimen of asceticism. On no account was he known to be offensive in the sense of wearing his faith on his sleeve. Even so, he steered clear of ribaldry and interlarded his speeches with references to God and the Bible. Expressions like *Deo volente* could be heard at Dulles press conferences. He once vouched for the efficacy of prayer in a radio interview, and during the grueling London conferences on Suez, he is said to have stolen away for a moment of prayer at St. Paul's. It was not out of character for a person of this type to slip cash to the needy child of his chauffeur or to share religious jokes with those of kindred spirit, just as he would burst out with an occasional "God bless you." Earlier, as a trustee of the Rockefeller Foundation, he had differed with his colleagues in wanting to deal with explicitly religious issues, and as secretary, he confided to Chiang Kai-shek, "My life is in the hands of God." It is all of a piece, along with his practice of saying grace before meals and reading sermons in his spare time.[17]

In the eyes of Dulles' critics, such practices were suspect. They smacked of hypocrisy. What is remarkable, however, is the number of times that Dulles' stance on the issues coincided with a private view of morality. Whether one takes his response to the Panama tolls controversy of 1913, in which he sided with Britain against a substantial number of his fellow citizens, or his opposition to war trials for Nazi prisoners in the wake of World War II, what one finds is a large measure of consistency. There were times when he proved more resistant than Eisenhower to the firing of State Department personnel for partisan political reasons, and if he strove for dependability at the highest level of statecraft, he tried to establish the same pattern on a lower level as well. After estimating that it would require approximately one year to negotiate the Japanese Peace Treaty, he accomplished it in exactly the time anticipated. His press conferences were well known for beginning on the minute, and aides could testify to the fact that his plane departed on schedule even if it meant leaving tardy staff members behind. His wife, Janet, used to tell the story of how he skipped a section of his law exam in order to keep a date with her, and his devotion as a husband never wavered down through the crowded years of a happy marriage. For a man who made a point of remembering Eisenhower's wedding anniversaries and who went out of his way to encourage foreign leaders to bring their wives on conference trips, it was second nature to use the marriage bond as an illustration of indissolubility when addressing a group of American ambassadors. What he said and what he did were, on balance, the same.[18]

Perhaps the sharpest attack on his integrity, relates to events leading up to Suez, in particular his alleged renege on an offer to finance the Aswan Dam. But here again, as difficult as the situation may have been, and as much as it may have tarnished his reputation, it proves no exception to the rule. There is a tendency to forget that Egyptian officials had already rejected the original American offer when they chose to hold out for better terms. In effect, they gambled and lost. Nasser also knew that Dulles' offer presupposed an agreement between Cairo and Tel Aviv, and he was unwilling to pay the price. Plans for Robert Anderson's secret mission to the Middle East and blueprints for American aid originated at about the same time, and when Anderson, a former secretary of the navy and deputy secretary of defense, sought to work out acceptable terms for an Arab-Israeli peace agreement, Egyptian leaders gave him the cold shoulder.[19]

Had Nasser seen his way clear on the key issue, Dulles would undoubtedly have approached Congress, at least for a renewal of his original offer. But with the passage of time, prospects for such an agreement faded. Cotton interests in California and the southern states had never been well disposed toward a dam that would increase the supply of overseas cotton. Moreover, between the fall of 1955 and spring of 1956, Cairo's financial status fell into limbo due to its purchase of Soviet bloc arms. It soon began to appear that the dam loan might be an albatross around the neck of recipient and donor alike. Egypt also became the first Arab nation to recognize Red China, thereby alienating the China lobby during an election year, even as it failed to reach agreement with the Sudan on water distribution rights. Nasser had passed the point of no return. But even if there had been progress on the Arab-Israeli issue, Dulles could not have retraced his steps without extreme difficulty and misgiving. First of all, he did not relish the idea of indulging a profligate and uncooperative neutral at the expense of allies like Turkey and Pakistan whose loyalty would have to go unrewarded. Secondly, he did not fancy the thought of being played off against Moscow once Nasser had put one foot in the Soviet camp, especially when he was hard pressed even to persuade Congress to vote aid to Yugoslavia. Faced with a choice between Tito and Nasser, there was no question which way Capitol Hill would go. On 15 July, the Senate Appropriations Committee adopted a report barring any allocation of funds from the 1957 Mutual Security Act without the express approval of the committee. Aid to Aswan was specifically barred in a separate rider, and the House Appropriations Committee showed itself similarly inclined.[20]

Contributing to the impression that Dulles "reneged" was Nasser's later assertion that Washington had "withdrawn" its offer peremptorily in such fashion as to embarrass him before his people and before the world. British officials, angry over Suez, were quick to second the charge. In their eagerness to find a scapegoat for the Suez fiasco, they described the American announcement as abrupt, claiming they had never been consulted. Israel's ambassador, Abba Eban, used the term "brutal" in referring to Dulles' action. And the president himself suggested that his secretary "might have been undiplomatic."[21]

Once again, however, there is more to the story than meets the eye. It was not until 19 July that Egyptian ambassador Ahmed Hussein formally "accepted" America's offer of the previous fall, at which point Dulles declared the offer null and void. Although Nasser affected surprise, he had been informed by the State Department two weeks earlier that funds originally ear-marked for Aswan had been reallocated. According to Foreign Secretary Lloyd, Egypt's president knew as early as March that he could no longer count on Anglo-American funding. On 13 July, three days before the meeting with Hussein, Dulles informed Nasser directly that the United States was no longer in a position to follow through due to rising opposition in Congress. Then, after discussing the situation with Hussein in frank and friendly terms, he invited Egyptian comment on the public statement he was about to make. London, which was to have matched Washington's offer, had long since decided against it. That Whitehall was as well informed as Nasser on the

American position, and fully in agreement, became apparent through a leak to the London *Times* which appeared on 14 July. Nor did Dulles act alone, as is sometimes suggested. After consulting his advisers, he cleared his decision with the National Security Council. Hussein himself later admitted that he could not fault the secretary in this or any other respect.[22]

Nasser was simply determined to take control. With British troops out of the way, all he needed was an incident to fire the popular imagination, and by "accepting" a defunct American offer, he managed to create such an incident. Ten days later, he took the action he had been planning for months. According to Tito, the Egyptian president had as much as told him that he intended to seize the canal regardless of what the United States decided in reference to Aswan. It was neither the first time, nor the last, that the dictator of a small country would try to justify policies little short of extortion by branding Uncle Sam a bully. Marroquín of Colombia had acted in precisely the same fashion at the time of Theodore Roosevelt when he made venal last-minute demands in connection with a canal treaty.[23]

More could be said about how a personal conception of morality affected Dulles' statecraft, but we should perhaps broaden the inquiry at this point and consider his general outlook on world affairs, which was one of guarded optimism. Although he viewed human nature as flawed and man's reason as having little impact on his decisions when acting en masse, he took it as a sign of progress that free institutions could claim an ever larger following. War, with its tragic record of recurrence, showed signs of receding as nations began to organize their economic and political lives on a more cooperative basis. People no longer regarded mass killing as normal or beyond the realm of legal sanction, nor was Europe, in Dulles' view, any longer the fire trap it had once been.[24]

At the same time, the world was unlikely to afford any kind of "safe haven" in the near future. Men had to "wage peace" with all the strength at their command because there were no easy solutions. In order to win appropriations for overseas aid as a cold war weapon, Dulles may have been tempted to play upon the common view of material privation as a standing invitation to left-wing violence and subversion. But that he harbored reservations as to the efficacy of campaigns to eradicate poverty is evident from the ambivalence of his public pronouncements. As for trade links between potential antagonists, they might attenuate the rigidity of political boundaries, but he did not expect them to reduce tension. Eisenhower tended to be more optimistic in this regard, but both men agreed on the reverse proposition. Pinprick measures of economic warfare directed against powerful aggressor states, as in the case of Germany, Italy, and Japan before the Second World War—especially without preparation for war and a clear willingness to wage it—were worse than useless, bringing on the very hostilities they were designed to avert. Despite the fact that Dulles was approached by congressmen and senators to maintain sweeping trade sanctions against Communist bloc countries, he succeeded in whittling down the number of items embargoed, and wherever possible, he declined to press America's allies for similar restrictions. Eisenhower, who was a strong booster of trade with Eastern Europe, agreed with his secretary that it was neither wise nor practical to attempt to dam up the natural channels of trade, whether between Germany and Poland or Malaya and Red China. In the case of Malaya, whose livelihood depended on the rubber trade, Moscow would merely become a privileged middleman between Kuala Lumpur and Peking. Trade sanctions were never more futile than in dealing with Communist countries where economic decisions were automatically taken by the state.[25]

World opinion, another weak reed in Dulles' opinion, had a way of bowing to force majeure and accepting the fait accompli. To be sure, he liked to quote the Declaration of Independence when he wanted to highlight the importance of a "decent respect" for the "opinions of mankind," and he was always ready to cite the facts about Russian colonialism knowing that Moscow's mandarins were vulnerable in their bid for international moral support. But he never expected a country as rich and powerful as the United States to be "loved." The most it could expect was a healthy measure of respect, and this only if it exercised its power justly and with restraint. One of the most vivid examples of how frail a reed world opinion could be was the case of Quemoy and the stance taken by leaders in India, Japan, Ceylon, Burma, and Indonesia. All supported American policy in private but hesitated to come out publicly for fear of alienating vocal constituencies at home. Much the same situation obtained in the Western Hemisphere, the Middle East, and North Africa. Only one or two leaders like Bourgiba of Tunisia volunteered public backing for the Eisenhower Doctrine (Jordan's foreign minister went out of his way to deny the existence of a power vacuum in the region and, by implication, the need for such a doctrine). When, therefore, George Allen of the Voice of America suggested to Dulles that Bourgiba's stand might make good public copy, Dulles replied: not unless you want him assassinated.[26]

During the 1950s, when the principal channel for world opinion was the United Nations, and when America and its allies could project their power almost anywhere in the name of world government, Dulles spent two weeks every fall encamped at New York's Waldorf Astoria for the opening sessions at Turtle Bay. He realized that the body would not remain forever under American sway and he anticipated the need for a system of weighted voting—membership was rocketing upwards as dozens of newly emerging nations took their seats in the General Assembly. Still, as one of the chief architects of the United Nations Commission on Human Rights, as well as the charter itself, he was understandably proud of the many times in which international machinery had operated in the interest of peace as, for example, when United Nations observers had exposed the subversive activities of Greece's Communist neighbors. UN troops also kept the peace in Iran, Korea, India, and

Pakistan, even as they staved off hostilities between Indonesia and the Netherlands by giving world opinion a chance to crystalize. Complications over Suez had led to the creation of the highly effective United Nations Emergency Force (UNEF), the same unit deployed in Lebanon two years later. Dulles would have liked to see the UN do even more. He saw no reason why it could not ease the French burden in Indochina, sponsor a cease-fire between Taipei and Peking, and defuse a Soviet ultimatum over Berlin in 1958.[27]

Success for the UN was neither instant nor automatic. Few, if any, chief executives have been more charismatic or more active than Secretary General Dag Hammarskjold. Yet he could no more put a dent in Moscow's resolve to crush the resistance in Budapest than he could prevail upon Nehru to hold a plebiscite in heavily Moslem Kashmir. Part of his problem stemmed from the fact that, owing to Soviet veto power, the United Nations never developed the standing police force envisioned by its charter. Nevertheless, he believed that the positive outweighed the negative. Significant contributions to the general welfare could be credited to the Trusteeship Council, the Social and Economic Council, and the International Court of Justice. If nothing else, the UN was a useful forum in which nations could voice their grievances and save face.[28]

Considering his strong legal background, it was probably to be expected that the secretary would remain a staunch advocate of international law, doing all he could to expand its parameters. Like Theodore Roosevelt, he was cognizant of the essential weakness of law unsupported by force. Nonetheless, he contributed to movements that would have extended international jurisdiction to outer space, as well as to Antarctica. He also believed in the principle of arbitration. Optimally, he would like to have institutionalized nonviolent shifts in the status quo on the basis of Article 14 of the UN charter for which he was largely responsible. In the long run, however, there could be no substitute for a truly effective form of world government, and this would not occur, he predicted, until a majority of the world's people came to live under free governments. At the same time, since democratic institutions, if they spread, would only spread gradually over a long period of time, he did not look for a legal solution to problems that impinged directly on a nation's vital interests or its *amour propre*. Neither did he expect arms control agreements, however attractive from a domestic political angle, to deter aggressor states or to strike at the root cause of war. It might be added that he was not the only skeptic at a time when problems of verification seemed well-nigh insuperable. Khrushchev later admitted that "as long as the US held a big advantage over us [as it did throughout the 1950s], we couldn't submit to international disarmament controls." Then, too, the British and French were no more anxious than the Russians to subscribe to test ban agreements while they were behind technologically, rhetoric notwithstanding.[29]

The most cursory examination of arms control proposals will reveal that they were generally slanted to favor the party making them and framed in such a way as to ensure rejection by the other side. Typically, the Kremlin waited until 1957, after completing an important series of explosions, to propose its nuclear test ban, while the United States, far ahead in the production of fissionable material and atomic weapons, offered to submit to a ban on further production if applied to both sides. Moscow, with an eye to the main chance, proposed to eliminate existing stockpiles even as a sanctimonious Washington invited Moscow to join in donating Uranium 235 to an international agency under UN (US) control knowing that this would cut sharply into Russia's slender stock. Fully aware that the Soviets counted secrecy and surprise among their most potent weapons, the United States sponsored systems of inspection. Likewise, when Eisenhower unveiled his "Open Skies" proposal at Geneva in July 1955, American reconnaissance planes were already overflying Moscow and he knew in advance that the Russians would not agree to have their skies, or any other part of their country, declared "open." He also knew that his démarche would prove highly effective as an exercise in public relations (the General Assembly endorsed it by a vote of 56–7). Two years later, when *Sputnik* blasted into orbit, removing any doubt as to which country held the lead in space technology, Washington piously invited Moscow to sign a convention guaranteeing the peaceful uses of outer space. As everyone knew, the Soviets relied upon their superiority in conventional ground strength to defend extensive frontiers with Europe and China. Washington therefore proposed that the ground forces of each side be equalized. There was room for skepticism once again when the United States, which depended on a sophisticated arsenal of nuclear weapons in Western Europe to offset the Soviet advantage in numbers of divisions, was invited by Poland's Rapacki to join in the elimination of all such weapons from Europe.[30]

But if arms control and the elimination of poverty, along with the promotion of trade and commerce, left something to be desired as antidotes to war, if world opinion and international law were found equally wanting, what then did Dulles recommend? Eisenhower, who once called himself a "TR republican," had on his desk in the Oval Office a plaque bearing the inscription "*Suaviter in modo, fortiter in re*" meaning "gently in manner, mightily in deed" or, to quote Theodore Roosevelt, "speak softly and carry a big stick." Such words could just as easily have appeared on the desk of the secretary, for both men believed implicitly in them.

Naturally, to "speak softly" in the 1950s meant speaking in ways that would not have been necessary, or even intelligible, at the time of TR. In an age when President Truman felt it essential to "scare hell" out of the country in order to bring about a break with isolationism, there could be no thought of refraining from rhetorical barbs designed to expose Soviet goals and underscore the incompatibility of Soviet and Western views of man. Thus, when Dulles gave Moscow unshirted hell at a United Nations forum in 1958, he was merely following the advice given to an earlier president by Senator Vandenberg. Long after congressional approval of the Marshall Plan and Truman Doctrine, legislators would not line up behind foreign aid packages unless the air positively crackled with polemics. At the same time, Dulles had to placate right-wing critics who advocated sterner measures than he was prepared to take, and he was among the first to recognize that the cold war called for a concerted effort to sway hearts and minds. International communism must be placed in the dock, he believed, and Russian accusations met with counteraccusations. If it was said in Moscow on Monday that democracy infringed on the rights of the worker, it must be said in Washington on Tuesday that the Kremlin trampled on God-given rights of spiritual and intellectual freedom.[31]

Dulles believed that the United States should strive, wherever possible, to take the offensive. Accordingly, when Moscow protested American bomber flights over the Arctic Circle, he proposed a system of polar inspection which the Russians felt obliged to reject. He was also anxious to use organizations like the CIA to counteract Communist subversion and to foster the growth of indigenous elements seeking the overthrow of pro-Communist governments. He wanted to see the Soviets under continual attack in the United Nations Security Council and elsewhere, not only for their uncivilized behavior but also for their record of lies and broken promises. Capitol Hill, he felt, must be prepared to spend more on the Voice of America and to appropriate generous sums for mutual security programs with an eye to promoting private investment and shoring up confidence within the "community of free nations."[32]

To the extent, therefore, that the phrase "speak softly" is applicable to the Eisenhower era, it is not synonymous with a low profile, and it most certainly did not imply ambiguity in defining the national interest. As Dulles told the Senate Foreign Relations Committee in April 1954, "the best preventive of war is to have it known in advance by any potential aggressor that if he tries to aggress he will suffer a loss greater than his potential gain." The secretary was convinced that misunderstanding had brought on three successive wars in the twentieth century. Had Britain and the United States expressed concern for the European balance of power in 1914, as well as during the 1930s, had they been prepared for war, and had Korea been declared within the American defense perimeter in 1950, instead of "beyond" it, hostilities could in all probability have been averted. Determined to avoid a repeat performance, he sponsored the Formosa Resolution and the Eisenhower Doctrine. He and Ike also negotiated defense treaties and deployed air and naval forces to crisis areas. Ambivalence there was at the time of Dien Bien Phu and Suez and with respect to the Baghdad Pact, but in the case of threatened attacks on Vietnam (1954), Israel (1956), and Turkey (1957), American determination was clearly articulated in the media as well as through diplomatic back channels, thereby eliminating any doubt as to how the United States would react if cornered. Similarly, when it appeared in 1955 that Peking might be targeting Quemoy for a full-blown invasion, Dulles was not content to rely on congressional resolutions. Indian officials passed word of Ike's intent to defend the threatened island with all the power at his command. The Formosa Resolution may have been deliberately vague, but in 1958, when Peking threatened Quemoy a second time, Dulles described the island as part of a vital network of interlocking defenses. Few could doubt American resolve when units of the Sixth and Seventh Fleets, sailing in tandem, began arriving on the scene.[33]

In positive terms, "speak softly" meant discretion and tact in crisis situations as opposed to posturing. Although the administration achieved a sizable margin of superiority over the Soviet Union, it hesitated to trade on its standing even when campaign charges in 1958 and 1960 alluded to a nonexistent "missile gap" in favor of Moscow. Dulles, who warned against "boasting of our own merit and seeing in others only demerit," declined to discuss any of the power plays involved in dislodging Soviet forces from Austria, and when asked what he thought of Molotov, he replied, "tops," adding with his usual gleam in the eye that the Soviet's efforts were directed against situations "which no amount of technical skill would surmount."[34]

As a rule, Dulles did not grandstand. Reporters found him hard to approach during international conferences, and when he or one of his representatives visited foreign capitals to lobby for policy changes with potentially embarrassing consequences for the host country, the talks were invariably confidential, the results unheralded. In this way, Spain's traditional harshness toward Protestant sects was softened and Peking agreed to the release of American prisoners; Moscow scaled back its campaign of subversive activity in France, and the Korean War was brought to an end. On one occasion, Henry Cabot Lodge made a well-publicized visit to the headquarters of the Strategic Air Command. But this is about as close as the administration ever came to the clenched fist. It would have been easy to allow public opinion to boil over during the Korean War leaving room for little but premature and risky measures resulting in a loss of face by the enemy. Yet this never happened. When veteran ambassador U. Alexis Johnson wrote in reference to Korea that Dulles should have been more mindful of TR's injunction to "speak softly," he missed the point. David Rees was closer to the mark when he called the Korean armistice a "magnificent performance" in crisis management.[35]

Over the years, the word "secrecy" has acquired a bad connotation among Americans, perhaps because it smacks of something undemocratic. Still, for Dulles it was an indispensable adjunct to the principle of "speaking softly." Conscious of public opinion, Dulles paid lip service to what he called "open covenants secretly arrived at," but not all of his covenants were so open. The Eisenhower-Rhee agreements were kept under the tightest of wraps.

Messages came and went through intermediaries and Rhee demanded, in at least one instance, that a written communication be shredded after the president had seen it. In the same way, years passed before newsmen learned of Anderson's missions to Egypt and Israel. When Anderson called on Ben Gurion, he did so incognito and the two met at the latter's residential hotel. Strict confidentiality was likewise a watchword in obtaining the release of the American prisoners held by Peking. By the same token, the inter-American foreign ministers conference of 1958, which Dulles described as the most successful meeting of its kind in ten years, was kept entirely off the record.[36]

Dulles often contacted his friends overseas by means of trusted middlemen just as Adenauer sometimes withheld vital information from a leaky foreign office by bypassing the bureaucracy and using American CIA agents as a conduit to Washington. America's guarantee of the Saar settlement never became common knowledge (in spite of French wishes), and in one situation, when Bonn's secretary of state Walter Hallstein conferred with Dulles in Washington, he did so at the latter's thirty-second street home to avoid reporters. In like manner, with Suez under attack and Eisenhower battling for reelection against Adlai Stevenson, trying to distance himself from the belligerents, Britain's Lord Harcourt called on Treasury Secretary Humphrey by the back door, and France's Alphand met with Dulles at "very unexpected hours." Finally, the Radford-Ely agreements of 1954, specifying how the United States would respond to a full-scale invasion of Indochina by China, were drawn up in the form of a *note verbale*. This, and much more, including the Cyprus settlement, proved possible because Dulles knew how to operate sub rosa. Initial discussions leading to the Trieste settlement of 1954 were held between Washington and London, later between the Western powers and each of the disputants, and as long as they remained confidential, they bore fruit. The moment word of their contents leaked, prospects for a diplomatic solution faded (until secrecy was restored).[37]

Regarding the "Big Stick" itself, there are again parallels between the turn of the century and the 1950s. Like TR, Dulles did not view world politics as exclusively military in nature. Moral, political, and socio-economic factors were every bit as critical in the eyes of a secretary who feared that defense outlays might undermine basic freedoms and work undue hardship on the economy, killing the goose that laid the golden egg. During the 1950s, despite a threefold increase in peacetime military spending compared with the period 1945–50, the nation's industrial sector continued remarkably healthy while living standards rose dramatically.[38]

One of the most effective ways, in the secretary's opinion, to economize on arms spending was to foster a stable equilibrium among the world's powers. During the 1930s, he had assumed that such a balance, as it obtained between five or six nations, might shift in the event of war, but not so much as to endanger the United States which, by remaining free and unentangled, could prosper as a neutral. By 1953, however, the world was an altogether different place; the rules had changed and Washington could no longer afford the luxury of nonentanglement. Titanic forces unleashed after 1939, coupled with American policy decisions, had ushered in a bipolar world in which two nations with competing ideologies were forced willy nilly to vie for the allegiance of the world's uncommitted until a new balance emerged in east and west. In practical terms, America's postwar dilemma called for German entry into the Western defense organization along with a revival of Japanese power. Dulles, as we have observed, was not slow to appreciate the potential of China as part of an Asian equipoise, but since Peking appeared to be an uncertain quantity he preferred to concentrate on restoring Tokyo to its former status as a makeweight against Soviet expansion.[39]

It would take time, of course, to rebuild all the balances destroyed by world war, and in the meantime there was no substitute for American leadership. Both president and secretary thought it wiser to overestimate the strength of one's enemy than to underestimate it, just as both believed that as long as one did not overspend, one could never be too strong. Ike liked to say that "we do not escape war by surrendering on the installment plan." Weakness, in other words, would invite attack. Dulles could not have disagreed more with leaders like Pineau who tended to regard power as provocative. The United States, he felt, should be well armed, well endowed with bases ringing the Soviet Empire, and above all well respected for its willingness to use such strength if necessary. Far from provoking one's adversary, power was more likely in his view to split it into rival factions and foment internal dissent. It was not appeasement, after all, that had saved Greece from a Communist takeover or provided the diplomatic backdrop against which Belgrade had severed its ties with Moscow. Then again, when Red China broke with Russia in the late 1950s, it came on the heels of two impressive demonstrations by the U.S. Navy, one in Vietnam and another in the Formosa Strait. While it is hard to generalize, it would seem safe to say that wherever the United States showed firmness, whether on the question of German rearmament or the landing of marines, the result was division within Communist ranks and a moderate Soviet line.[40]

Allied to the administration's principle of preparedness was the notion that one had to stand ready at all times to strike decisively and with overwhelming power. Public opinion would not tolerate protracted military engagement without a clear sense of movement along the road to victory. Secondly, even if certain weapons systems were of only marginal value, they could enhance America's image in the eyes of neutrals and underwrite success on the diplomatic chess board, if only indirectly. Thirdly, apart from the deterrent value of undisputed strength, Soviet aggression, whether by subversion or frontal attack, must be made to pay a price, for if successful it would undermine American credibility and "threaten peace everywhere."

This did not mean that the United States needed to go to extremes over a minor provocation. It did mean that appeasement was no formula for the avoidance of danger; only by running minor risks on a day-to-day basis could one forestall a more serious reckoning in the long run. Dulles also believed it advisable to engage in occasional demonstrations of strength as a matter of policy. During World War II, de Gaulle had asked Eisenhower to march directly through Paris, rather than around it, so that battle-hardened American veterans marching in impressive formation could be observed by groups on the political fence. During 1954, when Tito threatened violence in Trieste, Washington was able to restore calm by dispatching units of the Sixth Fleet. A month later, when fighting broke out in Trieste itself, this time instigated by Italian nationalists, the visit of an American destroyer worked wonders. One might add that King Hussein, badly shaken in April 1957, experienced the same kind of relief when American warships appeared in the eastern Mediterranean.[41]

If one is reminded of Theodore Roosevelt's "Big Stick," one also recalls the corollary that TR referred to as his "eleventh commandment": "Thou shalt not slop over." Atmospherics, whether in the form of rocket-rattling or maudlin sentimentality was to be avoided at all costs in Dulles' view, and it is doubtful if any other secretary of state has been more consistent in side-stepping the polar extremes. Secretary General Hammarskjold wanted Washington to allow the relatives of American prisoners being held by China to visit Peking for the cordiality this was expected to engender, but Eisenhower refused. Subsequently, Hammarskjold's relationship with the Chinese Communists soured while Dulles' improved. The same motive caused him to resist summitry, warning his countrymen not to regard it as some kind of "magic elixir." When newspapers gushed over the "spirit of Geneva," he replied with characteristic sangfroid that it was "a little premature to talk about the era of good feeling." Toasts were not enough and could prove dangerous to the extent that they were misleading. Eisenhower, more sanguine than his secretary in this regard and hoping for a new ethos, decided he would ask Americans to pray for the summit's success, but he did so over Dulles' objection.[42]

Bluff, another form of humbug under the general heading of atmospherics, was equally to be shunned. Britain had tried economic sanctions in an attempt to restrain Mussolini; FDR had experimented vis-à-vis Japan; and in each case the strategy had backfired. "Any man," Dulles warned, "who seeks by such measures as starvation to break the will of another, while at the same time . . . [proclaiming his] unwillingness to fight, is commonly judged to have the soul of a poltroon. He will be crowded and crowded until he finds himself in a corner where he will have to fight to prove the contrary." Dulles' detractors have charged him with bluffing in connection with his threat to "unleash" Chiang Kai-shek as in the case of his warning that American defense commitments would undergo an "agonizing reappraisal" should

Paris stand in the way of German rearmament. Enough has been said about public opinion and Pentagon planning to substantiate Dulles' sincerity and credibility when it comes to "agonizing reappraisal." As for Chiang, Washington had every intention of utilizing Nationalist armies in case of an escalation of the war in Korea, and Peking knew it. The mere possibility of an invasion mounted by Taipei, coupled with a series of hit and run operations along the coast, tied up approximately one million Communist troops. One can go further. Dulles never changed his tune on the matter of neutralism, as is sometimes alleged, nor was there anything hollow about his talk of liberating captive peoples. Liberation, as we shall have occasion to see, occurred to an extent unparalleled during the administrations that came before and after.[43]

There is, in fact, no instance on record of Dulles' hand being called and found wanting. When he packed his bags in 1950 and left London for Paris, declaring his readiness to negotiate a Japanese peace treaty with or without England—a crystal clear ultimatum—Britain's foreign secretary moved quickly to strike a deal. In 1955, he threatened on two occasions to cancel the summit unless Moscow made important eleventh-hour concessions and, as we have seen, both of his warnings were heeded.[44]

Vice President Nixon, who knew the secretary well, noted that one of his greatest strengths was his willingness to forego "decision-making by Gallup poll," and herein, it would appear, lies the key to much of what he was able to accomplish. From his earliest days, he admired Abraham Lincoln for releasing British nationals Mason and Slidell in the face of overwhelming popular desire to twist the lion's tail. It was a decision which, quite obviously, required courage, as well as prudence. Dulles also esteemed Woodrow Wilson for refusing to compromise with American senators on his plan for a League of Nations. Later in life, acutely aware of the need for strong executive leadership in the realm of foreign affairs, he would say that "it is not the business of a secretary of state to be popular." Both he and Eisenhower were willing on occasion to risk their standing at home in pursuit of the national interest abroad, whether this meant siding with Tokyo in the Girard case, resisting pressure to favor Italy over Yugoslavia on the issue of Trieste during an election year, or standing up to militant Protestants who were loathe to see Ike become the first president since Wilson to meet with the pope.[45]

The record for the years 1953–59 indicates that sizable chunks of political capital were plowed into contests over foreign policy. Almost every effort to obtain aid for neutralist governments involved an element of risk, and more than once Dulles emerged on the winning side by the slenderest of margins. Although executive agreements were controversial, this is how the government acquired its lease on Spanish air bases. The Bricker Amendment was defeated by a single vote. And when a question arose as to congressional checks on the president's power as commander-in-chief, Dulles was quick to recall that the framers of the Constitution distinguished between war-making and war-declaring powers, deliberately lodging the former with the executive to allow for swift action in emergencies. Paradoxically, Dulles found it relatively easy to enlist congressional support for continued U.S. involvement in Vietnam. Senator Jack Kennedy, speaking for the Democratic leadership in 1957, declared proudly that America's "increasingly successful policy in Indochina . . . has its origins within Congress."[46]

Like most presidents and secretaries of state, neither Eisenhower nor Dulles took it lightly when their prerogative was threatened. Ike, refusing to cooperate with Mike Mansfield when the senator called for a congressional committee to oversee the CIA, acted the same way several years later when Congress demanded information on covert operations involving anti-Castro exiles. A majority on the National Security Council favored compliance. Nonetheless, Ike refused. Again, when Senator Knowland wanted to make American withdrawal from the United Nations mandatory should Peking be seated in Taipei's place, Dulles recoiled. Deploring the loss of flexibility this would entail, he prevailed upon Knowland to substitute language which simply called upon the president to report to Congress on how Red China's admission to the UN would affect American policy together with any rec-ommendations the White House might have to make. It was a typical "pla-cating modification" which curbed Knowland's enthusiasm without silencing him and kept foreign policy in the hands of the executive. Thus, from the very start and throughout its eight-year tenure, the administration distin-guished itself for its independence from the legislative branch even as it cultivated congressmen and senators with remarkable success.[47]

Had Eisenhower and Dulles not subscribed to the principle of strong executive leadership in the field of foreign policy and possessed unusual ability to command, they would never have gone into Lebanon. Only a handful of congressional leaders supported the move initially. Objections ran the gamut from the alleged danger of alienating world opinion to the difficulty of justifying foreign intervention in what was supposedly a civil war. Dulles argued that the civil strife being generated by the Cairo-Da-mascus axis served as an opening wedge for Communist infiltration, and that this being the case, the question was not so much whether or not to intervene but rather whether Soviet intervention should go uncontested. Senator Ful-bright could not find sufficient evidence that Lebanese violence and insta-bility were Communist-inspired while Senator Russell doubted that American troops could move into Lebanon without bloodshed, to which the secretary replied that there might be some sniping, but little more. Rayburn wanted to know what would happen if Washington fumbled the ball and Moscow threatened all-out military intervention, to which Dulles rejoined that if the United States ever appeared in the eyes of the world as a nation unwilling to take chances, it would be riding for a fall. Within a matter of hours, Ike decided to act. Americans reacted nervously, as they are apt to do when faced suddenly with ticklish situations containing an element of risk. But the landings went well and before long John Q. Public was registering strong approval.[48]

One last example will suffice to illustrate the advantage of having a thick political skin. When Dulles insisted on Israeli withdrawal from the occupied territories in 1956–57, congressional leaders were determined to force a showdown. They did so by demanding his resignation—and by implication a more sympathetic stance toward Israel—as the price for passage of the Eisenhower Doctrine. Although Ike fought back gamely, taking his case to the American people over nationwide radio and television, Senators Morse, Fulbright, Humphrey, and Yarborough were equally committed. Throwing their full weight against the secretary and insisting that he step down, they nit-picked their way through congressional hearings and harpooned him mercilessly during two days of sworn testimony. Despite Eisenhower's promise to consult Congress hourly during a crisis, Senator Morse claimed he was "so frightened" of the consequences of the doctrine as to be "almost speechless." Senator Fulbright feared that it would lead to a dangerous aggrandizement of executive power by granting a "blank check" and setting dangerous precedents, while Senator Russell predicted an "absolute breakdown of Congressional control of expenditures." Asked by Russell why he had not sent Congressman Richards to the Middle East to ascertain how and where American money would be spent—we are being asked to "buy a pig in a poke," Russell exclaimed—Dulles is said to have flushed and pounded the table: "If Congress is not willing to trust the president to the extent he asks, we can't win the battle. If we have to pinpoint for every country, including the Communists, every step we are to take, this resolution will not serve its purpose. The emergency is great and the military situation is one of great danger."[49]

In the course of the hearings, Fulbright alleged that because Dulles had caused Britain and France to fail at Suez he had, in effect, split the North Atlantic Alliance. The senator from Arkansas then recalled the time when the secretary had presented Egypt's Naguib with .38 caliber pistols. Dulles, reportedly beet-red, sat doodling. However, when Humphrey inquired, "do you really know what you have in mind for Egypt?" he returned the senator's fire: "The more appropriate question is do we want to tell the Communists what we have in mind for Egypt and the answer to that is no." But, continued Humphrey, had the secretary not said that Russia should be informed in advance about how the United States would react to Communist aggression? "It is one thing," Dulles replied, "to warn the Communists of the penalties of aggression . . . quite another to let them know that we are going to employ so many men and at such and such a time in such and such a place." To make the picture complete, Senator Knowland charged the administration with a double standard in trying to punish Israel while allowing Russia to disregard UN resolutions on Hungary.[50]

In the end, Eisenhower stated that he was not about to fire his principal cabinet member even to obtain emergency legislation for the Middle East. The Eisenhower Doctrine was approved by a resounding vote of 355–61, and it was never invoked. Marines landed in Lebanon, but they did so on the basis of a verifiable threat to American life and property. Ike consulted Dulles as to whether or not he needed congressional authorization and Dulles thought not. It is interesting too that neither the Eisenhower Doctrine nor the Formosa Resolution, upon which Dulles rested his defense of Quemoy in 1958, affected executive prerogative in the way Senator Fulbright had predicted. If anything, while they may have afforded one or two presidents additional room for maneuver, they set a precedent for greater congressional involvement in an area traditionally regarded as an executive preserve, for what can be granted can also be withheld or confiscated. Along with the Gulf of Tonkin Resolution, the Formosa Resolution, and the Eisenhower Doctrine may have strengthened the hand of individual executives in the area of foreign affairs, but they also implied congressional veto power, and this was something that would affect the presidencies of Richard Nixon and Gerald Ford in unanticipated ways.[51]

CHAPTER 7

In the Final Analysis

I have always known him as decisive and inflexibly determined, just as history paints him, and at the same time warm, fond of good living, and an affectionate friend. One day the world will come to see him, alongside Eisenhower, as a man of great stature, a symbol of will power that aroused conflicting passions. But this was not Dulles the man. The Dulles I knew and loved was like many other men, but greater and more upright than most.

—Jean Monnet, *Memoirs*

The last year ended stormily, as it began, with calls for the secretary's resignation. Cyrus Sulzberger of the *New York Times* called him a "tragicomic figure" while Congressman Hamilton Fish suggested that he should be dismissed for inexcusable recklessness. As always, criticism came from the Right, as well as from the Left, and although important elements of the press, the public, and various committees on Capitol Hill began rallying to his side, Dulles remained what he had been for many years, a towering but essentially lonely and enigmatic figure. After addressing the National Council of Churches on 18 November 1958, the council repudiated his Far East policy by endorsing the recognition of Red China. This was a minor reverse, however, by comparison with the steady deterioration of his physical condition. Earlier, in the fall of 1958, it seemed that an individual who had survived typhoid at the age of thirteen and malaria less than a decade later, not to mention bouts of migraine, gout, and phlebitis, to name but a few of his infirmities, might turn yet another corner by overcoming the ravages of cancer, for although he continued to lose weight on a diet of baby food, he refused to alter his pace, embarking upon two flights to the Far East, several trips to Europe, one to Brazil, and another to Mexico for the inauguration of a new president.[1]

It was not to be. Dulles was denied the miracle of health for which he prayed. Nevertheless, his persistence on the diplomatic front paid a handsome dividend. Bilateral pacts were signed on 5 March 1959 with Turkey, Iran, and Pakistan. In the meantime, Khrushchev, who had been trying since late 1957 to arrange a freewheeling big-five conclave and who seemed on the verge of success, had to concede defeat. Initially, with *Sputnik* in orbit and Soviet propaganda at high tide, Dulles' views were pronounced "rigid" and, in return for Europe's offer of missile sites, the secretary had to agree to top level talks with Moscow. What he did, however, in the absence of an acceptable Soviet quid pro quo, was to resort to delaying tactics beginning with a demand for preliminary talks. These were eventually broken off by the USSR over the crisis in Lebanon, and by early May 1958 a NATO conference backed him overwhelmingly on the question of summitry.[2]

In the fall of 1958, he faced still another challenge, this time in the form of a Russian ultimatum; either the West agreed within six months to make West Berlin a free city under United Nations auspices and to withdraw its troops or Russia would sign a separate peace with East Germany, divesting itself of all responsibility for access routes and posing a serious dilemma for Allied policy. The date was 27 November. Dulles, impassive but stolidly determined as always to concert the Western response, walked out of a hospital where he was to undergo further treatment for his abdominal condition and, against doctors' orders, crossed the Atlantic to attend a NATO council session. Ashen gray, he was compelled to spend a portion of his nights stretched out on a bathroom floor; but the mere fact of his presence proved electrifying. Belgium's Spaak was later to recall that "after a speech by Foster Dulles, everything returned to normal. His calm, the impression of power emanating from him, the sincerity of his words and the firmness of his views restored the confidence of the entire Alliance. He spoke like a truly great statesman faced with an historic occasion." Once again, NATO beat back a Russian démarche and Khrushchev found it necessary to yield.[3]

The weakest link, perhaps, in the chain of Western unity at this point was the government of Great Britain. With a general election looming, Macmillan wished to appear more as a bridge between Washington and Moscow than as an ally of either. Dulles thus braced himself for yet another trip to European capitals. Once more, putting his life on the line, unable to keep down a single meal and wearing a surgical truss, he gathered what remained of his strength in one final effort to forge a united front. After giving his aides strict orders to monitor his performance at every step along the way and to alert him to any lapse in mental fitness, however slight, he seemed to go into overdrive. The negotiations appeared to lift him momentarily above the threshold of pain; he had never been more persuasive. French leaders gave him their full support as they conjured up images of Hitler crushing his adversaries piecemeal. Only the British stood fast despite a stirring appeal by Couve de Murville. Clinging to the argument that Washington should accept a transfer of operational control to East Germany, they plumped for a summit meeting and embraced portions of the Rapacki Plan which envisioned a neutral zone to the west of the Soviet Union that would remain open to inspection. But this was not England's last word. There were other meetings between the allies, some *à deux*, some *à trois*, others *à quatre*. Throughout the winter and spring, de Gaulle continued to depict Soviet offers as little more than a clever means of demoralizing Bonn, and eventually British qualms subsided. Measures were taken to deal with an attempt to isolate West Berlin militarily, the crisis passed, and for the time being at least, Allied harmony prevailed.[4]

Meanwhile, Dulles was steadily losing ground in his battle for life. After submitting to a second abdominal operation, he underwent a dozen radical radiation treatments. His stomach became a receptacle for implants of radioactive gold and he began to leave his office daily for lunch at his home, along with a nap. Finally, on 15 April 1959, following a brief spell in Florida, he submitted his resignation. It was not easy. For several weeks thereafter, he functioned as a special consultant to the White House, but even this taxed him to the limit. Refusing sedation as long as he could, he then requested reductions in dosage so as to remain mentally alert, and predictably, when the final curtain rang down on 24 May, there was a well-thumbed Bible close at hand, along with a last will and testament calling for a quickening of the nation's missionary impulse.[5]

Less predictable was how his reputation would fare with the passage of time. Voltaire, the French cynic, once remarked that history is a "pack of tricks we play on the dead." He might just as well have suggested the reverse, for the dead play tricks of their own. This is true not only in relation to what transpired behind closed doors during the 1950s, but also in terms of the many events since 1960 that have conspired to place Dulles in a less than positive light. Despite his campaign to retain French forces in the NATO field command, Paris eventually decided to withdraw. Not only did the American position in Indochina crumble under succeeding administrations, seeming to cast him in the role of false prophet, but SEATO, his personal creation and the legal buttress for American involvement, became defunct. The Baghdad Pact, with which he was less closely associated, expired with the overthrow of the Shah in 1979. One also recalls that he helped to multilateralize the Monroe Doctrine to meet modern-day threats of subversion, yet it suffered what is arguably its most serious reverse when President Kennedy accepted Soviet satellite status for Cuba and issued a self-denying noninvasion pledge.[6]

Nor is this all. The secretary fought for a position of influence in Lebanon, and within the space of a generation, Washington acquiesced in a Syrian-

Israeli condominium. Dulles' refusal to recognize the East German and Mainland Chinese regimes was superseded by *Ostpolitik* and a form of triangular diplomacy featuring the "China card." Castillo Armas of Guatemala and Diem of Vietnam, both allies of the United States in Dulles' time, were assassinated. Then, too, it was not long before the United Nations, for which he had worked so assiduously, became a vehicle for Soviet power so that by 1987 Moscow was introducing resolutions to broaden the scope of its operation. Even the tone of the Dulles era, with its stress on bipartisanship and executive prerogative, began to shift under Lyndon Johnson before sinking altogether beneath the weight of Nixon's Watergate scandal. The Formosa Resolution and Eisenhower Doctrine were, in effect, repealed by the War Powers Act of 1972.[7]

History has not been entirely unkind. Many of the concessions for which Dulles held out at the risk of appearing obtuse fell to his successors as a legacy of his stubbornness. Notable among them was a durable cease-fire in the Formosa Strait and German reunification on Western terms. Even the notion of "massive retaliation," which had begun to seem out of place by the late 1960s as Moscow proceeded to redress the missile gap in its favor, made a comeback in the 1970s. Hard bargaining was once again the order of the day. In addition, the positions that President Nixon took on such issues as summitry and containment, as well as his firmness in the face of Soviet provocation, can be seen as a throwback to the 1950s. The Carter Doctrine was essentially a corollary to the Eisenhower Doctrine (for which Dulles, rather than Ike, was responsible), and the Reagan Doctrine merely made explicit what had been implicit in such scenarios as Iran and Guatemala. The stunning 1990 victory in Nicaragua by Violeta Barrios de Chamorro and her UNO party over the Moscow-backed Sandinistas made Arbenz's downfall more intelligible by demonstrating that the popular vote of third world nations can no more be taken for granted by leftist dictators than by their right-wing counterparts. Lastly, in Egypt, the Aswan Dam project eventually soured, causing Russian leaders to regret the billions of rubles lavished on it without any commensurate strengthening of diplomatic and military ties between Cairo and Moscow.[8]

One way, perhaps, of gauging Dulles' competence is to compare his performance with that of contemporaries such as Dean Acheson, Christian Herter, and Dean Rusk. His celebrated penchant for "brinkmanship," a term coined by the media, must be viewed in the context of Truman's many trips to the edge of the abyss. During the 1960s, Kennedy staked out even more dangerous ground by mounting an invasion of Cuba and then blockading it in such fashion as to force the Soviets into a humiliating backdown. Within two years of JFK's election, America's half-baked intervention at the Bay of Pigs was followed by ineptness at the summit and the erection of the Berlin Wall, not to mention a renewed demand for Western withdrawal, accompanied by a Soviet ultimatum, and the mobilization of American reservists.

Canada's ambassador to the United States was astonished to find America's youngest elected president dangerously at loggerheads with Moscow and "totally fed up with . . . the uncommitted nations." Kennedy signed a limited test ban treaty; but détente, as practiced by Dulles, would not resume until Nixon began withdrawing the combat units sent to Vietnam by Presidents Kennedy and Johnson. During the early 1960s, Kennedy inaugurated Captive Nations Week, proclaimed anew the goal of a united Germany, and opposed Peking's admission to the United Nations. He had intended to follow a "soft" line on recognition but his hand was soon forced by public opinion so that in the weeks preceding his assassination he found himself on less cordial terms with Mainland China than Eisenhower had been. Secretary of State Rusk warned his countrymen not to take "premature comfort from arguments within the Communist world as to how to bury us" while Lyndon Johnson pulled out nearly all the stops in Vietnam and sent troops into the Dominican Republic. Thereafter, President Nixon had no sooner wound down the war in Vietnam than additional Communist insurgencies raged out of control in Laos, Cambodia, and Angola. Under President Carter, Soviet troops invaded Afghanistan and American hostages were held for ransom in Iran.[9]

In short, it is helpful to consider the historical context within which a given individual operated if one is to render a balanced judgment. One is less likely to attribute the ill-fated Hungarian uprising of 1956 to Dulles' talk of liberation in light of a similar revolt that occurred in Czechoslovakia twelve years later amid similar charges of Western provocation. By the same token, one could better appreciate Dulles' support for Castillo Armas after President Johnson's dispatch of 22,000 troops to the Dominican Republic. During the 1960s, democracy in Latin America vanished almost as rapidly as it had appeared during the preceding decade.[10]

It may be a trifle unfair to judge Christian Herter on the basis of his brief term of office under a lame duck president. Nevertheless, it is clear that as one who had been a professional politician for some twenty years and with few of Dulles' credentials, he did not accomplish a great deal. According to columnist Arthur Krock, Foggy Bottom appeared to fall apart after Dulles' death, with each separate division pursuing its own agenda and Herter giving little evidence of being in command. Ambassador Alphand noted that the new secretary "smiles and fumbles his responses in press conferences. . . . Where is the leadership?" With the exception of six good will trips by President Eisenhower, Herter's term produced virtually nothing. The Geneva negotiations on Germany and Central Europe ground to a halt; morale at NATO headquarters plummeted; relations between Washington and Ottawa began to cool. Trujillo's corrupt and repressive dictatorship came to a crashing end, owing in large measure to decisions taken by Eisenhower, and the new Dominican leadership proved just as distasteful and antagonistic from Washington's standpoint as the old. Prime Minister Macmillan observed that Herter seemed rather in awe of public opinion polls, never a healthy sign in the conduct of foreign policy. It was under Herter, too, that two thousand Panamanians invaded the Canal Zone and tore down the American flag.[11]

In Cuba, Ambassador Earl Smith, for all of his pains to distance himself from Batista and all his effort to undermine the old regime, was ridiculed by Castro and forced out of the country within three weeks of the revolution. Batista himself was refused entry into the United States, and when Castro paid a visit to Washington, he impressed Herter as being "like a child in many ways." The Cuban dictator added injury to insult with a sudden wave of confiscations, executions, and censorship. Finally, when Castro ordered Ike to reduce his embassy staff to eleven (1 January 1961), even as sympathetic an observer as Milton Eisenhower had to admit that "we . . . suffered indignities seldom before heaped on a nation by any power large or small." On 9 July 1960, Eisenhower assured the world that the United States "in conformity with its treaty obligations" would "not permit the establishment of a regime dominated by international Communism in the western hemisphere." The State Department, for its part, reaffirmed the validity of the Monroe Doctrine, and in August the Organization of American States condemned Soviet intervention. However, this is as far as it went. According to Robert Hill, an invasion by Cuban exiles scheduled for October 1960 was postponed, causing Frondizi of Argentina to despair of the drift in American policymaking. Words alone were insufficient to reassure Latin American leaders.[12]

Soon after Dulles died, North Vietnam ordered its forces in the south to resume guerrilla warfare and Herter's attempt to beguile Red China with offers of an exchange of newsmen and an increase in cultural contact fell on barren soil. Peking remained obdurate. In 1960, Mao's government imprisoned Bishop James Walsh of Maryknoll; indeed it was not until Nixon took office that the last of the American prisoners was released. It was under Herter also that East German authorities embarked upon a course of unprecedented interference with American convoys along the access routes to West Berlin. Eisenhower invited Khrushchev to an informal summit in the United States with the proviso that there be tangible signs of progress at Geneva. But things did not go as planned. Robert Murphy, who extended the invitation, either misunderstood his instructions or disregarded them because he failed to mention Eisenhower's stipulation. As the president was later to recall, it was a blunder resulting from the absence of "proper measures such as Foster Dulles had consistently employed." As a man of his word, Ike welcomed Khrushchev to Camp David (against the advice of Adenauer and de Gaulle) only to have a return invitation to Moscow cancelled on grounds that Washington had been caught red-handed in a U-2 spying operation. From this time onward, a White House aide was present whenever presidential directions were conveyed to a secretary or under secretary of state.[13]

As regards the U-2 incident itself, it may have been the first time in history that a head of state took personal responsibility for an act of espionage, and Khrushchev reciprocated by breaking off all contact with Eisenhower for the duration. Meanwhile, the situation created a furor in Japan where additional U-2s were based. Presidential plans for a visit to Tokyo had to be cancelled when Tokyo withdrew its invitation, the first cancellation of such an invitation to a president of the United States.[14]

Here, as elsewhere, Dulles might have been better than his successor at forecasting the outcome of various policy options. Among the many events that he had foreseen were de Gaulle's return to power, a short lifespan for the United Arab Republic, and the failure of American-style democracy to "take" in Vietnam. He also predicted that the tide of despotism would recede during the second half of the twentieth century just as it had during the first half of the nineteenth.[15]

In more concrete terms, when one considers a term in office that stretched over six years, it is plain that Dulles has some definite credits to his name. The Truman Doctrine and Marshall Plan, along with NATO and American entry into the Korean War, were all geared, as we noted earlier, to the forging of an effective makeweight against Soviet expansion. But European unity had yet to be realized under Acheson. NATO remained a paper tiger, for all practical purposes, until Dulles arranged the entry of German units and expanded its arsenal to include tactical nuclear weapons and intermediate range ballistic missiles. It was a viable NATO, then, coupled with the Austrian State Treaty, and a revival of Japanese power within the Western alliance, that should probably be regarded as Dulles' crowning achievements. The secretary's blunt criticism of European colonialism afforded de Gaulle an excuse to withdraw his naval forces from NATO and expel several fighter squadrons from French soil. However, given the Anglo-American "special relationship" and France's traditional independence, one is not surprised. Dulles made a concerted effort to include the French in Allied planning while satisfying de Gaulle's demand that consultation extend beyond the scope of immediate defense obligations. Three-power strategy sessions were expanded to cover a myriad of issues. The founding of the European Common Market and EURATOM constituted still another step forward as did the decline of communism as a political force in Italy and France (Communist deputies in the French National Assembly dropped in number from 150 to 10).[16]

In the Western Hemisphere, American relations with Canada soared to an all-time high under Dulles. A joint legislative committee was established to familiarize lawmakers on both sides of the border with problems of mutual interest, this in addition to a Joint Ministerial Committee on Defense Matters and an International Joint Commission dealing with problems involving common waters. Extension of the Reciprocal Trade Act to Ottawa delighted Canadian farmers, and when Dulles obtained an unprecedented four-year extension in 1958, he became one of the most sought-after speakers by Canadian chambers of commerce. On the secretary's death, there was speculation that eight hundred acres of Canadian land that he owned outright (his Duck Island estate) would go to the Canadian government, something unprecedented in the annals of American diplomacy, but not surprising; Dulles was one of the nation's leading internationalists.[17]

South of the border, American statecraft entered an equally constructive phase. Mexico turned a friendly face toward the United States while making impressive strides along the road to democratic government in the company of Argentina, Colombia, Venezuela, Bolivia, and Honduras. In Bolivia, a radical reformist regime received substantial aid from Washington and, on balance, dictatorial rule declined by about two-thirds throughout the region. Frondizi, who succeeded Perón in the Casa Rosada extended himself to encourage American investment in his country, and in 1957, the State Department negotiated several revisions in its treaty with Panama, all of which redounded to the latter's benefit.[18]

There were lapses, to be sure. Washington reneged on an agreement involving the purchase of Uruguayan meat, and soon after sending the popular and able Cecil Lyon as ambassador to Chile, it reassigned him to Paris at a lower rank. Montevideo and Santiago were not the only aggrieved parties. Clare Boothe Luce, after being named to succeed career ambassador Ellis Briggs in Rio de Janeiro, reconsidered after an altercation with Senator Morse and decided not to go.[19]

Generally, however, the tone was upbeat. It is true that the Chilean, Uruguayan, and Argentine assemblies voted to condemn American intervention in Guatemala, but American relations with these and other countries were either unaffected in the long run or showed signs of improvement. Vice President Nixon is remembered for the violent hostility he encountered in Venezuela, yet this was no more representative of his reception in Latin America as a whole than other outbursts of anti-Americanism that erupted during the same period in Taiwan and Japan. Soviet officials traveling abroad were not exactly immune from this type of reaction either. President Kliment Voroshilov, aged 76, was on a good will tour of Indonesia in the company of President Sukarno in May 1957, about a year before Nixon's unhappy experience in Caracas, when, on arrival at the presidential palace, a mob scene ensued. Indonesia's foreign minister had his limousine windows smashed; Russian flags were trodden underfoot, and an enormous picture of Voroshilov was trampled to pieces. By comparison, the Latin American response to visits by Nixon and Eisenhower proved quite friendly. Ike was greeted with such deafening acclaim during his 1960 trip to Argentina, Brazil,

Chile, and Uruguay that Tad Szulc of the *New York Times* was inspired to describe relations between the United States and Latin America as "on the highest plateau since the end of World War I." Szulc would have been even more accurate if, for purposes of comparison, he had chosen the year 1936 or, even more appropriately, the era of Theodore Roosevelt.[20]

There were no Latin American wars of consequence under Eisenhower, while a number of disputes which reached the boiling point proved amenable to U.S. mediation in cooperation with the OAS, the Inter-American Peace Committee, and a coalition of Argentina, Brazil, and Chile. Among the issues resolved were a border dispute between Peru and Ecuador, the Haya de la Torre asylum case involving Peru and Colombia, and a Nicaraguan invasion of Costa Rica mounted in retaliation for Figueres' alleged attempt on the life of Somoza. In the case of the Nicaragua-Costa Rica clash, Washington worked with the OAS to furnish Figueres with civilian and military aircraft at a nominal price, and peace was restored within a week's time. In 1957, when fighting flared along the frontier between Nicaragua and Honduras, OAS aircraft were able to spot the source of the trouble and order was promptly restored. Two years later, Nicaraguan exiles invaded their country from Costa Rica, hostile groups descended upon Panama from Cuba, and once more, the situation was brought quickly under control, this time by the OAS and the Inter-American Peace Commission acting with an assist from Washington.[21]

Milton Eisenhower later maintained that his brother's administration had "changed more fundamental policies affecting our relationships with Latin America than any other in American history." To be sure, not all of this was Dulles' doing, but he and his colleagues at State pioneered in founding the first American organization to aid less developed nations (with a fund capitalized at $300 million to meet the developing world's need for low interest loans). He also fostered the development of Latin American common markets, overturning a policy of a hundred years' standing. Hemispheric commodity study groups were formed to minimize fluctuations in the price of Latin American products on the world market. In addition, long-term aid programs replaced short-term programs under a new Economic Development Fund, and an Investment Guarantee Program, which underwrote insurance for noncommercial risks such as expropriation and war, benefited an estimated forty countries with over $200 million in insurance contracts. For the first time, American aid was not only channeled through such institutions as the Inter-American Bank and the United Nations; it was also offered with the proviso that it be used to support liberal programs of socioeconomic reform. Before bowing out in 1961, Eisenhower could claim to have doubled the flow of private and public capital going to Latin America.[22]

Granted, Ike's Act of Bogotá, with its experimental clauses mandating social reform, proved an abject failure almost immediately after Kennedy increased its budget tenfold and gave it a new name, the *Alianza para el*

Progreso. However, it did not materialize until after Dulles had passed from the scene and it is unlikely that he did much to support the concept while alive. Ike, who admitted that he had come to "lean heavily" on the advice of his brother Milton when it came to Latin America, tended to blame hemispheric unrest and Yankeephobia on such material conditions as a "feudal" class structure and Washington's neglect. Dulles did not agree, nor did he share Milton's views on the nexus between economic and political issues. Disinclined to believe that the United States should respond to anti-American demonstrations by granting more aid, he also rejected the idea that American support should be conditional upon the degree to which a government conformed to the pattern of American democracy. This was the so-called slide rule approach which struck him as a form of interference inconsistent with the practice of treating other peoples as equals. Henry Holland, who replaced Cabot as assistant secretary for inter-American affairs, spoke for Dulles, rather than the president's brother, when he said, "Each of us has something that other countries consider disadvantageous. The U.S., for example, is particularly criticized for its racial problem. What would be the reaction here if the racially tolerant Latin Americans were to announce that no further coffee would be shipped to the United States until we had straightened out our problem of segregation? We must follow a policy of live and let live."[23]

According to Milton, the man who had a decent home and therefore something worth preserving was "more apt to be moderate in his pursuit of other goals, more likely to favor democratic change over violent upheaval." Here again, Dulles would have had reservations based upon his reading of the historical record. His views would have coincided more nearly with those of Willard Beaulac, American ambassador to Paraguay, Colombia, Cuba, Chile, and Argentina. Beaulac believed that Nixon's misadventure in Venezuela had been blown out of all proportion: "Seldom," he observed, had "so much been made of so little."[24]

While it is true that Dulles made "neglect" of Latin America by the Democrats a campaign issue and continued to articulate the theme during his initial months at State, he had something very specific in mind: a lapse in the "courteous attentions" that are "highly valued by those of the Latin race." By this he meant that America's neighbors to the south should be treated less patronizingly, implying *less* financial aid rather than more. Anxious to abolish the Export-Import Bank, he succeeded in placing hemispheric aid on a loan basis because the policy of awarding outright grants that originated under FDR seemed to him demeaning. It was, first of all, a breach of gentlemanly decorum to raise expectations beyond one's ability to satisfy them; and second, it fostered a relationship of subservience.[25]

"Courteous attentions" implied a number of things. Ambassador Peurifoy, after helping to broker the pact between Castillo Armas and other claimants to the Guatemalan presidency, stepped aside at the signing of the final pact and yielded the limelight to the envoy from El Salvador. Two years later, the summit meeting that Dulles arranged between Canada, Mexico, and the United States, the first of its kind, was clearly a tonic to Mexican pride. It was also illustrative of a style that paid tribute to the "spiritual qualities," as well as the material accomplishments, of a neighboring nation of great "beauty and charm." Latin American leaders were consulted on such issues as the Korean Political Conference and Communist infiltration in British Guiana, problems of fairly wide import, and there were over a dozen conferences with the full corps of Latin American ambassadors for discussions covering a wide geographical spectrum. By 1958, Dulles was prepared to institute the practice of meeting regularly with Latin American foreign ministers; and, for good measure, Pan American Day was extended to Pan American week.[26]

During the years when Dulles handled Latin American policy, foreign aid was held to a minimum. Such funds as were earmarked generally went to the support of anti-Communist groups, and although there was an increase in strictly military aid, Assistant Secretary of State John Moors Cabot, who acted as unofficial mouthpiece for the hemisphere's pecuniary aspirations, was replaced and sent to Sweden. More and more, however, Milton's influence came to the fore as indicated by the peremptory tone of a 1956 note addressed by the White House to Dulles: "We are not really appreciative of Mexico's political and social problems." Thereafter, although Dulles continued to deny that the United States was "neglecting" Latin America, he began to make statements bearing a closer resemblance to Milton's philosophy than his own. Realizing that the president was turning more and more to his brother, he tended to concentrate on extrahemispheric issues. When Milton traveled to Latin America, he did so with the title of "special ambassador" and in the company of State Department experts serving as personal aides. He spent most of his weekends at the White House, enjoyed direct access to the president by phone, and was the recipient of at least one direct presidential favor. Ike lobbied Macmillan to give a commencement address at Johns Hopkins University, explaining in his letter to the British prime minister that it was "because of my sentimental attachment to the University and, of course, to my brother [its president]." It is not unlikely that the president said at the end of his second term, as is reported, that "I don't know why they're looking for my successor any further than my brother, Milton."[27]

Nowhere was the difference between Dulles and Milton Eisenhower more apparent than in American policy toward Cuba. Ambassador Arthur Gardner was removed in 1957 for being too closely linked with Batista, and two years later, Gardner's successor was relieved of his duties for not being sympathetic enough to Castro. Although one cannot be certain, this was likely at the behest of Milton Eisenhower, whose views were retailed by Dulles only weeks before Castro's victory—the secretary assured reporters that the most troubled state in the hemisphere was Venezuela, not Cuba. Dulles himself does not seem to have been so much hostile to Batista as simply resigned to his downfall. When he received the news of Castro's takeover, his initial reaction was, "I don't know whether this is good for us or bad." But Milton, who swayed his brother to ignore CIA warnings of significant Communist influence on the Castro movement, felt differently.[28]

On hindsight, one can see that the danger signals transmitted by Gardner and others had less force than they might normally have had because intelligence estimates failed to agree. As late as July 1959, two months after Dulles' funeral, Eisenhower was still not sure of Havana's political orientation. A third of the president's advisers labeled Castro a Communist, a third thought otherwise, while another third declined to hazard a guess. A second problem was that most American officials were incapable of viewing prosperous nations as anything other than stable. From Milton's standpoint, Cuba was among the least likely of all countries in the Western Hemisphere to take a turn to the left. True, Batista was corrupt and a dictator. But his regime appeared relatively mild in comparison with others. Personal freedom flourished on a scale unimaginable under Castro. There were remarkably few political executions and no death penalty despite widespread civil disorder. Cuba also boasted the highest per capita income in Latin America. It was surging ahead with the building of highways, hospitals, and schools of every kind, along with lower and middle income housing. With the lowest mortality rate in Latin America (infant and adult alike) and notable progress in the organization of labor unions (which Castro would later abolish), it stood third in per capita ratio of doctors, university students, and newspapers.[29]

Despite such a record, Washington set out to destroy the man under whom a large portion of it had been achieved. Earl Smith, who replaced Gardner and arrived in Havana with orders to distance himself from Batista, leveled harsh criticism against the government to which he was accredited. Denouncing it for its handling of native insurrection, he demanded the release of political prisoners and the firing of police officers guilty of alleged brutality. At the same time, he let it be known that he would receive any opposition leader who cared to see him. Meanwhile, the State Department, which had instituted an arms embargo against Batista, winked at unneutral shipments bound for Castro while pressuring America's allies to institute similar embargoes of their own. It would not even allow delivery of goods for which Batista had already paid. Thus, from the moment of Smith's arrival, there could be no doubt in the mind of informed Cubans that Washington wanted their government overthrown and would back no one but Castro. According to Smith, it should have been possible to promote the growth of a third political force, midway between Batista and Castro, but Washington failed to see the need.[30]

Turning for a moment to the Middle East, the results of the Eisenhower administration were problematical.[31] On the debit side, Dulles ignored repeated warnings from Turkey, Iran, and Pakistan that Afghanistan was being allowed to drift by default into the Soviet orbit. As Soviet aid to Kabul mounted, more and more American money was being funneled into coffers south of the Rio Grande. One could probably argue as well that refusal on the part of Washington to join the Baghdad Pact in deference to Israeli qualms doomed pro-Western forces in Iraq. The breach of a pledge to deliver military aid to Baghdad completes the picture of lost opportunity. And then there was Nasser.[32]

What is interesting about Suez is that the situation resulting from American intervention was not nearly as bleak as might have been expected. Although British and French influence plummeted in the short run and Soviet stock rose proportionately, Israel and the United States, along with the United Nations, all emerged stronger. *Fedayeen* raids ceased, not to resume for over a decade, and the Straits of Tiran were opened to Israeli trade and commerce. The United Nations derived an added measure of authority by virtue of the effectiveness of its emergency force which entered Gaza with Nasser's permission. This, incidentally, was the first use since Korea of Dulles' "Uniting for Peace" resolution, and as such, it provided a model for later UNEF peace-keeping operations in Cyprus and the Congo. Dulles could take satisfaction, too, in knowing that he had broken with the colonial past and demonstrated for the first time since World War II America's real power relative to its allies.[33]

The familiar argument that Suez damaged American ties with London and Paris holds little water. Anglo-American amity was restored under the government of Harold Macmillan, and NATO became stronger than ever. Of all the countries that Eisenhower visited on his European tour in 1959, none gave him a warmer welcome than England. Hundreds of thousands lined the roads from Gatwick Airport into the city. In the long run, British and French observers, almost to a man, came to regard Suez as a tempest in a teapot, if not a positive success for Eisenhower and Dulles. This is not to say that they approved of American ambivalence. But neither could they fathom their own national strategy. As one official remarked, what would Downing Street have done with Suez had it managed to prize it back?[34]

The irony is that Britain, in defeat, realized so many of her objectives. Provision was made for the clearing and proper maintenance of the canal while Syria agreed to restore damaged pipe lines between Iraq and the Mediterranean. Although Nasser had declared his intent to nationalize all Canal Company assets, both in Egypt and abroad, the company received $81 million for its stake in Egypt and wound up retaining all of its assets outside the country. Nasser, in fact, went even further, agreeing to pay off all debts to shareholders in installments not to exceed the revenue from canal tolls. He also allowed canal users to participate in the fixing of tolls along with regulations and, in addition, to play a role in the adjustment of disputes. British and French shipowners were eventually permitted to pay for the passage of their vessels in sterling and, as a final face-saver, Nasser sanctioned an appeal to the World Court on behalf of Israel (for its right to transit Suez).[35]

Egypt herself suffered untold losses including the bulk of her air force and an estimated £20 million worth of guns and ammunition. More damaging still, her political nakedness was laid bare for all the world to see. Not a single one of her friends and allies, including the Soviet Union, lifted a finger in her defense. During the entire first week, while the combined forces of Israel, France, and Britain bore down upon her, Moscow did nothing. It is true that Russia made inroads into the Middle East during the 1950s, but such gains would probably have occurred anyway, with or without Suez. Dulles, meanwhile, signed mutual security pacts with Teheran, as well as Karachi. Nasser was personally chastened by the Suez crisis, as in the case of the Lebanon landings a year and a half later. Care must also be taken not to confuse his opinion of the West generally, particularly of Anthony Eden, with his view of Dulles and Eisenhower. He used to say that whereas Dulles displayed "an iron fist in a velvet glove," Eden had shown a "velvet fist in an iron glove." He could deal with someone he hated but not with "someone I despise." In a telling footnote to history, Mahmoud Fawzi, Nasser's principal diplomatic adviser, was among those who attended Eisenhower's funeral in 1969 despite the absence of relations between Washington and Cairo.[36]

This is not to deny that there were moments of pathos. On 30 October, America lined up against England and France in the United Nations Security Council and, joining hands with the Soviet Union, co-sponsored a withdrawal resolution. Unfortunately, the timing was such that it appeared to implicate Washington in Moscow's decision to crush Hungary's freedom fighters for it was on the 30th, or the day after, that Moscow decided to teach Budapest a lesson. Elsewhere, a coup directed against the Syrian government and backed by Washington and London failed abysmally. In the process, Nasser's movement gained momentum with increased opportunities for Communist penetration. Syrian troops crossed the Jordanian border and King Hussein could feel the very pillars of his throne beginning to crumble as his prime minister, along with cabinet officials and leaders of the army, struck in open defiance. Nevertheless, Hussein persevered through sheer force of personality, his determination stiffened by Saudi aid and provisions of the Eisenhower Doctrine authorizing the use of American troops to shield Middle Eastern states against "overt armed aggression from any nation controlled by international communism." Eisenhower had based his doctrine on the assumption that Soviet control of Middle Eastern oil would be tantamount to control of Western Europe and Japan, and the doctrine represented a revolutionary commitment to an area never before regarded as one of primary American responsibility. Authorizing grants of up to $200 million in military and economic aid on a discretionary basis, with funds to be drawn from the mutual security appropriation of the current years there can be little doubt that, along with the landing of American marines in Lebanon in 1958, it did much to restore stability in the Middle East and North Africa. Although Eisenhower did not send troops to Jordan, he supported Macmillan's decision to do so, promising other forms of assistance and sending vessels of the Sixth Fleet to the eastern Mediterranean.[37]

By May 1957, Hussein had proven his mettle and the Eisenhower Doctrine had won the backing of Iraq, Iran, Turkey, Greece, and Pakistan. Israel and Jordan approved it implicitly even as anti-Communist declarations were signed by Lebanon, Libya, Saudi Arabia, and Ethiopia. Pro-Western governments in Lebanon and Saudi Arabia, as well as Jordan, were thus reinvigorated. King Saud, after renewing the American lease on Dhahran Airbase, ceased to denounce the Baghdad Pact and refused any longer to bankroll Nasser's public relations. Pro-Nasser candidates were likewise defeated in Lebanon where the bureau chief of one of Nasser's leading propaganda organs, *Middle East News*, was sent packing. By mid-June, American aid had begun to arrive in Lebanon—four planeloads of jeeps and recoilless rifles. A pro-Western premier, up for reelection, won handily, and later in the summer, Nasser appeared on British television to say that he regretted the rift between Cairo and London. British Airways was invited back to Egypt while ties between London and Amman were also on the mend.[38]

Indirectly, the Eisenhower Doctrine, in conjunction with American support for a three-power buildup along Syrian borders, sealed the fate of Syria's Communist party and put an end to the Soviet-Egyptian honeymoon. The United Arab Republic (UAR), which came into existence in February 1958 with the ostensible backing of Syria's Communists, was not, in fact, welcomed by them. Furthermore, Syria's Communist party, which had been the strongest in the area after electing the Arab world's first Communist deputy, stood to be suppressed when a non-Communist government came to power in Damascus early in 1958. By the end of the year, Nasser's friendship with the USSR was dying, and Russian hopes for a major military base in the Middle East had foundered. Despite Moscow's offer to assist in building the Aswan Dam and the formalization of the agreement on 23 October 1958, Egyptian elections in November of the same year were followed by wholesale arrests of Communists in Cairo, as well as in Damascus.[39]

Nasser, who had been in Yugoslavia on a visit to Tito when the Lebanon landings occurred, flew immediately to Moscow only to find Khrushchev uncooperative. This did not sit well in Cairo where officials, after refusing a Russian request for some Baghdad Pact papers they happened to have in their possession, began to attack the Communist party of Iraq, along with its president. Iraq signed economic and technical agreements with Moscow, but its leaders would go no further. Egyptian Communists were placed under arrest, and in December, Nasser made an insulting reference to Tartar hordes sweeping in from the east and threatening Syria after they had conquered Iraq. When Khrushchev assailed Nasser at the Twenty-First Congress of the Communist party, the latter returned the compliment, touching off a verbal slugging fest. By 1959, Nasser was instructing army officer Anwar Sadat to mount the rostrum in response to Soviet attacks on the UAR. He would go out of his way to transfer Egyptian students from Russian to American schools, anticipating the break between Cairo and Moscow that was to occur in 1972. Disillusioned with Moscow's refusal to guarantee the Iraqi coup, Nasser let Khrushchev know that he also disapproved of his shoe-pounding histrionics at Turtle Bay. It is for this reason, as well as others, that a bitter head of the Middle East department of the Soviet foreign ministry complained to an Egyptian delegation about nonalignment being "a myth." The Soviets castigated Egyptian leaders over Bulgarian radio, and it was not until 1964 that relations between Cairo and Moscow returned to anything like what they had been for a time during the 1950s.[40]

In sum, whatever shifts may have occurred in the political status quo on the aftermath of the Suez invasion were generally in favor of the West, and those who predicted a Middle Eastern "conflagration" owing to misguided American opposition to an Allied military expedition proved to be mistaken.

Much the same may be said of the Far East. Pundits warned that a political *Götterdämmerung* would ensue from America's refusal to recognize Peking. But despite every vicissitude and a number of obvious blunders, the picture that emerged was far from gloomy. Scanning the record of American diplomacy in Asia, one will not find an Eisenhower Doctrine or a landing of marines, but what one does find is an increased sense of Washington's presence. Dulles became the first secretary of state to visit the Far East while in office, as well as the first to stress the role of the United States as an Asian-Pacific power.[41]

As in any debut performance, there were errors of judgment. The Cuba of the Far East was not Vietnam, where Communist forces achieved little on paper that they had not already won on the battlefield, but rather Laos, where Washington maneuvered for a coalition of disparate political elements instead of backing pro-Western leaders as urged by Thai officials, the Pentagon, and the CIA. Things went from bad to worse with the arrival of Ambassador U. Alexis Johnson in early 1958. Eisenhower eventually threw his support to Prince Boun Oum, along with the outspokenly anti-Communist Nosavan Phoumi, but this was a decision that came late in the game and one that would soon be reversed by President Kennedy. The upshot was a victory for the opposition similar to what occurred in China when Chiang was pressured to coalesce with Communist rivals or suffer the loss of vital American aid. As Eisenhower admitted in his memoirs, "We left a legacy of strife and confusion." Elsewhere in the region, the administration helped to underwrite a guerrilla campaign aimed at the overthrow of Indonesia's Sukarno, but it was too little too late. Rebel operations stalled, and Washington had to retreat.[42]

On the positive side of the ledger, Dulles negotiated bilateral defense pacts with Korea and Taiwan; he played a key role in securing the Korean armistice; and he established the Southeast Asia Treaty Organization.

In Korea, a conflict which was expected to drag on for at least another year, ended suddenly, almost mysteriously, after Eisenhower ceased to call it a "police action" and began using the term "war." Ike reinforced his military position while considering the use of atomic weapons along with attacks on strategic targets in China proper. He also let it be known that, if need be, he would enlist the assistance of Chiang Kai-shek. As a war hero with a reputation for straight talk, he spoke with a certain amount of credibility when he said that the least he would be willing to accept was an armistice based on the status quo. Finally, he bombed North Korean dikes and exacted a heavy civilian toll, something Truman had never been willing to do.[43]

Certain commentators, including Churchill, have cited Stalin's death on 5 March as a major factor in the Korean armistice. Most observers, however, did not see it this way, certainly not Eisenhower, Nixon, or the CIA; nor, for that matter, Adenauer, the British foreign office, or George Kennan (who agreed with Dulles that a shakeup in the Soviet bureaucracy was just as likely to strengthen the hand of Kremlin hawks). In spite of all the post-Stalin liberalization that occurred in satellite regimes, there is no indication that the Soviet Union was any less willing to risk war for minor gains after March 1953 than it had been before. It was, after all, under Stalin's successors that the Berlin Conference of early 1954 ended in stalemate, that Moscow's position on Austria hardened, that Soviet forces put down the Hungarian Revolution, and that Peking attacked Chiang's offshore islands with the blessing of its northern neighbor. During this same period, offensive missiles were shipped to Cuba, ultimatums were issued to force the West out of Berlin, and the Berlin Wall went up. Within a few weeks of Stalin's death, two allied aircraft were downed in German air corridors and Vietnamese Communists invaded Laos. It was not, moreover, until the very end of the Korean War, long after the death of Stalin, that P'yŏngyang landed its heaviest blows—in April and July. Far from being the byproduct of favorable shifts in the Kremlin, Korea's deliverance appears to have been the fruit of such classic diplomatic techniques as compromise, quiet persuasion, negotiation from strength, and an astute handling of public opinion.[44]

There may be some merit in Dulles' argument that Washington should have persevered on the battlefield until its adversaries were clearly vanquished. Under Secretary Smith, Assistant Secretary Robertson, Vice President Nixon, General MacArthur, and many others were of this mind. As it was, *Pravda* could speak of America's "disgrace" while Peking boasted of a "victory." America's ambassador to Korea, Ellis Briggs, regarded the armistice as a definite triumph for China and Russia, predicting that it would breed neutralism and undermine the French cause in Indochina. Approaching it from still another angle, Henry Kissinger felt that a harder line, besides saving Indochina, might have split Moscow and Peking in 1953 rather than 1959.[45]

Proponents of the soft line are quick to point out that boldness of the type recommended by Dulles and Kissinger might have led to prolonged and bitter hostilities which, in turn, could have alienated America's allies, aborted NATO, deprived the United States of its economic boom, and opened Europe to Communist penetration. Eisenhower's reputation for statesmanship might have suffered, thereby loosening his grip on Congress and placing his domestic program in jeopardy. While David Rees may have exaggerated in calling the Korean armistice "the greatest achievement of the Eisenhower years," there can be little doubt that much was accomplished, especially toward the end of the talks when both sides were bedeviled by violent resistance on the part of Rees. North Korea, after sustaining two million casualties and witnessing the destruction of a third of its population, suffered a slight loss of territory and saw its army virtually obliterated. Dulles and Eisenhower were also able to vindicate the principle of voluntary repatriation, no minor coup considering that the United Nations, under the influence of Britain, France, Canada, and India, was willing to concede on this score. Prisoners of war could decide whether or not to return to their native land, and because several thousand Chinese and North Koreans chose not to return, Communists everywhere stood to be less certain in future contests of the loyalty of their armies.[46]

A second major accomplishment in the Far East was the formation of the Southeast Asia Treaty Organization. With a membership of the United States, Britain, France, Australia, New Zealand, Thailand, and the Philippines, it was an institution for which the secretary had long seen a need. It was also controversial.

Significantly, Dulles made sure that America's responsibility to extend military support in time of war was couched in the vaguest of terms. Publicly, he may have oversold SEATO's potential in order to win votes in Congress, but privately, he was under no illusion as to what the organization could be expected to achieve. Aware that it would not even be an automatic antidote to subversion, what he envisioned was a psychological climate within which politicians of like disposition could associate without fear of intimidation, and in this respect his plan seems to have succeeded. Malaya, after putting down a Communist insurgency in the years 1955–57, conducted orderly elections, as did other nations in the region. Taiwan advanced from relative obscurity to become one of the world's most prosperous and financially stable countries. As for Japanese growth, it proved phenomenal considering the ravages of war. Between 1952 and 1960, Tokyo tripled its exports, becoming in the process the world's premier shipbuilder. As noted earlier, Britain and France prevented SEATO from backing the government of Laos against

Communist Pathet Lao incursions after Dulles had pledged such support. Even so, the Thais knew they could count on Washington in an emergency and this made a difference when the Vietminh advanced to within ten miles of their border in 1954. Although Vietnam, Laos, and Cambodia could not join without violating the Geneva accords and incurring British displeasure, they were indirectly covered because the council adopted a protocol allowing it to respond to outside requests for aid; indeed, this is what laid the groundwork for later American intervention. Diem's miracle, however shortlived, owed much to SEATO's mantle of protection—a mantle which, in Dulles' words, could be woven into a "coat of defensive chain mail." In addition to providing a legal framework for American involvement, SEATO acted as a shield against Chinese invasion. One might add that President Magsaysay of the Philippines felt that SEATO's Pacific Charter, which he had drafted, did much to lay the ghost of Western colonialism, and he himself put it to good use in fighting the insurrectionary Huks.[47]

Subsequent developments ascribable either in whole or in part to SEATO include: Indonesia's anti-Communist countercoup of 1965; the Asian Development Bank founded in 1965–67; the Asian and Pacific Council established in Seoul in 1966; and the Association of Southwest Asian Nations (ASEAN) launched from Bangkok in 1967 for the purpose of economic development with a membership of the Philippines, Thailand, Indonesia, Singapore, and Malaysia. In addition to sponsoring scholarships, visiting professorships, and Operation Rice Bowl, SEATO generated the impetus for a council of education ministers and a Parliamentarians Union, as well as a highly respected Asian Institute of Technology in Bangkok, an agricultural research center, and an Asian labor education center in the Philippines. At the same time, France, Britain, Australia, and New Zealand offered basic training courses for the development of skilled labor.[48]

Above all, SEATO bought time and filled the vacuum left by a no-war, no-peace situation in Korea, Indochina, and the Formosa Strait. In 1958, it unveiled its cultural program and formulated plans for economic cooperation even as it began to benefit from close multilateral defense planning. Australia made over $6 million available for the defense of fellow pact members, and the United States contributed substantial sums of its own. The Burmese, skeptical at first, changed their tune by the late 1950s. Rangoon urged Washington to maintain a firm military posture and, unlike London and Paris, would have been happy to see SEATO's protection extended to Taiwan.[49]

On the strategic front, Thai airfields were lengthened to accommodate jet squadrons and a number of military exercises were held. *Firm Link* involved a U.S. carrier and two destroyers, along with ground forces from Thailand and the Philippines. The British sent two destroyers and a light cruiser, while Australia contributed two additional destroyers. Observers were also on hand from Laos, Vietnam, Cambodia, Burma, and Indonesia. After U.S.

naval units landed Philippine troops in Bangkok, the staging of a military parade attracted 750,000 spectators. Later the same year (1956) came operation *Sea Link*, co-sponsored by Washington and Manila for the training of SEATO personnel in both amphibious tactics and naval gunfire for the support of ground combat. The following year, American servicemen participated in two more exercises: *Astra*, sponsored by the United Kingdom to simulate the escort of a convoy from Singapore to Bangkok against air and submarine opposition; and *Albatross*, sponsored by Australia to improve combined air-surface operations for the protection of shipping in the South China Sea. Apart from the major exercises, there were also minor operations involving two or more nations. *Teamwork*, for example, was sponsored by the United States and Thailand; *Phiblink* was a U.S.-Philippine project; and in 1958 came *Ocean Link* which featured carriers from the United States, Britain, and Australia, followed by additional maritime and amphibious maneuvers, all serving in one or another way to raise the level of teamwork and understanding.[50]

Early in the century, Theodore Roosevelt won universal acclaim and a Nobel Peace Prize for being the world's "honest broker," yet he was not nearly as active on the diplomatic scene as Dulles. In addition to the latter's leadership in Western European Union, the Austrian State Treaty, and SEATO, he played a significant mediatory role in settling the Saar dispute, along with a bitter quarrel between France and Tunisia. One has the feeling that here was another individual who, like TR, could think dispassionately, grasp both sides of a dispute, and arrive at an equitable solution. In Cyprus, a plan that he conceived for the reconciliation of ethnic Greeks and Turks succeeded, at least temporarily, in calming some very troubled waters. Along the way, he had to resist pressure from the Greek lobby, which demanded *enosis*, the Turks, who insisted on partition, and the British, who wanted to retain their colony. None of the parties could be fully satisfied. Another trouble spot was Trieste where Italian-Yugoslav friction threatened the peace of the Mediterranean, not to mention Italy's position on EDC. Lengthy negotiations conducted jointly by London and Washington with each of the disputants threatened repeatedly to collapse. There were conferences almost nightly at the State Department, with Dulles involving himself in every phase of the process from the drafting of day-to-day instructions to the taking of decisions on arms shipments and economic assistance. A settlement was reached late in 1955, facilitated in part by the promise of American grain shipments to Belgrade, and Italy was able to cast its vote for German membership in NATO on schedule. Again, the path had been rockstrewn.[51]

Mediation of this kind presupposed an ability to strike delicate balances. In earlier chapters, we alluded not only to Dulles' pragmatic approach but also to the example that is perhaps most telling in this regard, namely, his strategy of straddling when it came to colonialism. On the one hand, he did much to promote the anticolonialist cause, realizing that it was popular at home and that any other posture abroad would be so much grist for Com-

overboard. Under the heat of a congressional hearing and in reply to a suggestion that, before passage of the Eisenhower Doctrine, he should seek French and British backing to ensure that American boys would not be sent overseas to fight alone, he replied, "If I were an American boy, as you term it, I'd rather not have a French and British soldier beside me, one on my right and one on my left." That such a gaffe should have occurred under such circumstances is suggestive of the larger picture. Sighed the French ambassador, "It is enough to be a leader of . . . [an anticolonialist] revolution to be regarded here [in the American capital] as a George Washington." One is also reminded of Nixon's observation that "obsessive fear of associating with European colonial powers blinded successive American administrations to a very simple fact: Communism, not colonialism, was the *principal* cause of the war in Indochina."[52]

At the same time—and here one sees the balance—Dulles was capable, as mentioned earlier, of subordinating the anticolonialist cause to more pressing goals such as EDC and WEU. For the benefit of reporters, he once declared that "We can get ourselves into a hell of a lot of trouble by just dipping into things which are not primarily our concern . . . we have enough responsibility without running around the world trying to take on everybody else's." He could discern an inclination on the part of his countrymen to substitute one form of dependency for another without really intending it, as well as a tendency to appear self-righteous, "thanking God that we are not as other men." Were the UN trusteeships under which America ruled its dependencies not de facto imperialism, he wanted to know? And why should Americans pay more attention to the French presence in Algeria than to what the Russians were doing in Latvia, Lithuania, and Estonia? As usual, though, he entered a caveat: not everyone within the Soviet orbit had been coopted by force. The Czechs had made a conscious decision to align themselves with the Kremlin after their leaders, Beneš and Masaryk, lost faith in the Western powers and the League of Nations.[53]

The safest thing to say about Dulles as a diplomat is that he was unpredictable except when it came to his public persona. He was also shrewd, and historians striving for an accurate assessment of the man and his era will find that the ruses of an artful secretary are still capable of misleading.

Russian leaders, when informed of his death in 1959, must surely have wondered about the hidden side of a man who, for so many years, had been their chief nemesis. Was it not under his stewardship that people the world over had witnessed the first flowering of Soviet-American détente? After careful coaching by Dulles (from his deathbed) and in spite of a congressional resolution inaugurating Captive Nations Day, an American vice president would fly to Moscow to deliver an address over Soviet television. A Russian premier would soon be sitting with an American president in shirt sleeves around a fireplace at Camp David. By 1959, a genuine thaw had developed in superpower relations, with Moscow and Washington serving together on a twenty-four-member committee for the peaceful uses of outer space, co-sponsoring an Atomic Energy Agency to promote peaceful uses of the atom, and signing the Antarctica Treaty which, by means of a unique system of policing, reserved an entire continent for nonmilitary use. After some thirty months of negotiation, the United States and the Soviet Union had agreed on a vastly expanded program of cultural exchange, and Moscow had disbanded its propaganda bureau, the Cominform (Information Bureau of the Communist and Workers' Parties). Earlier, in 1955, British and Russian fleets had exchanged visits in a modestly upbeat atmosphere while Bulgaria welcomed a British football team. Progress was also recorded in talks leading to a test ban treaty.[54]

Equally striking is the fact that as Soviet-American relations improved, the underlying strategic position of the Kremlin continued to erode. Tito, after liberalizing his ties with the West, joined with Greece and Turkey in a defensive pact at the same time that he insisted on his right to buy arms from Washington. So confident, in fact, was Yugoslavia of its status as an independent regime during the period 1953–56 that it saw fit to resist Kremlin pressure for the recognition of East Germany. Albania, across the border, nearly upstaged its neighbor by breaking out of the Soviet straitjacket entirely and attaching itself to Peking. By 1960, Moscow was obliged to give up its submarine base on the Adriatic. In the meantime, the Matsu-Quemoy crisis of 1958, which some feared might split the Western alliance, served only to widen the rift between Peking and Moscow.[55]

Every one of the above geopolitical developments, it should be said, occurred while Dulles was facing down Kremlin ultimatums, planning covert activity aimed at the overthrow of Communist-dominated governments, and generally sapping the underpinnings of the Russian-built edifice. His success as a midwife to German rearmament impelled the Soviets to sever some of their ties with Britain and France. Simultaneously, riots and revolts in East Germany, Poland, and Hungary led to a massive hemorrhaging of Communist brainpower. Escapees from East Germany alone numbered 250,000 a year, bringing the total in this area to about three million from 1953 to 1959. From North Korea came another two million refugees, from North Vietnam one million, and from Hungary an estimated two hundred thousand. West Berlin's production and trade with the outside world tripled, while hostile regimes in Iran and Guatemala came tumbling down. Moreover, at a time when Communist alliances were riven by disputes and bickering, as Mao Tse-tung was dispatching anyone quixotic enough to accept his invitation to "let a thousand flowers bloom," as Russian bosses were plotting the liquidation of Beria and Kaganovich, along with the purging of Malenkov, Molotov, and Shepilov, and as Marshal Zhukov was accepting demotion, Dulles was forging a new consensus and fine-tuning his approach to the United Nations.[56]

Americans marvelled at the apparent contradiction between sudden gains in the cold war and a winding down of the war itself. For the first time since 1917, Soviet officials allowed the publication and dissemination of the Christian Bible just as they and their allies in Eastern Europe undertook to curb the power of the secret police. German prisoners of war returned from Russia in exchange for a partial restoration of trade between Moscow and Bonn. Gomulka of Poland, then Kadar of Hungary, moved to expand freedom of the press and religion. Curiously, after Washington took the lead in reducing its ground forces, Moscow did the same; and while the United States acquired military installations in Morocco and Spain, the Soviet Union withdrew from Porkkala naval base in Finland. With the occupation of Austria at an end, Hungary began to dismantle its border fortifications commanding the approaches to Austria and Yugoslavia, and Russia renounced its claims on Turkey, including the right to special privileges in the Straits. It was all rather remarkable, beginning with the year 1955, when Molotov declared that the road from Moscow to New York was becoming "better and smoother." Only a few months before Molotov spoke, Kremlin leaders had apologized for the downing of an American naval aircraft over the Bering Strait and offered to pay half the damages, something unparalleled in the recent past. The phrase "Spirit of Geneva," however suspect as a catchword, would prove to be something more than mere fiction.[57]

It is the irony of fate that John Foster Dulles should have gained a reputation for constant stirring of the pot of Soviet-American discord when the historical record indicates otherwise. To be sure, Dulles intended to hold his own and, wherever possible, to enhance Western prospects. He was not one to yield without a struggle. Still, he never ceased to aim at détente because he believed that competition and conciliation were always reconcilable. Within two short years of taking office, he succeeded in establishing a relationship with Moscow that helped to move the country away from confrontational politics.[58]

This, too, might have crossed Gromyko's mind on the day that he stood musing beneath the yellowwood tree at Arlington National Cemetery.

Notes

HCKMT	Historical Commission of the Kuomintang Archives, Yang-mingshan, Taiwan
IS	International Series, DDE Papers
JFD	John Foster Dulles
JFDOH	John Foster Dulles Oral History Collection
JFDP	John Foster Dulles Papers
MHCBHL	Michigan Historical Collections, Bentley Historical Library, Ann Arbor, Michigan
NA	National Archives
NSC	National Security Council
OHI	Oral History Interview
PAC	Philip A. Crowl, Oral History Interviewer
PRO	Public Record Office, Kew, England
PU	Princeton University
RDC	Richard D. Challener, Oral History Interviewer
SS	Subject Series, DDE Papers
TCM	Telephone Conversations Memoranda, DDE Papers
UG	University of Georgia
UP	United Press
WHMS	White House Memoranda Series, DDE Papers
WHOSANSA	White House Office, Special Assistant for National Security Affairs
WKP	Wellington Koo Papers, Columbia University

PROLOGUE

1. Wiley T. Buchanan Oral History Interview (hereafter OHI) by Philip A. Crowl (hereafter PAC), 15 June 1966, pp. 28–29; David Waters OHI by PAC, 12 February 1966, p. 49, John Foster Dulles Oral History Collection, Princeton University Library (hereafter JFDOH); newspaper clippings, along with K. Okazaki Speech of 9 September 1959, Department of State Press Dispatch #488 (hereafter DSPD), United Press (hereafter UP) Dispatch, 26 May 1959, box 83, Allen Dulles Papers, Princeton University (hereafter PU); *New York Herald Tribune*, 28 May 1959, pp. 1–2; *Time*, 8 June 1959, p. 18; Arnold Heeney, *The Things That Are Ceasar's: Memoirs of a Canadian Public Servant* (Toronto: University of Toronto Press, 1972), 159. See also box 143, John Foster Dulles Papers, Princeton University (hereafter JFDP). It was the first "official" funeral for a secretary of state. To this day, only two other funerals, those of John F. Kennedy and Dwight D. Eisenhower, may be regarded as comparable, and the circumstances surrounding Kennedy's death were unique—an incumbent head of government and chief of state felled by an assassin's bullet. Although Eisenhower's funeral attracted more heads of government and chiefs of

state than that of his secretary, the ex-president was not accorded as high a level of representation by Britain, the Soviet Union, or Japan.

2. David and Deane Heller, *John Foster Dulles: Soldier for Peace* (New York: Harcourt Brace, 1960), 316; *Life*, 8 June 1959 (clipping), box 81, Allen Dulles Papers, PU; foreign press clippings on Dulles' funeral and UP dispatch, 26 May 1959, box 83, ibid.; *New York Herald Tribune*, 28 May 1959, p. 1.

3. For Dulles' early views on Europe and China, see John Foster Dulles (hereafter JFD), "Notes on the Situation in Europe," 7 October 1944; *Christian Science Monitor*, 7 July 1948, section 2, p. 1, boxes 282 and 398, JFDP; Koo-JFD Conversations (hereafter Conv.), 12 June 1950 and 27 December 1951, boxes 180, 184, Wellington Koo Papers, Columbia University (hereafter WKP).

4. George R. Packard III, *Protest in Tokyo: The Security Treaty Crisis of 1960* (Princeton: Princeton University Press, 1960), 5, 184, 233; Eleanor Lansing Dulles, *John Foster Dulles: The Last Year* (New York: Harcourt Brace, 1963), 232. The Kremlin fired rockets almost directly over Japan. It also took a hard line on the fishery talks, letting it be known that it regarded the security treaty as an intolerable provocation and that if Japan remained neutral, Moscow would guarantee such neutrality and create a nuclear-free zone in East Asia. At the same time, Japan would receive back certain islands taken from it after World War II. Soviet Defense Minister Malinovsky sent the Tokyo stock market into a tailspin with the announcement that his rocket commanders had been ordered to strike bases harboring American U-2s. Nor was this unusual. Again and again, Soviet officials threatened to destroy Japan if it continued to lean Westward.

INTRODUCTION

1. For a stunning example of how the centrality of Dulles' role in the Austrian State Treaty has escaped scholarly notice, see Audrey Kurth Cronin, *Great Power Politics and the Struggle over Austria, 1945–1955* (Ithaca: Cornell University Press, 1986). For examples of the prevailing historiography that depicts Dulles as anxious to involve the United States militarily in Vietnam (setting him off against an allegedly more restrained and statesmanlike Eisenhower), see Elmo Richardson, *The Presidency of Dwight D. Eisenhower* (Lawrence: University of Kansas Press, 1979), 76; Stephen E. Ambrose, *Eisenhower the President* (New York: Simon and Schuster, 1984), 177–79, 185 (hereafter *EP*); Townsend Hoopes, *The Devil and John Foster Dulles* (Boston: Little, Brown, 1973), 209–12; and Richard H. Immerman, "Prologue: Perceptions by the U.S. of Its Interests in Indochina," and Denise Artaud, "France Between the Indochina War and the European Defense Community," in Lawrence S. Kaplan, Denise Artaud, and Mark Rubin, eds., *Dien Bien Phu and the Crisis of Franco-American Relations, 1954–1955* (Wilmington: Scholarly Resources Press, 1990), 15–17, 269, 271, 273 (Artaud sees Dulles as intransigent, simplistic, and one-dimensional). For current (and conventional) accounts of Guatemala in 1954, see Richard H. Immerman, *The CIA in Guatemala: The Foreign Policy of Intervention* (Austin: University of Texas Press, 1982) along with Stephen Schlesinger and Stephen Kinzer, *Bitter Fruit: The Untold Story of the American Coup in Guatemala* (Garden City: Doubleday, 1982). For an example of the kind of punishment Dulles has received for his alleged policy on Suez, see Herman Finer, *Dulles over Suez* (Chicago: Quadrangle, 1964), 492–96; and William Bragg Ewald, Jr., *Eisenhower the President:*

Crucial Days, 1951–1960 (Englewood Cliffs: Prentice Hall, 1981), 212–13. For an analysis that reflects an astute awareness of the constraints imposed upon Dulles by American public opinion, see Michael A. Guhin, *John Foster Dulles: A Statesman and His Times* (New York: Columbia University Press, 1972). Guhin furnishes the best overall scholarly evaluation to date. Another outstanding volume, even if somewhat dated, is Louis Gerson, *John Foster Dulles* (New York: Cooper Square, 1967), especially valuable for its treatment of a number of specific issues such as the Matsu-Quemoy crisis of 1955. For still other works that demonstrate the high degree of restraint and sophistication that characterized Dulles' statecraft (in selected areas), see Kenneth T. Young, *Negotiating With the Chinese Communists: The United States Experience, 1953–1967* (New York: McGraw Hill, 1968); Leonard H. D. Gordon, "United States Opposition to the Use of Force in the Taiwan Strait, 1954–1962," *Journal of American History* 72 (December 1985): 637–60.

2. Barton Bernstein, "Foreign Policy in the Eisenhower Administration," *Foreign Service Journal* 50 (May 1973): 17–20, 29–30, 38, is excellent on early historiography. Richard H. Immerman is virtually alone in presenting Eisenhower and Dulles as working in close collaboration, with neither side dominant and Dulles having a relatively free hand. See Immerman, *CIA*, 14, 123; idem, "Eisenhower and Dulles: Who Made the Decisions?" *Political Psychology* 1 (Autumn 1979): 21–38. For accounts that portray Eisenhower as boss, see Chalmers M. Roberts, *First Rough Draft* (New York: Praeger, 1973), 107, 111; Hoopes, *Dulles*, 283, 307; Arthur Krock, *Memoirs: Sixty Years on the Firing Line* (New York: Funk and Wagnalls, 1968), 281; Milton Eisenhower, *The President is Calling* (Garden City: Doubleday, 1974), 274; R. Gordon Hoxie, "Eisenhower and Presidential Leadership," *Presidential Studies Quarterly* 13 (Fall 1983): 589–612; Donald Neff, *Warriors at Suez: Eisenhower Takes America into the Middle East* (New York: Simon and Schuster, 1981), 39; Burton I. Kaufman, *Trade and Aid: Eisenhower's Economic Policy, 1953–1961* (Baltimore: Johns Hopkins University Press, 1982), 7, 209; Warren I. Cohen, ed., *New Frontiers in American-East Asian Relations* (New York: Columbia University Press, 1983), 158–59; Bernstein, "Foreign Policy"; Richardson, *Eisenhower*, 99, 102 (and chaps. 5 and 8); Ambrose, *EP*, 185, 226, 229, 232, 442, 643; Stephen G. Rabe, *Eisenhower and Latin America: The Foreign Policy of Anticommunism* (Chapel Hill: University of North Carolina Press, 1988), 136; and Fred I. Greenstein, *The Hidden-Hand Presidency: Eisenhower as Leader* (New York: Basic Books, 1982). Greenstein likens Eisenhower to a "senior colleague" (p. 87) and portrays him as one who exerted himself decisively in successive crises without really appearing to (hence the term "hidden-hand"). For works that describe Dulles as the "prime mover," "creator," and "architect" of American foreign policy, see Richard Goold-Adams, *The Time of Power: A Reappraisal of John Foster Dulles* (London: Weidenfeld and Nicolson, 1962), 70; David Mayers, "Eisenhower's Containment Policy and the Major Communist Powers, 1953–1956," *International History Review* 5 (February 1983): 59–83; Andrew H. Berding, *Dulles on Diplomacy* (Princeton: Van Nostrand, 1965), 120, 172–73; Abba Solomon Eban, *Abba Eban: An Autobiography* (New York: Random House, 1977), 175; Roscoe Drummond and Gaston Coblentz, *Duel at the Brink: John Foster Dulles' Command of American Power* (Garden City: Doubleday, 1960), 25; Jacob D. Beam, *Multiple Exposure: An American Ambassador's Unique Perspective on East-West Issues* (New York: Norton, 1978), 44–45; John F. Kennedy,

"A Democrat Looks at Foreign Policy," *Foreign Affairs* 36 (October 1957): 56; and Chester Cooper, *The Lion's Last Roar: Suez 1956* (New York: Harper, 1978), 75.

3. Veteran journalist Arthur Krock referred to Dulles as the most widely misunderstood public official of his time. See Krock OHI by PAC, 20 February 1965, p. 6, JFDOH.

CHAPTER 1

1. For the Middle East, see Eban, *Autobiography*, 172; Janice Patricia Dooner, "John Foster Dulles, Anti-communism, and the Suez Canal Crisis of 1956–57" (Senior Thesis, Princeton University, 1981), 24.

2. For the opinion of Generals Twining and White (on preparedness for conventional warfare), see record of National Security Council Meeting, 1 May 1958, box 10, NSC Series, Ann Whitman File, Eisenhower Library, Abilene, Kansas (hereafter NSC). According to statistics on file at the U.S. Army Military History Institute at Carlisle Barracks, Pennsylvania, there were approximately 77,000 army officers in 1949 as compared with 105,000 in 1958. Enlisted army personnel increased from 583,000 (1949) to 794,000 (1958), and counting all services, the figure rose from 1,615,000 (1949) to 2,601,000 (1958).

3. For the bonanza in oil, see Christian Pineau, *1956/Suez* (Paris: R. Laffont, 1976), 194; *Time*, 28 January 1957, p. 33.

4. Kaufman, *Trade*, 208; Eisenhower (hereafter DDE) State of the Union Message, 12 January 1961, in Robert L. Branyan and Lawrence H. Larsen, eds., *The Eisenhower Administration, 1953–1961: A Documentary History* (New York: Random House, 1971), 2:1349; JFD Speech, 9 June 1956, box 102, JFDP; JFD, "Policy for Security and Peace," *Foreign Affairs* 32 (April 1954): 363.

5. *Daily Telegraph* (London), 25 May 1959, and London *Times* editorial, foreign press clippings on JFD funeral, box 83, Allen Dulles Papers, PU; quotation from Alexander DeConde, *The American Secretary of State*, in Berding, *Dulles*, 172.

6. See, for example, Paul-Henri Spaak, *The Continuing Battle: Memoirs of a European, 1936–1966*, trans. Henry Fox (London: Weidenfeld and Nicolson, 1971), 130–31; William B. Macomber, Jr. OHI by PAC, 12 and 19 January 1966, p. 40; Richard M. Nixon OHI by Richard D. Challener (hereafter RDC), 5 March 1965, p. 10, JFDOH; foreign press clippings on JFD funeral (quotation from Brazilian foreign minister), box 83, Allen Dulles Papers, PU; Maurice Couve de Murville, *Une politique étrangère 1958–1969* (Paris: Plon, 1971), 29.

7. John Robinson Beal, *John Foster Dulles: A Biography* (New York: Harper, 1957), 29–30; Eleanor Lansing Dulles OHI by PAC, 26 March to 22 April and 19 October 1965, pp. 32–33; John M. Allison OHI by RDC, 20 April 1969, p. 25, JFDOH; JFD Paper on Rogers Lamont, 14 September 1948, box 284, JFDP.

8. Macmillan was generally positive. See Richard M. Nixon, *Leaders* (New York: Warner, 1982), 151–53; Harold Macmillan, *Tides of Fortune, 1945–1955* (New York: Harper, 1969), 587–88, 634, 643, 651; idem, *Riding the Storm, 1956–1959* (London: Macmillan, 1971), 478, 589, 650; Georges Bidault, *Resistance: The Political Autobiography of Georges Bidault* (New York: Praeger, 1967), 94, 170; Drummond and Coblentz, *Duel*, 213; George V. Allen OHI by PAC, 29 July 1965, pp. 21–22; Couve de Murville OHI by PAC, 19 June 1964, p. 34; René Mayer OHI by Loftus Becker, 28 June 1967, p. 12, JFDOH; DSPD #488 and 1432, box 83, Allen Dulles Papers,

PU; Winthrop Aldrich OHI #250 by David Berliner, 16 October 1972, p. 18, Dwight D. Eisenhower Library, Abilene, Kansas (hereafter EL), Columbia University Oral History copyright (hereafter CUOHC); Couve de Murville, *Politique*, 29; Lord Moran, *Churchill: Taken from the Diaries of Lord Moran, 1940–1965* (Boston: Houghton Mifflin, 1965), 540, 580. De Gaulle was not an uncritical admirer of Dulles. For his reservations, see Charles de Gaulle, *Memoirs of Hope: Renewal and Endeavor* (New York: Simon and Schuster, 1971), 208–9.

9. Meir did not always speak critically of Dulles, but the reservations are clear in her autobiography. See Mary Pillsbury Lord OHI by RDC, 21 June 1966, p. 31; Christian Pineau OHI by PAC, 16 June 1965, JFDOH; London *Evening Standard*, 1 April 1957 (clipping) and John Hay Whitney to JFD, 25 March 1957, box 113, JFDP; Heeney, *Memoirs*, 145; Golda Meir, *My Life* (New York: Putnam's Sons, 1975), 306.

10. Camille Chamoun OHI by Dr. R. Bayly Winder, 28 August 1964, p. 6; Chiang Kai-shek OHI by Spencer Davis, 24 September 1964, p. 33; Couve de Murville OHI, p. 32; Paik Too-Chin OHI by Spencer Davis, 28 September 1965, p. 21; Katsuo Okazaki OHI by Spencer Davis, 2 October 1964, p. 29; Yung Tai Pyun OHI by Spencer Davis, 29 September 1964, p. 21; Admiral Sohn Won Yil OHI by Spencer Davis, 29 September 1964, p. 1; General Carlos P. Romulo OHI by Spencer Davis, 28 October 1965, p. 47; Nixon OHI, p. 16 (on Dulles' craftiness); Shigeru Yoshida OHI by Spencer Davis, 30 September 1964, pp. 22–23, JFDOH; Hoopes, *Dulles*, 53; Bidault, *Resistance*, 94, 170; Drummond and Coblentz, *Duel*, 19, 179; Christian Pineau, *Nikita Serguéevitch Khrouchtchev* (Paris: Perrin, 1965), 186; Hervé Alphand, *L'Etonnement d'être: journal, 1939–1973* (Paris: Fayard, 1977), 288–89; Herbert Morrison, *Herbert Morrison: An Autobiography* (London: Odham's Press, 1960), 280, 282, 298; Sir William Hayter, *A Double Life* (London: Hamilton, 1974), 156–57; Robert Cutler, *No Time for Rest* (Boston: Little, Brown, 1966), 334 ("there was no trace in him of the devious or the chicane").

11. John Emmet Hughes, *The Ordeal of Power* (New York: Atheneum, 1963), 105, 112, 119, 169, 207–8 (views Dulles as disturbingly hawkish); Charles E. Bohlen, *Witness to History, 1929–1969* (New York: Norton, 1973), 473 (portrays Dulles as overextending the United States by way of treaty networks and bases); C. M. Woodhouse, *British Foreign Policy Since the Second World War* (New York: Praeger, 1962), 73; Adam Ulam, *The Rivals: America and Russia Since World War II* (New York: Viking, 1971), 132, 147, 214, 231; Stewart Alsop OHI by RDC, 4 February 1966, p. 7; Marquis Childs OHI by RDC, 12 January 1966, p. 22; Joseph Sisco OHI by PAC, 12 August 1966, p. 24, JFDOH; *Harper's* (August 1956): 31, box 5, George F. Kennan Papers, PU; Ambrose, *EP*, 621; Waldemar J. Gallman, *Iraq Under General Nuri* (Baltimore: Johns Hopkins University Press, 1964), 184–92, 194, 198; Roberts, *Rough Draft*, 111 (sees Ike as having brought a thaw to the cold war); Henry A. Kissinger, "Reflections on American Diplomacy," *Foreign Affairs* 35 (October 1956): 51–52 (critical of pacts); Heeney, *Memoirs*, 115, 178 (agrees with Roberts); Cooper, *Lion's Last Roar*, 64 (critical of pacts).

12. Lord Home of the Hirsel OHI by author, 23 July 1986. For an example of recent trends in academia reflecting skepticism as to the validity of the Monroe Doctrine, see Immerman, *CIA*, 7–19.

13. For gaps in the Alphand diary, see Alphand, *Journal*, comparing the first six months of 1954 with other periods. Box 191 of the Koo Papers (WKP) was found to contain no Robertson-Koo conversations for the critical period 12 February through

7 April 1954. For Iran and Britain, see FO 371/104567, Public Record Office, Kew, England (hereafter PRO). For an example of the withholding of confidential annexes, see CAB 128/27, PRO (which, at the time that the present research was in progress, contained very few confidential annexes). Box 10 of the Eisenhower Library's Dulles Files, Telephone Conversations Memoranda (Princeton University transcripts), was found to contain nothing for the important interval 27 February through 17 March 1954. Then, too, the Foreign Relations series reveals another gaping hole in connection with the fall of Dien Bien Phu: volume 5 (pt. 1) becomes increasingly thin after 29 April 1954. In fact, the actual fall of Dien Bien Phu is never reported. There is also nothing on the period 20 May to 2 June. See United States Department of State, *Papers on the Foreign Relations of the United States, 1952–1954*, vol. 5, pt. 1 (Washington, D.C.: U.S. Government Printing Office, 1983)—hereafter FR.

14. See DDE, *Mandate for Change, 1953–1956* (Garden City: Doubleday, 1963), 341; idem, *Waging Peace, 1956–1961* (Garden City: Doubleday, 1965), 39, 73, 295.

15. For a relatively recent work that helps to bridge the gap, see Eleanor Dulles' authoritative *John Foster Dulles: The Last Year*. For earlier works on the side of Dulles, see Berding, *Dulles*; Beal, *Dulles*; Drummond and Coblentz, *Duel*; Heller and Heller, *Dulles*; and Henry P. Van Dusen, ed., *The Spiritual Legacy of John Foster Dulles* (Philadelphia: Westminster Press, 1960). For works by State Department officials and members of the Foreign Service, see Bohlen, *Witness*; Winthrop Aldrich, "The Suez Crisis: A Footnote to History," *Foreign Affairs* 45 (April 1967): 541–52; Robert R. Bowie, *Suez, 1956* (London: Oxford University Press, 1974); Beam, *Multiple Exposure*; John M. Allison, *Ambassador from the Prairie, or, Allison Wonderland* (Boston: Houghton Mifflin, 1973). For works written by Eisenhower's lieutenants or by the president himself (in addition to his two-volume memoirs), see DDE, *At Ease* (Garden City: Doubleday, 1967); Milton Eisenhower, *The Wine is Bitter* (Garden City: Doubleday, 1963); idem, *The President is Calling* (Garden City: Doubleday, 1974); John S. D. Eisenhower, ed., *Letters to Mamie* (Garden City: Doubleday, 1977); Robert H. Ferrell, ed., *The Eisenhower Diaries* (New York: Norton, 1981); idem, *The Diary of James C. Hagerty: Eisenhower in Mid-Course, 1954–1955* (Bloomington: Indiana University Press, 1983); Sherman Adams, *Firsthand Report* (New York: Harper, 1961); Cutler, *No Time for Rest*; James Rhyne Killian, *Sputnik Scientists and Eisenhower: A Memoir of the First Special Assistant to the President for Science and Technology* (Cambridge: MIT Press, 1977); Arthur Larson, *Eisenhower: The President Nobody Knew* (New York: Scribner's, 1968); Henry Cabot Lodge, Jr., *As It Was* (New York: Norton 1976); idem, *The Storm Has Many Eyes* (New York: Norton, 1973); Matthew B. Ridgway, *Soldier: The Memoirs of Matthew R. Ridgway* (New York: Harper, 1956); Arthur W. Radford, *From Pearl Harbor to Vietnam: The Memoirs of Admiral Arthur W. Radford*, ed. Stephen Jurika, Jr. (Stanford: Stanford University Press, 1980).

16. Mark G. Toulouse, *The Transformation of John Foster Dulles* (Macon: Mercer University Press, 1985); Albert N. Keim, "John Foster Dulles and the Protestant World Order Movement on the Eve of World War II," *Journal of Church and State* 21 (Winter 1979): 73–89; John M. Mulder, "The Moral World of John Foster Dulles," *Journal of Presbyterian History* 49 (Summer 1971): 157–82. In the case of Adenauer, for example, only the first volume of his mutlivolume set of memoirs has been translated into English. Among French sympathizers whose works are not available in English, one can cite Christian Pineau, Couve de Murville, and Paul Ely. For

the British side, see Morrison, *Autobiography*; Macmillan, *Riding the Storm* and *Tides of Fortune* (Macmillan is sometimes complimentary, but not by any means always); Baron Richard Austen Butler, *The Art of the Possible: The Memoirs of Lord Butler* (London: Hamish Hamilton, 1971); Anthony Nutting, *I Saw for Myself: The Aftermath of Suez* (Garden City: Doubleday, 1958); idem, *No End of a Lesson: The Story of Suez* (New York: Clarkson N. Potter, 1967); David Dilks, ed., *The Diaries of Sir Alexander Cadogan* (New York: Putnam's, 1972); Ivone Kirkpatrick, *The Inner Circle* (London: Macmillan, 1959); Earl of Kilmuir, *Political Adventure: The Memoirs of the Earl of Kilmuir* (London: Weidenfeld and Nicolson, 1964); Lieutenant General Sir John Bagot Glubb, *A Soldier With the Arabs* (London: Hodder and Stoughton, 1957); Glubb, *Britain and the Arabs* (London: Hodder and Stoughton, 1957); Anthony Eden, *Full Circle: The Memoirs of Anthony Eden* (Boston: Houghton Mifflin, 1960); Selwyn Lloyd, *Suez 1956: A Personal Account* (London: Jonathan Cape, 1978). Lloyd is an exception as far as the British are concerned since he is basically friendly.

17. Gerard Smith OHI by PAC, 13 October 1965, pp. 8–9, JFDOH; JFD Press Conference (hereafter Conf.), 10 January 1958, box 125, JFDP; James Russell Wiggins, "Notes," 4 April 1958, box 2, Additional Papers, JFDP (hereafter DAP); JFD-DDE Conv., 12 August 1958, box 7, White House Memoranda Series (hereafter WHMS), EL; Gerson, *Dulles*, 309. For the British position see Macmillan, *Storm*, 464–65, 476; Wiggins, "Notes," 4 April 1958, box 2, DAP; JFD-Gruenther Conv., 19 February 1958, box 1, General Correspondence and Memoranda Series (hereafter GCMS), EL; Ambrose, *EP*, 403 (Macmillan's position seems to have shifted by late 1959; ibid., 538).

18. Robert Richardson Bowie OHI by RDC, 10 August 1964, p. 8; Philip Kingsland Crowe OHI by RDC, 4 October 1965, p. 12, JFDOH; Berding, *Dulles*, 123; Hugh Thomas, *Suez* (New York: Harper, 1966), 156 (re: "a remarkable capacity"); Vandenberg to JFD, 16 September 1949, box 3, Arthur H. Vandenberg Papers, Michigan Historical Collections, Bentley Historical Library, Ann Arbor, Michigan (hereafter MHCBHL). Niebuhr and Kennan are discussed in a later chapter.

19. George F. Kennan letter to the *New York Times*, 28 October 1956; *Sunday Patriot News*, 7 September 1958, p. 9; *New York Herald Tribune*, 21 September 1958 (clipping); idem, "Foreign Policy and Christian Conscience," *The Atlantic* 203 (May 1959): 47–49; *New York Times* Magazine, 12 September 1954, and *U.S. News and World Report*, 29 June 1956, boxes 4, 5, and 7, George F. Kennan Papers, PU; idem, *Russia, the Atom and the West* (New York: Harper, 1957), 62–63, 70–71, 105 (originally, Kennan opposed Peking's admission to the United Nations, but he soon changed his mind).

20. Heller and Heller, *Dulles*, 56; Christian Herter OHI by RDC, 31 August 1964, p. 2; Eustace Seligman OHI by RDC, 26 March 1965, p. 10; Edward J. Shedd OHI by Gordon A. Craig, February 1966, p. 20, JFDOH; Philip K. Crowe, "Recollections of John Foster Dulles," July 1962, box 2, DAP; Introduction to "Eleven Documents Relating to John Foster Dulles' Work With the War Trade Board and Paris Peace, Including Correspondence with President Wilson," AM 16001, General Manuscripts, bd., PU (hereafter ED); JFD Memorandum (hereafter Memo), 1 April 1919; Baruch and Lamont to Lansing, 30 May 1919; Wilson to JFD, 27 June 1919, ED.

21. Roswell Barnes OHI by PAC, 24 July 1964, p. 9; George S. Franklin, Jr. OHI by RDC, 12 March 1965, pp. 10–11, JFDOH; Gerson, *Dulles*, 24–26. Dulles was

employed as legal counsel by the banks of England, France, China, Spain, and Poland. He was also retained by the governments of the Netherlands, Panama (to draft a new legal code), and Britain (for its wartime purchasing mission). He worked closely with Beneš at Versailles and personally accompanied Masaryk to the U.S. Treasury Department to draw a check that established the new nation of Czechoslovakia; JFD, *War or Peace* (New York: Macmillan, 1950), 142. After the war, he represented a wide array of clients including Ruhr industrialists on trial before French courts martial (he persuaded them to cease resistance) and American bankers unable to collect principal or interest on their German bonds. See Heller and Heller, *Dulles*, 74–75; miscellaneous undated manuscript in handwriting (author unknown) in box 279, JFDP. He also participated in the financing of the Young Plan, served as special counsel to the underwriters of the Dawes loan, and helped to work out a stabilization plan for the Polish zloty. In addition to big cases such as those involving Credit Lyonnais and bondholder claims against the match empire of Kreuger and Toll, he helped to organize Brazil's Port of Para Company and to recover deposits of Polish gold from Nazi-occupied France. In Berlin, he dealt mainly with Reischsbank President Hjalmar Schacht. On one occasion, he accepted an invitation from Hitler to attend a piano recital by Walter Gieseking. At the same time, sensitive to the anti-Semitic tone of the German government, he closed down his Berlin branch office in 1934. It was as chairman of the Federal Council's Commission for a Just and Durable Peace that he held the study conferences at his home, and in 1941 his commission published "Six Pillars of Peace," bringing the first significant organized criticism to bear upon Roosevelt's Atlantic Charter for its failure to stipulate a successor to Wilson's League. Following the Dumbarton Oaks Conference in the fall of 1944, Dulles again took aim at the Roosevelt administration for neglecting the rights and wishes of smaller nations; Barnes OHI, pp. 5–6, 9, JFDOH; Arthur Dean, "John Foster Dulles, 1888–1959: An Appreciation" (acknowledged by PU as a gift, 4 February 1960), box 1, DAP.

22. See box 278, JFDP for the pre-1953 corpus of Dulles' work.

23. Vandenberg Diary, 4, 5, 7, 8, 20, 23 June 1945; JFD to Vandenberg, 5 December 1949, boxes 3 and 6, Vandenberg Papers, MHCBHL; JFD, *War or Peace*, chap. 11; Theodore C. Achilles OHI by PAC, 7 May 1966, pp. 1–3; Clarence Dillon OHI by RDC, 21 October 1965, p. 8, JFDOH; JFD Press Conf., 24 January 1954, box 78, JFDP; Gerson, *Dulles*, 42; Dean, "Appreciation," box 1, DAP. At the 1948 session of the United Nations, Dulles diverged from the line taken by his superiors, Marshall and Rusk. In so doing, he helped Israel to defeat the Bernadotte Plan which would have (1) deprived the new state of land in Galilee and the Negev, (2) internationalized Jerusalem, and (3) made Haifa a free port with a corridor to Jordan. Instead, Dulles supported a resolution leaving the determination of frontiers to Arab and Jew, and he did much to secure its acceptance. He also played a large part in winning approval for the pro-Jewish Genocide Convention which was opposed by Moscow; JFD Memo in JFD to Vandenberg, 5 December 1949, box 3, Vandenberg Papers, MHCBHL; Ernest Gross OHI by RDC, 1964, pp. 6, 8–13, JFDOH; U.S. Senate "Hearing Before the Committee on Foreign Relations, 83rd Congress, 2nd Session: Statements of Secretary of State John Foster Dulles and Admiral Arthur Radford, Chairman of the Joint Chiefs of Staff" (Washington, D.C.: United States Government Printing Office, 1954), 34; Henry Cabot Lodge OHI by RDC, 16 Feb-

ruary 1965, p. 2; Abba Eban OHI by Louis L. Gerson, 28 May 1964, pp. 3–6, JFDOH; Paper on Rogers Lamont, 14 September 1948, box 284, JFDP.

24. Eban, *Autobiography*, 188 (on Rayburn); *Time*, 21 January 1957, p. 27.

25. Theodore C. Sorensen, *Kennedy* (New York: Bantam, 1966), 276.

26. Stephen E. Ambrose, *Nixon: The Education of a Politician* (New York: Simon and Schuster, 1987), 148; Norman A. Graebner, ed., *Ideas and Diplomacy* (New York: Oxford University Press, 1964), 88; John L. Gaddis, *The United States and the Origins of the Cold War* (New York: Columbia University Press, 1972), 349–52.

27. A 1952 National Security Council Memorandum (hereafter NSC Memo) envisioned the fall of one Southeast Asian nation as an event leading to the fall of others and then to the communization of India, the Middle East, and even Western Europe: Richard M. Nixon, *No More Vietnams* (New York: Arbor House, 1985), 29. For Trieste, see Roberto Rabel, "Prologue to Containment: The Truman Administration's Response to the Trieste Crisis of May 1945," *Diplomatic History* 10 (Spring 1986): 155, 159n.

28. Trevor Barnes, "The Secret Cold War: The C.I.A. and American Foreign Policy in Europe, 1946–1956, Pt. II," *The Historical Journal* (of England) 25 (September 1982): 656–59; Schlesinger and Kinzer, *Bitter Fruit*, 102–3 (on Truman's support of "Operation Fortune" in Guatemala); DDE, *Mandate*, 166–68. Dulles, one might add, was entirely in sympathy with the French effort in Vietnam. See JFD Speech to the French National Political Science Institute, 5 May 1952, and Speech to the National Conference of Christians and Jews, 12 May 1952, box 107, H. Alexander Smith Papers, PU. For the link between Korea and Vietnam, see Bernard B. Fall, *Hell in a Very Small Place: The Siege of Dien Bien Phu* (New York: Vantage, 1967), 294.

29. George C. Herring and Richard H. Immerman, "Eisenhower, Dulles and Dienbienphu: 'The Day We Didn't Go to War' Revisited," *Journal of American History* 71 (September 1984): 353; Branyan and Larsen, eds., *Eisenhower*, 1:233–34; Memo on Congressional Leadership Conference, 3 April 1954, box 7, Chronological Series, EL (hereafter CS); Makins to Eden, 11 April and 25 May 1953, FO 371/103495, PRO (on Bricker, Dulles, and the *Washington Post*); Makins to Foreign Office (hereafter FO), 3 August 1953, FO 371/103496, PRO; Melvin Gurtov, *The First Vietnam Crisis: Chinese Communist Strategy and United States Involvement, 1953–1954* (New York: Columbia University Press, 1967), 34.

30. DDE Diary, 22 January 1952, in Ferrell, ed., *Eisenhower*, 212. According to Robert Cutler, Ike's special assistant for national security affairs, the amount spent on missile development soared from $1 million annually under Truman to some billions a year under Eisenhower ("We had to catch up for seven 'lost years'"); Cutler, *No Time for Rest*, 349. See also DA to SCAP, 5 August 1950, #042322Z, Messages State Department In, RG 9, Douglas MacArthur Papers, MacArthur Memorial Archives, Norfolk, Virginia (on Korean military equipment).

31. According to Congressman Walter Judd, the Russians, at one stroke, gave the Red Chinese more military equipment than Washington had furnished to Chiang throughout the period (Mao received enough in a single year, 1945, to keep a million men under arms for five years). See Judd OHI by PAC, 11 December 1965, JFDOH; Knowland-DDE Phone Conv., 31 October 1956, DDE Diaries, Ann Whitman File (hereafter AWF), EL; Ambrose, *EP*, 202; DDE-JFD-Yeh Conv., 2 January 1953, box 187, WKP.

32. Alexander Smith OHI by PAC, 16 April 1964, p. 38, JFDOH; U. Alexis Johnson, *The Right Hand of Power* (Englewood Cliffs: Prentice Hall, 1984), 231; DDE to Churchill, 10 February 1955, PREM 11/879, PRO. For the battle over Quemoy in 1949, see box 137, JFDP. Chou continued even after 1954 to shun Trevelyan; indeed the British envoy was kept waiting for another decade before finally receiving full recognition. See also Walter Robertson OHI by PAC, 23–24 July 1965, pp. 49–52, JFDOH. Robertson speaks bitterly of the fact that (1) Marshall cut off the flow of American ammunition to Chiang in order to induce the latter's acquiescence in a coalition government; (2) Marshall withheld a $500 million loan to Chiang for some thirteen critical months, again with the idea of forcing coalition; and (3) Europe received $14 billion while Chiang could not obtain $500 million (ibid., pp. 6–8).

33. Roberts, *Rough Draft*, 110; Makins to Eden, 2 May 1953, FO 371/103495; Makins to FO, 3 August 1953, FO 371/103496, PRO (on the *New York Times'* position).

34. The figure 33 percent comprised a total of fifteen nations. According to the Sino-Soviet treaty of alliance (1950), both parties would render "military and other assistance with all the means at their disposal" should either party be attacked by Japan or by one of Japan's allies. See DDE to Churchill, 10 February 1955, PREM 11/879, PRO. With reference to White, Attorney General Brownell revealed on 6 November 1953 that the FBI had conclusive evidence to substantiate charges of disloyalty—evidence which Eisenhower later described in his memoirs as "incontrovertible." According to Walter Judd, White took poison. See DDE, *Mandate*, 315; Judd OHI, p. 34, JFDOH.

35. Judd OHI, pp. 19–25, JFDOH. According to Donald B. Lourie, under secretary of state for administration, Senator Hickenlooper received an anonymous letter naming twenty-one homosexuals in the State Department. Truman, who was then president, let seventeen of them go. Ike then passed judgment on four more who held influential posts (Lourie OHI by RDC, 8 April 1965, p. 32, JFDOH). According to Congressman Judd, only a very small percentage of the hundred that were dismissed by Truman filed any formal protest. Then, following the election of 1948 in which Democrats won a House majority, the subcommittee was abolished. It still had a roster of over a hundred names to investigate, and it was this list that was leaked to Senator McCarthy (who sat on the corresponding Senate Government Operations Committee). This was also the list that the senator from Wisconsin imprudently brandished in a speech at Wheeling, West Virginia. McCarthy did not have any actual names at the time, only State Department numbers, and when pressed he could not produce. Moreover, the individuals in question were merely suspects at the time (Judd OHI, pp. 31–36, JFDOH).

36. John J. Bly, "The Diplomacy of John Foster Dulles in Negotiating the Japanese Peace Treaty" (Master's Thesis, East Texas State University, 1979), pp. 24–26, 32–34; Roberts, *Rough Draft*, 102.

37. Lodge, *As It Was*, 35; National Security Council (hereafter NSC) Meeting, 11 February 1953, box 4, NSC Series, AWF (hereafter simply NSC); Gerson, *Dulles*, 96; JFD to DDE, 12 November 1954, FR (1952–54), 5:1471; Makins to Eden 17 January 1953, FO 371/103495, PRO.

38. Vernon A. Walters, *Silent Missions* (Garden City: Doubleday, 1978), chap. 8; Schlesinger and Kinzer, *Bitter Fruit*, 103; Miguel Ydígoras Fuentes, *My War With*

Communism, As Told to Mario Rosenthal (Englewood Cliffs: Prentice Hall, 1963), 8; JFD confirmation testimony, FO 371/103510, PRO.

39. Richard M. Nixon, *Memoirs of Richard Nixon* (New York: Grosset and Dunlap, 1978), 118; Woodhouse, *British Foreign Policy*, 39, 56; William Colby and Peter Forbath, *Honorable Men: My Life in the CIA* (New York: Simon and Schuster, 1978), 110–11; Loy Henderson OHI by Don North, 14 December 1970, pp. 42–43, EL (CUOHC); Packard, *Tokyo*, 25; Makins to FO, 6 March 1953, PREM 11/431, PRO; Peter L. Hahn, "Containment and Egyptian Nationalism: The Unsuccessful Effort to Establish a Middle East Command, 1950–53," *Diplomatic History* 11 (Winter 1987): 23–40.

40. Drummond and Coblentz, *Duel*, 183; Stephen E. Ambrose, *Ike's Spies* (Garden City: Doubleday, 1981), 272; JFD-DDE Conv., 30 July 1958, box 7, WHMS; miscellaneous item, August 1957, DH; Packard, *Tokyo*, 59; Ambrose, *EP*, 168, 341–42; Kennan, *Russia*, 2–3; M. L. Oliphant, "Confidential Report on Visit to Russia, May 1956," CHAN II 4/15-3, Viscount Chandos Papers (Oliver Lyttelton), Churchill College, Cambridge; H. W. Brands, Jr., "Blueprint for Quagmires, or Keeping the SOBs on Our Side: The Eisenhower Administration and Third World Authoritarianism," Society for Historians of American Foreign Relations *Newsletter* 17 (March 1986): 5.

41. Joseph Stalin, *Problems in Leninism* (New York: International Publishers, 1934), 19–20, 26–27, 64, 66; idem, *Leninism* (New York: International Publishers, 1928), 354–55.

42. Drummond and Coblentz, *Duel*, 158; Kaufman, *Trade*, 63–65; Woodhouse, *British Foreign Policy*, 51; Neff, *Warriors*, 256–57; Krock Notes (7 October 1959?), #331A, bk. 2, box 1, Arthur Krock Papers, PU.

43. Unidentified Memo read by Dulles and dated 14 June 1957, box 114, JFDP. See also International-General File, Richard Russell Papers, University of Georgia (hereafter UG).

CHAPTER 2

1. For Eisenhower's cosmopolitan instincts and background, see DDE Diary, 5 July 1942, in Ferrell, ed., *Eisenhower*, 70; DDE, *Mamie*, 21, 56, 79, 87, 155, 163, 181, 205; idem, *At Ease*, 272, 278–80, 309–10, 377; idem, *Mandate*, 143, 241; idem, *Waging Peace*, 420; idem, *Crusade in Europe* (Garden City: Doubleday, 1948), 61, 77, 79, 85, 100–101, 186, 194, 220, 241, 248, 309, 362–63, 461, 466, 473–74; Harry C. Butcher, *My Three Years with Eisenhower* (New York: Simon and Schuster, 1946), 76, 109, 114; Robert R. Bowie OHI #102 by Ed Edwin, 10 August 1967, pp. 1–7, EL (CUOHC).

2. DDE Diary, 7 February 1954, in Ferrell, ed., *Eisenhower*, 273–74; DDE, *Crusade*, 458, 466, 472; James C. Hagerty OHI by Ed Edwin, 2 February 1968, p. 194, EL (CUOHC), NSC Meeting, 4 March 1954, box 5, NSC.

3. Merriman Smith, *A President's Odyssey* (New York: Harper, 1961), 269; DDE, *Waging Peace*, 21, 104, 287, 439, 484, 493, 510; Ambrose, *EP*, 543. For Dulles, as opposed to Eisenhower, on such issues as poverty, social reform, communism, and Latin America, see Adams, *Firsthand Report*, 66; Larson, *Eisenhower*, 100–101.

4. DDE, *Crusade*, 300; Butcher, *Eisenhower*, 137–38, 150, 377, 383–84, 487; Lloyd, *Suez*, 37; Hagerty OHI, pp. 193–94, EL (CUOHC).

5. John Gunther, *Eisenhower: The Man and the Symbol* (New York: Harper, 1951), 27, 54, 59, 140; Eisenhower, *Wine*, 187; DDE Farewell Message, 17 January 1961, in Branyan and Larsen, eds., *Eisenhower*, vol. 2, 1375; Andrew J. Goodpaster OHI #37 by Ed Edwin, 2 August 1967, p. 113, EL (CUOHC); Goodpaster OHI #477 by Malcolm McDonald, 10 April 1982, pp. 13–14, EL; Russell "Notes on Legislative Leaders' Meeting," 13 December 1955; Richard Nixon OHI by Hugh Cates and Robert Stevens, Jr., 13 April 1978, p. 17, Russell Papers, UG.

6. Goold-Adams, *Dulles*, 38; Avery Dulles letter to the *New York Times*, 28 September 1975, DAP, JFDP; Allen Dulles OHI by PAC, 17 May and 3 June 1965, pp. 3, 8–9, 12, 36; Eleanor Dulles OHI, p. 11; Richard K. Benson OHI by PAC, 8 July 1965, p. 21; Mrs. W. Randolph Burgess OHI by PAC, 24 August 1966, p. 42; Crowe OHI, p. 30; Gene C. Stanton Babcock OHI by PAC, 23 July 1964, pp. 14–15; Clarence Dillon OHI by RDC, 21 October 1965, p. 7; Margaret Dulles Edwards OHI by RDC, 23 April 1965, p. 39; Arthur Eldridge OHI by PAC, 8 July 1965, pp. 20–21; Hagerty OHI, p. 41; John W. Hanes, Jr. OHI by PAC, 29 January and 22 August 1966, pp. 220, 232; Robert F. Hart OHI by PAC, 6 July 1965, p. 25; Charles Lucet OHI by PAC, 18 July 1966, pp. 2–3; Phyllis Bernau OHI by PAC, 8 January 1966, p. 44; Sir Thomas MacDonald OHI by PAC, 11 June 1964, p. 4; Nixon OHI, p. 17; George D. Woods OHI by RDC, 3 March 1966, p. 5, JFDOH; *Washington Post Parade*, 20 February 1955 (clipping); *Daily Princetonian*, 24 May 1959, p. 1, boxes 66 and 83, Allen Dulles Papers, PU; JFD Diary, 6, 10, 18 January 1911 and 28 January 1919, box 278, JFDP; Richard Harkness, "Memoranda and Notes on Visits and Interviews with JFD" (second half of 1958 or 1959); Dean, "Appreciation," pp. 14–16, box 1, DAP; "Commission des Réparations des dommages Procès-Verbal, No. 114," ED; *Reader's Digest* clipping (November 1951), box 399, JFDP; Eleanor Lansing Dulles to her father, 21 March (1909?); JFD to his grandfather, 27 December 1908; JFD to Eleanor, 31 January 1909, box 20, Eleanor Lansing Dulles Papers, PU; *Time*, 1 June 1959, p. 12; Lord Home of the Hirsel, *The Way the Wind Blows: An Autobiography* (New York: Quadrangle, 1976), 109; Dulles, *Dulles*, 125.

7. DDE Diary, 16 September 1947, 6 November 1950, 17 March 1951, 22 January 1952, 18 January 1954, in Ferrell, ed., *Eisenhower*, 143, 181, 190, 210, 212, 271; DDE, *At Ease*, 126, 229; Lodge, *As It Was*, 105, 113; Sir John Wheeler-Bennett, ed., *Action This Day: Working with Churchill* (New York: St. Martin's, 1968), 133 (Lord Salisbury found Ike to be more of a Russophobe than Dulles); DDE, *Mandate*, 8, 33, 139, 148, 357, 446; idem, *Waging Peace*, 368; idem, *Crusade*, 4, 473; Gunther, *Eisenhower*, 43; DDE Farewell Message, 17 January 1961, in Branyan and Larsen, eds., *Eisenhower*, 2:1374; DDE OHI by Raymond Henle, 13 July 1967, pp. 10, 26, EL; Moran, *Churchill*, 537; JFD, *War or Peace*, 262.

8. DDE Diary, 26 May 1946, 16 September 1947, in Ferrell, ed., *Eisenhower*, 137, 144; Lodge, *As It Was*, 62; Adams, *Firsthand Report*, 65; Herbert S. Parmet, *Eisenhower and the American Crusades* (New York: Macmillan, 1972), 161; DDE, *Waging Peace*, 125, 239; Butcher, *Eisenhower*, 118, 257, 273; Cutler, *No Time for Rest*, 302; DDE State of the Union Address, 6 January 1955; DDE Second Inaugural Address, 21 January 1957; DDE Message to the U.S. Armed Forces in Lebanon, 19 July 1958; DDE Address to the UN General Assembly, 13 August 1958, in Branyan and Larsen, eds., *Eisenhower*, 1:448, 463, 628–29; 2:728, 742; Walters, *Silent Missions*, 223; "Back to God" Program, 3 February 1957, box 116, JFDP; Emmet Hughes, Diary Notes of Meetings, box 3, Emmet Hughes Papers, PU (for Ike's

profanity); Vernon Walters OHI by Dr. John Wickman, 21 April 1970, p. 61, EL; Ambrose, *EP*, 38; JFD Address, 22 October 1958, file 556–122, Historical Commission of the Kuomintang, Yangmingshan Archives (hereafter HCKMT).

9. DDE, *Waging Peace*, 610; idem, *At Ease*, 311; idem, *Mandate*, 248; George M. Humphrey OHI by PAC, 5 May 1964, pp. 8, 10–11, JFDOH; JFD Meeting with Aides, 28 March 1955; JFD-DDE Conv., 26 December 1955, boxes 2 and 3, WHMS; Ambrose, *EP*, 399, 404, 448–50, 453, 608–9, 615, 643, 656–57, 660, 664–65; Toulouse, *Dulles*, 111; Dean Rusk OHI by Karen Kelly, 15 August 1980, Russell Papers, UG; Edward C. Keefer, "President Dwight D. Eisenhower and the End of the Korean War," *Diplomatic History* 10 (Summer 1986): 271–72, 276–77. By mid-February 1953, Dulles was paying lip service to Eisenhower's position on atomic weapons (NSC Meetings, 11 and 18 February 1953, box 4, NSC). Yet, he did so reluctantly. As late as 1958 he still recoiled from the idea of using tactical atomic weapons, even in the Quemoy theater. It is interesting to recall, too, that just as Dulles had urged Ike to consult his allies on the use of atomic weaponry and the widening of the war in Korea, he also had recourse to an alleged sense of Congress in trying to sell his chief a softer line on Rhee. See Keefer, "Korean War," 271, 285; DDE, *Waging Peace*, 295.

10. Winthrop W. Aldrich OHI by RDC, 15 July 1964, p. 2, JFDOH; Gerson, *Dulles*, 133–35; Makins to Eden, 28 February 1953, FO 371/103495; Makins to FO, 8 January 1953, PREM 371/422, PRO.

11. Eden to Steele, 20 November 1952, PREM 11/323; DDE to Churchill, 5 May 1953, PREM 11/421; Churchill to DDE, 10 and 12 April 1953, PREM 11/429, PRO. Churchill was aptly described by one official in the foreign office as "an old man in a hurry" who seemed "afflicted by a strange mixture of conscience and conceit"—a "formidable psychological fortress" against which "the weapons of logic and caution make little, if any, impression." His general line was, "Don't let's be beastly with the Bear," and he clearly felt not only that the Russians were willing to let go of their zone (politically) but also that a divided Germany was a greater risk than a neutral Germany united. See (Nutting?) to Eden, 25 June 1953, AP 20/16, 127, Avon Papers, Birmingham University, England (hereafter AP). Eden described Churchill's lust for summitry as his "lunatic obsession." See Robert Rhodes James,' *Anthony Eden* (London: Weidenfeld and Nicolson, 1986), 392.

12. Hughes, *Ordeal*, 105, 112; Larson, *Eisenhower*, 74–75; JFD Memo, 30 April 1954, box 2, DH; NSC Meetings, 31 March, 8 April, and 13 May 1953, box 4, NSC; JFD to Nitze, 14 July 1950, FR (1950), 7:386–87; Makins to Eden, 11 April 1953, FO 371/103495, PRO; JFD-Pearson Conv., 15 February 1953, vol. 4, Lester D. Pearson Papers, MG26N1, PAC.

13. Gerald de Gaury, *Faisal* (New York: Praeger, 1967), 80; DDE, *Mandate*, 150–59; *Time*, 25 May 1953, p. 29; Hagerty Diary, 23 June 1954, box 1, EL; NSC Meeting, 1 June 1953, NSC; Walters OHI, p. 66, EL; Gerson, *Dulles*, 128, 244; (?) to Eden, 25 June 1953, AP 20/16/127 (Dulles, as compared with Ike, on Suez).

14. Berding, *Dulles*, 34–35; Humphrey OHI, p. 10; Nathan F. Twining OHI by PAC, 16 March 1965, p. 31; Andrew J. Goodpaster OHI by RDC, 11 January 1966, p. 11; Mr. and Mrs. Richard Harkness OHI by RDC, 30 March 1966, p. 27, JFDOH; Krock Memo, 5 June 1953, box 24, Krock Papers, UP; JFD-DDE Conv., 22 December 1954 and 24 May 1957; JFD Memo for DDE, 21 October 1953; JFD-DDE

Conv., 25 May 1954, boxes 1, 2, 8, WHMS; Goodpaster OHI #378, pp. 106–7, EL; Ambrose, *EP*, 60, 64, 455, 551.

15. Bacon to Weeks, 21 July 1953, box 71, JFDP; Ambrose, *EP*, 79, 124, 128; Pearson Memo, 16 November 1953 (for St. Laurent), vol. 174 (D-16-12-E), Louis St. Laurent Papers, MG26L, PAC; Roberts, *Rough Draft*, 141.

16. DDE, *Waging Peace*, 337; Drummond and Coblentz, *Duel*, 28–29; JFD-DDE Conv., 17 August 1954, 17 January, 20 June 1955, 22 July 1957, boxes 1, 3, 5, WHMS; Scott to Allen, 9 January 1954, FO 371/110222, PRO; C. L. Sulzberger, *A Long Row of Candles: Memoirs and Diaries* (New York: Macmillan, 1969), 750.

17. DDE,*Waging Peace*, 266, 270, 286n; Nikita Khrushchev, *Khrushchev Remembers: The Last Testament*, trans. Strobe Talbot (Boston: Little, Brown, 1974), 362–63; Cutler, *No Time for Rest*, 363–64; Arleigh Burke OHI by RDC, 11 January 1966, p. 11; James C. Hagerty OHI by RDC, 14 October 1965, p. 25, JFDOH; JFD-Lodge-Hammarskjold Conv., 7 July 1958, box 1, GCMS; Goodpaster Memo of Conf., 21 July 1958, box 35, DDE Diary, AWF; NSC Meeting, 8 April 1953, box 4, NSC; JFD to DDE, 19 March 1956, box 5, DH; John W. Hanes OHI by Don North, 30 December 1970, p. 20, EL (CUOHC); Schlesinger and Kinzer, *Bitter Fruit*, 162. See also Ambrose, *EP*, 464–65. For a dissenting view on Lebanon, see Drummond and Coblentz, *Duel*, 191 (it was all Dulles) and Bernard M. Shanley OHI by RDC, 14 July 1966, pp. 19–20, JFDOH (finds no difference between JFD and DDE).

18. Others who saw Ike as the driving force behind American policy on Suez included Winthrop Aldrich U.S. ambassador to Britain; Christian Pineau, French foreign minister; Robert Bowie, director of policy-planning at State; Allen Dulles, head of the CIA; his aide, Richard Bissell; Philip Crowe, later State Department special assistant on press relations; Abba Eban, Israeli ambassador to the United States; General Andrew Goodpaster, White House staff secretary; Gordon Gray, director of defense mobilization; James Hagerty, Eisenhower's press secretary; Walter B. Kerr, journalist; Charles Malik, Lebanese ambassador to the United States; Herman Phleger, State Department legal adviser; and Bernard Shanley, Eisenhower's secretary. See Eden, *Full Circle*, 635; Hoopes, *Dulles*, 381; DDE, *Waging Peace*, 39; Pineau, *Suez*, 195; Bowie, *Suez*, 29; Kennett Love, *Suez: The Twice-Fought War* (New York: McGraw Hill, 1969), 652; Allen Dulles OHI, p. 71; Aldrich OHI, p. 24; Richard M. Bissell, Jr. OHI by RDC, 7 September 1966, pp. 27–28; Eban OHI, pp. 35–36; Goodpaster OHI, p. 38; Gordon Gray OHI by RDC, 4 March 1966, p. 19; Hagerty OHI, p. 24; Richard Harkness OHI by RDC, 30 March 1966, p. 11; Walter B. Kerr, Jr. OHI by PAC, 25 June 1964, p. 32; Lodge OHI, p. 21; Charles Malik OHI by R. Bayly Winder, 27 August 1964, pp. 41–42; Herman Phleger OHI by PAC, 21 July 1964, p. 80; Shanley OHI, p. 46; Couve de Murville OHI, p. 40; Crowe OHI, pp. 35–36, JFDOH; Harkness Notes, 31 October 1956; James Russell Wiggins, "Notes on Conversations with John Foster Dulles Relating to Russia, 1955–1958"; Press Backgrounder, 30 October 1956, pp. 5–6, boxes 1 and 2, DAP; Hughes Diary Notes of Meetings, 31 October 1956, box 3, Hughes Papers, PU; Lloyd, *Suez*, 202, 219; Berding, *Dulles*, 100; Sir William Hayter OHI by author, 21 July 1986. Macmillan errs when he depicts Dulles as frenzied in his hostility (*Storm*, 157). Others who leave an erroneous impression include Sherman Adams (OHI by RDC, 15 August 1964, pp. 22–23, JFDOH); Walworth Barbour (OHI by PAC, 5 August 1966, p. 13, JFDOH); and Emmet John Hughes (OHI by RDC, 22 April 1965, p. 35, JFDOH). It should be noted that Hughes' recollection does not coincide with the

notes he took on 31 October 1956. Eden's biographer, Robert James, notes that "although Dulles might be variable, Eisenhower had been consistently hostile towards military action throughout" (*Eden*, 543).

19. Neff, *Warriors*, 301; JFD-DDE Conv., 6 and 14 August 1956, box 5, WHMS; Henderson OHI, p. 48, EL (CUOHC); Notes on Bipartisan Legislative Leaders Meeting, 12 August 1956, Russell Papers, UG; JFD-DDE Phone Conv., 30 October 1956 (11:37 A.M.); Allen Dulles-JFD Phone Conv., 1 November 1956 (11:58 A.M.); Knowland-JFD Phone Conv., 31 October 1956 (9:19 A.M.); JFD-Wilcox Phone Conv., 1 November 1956 (8:30 A.M.); JFD-Lodge Phone Conv., 31 October 1956 (1:06 and 5:13 P.M.); JFD-George Phone Conv., 30 October 1956 (12:48 P.M.), boxes 5 and 11, Telephone Conv. Memoranda, DDE Papers, EL (hereafter TCM).

20. DDE-Nixon-Hoover-Phleger-Hagerty-Goodpaster Conf., 5 November 1956, box 4, WHMS; Notes on Bipartisan Legislative Leaders Meeting, 9 November 1956, Russell Papers, UG.

21. Merry and Serge Bromberger, *The Secrets of Suez* (London: Pan Books, Ltd., 1957), 18; Greenstein, *Hidden-Hand*, 96; Lloyd, *Suez*, 168; Pineau, *Suez*, 124 (Eden told Pineau that Ike *"nous demandait de retarder toute operation jusqu'a l'élection présidentiele américaine du 6 novembre—Après quoi il s'engageait à réaliser un front commun* [sic] *avec nous pour obtenir de l'Egypte un réglement satisfaisant de l'affaire de Suez"*). During the 1956 campaign, Eisenhower was warned against the danger of alienating powerful pro-Israel lobbies if he tried to block an Allied invasion of Suez. But the president never hesitated, remarking that "we thought the American Jew was . . . an American before he was a Jew so we'll just take the salt thataway"— he won New York State by 1,600,000 votes. See Hoopes, *Dulles*, 390; Lodge, *As It Was*, 95; Arthur Radford OHI by PAC, 8 May 1965, p. 65, JFDOH. The 1950 Tripartite Pact, which provided unilateral guarantees of Middle East borders for pledges of nonaggression, dealt with conditions under which violations of the Arab-Israeli armistice would be punished.

22. Lodge, *As It Was*, 94–95; Mohamed Hassanein Heikal, *The Cairo Documents* (Garden City: Doubleday, 1973), 148; Hughes Diary of meeting with DDE, 30 October 1956, box 3, Hughes Papers, PU; Goodpaster OHI #378, p. 111, EL.

23. Hoopes, *Dulles*, 346–47, 369–70, 372; Andre Beaufré, *The Suez Expedition* (New York: Praeger, 1969), 37, 62–64, 79–80; Woodhouse, *British Foreign Policy*, 86; Nutting, *No End*, 132–33.

24. Beaufré, *Suez*, 97; Neff, *Warriors*, 407; Cooper, *Lion's Last Roar*, 207.

25. DDE OHI by PAC, 28 July 1964, pp. 37–38; Twining OHI, p. 17, JFDOH; DDE-JFD Conf., 30 October 1956, box 18, DDE Diaries, AWF.

26. DDE-JFD Phone Conv., 6 August and 6 September 1956, boxes 4 and 5, WHMS; DDE-JFD Phone Con., 7 and 10 September 1956, 30 October 1956 (3:40 P.M.), box 18, DDE Diaries, AWF; JFD to DDE, 31 August 1956, box 5, DH; Notes on Bipartisan Legislative Leaders Meeting, 12 August 1956, Russell Papers, UG.

27. Home, *Autobiography*, 141; Eban, *Autobiography*, 207; Beaufré, *Suez*, 25; Bohlen, *Witness*, 428–29, 433; JFD Address at Williamstown, 6 October 1956, box 106, JFDP; Paul Ely, *Mémoires: Suez . . . le 13 Mai* (Paris: Plon, 1969), 144–45; Thomas, *Suez*, 54, 59, 82, 95–96, 102; Lloyd, *Suez*, 88, 92; Roberts, *Rough Draft*, 142; Heeney to Department of External Affairs (hereafter DEA), 29 March 1956 (tel. #615), box 219, U-15, vol. 6, St. Laurent Papers, MG26L, PAC (this material was declassified by request of the author).

28. Sir Robert G. Menzies, *Afternoon Light: Some Memoirs of Men and Events* (New York: Coward-McCann and Geoghegan, 1967), 165–66; Beaufré, *Suez,* 62–63; Macmillan, *Storm,* 116–17, 122, 125; Nutting, *No End,* 69; Kilmuir, *Memoirs,* 271; Lloyd, *Suez,* 76, 152, 160; Roberts, *Rough Draft,* 140.

29. Beaufré, *Suez,* 96; Lloyd, *Suez,* 123; Cooper, *Lion's Last Roar,* 181.

30. Kerr to Dulles, 10 April 1954, box 81, JFDP; FO to Geneva (U.K. delegation), 27 April 1954, PREM 11/645, PRO.

31. DDE, *Mandate,* 351 (refers to "united action" as "Foster's position"); JFD Press Conference, 13 April 1954, box 79, JFDP; JFD-DDE Conv., 24 March 1954; Dulles to U.S. ambassador at Paris, 6 April 1954, box 7, CS; NSC Meetings, 23 December 1953, 11 January and 25 March 1954, box 5, NSC; Ely, *Indochine,* 65–67, 69, 88; Greenstein, *Hidden-Hand,* 137; Eden to Churchill, 16 May 1954, PREM 11/666; Eden to FO, 17 May 1954; Eden to Makins, 12 June 1954, PREM 11/649, PRO. See also Ernest May, *"Lessons" of the Past* (New York: Oxford University Press, 1973), 95. According to Cyrus Sulzberger, Dulles was opposed to the use of American troops on the Mainland before he ever became secretary of state (Sulzberger, *Candles,* 747). For examples of the current assumption that Ike was more of a restraining force than Dulles (in seeking British support for American involvement), see Gregory J. Pemberton, "Australia, the United States and the Indochina Crisis of 1954," *Diplomatic History* 13 (Winter 1989): 51; Larson, *Eisenhower,* 75; Fall, *Hell,* 297, 300; Richardson, *Eisenhower,* 76; Hoopes, *Dulles,* 209–12; Roberts, *Rough Draft,* 115; Ambrose, *EP,* 177–79, 185; Richard M. Saunders, "Military Force in the Foreign Policy of the Eisenhower Presidency," *Political Science Quarterly* 100 (Spring 1985): 108, 111–12, 115; and David L. Anderson, "Eisenhower, Dienbienphu, and the Origins of United States Military Intervention in Vietnam," *Mid-America* 71 (April–July 1989): 101–17. Although Anderson recognizes Dulles as the originator of "united action" as a phrase and notes that he was inclined to favor Allied intervention over a unilateral U.S. strike (pp. 106–8), he nevertheless views Ike as preeminently cautious and in command (pp. 104, 115). Richard Immerman, who has painted Ike as occasionally on the hawkish side, also credits him with almost all of the restraining influence. See Richard Immerman, "Between the Unattainable and the Unacceptable: Eisenhower and Dienbienphu," in Richard Melanson and David Mayers, eds., *Reevaluating the Eisenhower Presidency in the 1950s* (Urbana: University of Illinois Press, 1987), 120–21, 123, 129, 134, 136, 138–40, 143–44. Earlier, in an article that he co-authored with George C. Herring, Immerman was not sure that any top American officials were ever enthusiastic about intervention (i.e., the whole thing may have been a form of "bluff"—a "grand charade," in other words)— see George C. Herring and Richard H. Immerman, "Eisenhower, Dulles, and Dienbienphu: 'The Day We Didn't Go To War' Revisited," *Journal of American History* 71 (September 1984): 349–50, 363. Ike's position is described as "elusive" (p. 349), and Dulles, while presented as "quite cautious" (p. 349), is nevertheless seen as pressing relentlessly for the British backing needed to satisfy Congress (pp. 358–59). The most recent, as well as the most extensive analyses of Dien Bien Phu and American diplomacy also follow the conventional line: Melanie Billings-Yun, *Decision Against War: Eisenhower and Dien Bien Phu, 1954* (New York: Columbia University Press, 1988), and Kaplan et al., eds., *Dien Bien Phu.* See, in particular, Immerman, "Prologue," and Artaud, "France Between the Indochina War and the European Community," ibid., 15–17, 269, 271, 273. Billings-Yun portrays Eisenhower as cau-

tious (pp. xii, 15, 36, 93, 95, 101–11) and very much in command (pp. 20, 76). Dulles, on the other hand, is viewed as provocative although generally "obedient" (pp. 19, 61–64, 137). Only two cases of insubordination on the secretary's part are recorded (pp. 145, 150). While the volume is commendable in many ways and brilliantly written, it suffers from a lack of British documentation and presents a good deal in the way of countervailing evidence. For example, Dulles' conservative side is given extensive play (pp. 37, 39, 41–42, 54, 57–58, 82, 106, 142). There is also much to confirm Ike's interventionist instinct (pp. 43, 81–82, 108–9, 119, 142–43). Congress is viewed as decisively and independently dovish (pp. 26–27); however, the key reference is to early February, before the crucial battle for Dien Bien Phu had even begun. Subsequently, Congressional opinion shifted considerably and would remain fluid, subject to executive pressure (pp. 95, 113, 118). William Conrad Gibbons, *The United States Government and the Vietnam War: Executive and Legislative Roles and Relations, pt. 1: 1945–1960* (Princeton: Princeton University Press, 1986), is cited by Billings-Yun (p. 169) as indicative of congressional opposition to American intervention even though Gibbons himself frequently argues the reverse (see, for example, Gibbons, *Vietnam*, 175, 204, 216, 244–45, 258–59). Blame is laid on Dulles for his "united action" address; yet the author admits that this particular speech was just as much Eisenhower's idea as anyone else's (p. 64). Dulles is portrayed as jumping suddenly onto the bandwagon of immediate intervention (p. 137) and then, just as suddenly, jumping off without any convincing explanation. Moreover, Eisenhower is identified as at once a respecter of Congress and one whose respect was more apparent than real (pp. 159–60). Lloyd C. Gardner, in *Approaching Vietnam: From World War II Through Dienbienphu, 1941–1954* (New York: Norton, 1988), is ambivalent much of the time on the exact relationship between Eisenhower and Dulles. Although he sketches Dulles as a hawk (pp. 228, 250, 278–79), he is not always sure of Ike's caution (p. 228; also pp. 167, 199, 203), and he winds up, even in the case of Dulles, admitting some uncertainty as to whether the secretary really wanted to intervene to save Dien Bien Phu: "Probably, Dulles was unsure himself" (p. 246). No persuasive explanation is given for Radford's striking about-face on 2 April (p. 205) while Congress is portrayed as by turns dovish, hawkish, and mixed in sentiment (e.g., pp. 174, 216). John Prados, *The Sky Would Fall: Operation Vulture: The U.S. Bombing Mission in Indochina, 1954* (New York: Dial, 1983), once again, views Dulles as the stereotypical hawk and Ike as more on the dovish side (pp. 26–27, 109, 111, 171, 184, 201–2, 207). Still, Prados admits contradictory evidence (pp. 48–49, 87, 104, 161). It is interesting to note that France had insisted on arms support in Indochina as the price for joining NATO. See Ferrell, ed., *Hagerty*, 16. In dealing with the linkage between EDC and an American air strike at Dien Bien Phu, scholars tend to emphasize French demands (no air strike, no EDC) while paying little, if any attention to what was being demanded by Washington (no EDC, no air strike). See, for example, Immerman, "Prologue," and Kaplan, "Indochina," in Kaplan et al., eds., *Dien Bien Phu*, 13–14, 231, 233–35, 237–38, 240, 242, 246, 247n. Kaplan and Artaud hint at Dulles' position (pp. 239–41, 260), but it is never clarified. George C. Herring's essay, "Franco-American Conflict in Indochina, 1950–1954" (in the same collection), has Dulles telling Eisenhower that an air strike should be used as leverage to insure French ratification of EDC, but the author does not develop the point any further (ibid., 43).

32. DDE OHI, 28 July 1964, pp. 25–26; Matthew B. Ridgway OHI by PAC, 1

May 1964, p. 20, JFDOH; Ely, *Indochine*, 73–75; Henri Navarre, *Agonie de L'Indochine, 1953–1954* (Paris: Plon, 1956), 96–98; JFD-DDE Conv. (Wilson and Radford present), 2 April 1954, box 7, CS; Roberts, *Rough Draft*, 121; JFD-Koo Conv., 19 May 1954, box 191, WKP; Makins to FO, 3 April 1954; Jebb (U.K. Embassy, Paris) to FO, 23 April 1954, PREM 11/645, PRO; Arthur Radford, "Personal Log," 19 March 1954; JFD-Radford Phone Conv., 24 March 1954, box 2, Radford Papers, Operations Archives, U.S. Naval Historical Center, Washington Navy Yard. Eisenhower never mentioned Dulles as being among those who favored an air strike; indeed he told the NSC that British concurrence was a condition attached by the secretary of state (rather than the president, by implication). See NSC Meeting, 29 April 1954, box 5, NSC. It should be noted that the buzz word "united action" is interpreted by Billings-Yun as a modification of something Eisenhower said at a strategy session bearing on his hope for a Southeast Asian defense pact (p. 64). This follows Ambrose (*EP*, 178). But there is a problem: the available evidence does not pinpoint Ike, any more than Dulles, as the pact's originator. Secondly, Dulles' phrase "united action" had much less to do with plans for SEATO, as the defense organization eventually came to be known, than it did with affording the British some kind of a veto on U.S. military intervention. According to Gibbons, Dulles was more insistent, as a champion of united action, than Eisenhower (*Vietnam*, 195, 200). Hoopes (*Dulles*, 212) hypothesizes correctly that "united action" was a ploy by Dulles (not Ike) to put the brakes on Radford and retain control of American policy. But Hoopes' explanation leaves something to be desired because he does not explain why and what Dulles had in mind (i.e., EDC). Richard Nixon, in his memoirs, refers to "united action" as Dulles' plan and describes Ike as singing like a dove on 6 April after being hawkish a week earlier. See *Memoirs of Richard Nixon* (New York: Grosset and Dunlap, 1978), 151, 155.

33. Makins to FO, 24 April, 1, 8, 15 May, 5 and 12 June 1954, FO 371/109100, PRO; Roberts, *Rough Draft*, 117. According to Pemberton, Canberra was not as well disposed toward a course of action independent of London as Dulles may have supposed or given the impression of supposing. See Pemberton, "Indochina," 62. In the account by Herring and Immerman, Congress resisted efforts by Dulles, as well as Eisenhower, to manipulate it into authorizing military intervention (Herring and Immerman, "Dienbienphu," 353). Yet, according to Prados, "the American press exhibited unqualified approval for intervention" by 7 April, including Walter Lippmann and the *New York Times*, and by 16 April Senator Knowland thought Congress was ready to authorize American intervention independently of Britain, assuming a grant of freedom to the associated states (*Vulture*, 116, 140). By Gibbons' account, Congress was more enthusiastic about intervention by early spring than the administration (*Vietnam*, 203–4, 216–17). Even after the fall of Dien Bien Phu, Congress continued to appear flexible (ibid., 258–59).

34. Hagerty Diary, 8 February and 1 April 1954, in Ferrell, ed., *Hagerty*, 15, 39; JFD-DDE Phone Conv., 5 April 1954 (8:22 A.M.), box 10, TCM; NSC Meetings, 23 December 1953, 11 January and 4 February 1954, box 5, NSC. See also Billings-Yun, *Dien Bien Phu*, 142. Lord Salisbury, leader of the House of Lords in England, wrote Eden that Eisenhower "whom I'm beginning to think, though well meaning, is a prize noodle" seemed to be much attracted to Walter Judd's line on Indochina: that Washington would be better off intervening alone than alongside a colonial power like Britain (9 May 1954, AP 20/17/118). This reflects the concern that had

been voiced by Churchill at Bermuda (in December) when Ike had used extremely strong language threatening the use of atomic weapons in the Far East and Indochina (James, *Eden*, 374). When Churchill suggested that Russia had changed, Eisenhower spoke of her as a whore, who might have changed her dress, but who should be chased from the streets—she was out to subvert the entire free world. See David Carlton, *Anthony Eden* (London: Allen Lane, 1981), 335.

35. JFD Conv. with Radford, Judd, Wiley, and Smith, 24 and 29 March, 7 and 19 April 1954, box 7, CS; JFD Memo, 24 April 1954, box 2, DH; NSC Meeting, 6 April 1954, box 5, NSC: Gibbons, *Vietnam*, 179–80; Makins to FO, 7 April 1954, PREM 11/645; Eden to Makins, 12 June 1954, PREM 11/649, PRO; JFD-Radford Phone Conv., 24 March 1954; Radford Personal Log, box 2, Radford Papers, U.S. Naval Historical Center; JFD Phone Conv. with Wiley, Smith, and Radford, 24 and 25 March, 7 and 19 April 1954, box 2, TCM. According to Billings-Yun (*Dien Bien Phu*, 86), congressional opinion was "uninfluenced" when consulted on 3 April. But this does not square with Gibbons, *Vietnam*, 176–81. When queried by French general Ely, Dulles was noncommittal even on the question of an American response should Peking decide to send jet fighters into Indochina. See JFD Memo, 23 March 1954, 751g.00/3–2354, microfilm LM 71, roll 11, National Archives (hereafter NA). One might add that Dulles continued to sound dovish. In a cable from Paris dated 23 April and addressed to the acting secretary of state, he said he saw no reason why the fall of Dien Bien Phu had to be disastrous for the prospects of EDC or even with regard to the rest of Indochina. See Kaplan, "The United States, Nato, and French Indochina," in Kaplan et al., eds., *Dien Bien Phu*, 241–42 (and, of lesser interest, ibid., 239). According to the official history of the Joint Chiefs of Staff (*The War in Vietnam: History of the Indochina Incident*) declassified in 1981, Dulles rejected a NSC Planning Board recommendation for a decision on whether or not to intervene, preferring instead to work for a broad-based political coalition (SEATO). See p. 382 of the original mimeographed version at the Military History Branch, NA.

36. JFD-DDE Conv., 24 March and 2 April 1954, box 7, CS; JFD-DDE Meeting, 2 April 1954, box 2, WHMS; NSC Meetings, 25 March, 1 and 6 April 1954, box 5, NSC; FO (Eden) to U.K. Embassy, Paris, 25 April (6:25 P.M.) 1954; Memo of Meeting at 10 Downing Street, 25 April (4:00 P.M.) 1954, PREM 11/645, PRO.

37. Memo on Congressional Leadership Conf., 3 April 1954 (for Radford's denial of the efficacy of an air strike); JFD-DDE Conv. (Wilson and Radford present), 2 April 1954; JFD-DDE Phone Conv., 3 April 1954, box 7, CS; JFD-DDE Meeting, 2 April 1954, box 2, WHMS. Although it is not entirely clear, it would appear that legislators present at the 3 April meeting heard, among other things, that France was shaky in terms of staying power; that the Quai D'Orsay had refused to make important political concessions; that Downing Street remained on the fence; that Thailand could not be expected to make much of a contribution; and that the Philippines might not send troops. See Richard B. Russell Notes on a State Department Meeting, 3 April 1954, Red Line File, Russell Papers, UG. The argument put forth by Billings-Yun that Radford did a complete volte-face on the issue of relieving Dien Bien Phu merely because Ike suggested that, if possible, the initiative for a congressional resolution should seem to come from congressional leaders themselves (Dulles said he was planning to do this) seems less than convincing (*Dien Bien Phu*, 84–85). It has also been suggested that Radford may have shifted his stance owing in part

to the opinion of various chiefs of staff (e.g., Gibbons, *Vietnam*, 185). This would appear unlikely as well. Radford had polled the chiefs three times by 2 April and he could see that the air force and navy were prepared by that time to offer conditional support (Prados, *Vulture*, 92–93). Ridgway, it is true, was opposed to an air strike and he was supported in this stance by Marine Commandant Shepherd; but the two of them were opposed not only by Radford, but also by Air Force General Nathan Twining, who endorsed the air strike with provisos which could easily have been satisfied (he gave a qualified "yes") and Navy Chief Admiral Carney who, while he did not want to advocate intervention until consulted by the White House, was perfectly willing to indicate U.S. military capability and reiterate his view of the importance of holding East Asia. Ridgway himself was not so much opposed to intervention itself as to intervention in a backwater area (which he viewed as a dangerous diversion). His emphasis was on cutting the links between China and the Vietminh by means of an ultimatum to Peking which Washington would have to be prepared to back up. See Ridgway Memos of 2, 6, and 24 April 1954; Carney Memo of 2 April; and Twining Memo of (2?) April, box 30, Matthew B. Ridgway Papers, U.S. Army Military History Institute, Carlisle Barracks, Pennsylvania. As regards the line that Congress, rather than the executive, kept the United States at peace, it is curious that at a meeting that was presumably staged by a hawkish administration to gain congressional backing for intervention, there were three key Republican figures who failed to attend: House Majority Leader Charles A. Halleck, House Majority Whip Leslie C. Arends, and Senate Majority Whip Leverett Saltonstall. As a result, those Republicans who did attend were outnumbered 5–3 by their Democratic colleagues (Gibbons, *Vietnam*, 189). It might be noted in addition that although Chalmers Roberts' article "Airstrike" and Bernard Fall's *Hell* (475n) followed the conventional line at the time (i.e., that Dulles and Radford approached congressional leaders to make a case for an air strike to be preceded by passage of a joint congressional resolution authorizing the use of the American military in Indochina—similar to the Gulf of Tonkin Resolution voted under President Johnson) both accounts confirm Senator Russell on Radford's admission of the possible need for U.S. ground troops.

38. JFD Press Conf., 13 April 1954, box 79, JFDP; JFD-Radford-Merchant-Eden-Caccia Conv., 24 April 1954, box 9, Subject Series, DDE Papers, EL (hereafter SS); Churchill to Eden (27 April 1954?); Colville to Makins, 28 April 1954; Eden to Churchill, 16 May 1954, PREM 11/666; Jebb to FO, 24 April 1954, PREM 11/645, PRO; Lord Home OHI by author, 23 July 1986. According to Herring and Immerman, Radford continued, while abroad, to press hard for an air strike ("Dienbienphu," 358). Perhaps, but the authors do not utilize European sources and their version is therefore limited since it relies on American records of what was said in Paris. It would appear that what Radford told the British in Paris, with French officials looking on, was quite different from what he said to them confidentially while in England at Chequers (based on British sources).

39. Ely, *Indochine*, 67, 69, 76–77, 83; Fall, *Hell*, 297; Ewald, *Eisenhower*, 109–10; JFD-DDE Phone Conv., 5 April 1954, box 7, CS; JFD-Radford Phone Conv., 24 March 1954, box 2, Radford Personal log, Radford Papers, U.S. Naval Historical Center.

40. JFD to U.S. ambassador at Paris, 6 April 1954; JFD-DDE Phone Conv., 5

April 1954; JFD Memo for DDE, 23 March 1954, box 7, CS; Ely, *Indochine*, 67, 69; Eden to FO, 1 May 1954, PREM 11/649, PRO.

41. Nixon OHI, p. 45, JFDOH; JFD-DDE Phone Conv., 5 April 1954; JFD-Smith Phone Conv., 19 April 1954, box 7, CS; Makins to FO, 17 April 1954, FO 371/109100, PRO; NSC Meeting, 6 May 1954, box 5, NSC; DDE Press Conf., 7 April 1954, in Branyan and Larsen, eds., *Eisenhower*, vol. 1, 330–31; Gurtov, *Vietnam*, 121. See also DDE to Churchill, 5 April 1954 (on dominoes), PREM 11/645, PRO. Radford confirmed Ely's interpretation of the Washington talks when he recalled that Ike had made it clear that the French were to have virtually anything and everything they might want. See Radford, *Memoirs*, 401. According to Radford, the French made two requests in April for U.S. ground forces—on one occasion for twenty thousand marines, on another for six marine divisions (ibid., 421).

42. Hagerty Diary, 24 April 1954, box 1, James Hagerty Papers, EL; Roberts, *Rough Draft*, 114; DDE to Churchill, 5 April 1954 (hand-delivered by Aldrich), PREM 11/645; FO to U.K. Embassy, Paris, 25 April 1954 (6:25 P.M.); Memo of 10 Downing Street Meeting, 25 April 1954 (4:00 P.M.); British Cabinet Meeting, 24 May 1954, CAB 128/27 (part 1), PRO.

43. Hagerty Diary, 26 March 1954, in Ferrell, ed., *Hagerty*, 35; JFD-DDE Meeting, 19 May 1954, box 2, WHMS.

44. DDE, *Mandate*, 341, 345, 351; Bidault, *Resistance*, 198–99; Pineau, *Suez*, 92; JFD-McCardle Phone Conv., 23 July 1954, box 2, TCM; Ely, *Indochine*, 87–88; Navarre, *Indochine*, 243; Chalmers Roberts, "United States Twice Proposed Indochina Air Strike," *Washington Post and Times Herald*, 7 June 1954, pp. 1, 4; Herring and Immerman, "Dienbienphu," 343.

45. Berding, *Dulles*, 120; Eban, *Autobiography*, 175; Drummond and Coblentz, *Duel*, 25; Adams OHI, p. 13; George D. Aiken OHI by PAC, 5 February 1966, p. 7; Aldrich OHI, p. 41; Allen OHI (pt. 2), p. 6; Dillon Anderson OHI by RDC, 13 June 1966, pp. 2, 46; Sir Howard Beale OHI by Gerard C. Smith, 6 May 1964, p. 15; Eugene Black OHI by RDC, 15 July 1964, p. 26; Crowe OHI, p. 44; John B. Hollister OHI by PAC, 6 May 1964, p. 36; David W. Wainhouse OHI by PAC, 24 July 1965, p. 43; James Reston OHI by PAC, 23 June 1965, p. 18; Lodge OHI, p. 32; Nixon OHI, p. 8; W. B. Macomber OHI, p. 113, JFDOH; Clare Boothe Luce OHI by John Luter, 11 January 1968, p. 62; Aldrich OHI, p. 29; Bowie OHI, p. 19, EL (CUOHC); JFD, "Not War, Not Peace" (Address to the Foreign Policy Association, 17 January 1948), p. 11; idem, *War or Peace*, 17 ("waging peace"); DDE to JFD, 8 January 1954, box 80, JFDP; DDE Corrections on JFD Speech draft, 16 July 1957, box 116; JFD-DDE Conv., 22 January and 13 May 1958, box 6, WHMS; DDE-JFD Phone Conv., 28 July 1958, box 34, DDE Diaries, AWF; Love, *Suez*, 282.

46. Nikita Khrushchev, *Khrushchev Remembers I* (Boston: Little, Brown, 1970), 397; idem, *Testament*, 454–55; Eban, *Autobiography*, 175; Pineau, *Suez*, 91, 175; Macmillan, *Tides*, 634; idem, *Storm*, 94; Drummond and Coblentz, *Duel*, 13; David Wise and Thomas B. Ross, *The U-2 Affair* (New York: Random House, 1962), 138; *Jours de France* 53 (19–26 November 1955): 19, box 66, Allen Dulles Papers, PU; Arnold Heeney, "Washington Under Two Presidents: 1953–57; 1959–62," *International Journal* 22 (Summer 1967): 502; Moran, *Churchill*, 540, 579; Makins to Eden, 18 June 1954, AP 20/17/18.

47. Dulles, *Dulles*, 149; Memo on Conf. at JFD Residence, 31 October 1954, "Indochina 1954," Briefing Notes Subseries, NSC Series, White House Office of the

Special Assistant for National Security Affairs, EL (hereafter WHOSANSA); JFD News Conf., 28 July 1953, box 68, JFDP; Gerard C. Smith OHI, p. 31, JFDOH; Drummond and Coblentz, *Duel*, 209.

48. Richard Delo Challener and John Fenton, "Which Way America? Dulles Always Knew," *American Heritage* 22 (June 1971): 90; Adams, *Firsthand Report*, 73; Drummond and Coblentz, *Duel*, 21–22, 25–26, 31–32; Larson, *Eisenhower*, 76, 78; Berding, *Dulles*, 17; W. Macomber OHI, pp. 112, 118, JFDOH: Eleanor Lansing Dulles, *Chances of a Lifetime* (Englewood Cliffs: Prentice Hall, 1980), 312; Shanley OHI, p. 2; Gerald D. Morgan OHI by RDC, 7 December 1966, p. 5, JFDOH; Crowe, "Reflections," p. 58, box 2, DAP; Krock Memo, 7 December 1959, bk. 2, box 1, Arthur Krock Papers, PU; Milton Eisenhower OHI #345 by Maclyn Burg, 6 November 1975, pp. 31–32, EL; Milton Eisenhower OHI #292 by John Luter, 21 June and 6 September 1967, p. 15; Andrew Berding OHI by John Luter, 13 June 1967, pp. 28–30; Bowie OHI, pp. 18–19, EL (CUOHC); Robert C. Hill OHI by John Mason, Jr., October 1972, pp. 41 and 45, Columbia University Oral History Collection (hereafter CUOH).

49. Macmillan, *Storm*, 178; DDE Press Conf., 15 April 1959, in Branyan and Larsen, eds., *Eisenhower*, 2:1152; Adams OHI, pp. 2–3, 9; DDE OHI, p. 10; John M. Hightower OHI by PAC, 8 June 1965, p. 20, JFDOH; Krock Notes on White House Dinner, 28 July 1959, bk. 2, box 1, Krock Papers, PU; Greenstein, *Hidden-Hand*, 89–91; Paterson to Churchill, 6 May 1954, PREM 11/649. There were tears in Ike's eyes once more when he attended Dulles' funeral.

50. Heller and Heller, *Dulles*, 284; Berding, *Dulles*, 148; John R. Beal OHI by RDC, 9 September 1965, pp. 2–3; Childs OHI, pp. 10–13, 17, 36; Ernest Kidder Lindley OHI by PAC, 6 November 1965, pp. 2–3, 10–11, 25; Peter Lisagor OHI by RDC, 3 February 1966, p. 10; Phleger OHI, p. 91; David Schoenbrun OHI by PAC, 23 June 1964, p. 53; William J. Sebald OHI by PAC, 22 and 27 July 1965, p. 116; Sir Thomas MacDonald OHI by PAC, 11 June 1964, p. 21; Michael J. Mansfield OHI by RDC, 10 May 1966, p. 3, JFDOH; JFD Press Conference, 18 December 1956, box 106, JFDP (for Dulles' admission of ignorance, see also Press Backgrounder, 7 May 1955, and Press Conf., 26 March 1957, boxes 93 and 113, JFDP); JFD Press Conf., 23 April 1957, box 114, JFDP (outfoxing reporters); Carl McCardle OHI by John Luter, 29 August 1967, p. 26; Chalmers Roberts OHI by John Luter, 29 August 1967, pp. 2–5, EL (CUOHC); Roberts, *Rough Draft*, 108; William Sebald, *With MacArthur in Japan: A Personal History of the Occupation* (New York: Norton, 1965), 250–51. According to James R. Wiggins (OHI by PAC, 9 August 1965, pp. 16, 21, JFDOH), Charles Evans Hughes held daily press briefings. But the issues were neither as wide-ranging nor as critical. According to Richard Wilson (OHI by RDC, 3 March 1966, p. 12, JFDOH), Hull did the same thing—but he was perfunctory and his conferences lasted only a few minutes.

51. Heller and Heller, *Dulles*, 245; Childs OHI, p. 17; Hightower OHI, p. 7; MacDonald OHI, p. 21; Mansfield OHI, p. 3, JFDOH; JFD Press Conf., 19 January 1954 and 25 March 1958, boxes 78 and 129, JFDP.

52. Beal OHI, pp. 6–7; Childs OHI, pp. 9–10, 21, 36; Kerr OHI, p. 29; Krock OHI, p. 28; Malik OHI, pp. 8–9; O. Frederick Nolde OHI by RDC, 2 June 1965, pp. 39–40; Sebald OHI, p. 116; James P. Shepley OHI by RDC, 13 May 1965, pp. 7, 14; Sir Percy Spender OHI by PAC, 22 June 1964, p. 3, JFDOH; JFD Press Conf., 19 January 1954, box 78, JFDP.

53. McCardle OHI, p. 5 (CUOHC); Krock OHI, pp. 25–26; Lindley OHI, pp. 10, 12, 25; Lisagor OHI, p. 21; Babcock OHI, pp. 16–18; Crowe OHI, p. 15; Hanes OHI, p. 247; Robert W. Purcell OHI by RDC, 15 July 1965, pp. 7–8, 23; Ogden Reid OHI by PAC, 9 May 1967, pp. 5–6; Reston OHI, pp. 19–24; Richard Rovere OHI by RDC, 21 January 1965, pp. 22–23; Schoenbrun OHI, p. 80; Shepley OHI, p. 6; Edward Weintal OHI by PAC, 11 May 1967, p. 18, JFDOH (Dulles had "a very good press" as a result of the backgrounders he gave—so much so that Acheson wondered how he ever managed to pull it off); UP Dispatch, 2 December 1954 (on 1300 radio stations), JFD Press Conf., 16 January 1958 (on certificate of appreciation) boxes 78, 127, JFDP; Crowe, "Reflections," p. 46, box 2, DAP; D. E. Boster Memo, 30 October 1958, box 5, GCMS; Makins to FO, 3 July 1954, FO 371/109101; Makins to FO, 12 December 1953, FO 371/103496, PRO; Memo on Discussion at Canadian Embassy, 28 June 1954, vol. 34, Pearson Papers, MG26N1, PAC. Beal's biography, with its misleading chapter title, "The Unpopular Man," came out in 1957, just after Suez, at a time when Dulles' fortunes were at rock bottom and before all the returns were in.

54. Stewart Alsop OHI, p. 19 (on Acheson); Loftus E. Becker OHI by PAC, 25 June 1964, p. 38; Childs OHI, pp. 19–20 (also on Acheson as a point of comparison); Crowe OHI, pp. 17, 25–26; Weintal OHI, p. 18 (on Acheson as well), JFDOH; Crowe, "Reflections," p. 49, box 2, DAP; Makins to FO, 13 November 1953, FO 371/103523; Makins to Strang, 4 September 1953, FO 371/103514, PRO: JFD-DDE Phone Conv., 1 November 1956 (8:40 A.M.), box 11, TCM; Wilbur Crane Eveland, *Ropes of Sand: America's Failure in the Middle East* (New York: Norton, 1980), 70, 74; Dooner, "Dulles," pp. 21–22; Love, *Suez*, 277; Neff, *Warriors*, 43, 433–35.

55. Crowe OHI, pp. 7–8; Roscoe Drummond OHI by RDC, 13 January 1966, pp. 34–35; Lindley OHI, pp. 2–3; Reston OHI, pp. 21–22; Rovere OHI, p. 3; Waters OHI, pp. 26–27; Wilson OHI, p. 24; Weintal OHI, pp. 18, 20, JFDOH; Harkness "Notes," 31 October 1956 and 21 July 1958; Crowe, "Reflections," pp. 46–48; Wiggins "Notes" on JFD backgrounders, 29 December 1956 and 3 April 1958, boxes 1 and 2, DAP; JFD to Krock, 12 December 1957, box 24, Krock Papers, PU; Roberts, *Rough Draft*, 146. According to Lisagor, Dulles usually gave no more information in a backgrounder than he was willing to give in public, but he had a way of "making us feel as if we were privy to things he wouldn't say in public" (OHI, p. 22, JFDOH).

56. Berding, *Dulles*, 28–29; John M. Vorys OHI by RDC, 9 June 1966, pp. 44, 46, 53, 56; James P. Richards OHI by RDC, 23 September 1965, pp. 17, 19; Alexander Wiley OHI by RDC, 19 July 1966, pp. 3–5, JFDOH; JFD Speech to the Council on Foreign Relations, 7 June 1957, box 122, JFDP; Hill OHI, p. 33, CUOH. See also JFD Day Book, box 382, JFDP.

57. Branyan and Larsen, eds., *Eisenhower*, 1:234: Jacob K. Javits OHI by PAC, 2 March 1966, p. 14; Wiley OHI, pp. 5, 7, JFDOH; Makins to FO, 16 January 1954, FO 371/109100, PRO.

58. Everett McKinley Dirksen OHI by RDC, 19 July 1966, pp. 2–3; W. Macomber OHI, p. 39; Richards OHI, pp. 4, 6–7, JFDOH; JFD Day Book, 7 April 1954, box 380, JFDP.

59. DDE OHI #106 by Raymond Henle, 13 July 1967, pp. 24, 28, EL; Richard Nixon OHI by Hugh Cates and Robert Stevens, Jr., 13 April 1978, p. 17, Russell Papers, UG; Makins to Eden, 23 February 1954, FO 371/109099, PRO.

60. Milton Eisenhower, *President*, 366; John W. McCormack OHI by PAC, 12

February 1966, pp. 2–3, JFDOH; Ambrose, *EP*, 207; JFD to DDE, 12 November 1954, FR (1952–54), 5:1471–72; Makins to FO, 27 June 1954, FO 371/109101, PRO; Koo-Rankin Conv., 5 June 1953, box 187, WKP; Press Opinion Summary, 26 August 1958, file 1415–40, vol. 6, RG25, DEA. See also boxes 89 and 91, JFDP.

61. Statements by Dulles and Radford, *U.S. Senate Hearing Before the Committee on Foreign Relations, 83rd Congress, 2nd Session* (Washington, D.C.: U.S. Government Printing Office, 1954), p. 44; Anna Kasten Nelson, "John Foster Dulles and the Bipartisan Congress," *Political Science Quarterly* 102 (Spring 1987): 43–64. For Dulles' funeral, see material in box 83, Allen Dulles Papers, PU.

62. JFD Press Conf., 12 September 1954, box 79, JFDP; JFD Press Backgrounder, 15 May 1955, box 89, JFDP; Gerson, *Dulles*, 113–15; Makins to Eden, 28 February 1953 and 7 March 1954, FO 371/103495, PRO; Makins to FO, 13 February 1953, FO 371/103512; DDE State of the Union Message, 1953; Eden to Churchill, 20 February 1953, PREM 11/432, PRO; Memo of JFD-Pearson Conv., 15 February 1953, vol. 4, Pearson Papers, MG26N1, PAC. On the Hull portrait, see material in box 81, Allen Dulles Papers.

63. Ambrose, *Ike's Spies*, 240; Love, *Suez*, 271; Patrick Seale, *The Struggle for Syria: A Study of Post-War Arab Politics, 1945–1958* (London: Oxford University Press, 1965), 286; Allison OHI, pp. 3–4; Bowie OHI, p. 2, JFDOH; Berding OHI (introduction), EL (CUOHC); Ambrose, *EP*, 320–21; Warren Cohen, *Dean Rusk* (Totowa: Cooper Square Publishers, 1980), 71, 82; *Time*, 21 January 1957, p. 12; 11 February 1957, p. 17; 11 March 1957, p. 16.

64. Heller and Heller, *Dulles*, 242; John Milton Cooper, *The Warrior and the Priest: Woodrow Wilson and Theodore Roosevelt* (Cambridge, Mass.: Harvard University Press, 1983), xii; McCardle OHI, p. 23, EL (CUOHC); JFD, "Challenge and Response in United States Policy," *Foreign Affairs* 36 (October 1957): 42; JFD Press Conf., 30 September 1958, box 127, JFDP. For Dulles' speeches, see material in box 95, JFDP.

CHAPTER 3

1. George F. Kennan OHI by RDC, 3 March 1967, p. 6, JFDOH; JFD Press Conf., 27 November 1953, box 71, JFDP; Makins to FO, 19 May 1953, PREM 11/421, PRO.

2. DDE Diary, 11 January 1956, in Ferrell, ed., *Eisenhower*, 308; Konrad Adenauer, *Memoirs, 1945–53*, trans. Beate Rum von Oppen (Chicago: Regnery, 1965), 444–47, 449; Love, *Suez*, 305, 307; Neff, *Warriors*, 93; Anwar el-Sadat, *In Search of Identity: An Autobiography* (New York: Harper Colophon Books, 1978), 126–27; Nelson, "Dulles," pp. 58–59. Bonn's denial of rolling mill parts to Hungary at Washington's request would be an example of trade restraint.

3. Beal, *Dulles*, 123; Heikal, *Cairo Documents*, 41–43; Memo of Conv. between JFD and Lloyd at Bermuda, 20 March 1957, box 113, JFDP; Memo of White House Conf., November 1956, box 4, WHMS; JFD-Caccia Conv., 24 December 1956, box 1, GCMS; Unidentified Summary Briefing Paper, box 7, DH; JFD-DDE Phone Conv., 8 December 1956, box 20, Dwight D. Eisenhower Series, AWF, EL; Churchill to DDE, 21 June 1954, PREM 11/649, PRO; Salisbury to Eden, 24 September 1953, AP 20/16/155 (on Buraimi).

4. Konrad Adenauer, *Mémoires: 1953–1956*, trans. Geneviève Teissèdre and

Georgette Chatenet (Paris: Hachette, 1967), 432–33, 472; *Time*, 7 January 1957, p. 14; FO Northern Department Memo, 18 March 1955, FO 371/116665; Record of Tripartite Meeting of Quai d'Orsay, 25 April 1953, PREM 11/429, PRO.

5. Macmillan, *Storm*, 475, 477–78; JFD-Alphand Conv., 7 January 1958, box 1, GCMS; Adenauer, *Mémoires: 1953–1956*, 189–90, 200.

6. Transcript of JFD Remarks, 21 April 1956, box 106, JFDP; Crowe, "Reflections," box 2, DAP; JFD Manuscript, 21 April 1956, box 287, JFDP; DDE to Churchill, 14 December 1954, FR (1952–54), 5:1499; Hayter to FO, 28 March 1955, PREM 11/893; DDE to Churchill, 5 and 8 May 1953; *Pravda* editorial quoted by *Tass*, 24 May 1953, PREM 11/421, PRO; Makins to FO, 8 January 1953; Jebb to FO, 12 March 1953; Churchill to DDE, 21 April 1953 (for DDE's position, as opposed to JFD); DDE to Churchill, 27 April 1953, PREM 11/422, PRO; Berding, *Dulles*, 23, 47; JFD Press Conf., 10 January 1958, box 125, JFDP.

7. Adenauer, *Mémoires: 1953–1956*, 452–53; Bohlen, *Witness*, 390–91; Draft of JFD Statement, 13 August 1955, box 91, JFDP; Gerson, *Dulles*, 235–36; JFD to DDE, 7 November 1955, box 5, DH.

8. Berding, *Dulles*, 25; DSPR, 6 June 1955, box 92, JFDP; Wiggins, "Notes," 4 April 1958, box 2, DAP.

9. Leonard Hall OHI by RDC, 29 July 1966, p. 17, JFDOH; Draft of JFD Statement, 13 August 1955, box 91, JFDP.

10. Harkness, "Notes," 17 August 1953, box 1, DAP; JFD Address, 10 October 1952, box 107, Alexander Smith Papers, PU; NSC Meeting, 25 June 1953, box 4, NSC.

11. JFD-DDE Conv., 10 July 1954, box 1, WHMS; Krock Notes on Visit to White House, 16 November 1956, bk. 2, box 1, Krock Papers, PU; JFD to Mendès-France (c/o U.S. Embassy, Paris), 10 July 1954, box 3, DH; JFD Memo for DDE, 21 October 1953, WHMS; Makins to FO, 17 July and 7 August 1954; Minutes on Watson to Mann, 9 August 1954; Makins Memo on Conv. with JFD, 4 August 1954; Scott to FO, 21 August 1954; Wenner Minute on Makins to FO, 18 September 1954; Makins to FO, 18 September and 2 October 1954, FO 371/109101; Churchill to Eden, 18 August 1954; Memo of Churchill–Mendès-France Conv., 23 August 1954, PREM 11/672; Makins to FO, 25 September and 24 October 1953, FO 371/103496, PRO; Moran, *Churchill*, 614; Massigli to Mendès-France, 7 September 1954 (re: British fear of U.S. disengagement); Bonnet to Mendès-France, 27 August and 16 September 1954 (on French fears) in Ministère des Affaires Étrangères, *Documents diplomatiques français*, 1954 (Paris: Imprimerie Nationale, 1987), 219, 284, 378–79 (hereafter *DDF*, 1954).

12. JFD, *War or Peace*, 218, 222; JFD to U.S. Embassy, Paris, 13 July and 5 October 1953; JFD to Chiperfield, 18 June 1953; Hagerty Diary, 24 December 1954 (on Mendès-France's position), FR (1952–54), 5:793n, 796, 819, 996n, 1523. See also ibid., 1117, 1619, 1764, 1770; *New York Herald Tribune*, 15 and 16 December (clipping charging Dulles with a gaffe); Memo to Murrow, undated; JFD Address to National Press Club, 22 December 1953; JFD Address to NATO Conference, December 1953, boxes 69 and 73, JFDP; David K. E. Bruce OHI by PAC, 9 June 1964, p. 7, JFDOH; Ambrose, *EP*, 207; *China Post* (Taipei), 28 December 1954; Gerson, *Dulles*, 141–42; Scott to FO, 28 August 1954; Makins to FO, 18 September and 2 October 1954, FO 371/109101; Makins to Eden, 13 June 1953, FO 371/103495; Makins to FO, 19 December 1953, FO 371/103496; Jeff to FO, 3 January 1955, FO

371/118107; Churchill to DDE (19 December?) 1953, 25 December 1953, PREM 11/699, PRO (Churchill called the tactic "blunt but salutary").

13. Goold-Adams, *Dulles*, 117; Lodge, *As It Was*, 67; DDE, First Inaugural Address, in Branyan and Larsen, eds., *Eisenhower*, 1:29–30; JFD, "Challenge and Response," 25; Frederick E. Nolting, Jr. OHI by RDC, 2 June 1966, p. 33, JFDOH; Transcript of JFD Remarks, 21 April 1956; JFD Address to Council on Foreign Relations, 7 June 1957; JFD Manuscript, 21 April 1956, boxes 109, 122, 287, JFDP; NSC Meeting, 18 February 1953, box 4, NSC.

14. Humphrey OHI, p. 24; Romulo OHI, pp. 10–11, JFDOH; *Sunday Star*, 6 March 1955 (clipping), box 95, JFDP; JFD to DDE, 16 March 1956, box 5, DH; Ellis Briggs OHI by Douglas Scott, 19 June 1970, p. 122, EL (CUOHC); Churchill to DDE, 22 December 1953 (draft), PREM 11/699, PRO; Radford Memo on meeting with Churchill at Chequers, 26 April 1954, Radford file, 091 Indochina, April, RG 218, NA (Churchill's response to a plea for "united action" in Indochina [SEATO] was the lament that Washington had not "stood by the British in their crisis with Egypt"); Memo of Conv. between DDE, JFD, Churchill, Eden, et al., 25 June 1954, box 91 (Records of the Council of Foreign Ministers), RG 43, NA (discussion of Britain's position in Egypt and the possibility of American aid was followed immediately by discussion of British support for the Franco-American position in Indochina—i.e., SEATO).

15. James W. Riddleberger OHI by Gordon A. Craig, September 1965, pp. 62, 64–65, JFDOH; JFD Backgrounder, 14 February 1954; JFD Statement, 16 February 1954; JFD Statement Before Senate Foreign Relations Committee, 10 June 1955; DSPR #338, boxes 78 and 89, JFDP; Beam, *Multiple Exposure*, 42–43; Makins to FO, 17 April 1953; Hayter to FO, 15 April 1955, PREM 11/818; British Embassy, Austria, to FO, 25 February and 16 March 1955, FO 371/117779; Hayter to FO, 7 March 1955; FO to Wallinger, 12 March 1955, FO 371/117786; Hayter to FO, 9 February 1954; FO Northern Department Memo, February 1955, FO 371/116650, PRO; Cronin, *Austria*, 145–46; Chauvel to Mendès-France, 27 October 1954 (re: *Anschluss*), *DDF* (1954), 623–25; Couve de Murville to Pinay, 25 March 1955 (re: *Anschluss*), Ministère des Affaires Étrangères, *Documents diplomatiques français*, 1955, pt. 1 (Paris: Imprimerie Nationale, 1988), 351 (hereafter *DDF*, 1955, pt. 1).

16. Thompson to Austrian Government, 12 January 1954; JFD Press Backgrounder, 13 May 1955, boxes 78 and 89, JFDP; Crowe, "Reflections," DAP; Makins to FO, 5 May 1953; Harvey to FO, 6 May 1953; Lloyd to Churchill, 6 May 1953; FO to U.K. Embassy, Washington, 18 April 1955; Scott to FO, 19 April 1955, PREM 11/818; Makins to FO, 1 April 1955; FO to U.K. Embassy, Washington, 12 April 1955; Scott to Eden, 20 April 1955, PREM 11/893; Colville Memo, 26 July 1954; Makins to FO, 4 August 1954; Scott to FO, 19 August 1954; FO to U.K. Permanent Delegation, Paris, 2 September 1954, PREM 11/670; Wallinger to FO, 27 February 1955, FO 371/117785; Hayter to FO, 7 March 1955; FO to Wallinger, 12 March 1955, FO 371/117786; Transcript of Fifth Tripartite Meeting, 14 July 1953, PREM 11/425; Cabinet Conclusions (hereafter CC) [55] 27–28, 30 March 1955, PRO; Cronin, *Austria*, 156; Couve de Murville to Pinay, 7 April 1955, *DDF* (1955, pt. 1), 416.

17. On Austria's reluctance to press its case see Nutting to Eden, 24 November 1954, AP 20/17/28. See also Macmillan, *Tides*, 596; JFD to DDE, 12 May 1955, box 4, DH; Adenauer, *Mémoires: 1953–56*, 432–33; Llewelyn E. Thompson OHI by PAC, 29 June 1966, pp. 12–15, JFDOH; U.K. Embassy, Austria, to FO, 25 February

1955, FO 371/117779; CC, Minute 4, 30 September 1952; Caccia to FO, 10 April 1953; Caccia to FO, 16 April 1953; Makins to FO, 17 April 1953; Hayter to FO, 18 April 1953; Makins to FO, 5 May 1953; Harvey to FO, 6 May 1953; Lloyd to Churchill, 6 May 1953; U.K. Embassy, Berlin, to FO, 5 February 1954, PREM 11/818, PRO; Chauvel to Mendès-France, 27 October 1954, *DDF* (1954), 622; Lalouette to Pinay, 6 April and 11 May 1955, *DDF* (1955, pt. 1), 408, 618–19. For the theory that Stalin's death was pivotal (similar to the argument discussed in chapter 1 that would deny Dulles credit for ending the Korean War), see Cronin, *Austria*, 123, 160, 164. Cronin scarcely mentions Dulles by name, although it was he, more than anyone else, who made rapprochement something to be bought by the Soviet Union, rather than something to be had for the asking, and even though it was he who held the Western coalition together long enough to arrive at WEU without a preliminary summit. The Cronin account would be more complete, as well as more convincing in part, if it: (1) alluded to the Soviet craving for respectability and Dulles' strategy of parlaying American support on the summit for Austrian freedom; (2) recognized Soviet fears of *Anschluss*—Moscow is portrayed as more on the offensive than defensive; (3) suggested that the summit may have been something of a consolation prize intended to save face for the Kremlin after its crushing defeat on WEU; (4) credited Dulles with successful delaying tactics, ensuring the achievement of his first goal, WEU (by Cronin's account, he appears obstructionist); (5) differentiated between the Western position and that of Dulles—the latter being responsible for all of Vienna's last-minute gains (had it not been for Dulles, Western leverage, as derived from the power to give or withhold assent to a summit, would have been squandered at the outset); (6) supplied hard documentation for the book's central thesis, namely, that internal Soviet politics, as opposed to external factors, played the key role.

18. Bohlen, *Witness*, 362; Barbour OHI, pp. 5–6; Livingston T. Merchant OHI by PAC, 13 March–17 April 1965, pp. 92–94; Thompson OHI, p. 21, JFDOH; JFD News Conf., 26 April 1955; JFD Press Backgrounder, 13 May 1955; TV Report by JFD to DDE, 17 May 1955; JFD Statement Before the Senate Foreign Relations Committee, 10 June 1955; DSPR #338, box 89, JFDP; JFD–George Conv., 6 May 1955, box 5, SS; JFD to DDE, 12 May 1955, box 4, DH; Hayter to FO, 13 and 15 April 1955; FO to U.K. Embassy, Washington, 18 and 19 April 1955; Scott to FO, 19 April 1955, PREM 11/818; Memo from U.K. Embassy, Vienna, 27 May 1955, FO 371/117777, PRO; Cronin, *Austria*, 156–59; Lalouette to Pinay, 11 May 1955, *DDF* (1955, pt. 1), 618–19.

19. *New York Times*, 16 May 1955, p. 8 (treaty text); Thompson OHI, pp. 15–16, JFDOH; Livy Merchant, "Recollections of the Summit Conference, Geneva, 1955" (1957), pp. 4–5; JFD Interview on BBC, 3 December 1957, boxes 92 and 119, JFDP; JFD to DDE, 7 November 1955, box 5, DH; Cronin, *Austria*, 159.

20. DDE, *Mandate*, 15; NSC Meeting, 5 March 1954, FR (1952–54), 5:888; NSC Meeting, 11 February 1953, box 4, NSC; Goodpaster OHI #37, pp. 98–99, EL (CUOHC).

21. JFD Memo for DDE, 15 May 1954, box 8, WHMS; Spaak, *Memoirs*, 178; Memo of State—Mutual Security and JCS Meeting, 28 January 1953, FR (1952–54), 5:713; DDE, *Mandate*, 404.

22. Lodge, *As It Was*, 22; DDE, *Mandate*, 360; Paul Weymar, *Adenauer, His Authorized Biography*, trans. Peter de Mendelsohn (New York: Dutton, 1957), 475–76; Bruce to State, 12 March 1953; State Department Paper (January 1954?); Bidault-

Alphand-Merchant Conv., 17 February 1954; MacArthur Memo, 23 April 1954, FR (1952–54), 5:767–69, 874–76, 943n, 944; JFD Memo for DDE, 21 October 1953, box 8, WHMS; Alphand, *Journal*, 26 April 1954, 246, 267n; *China Post*, 5 December 1954, p. 1.

23. JFD to U.S. Embassy, Paris, 24 January and 22 March 1953; Dillon to State, 22 March 1954; JFD to DDE, 29 September 1954, FR (1952–54), 5:707–8, 905–7, 1366; Kilmuir, *Memoirs*, 222; Makins to FO, 19 September 1953, FO 371/103496; CC 10 (54), 22 February 1954; CC 17 (54), 10 March 1954; CAB 128/27, pt. 1; Makins to FO, 17 March 1954, PREM 11/910, PRO.

24. JFD to Bidault, 23 February 1954; JFD to State, 3 March 1954; Bidault to JFD, 7 March 1954, FR (1952–54), 5:879, 885, 895; JFD Statement at Berlin Conf., 26 January 1954 (DSPR #38); JFD Press Conf., 31 January 1954, box 78, JFDP; U.K. Embassy, Washington, to FO, 27 March 1954, FO 371/109100; Makins to FO, 11 July 1953, PREM 11/425, PRO; Geoffrey Warner, "Britain and the Crisis over Dien Bien Phu, April 1954: The Failure of United Action," and Kaplan, "United States, NATO, and French Indochina," in Kaplan et al., eds., *Dien Bien Phu*, 59, 240. On the link between Indochina and EDC (made explicit by Dulles), see JFD Memo, 16 February 1954, box 2, DH. The Netherlands ratified EDC on 20 January 1954, Belgium on 11 March, Germany on 29 March, and Luxembourg on 7 April. See FR (1952–54), 5:927. See also Makins to Eden, 21 May 1954, AP 20/17/18A (the Americans have "swallowed their scruples and on the whole have used their influence to support the colonial system").

25. JFD Memo, 16 February 1954, box 2, DH; JFD to Bidault, 23 February 1954; Smith to U.S. Embassy, Paris, 9 and 11 March 1954; Dillon to State, 17 March 1954; JFD to U.S. Embassy, Paris, 20 and 22 March 1954; Dillon to State, 22 March 1954, FR (1952–54), 5:879, 896–900, 905–7; Adenauer, *Mémoires: 1953–1956*, 221; Makins to FO, 5 December 1953, FO 371/103496; CC 17 (54), 10 March 1954; CAB 128/27 pt. 1, p. 133; Makins to FO, 17 March 1954, PREM 11/910, PRO; Kaplan, "United States, NATO, and French Indochina," in Kaplan et al., eds., *Dien Bien Phu*, 239–40. For additional information on the American effort to secure a Saar settlement satisfactory to France, see JFD to U.S. High Commissioner to Germany, 8 April 1953; Conant to JFD, 9 October 1953; JFD to Bidault, 23 February 1954, FR (1952–54), 5:787, 819, 880. For more on Dulles' strategy of linkage, see Kaplan, "United States, NATO, and French Indochina," and Artaud, "Indochina War," in Kaplan et al., eds., *Dien Bien Phu*, 233, 260.

26. Adams, *Firsthand Report*, 120, 122; MacArthur Memo of talk with Laniel, 14 April 1954, FR (1952–54), 5:934, 940n. See also JFD to American ambassador at Paris, 6 April 1954, box 7, CS; NSC Meeting, 6 May 1954, box 5, NSC; Alphand, *Journal*, 8 May 1954, p. 247; U.K. Embassy, Washington, to FO, 3 and 10 April 1954; Makins to FO, 17 and 24 April, 1 May 1954, FR 371/109100, PRO; Robert F. Randle, *Geneva 1954: The Settlement of the Indochinese War* (Princeton: Princeton University Press, 1969), 89. For France's two requests for an American bombing strike (in early and late April, circa 3 and 23 April), see JFD to DDE, 22 April 1954; MacArthur Memo, 23 April 1954, FR (1952–54), 5:940–46; JFD Longhand Notes on Dien Bien Phu (n.d.), box 8, SS; Eden to Makins, 12 June 1954, PREM 11/649, PRO; Prados, *Vulture*, 139. The original date that had been suggested for the opening of debate was 1 May. See JFD to U.S. Embassy, Paris, 20 March 1954, FR (1952–54), 5:900. According to Gardner, Nixon spoke without White House approval (*Viet-*

nam, 231). But this seems highly unlikely and is belied by the findings of other historians, for example, Prados, *Vulture*, 140; Billings-Yun, *Dien Bien Phu*, 133 (Nixon spoke from a prepared statement).

27. JFD to DDE, 22 April 1954; MacArthur Memo, 23 April 1954; JFD to U.S. Embassy, Paris, 18 May 1954; Dillon to State, 19 May 1954, FR (1952–54), 5:940–41, 943, 955, 957–59; Weymar, *Adenauer*, 476; JFD-DDE Luncheon Conv., 11 May 1954, box 1, WHMS; JFD Memo, 24 April 1954; JFD to Smith, 23 April 1954, box 2, DH; Joseph Laniel, *Le drame Indochinois: De Dien-Bien-Phu au pari de Genève* (Paris: Plon, 1957), 110; Makins to FO, 1 May 1954, FO 371/109100; Makins to FO, 12 and 19 June, 17 July 1954, FO 371/109101, PRO. For data on American offers to aid France with ground forces in return for certain concessions, see Neil Sheehan, Hedrick Smith, E. W. Kenworthy, and Fox Butterfield, eds., *The Pentagon Papers* (New York: Bantam, 1971), 10–13; DDE-JFD Conv., 11 May 1954, box 1, WHMS. Billings-Yun notes that Dulles' interventionist rhetoric seemed to subside in late April and early May, coinciding with the course of political events in Paris (*Dien Bien Phu*, 153–54).

28. For documentation and more on tripartitism, see Frederick W. Marks III, "The Real Hawk at Dienbienphu: Dulles or Eisenhower?" *Pacific Historical Review* 59 (August 1990): 317–18n. 25.

29. For American and Chinese opinion on French bargaining at Geneva, see Dillon to State, 19 May 1954, FR (1952–54), 5:958; JFD-Judd Conv., 14 September 1954, box 9, CS; JFD to Bruce, 31 August 1954, box 2, GCMS; Johnson, *Right Hand*, 218; Cheng Paonan to Koo, 25 April 1954, box 150, file 119, WKP.

30. Carlton, *Eden*, 337; Beal, *Dulles*, 267, 307; Dooner, "Dulles," 43–44; Hollister OHI, p. 70, JFDOH ("he never would try to take all the credit for anything"). Typical of the credit Eden has received are the following accounts: Spaak, *Memoirs*, 178–79, 181–82; Macmillan, *Tides*, 481–82; Weymar, *Adenauer*, 484–85; Kirkpatrick, *Inner Circle*, 261; and Geoffrey Warner, "The Anglo-American Special Relationship," *Diplomatic History* 13 (Fall 1989): 485–86.

31. JFD to State (12 September 1954?); JFD to DDE, 17 (18?), 28, 29 September 1954, box 3, DH; JFD to Eden, 8 September 1954; Eden to JFD, 8, 9 September 1954; JFD to Eden, 14 September 1954; Dillon to State, 15 September 1954; JFD to Adenauer, 18 September 1954; JFD to DDE, 18 September 1954; NSC Meeting, 24 September 1954, FR (1952–54), 5:1155–56, 1193–94, 1196, 1226–27, 1266; Carlton, *Eden*, 361 (on the origin of the so-called Eden Plan). Dulles' snub of Mendès-France seems to have had a positive effect. See JFD to Dillon, 16 September (10:00 P.M.) 1954, box 3480, file 740.5, RG 59, NA. On disappointment with Eden's tour and postponement, see Smith to U.S. Embassy, London (for Eden from JFD), 8 September 1954; JFD to DDE, 18 September, ibid. One of the reasons why WEU was pushed harder and earlier by London than by Washington is that the British never liked EDC. Dulles, by contrast, was fully committed to it and therefore hesitant to prejudice its chances by playing into the hands of compromisers as long as there was any chance of its acceptance. He also wanted to appear reserved on the aftermath of EDC's defeat in order to impress London, as well as Paris, with the seriousness with which Washington was considering "disengagement." See "Comments on British Proposal for German Membership in NATO" (n.d.) and Smith to U.S. Embassy, Manila (Dulles), 7 September 1954, boxes 3477 and 3480, ibid.

32. JFD to DDE, 3 October 1954, box 3, DH; NSC Meeting, 24 September 1954;

JFD to DDE, 3 October 1954; NSC Draft Statement of Policy, 16 September 1954; Report on JFD Conv. in Bonn and London, 20 September 1954; Bowie Memo, 27 September 1954; JFD to DDE, 28 September 1954; JFD to DDE, 12 November 1954; JFD to U.S. Embassy, Paris, 14 December 1954, FR (1952–54), 5:1207, 1222, 1266, 1277, 1293, 1370, 1479, 1497–98; Goold-Adams, *Dulles*, 164; James B. Conant OHI by Gordon A. Craig, 11 July 1964, pp. 30–32, JFDOH; Adenauer, *Mémoires: 1953–1956*, 332–33; Makins to FR, 2 October 1954, FO 371/109101, PRO; Ambrose, *EP*, 216; Record of Meeting at Hotel Talleyrand, 23 September 1954, box 3480, file 740.5, RG 59, NA; Carlton, *Eden*, 362–63. Carlton, without benefit of American documentation, can only guess that Eden's conversation on the eve of the London Conference was motivated by U.S. pressure—he uses the word"probably" and refers more specifically to Eden's fear of a recrudescence of the "Asia First" mentality. To the question, what if Eden had offered the same thing earlier, would it have saved EDC, Carlton replies that "the French assembly probably had a deep psychological need to reject at least once a European settlement involving the Germans" (ibid., 363).

33. Adenauer, *Memoirs, 1945–53*, 443; JFD to DDE, 17 September 1954, box 3, DH; Ambrose, *EP*, 216; Adenauer, *Mémoires: 1953–1956*, 288, 325, 332, 355–56; First Meeting of Four-Power Conf., Paris, 20 October 1954; JFD to DDE, 23 October 1954; JFD Report to Cabinet, 25 October 1954; Dillon to State, 16 October 1954; JFD to DDE, 12 November 1954; Minutes of Meeting with Mendès-France at White House, 18 November 1954; DDE to Churchill, 14 December 1954; Merchant Memo, 16 December 1954; Martin Memo, 27 September 1954, FR (1952–54), 5:1292, 1395, 1409, 1463–65, 1473, 1481–85, 1499, 1506; Memo of Conv. between Mendès-France, JFD, and Eden, 3 October 1954, box 9, CS.

34. JFD-DDE Conv., 30 October 1954, box 1, WHMS; Memo of Conv. between Mendès-France, Eden, and JFD, 3 October 1954, box 9, CS; Adenauer, *Mémoires: 1953–56*, 355–57; JFD to DDE, 23 October 1954 (two reports); JFD to DDE, 12 November 1954, FR (1952–54), 5:1463–64, 1473.

35. Weymar, *Adenauer*, 486–87; Merchant to JFD, 31 March 1954; Acting Secretary to U.S. Embassy, France, 13 April 1954; U.S. Delegation at NATO Meeting to State, 17 December 1954; NSC Memo, 22 December 1954; Minutes of U.S.-U.K. Talks, 5 March 1953; JFD to U.S. Embassy, London, 13 January 1954; Bohlen to State, 23 December 1954; DDE to Churchill, 14 December 1954, FR (1952–54), 5:488, 503, 551–52, 562, 749, 872–73, 1499, 1518, 1510n; White House Meeting, 11 March 1955, box 2, WHMS; JFD-DDE Phone Conv., 12 January 1955, box 1, Hagerty Diary, EL; Jebb to FO, 12 March 1953, PREM 11/422, PRO; Memo of JFD-Pearson Conv., 15 February 1953, vol. 4, Pearson Papers, MG26N1, PAC; Bonnet to French foreign minister, 15 November 1954, *DDF* (1954), 722.

36. Hagerty Diary, 24, 25, 29 December 1954, in Ferrell, ed., *Hagerty*, 148–51; Hagerty OHI, pp. 28–29, JFDOH; JFD to Dillon, 14 December 1954; Dillon to JFD, 31 December 1954; Hoover to DDE, 1 February 1955, box 3, DH; Alphand, *Journal*, 239–40; *China Post*, 25 December 1954; NSC Meeting, 24 September 1954; Hagerty Diary, 24 December 1954, FR (1952–54), 5:1267, 1519–23; Jebb to FO, 3 January 1955, PREM 11/118107, PRO; Makins to Eden, 21 May 1954, AP 20/17/18A (on colonialism); Mendès-France to Bonnet, 29 December 1954, *DDF* (1954), 977 (wants to convey his thanks to Dulles for Washington's quiet, diplomatic response to the Deputies' initial, adverse vote, terming the low-key U.S. reaction "indispen-

sable" to his success). For the importance of the American promise on troop commitment, see Bonnet to Mendès-France, 4 January 1955; Juniac to Mendès-France, 11 January 1955, *DDF* (1955, pt. 1), 8, 58–59.

37. Martin Memo, 27 September 1954; Barbour Memo, 6 October 1954; NSC Meeting, 6 October 1954; Summary of Nine-Power Conf. (21 October 1954), 22 October 1954; Anderson Report, 22 October 1954; JFD to DDE, 12 November 1954, FR (1952–54), 5:1292, 1376, 1382–83, 1417–20, 1477–78.

38. FO to U.K. Embassy, Paris, 13 April 1954, PREM 11/645, PRO (gives the precise wording of the U.S.-U.K. communiqué—"We are ready to take part, with the other countries principally concerned, in an examination of the possibility of collective defensive measures to assure the peace, security, and freedom of Southeast Asia"). See also Evelyn Shuckburgh, *Descent to Suez: Diaries, 1951–1956* (London: Weidenfeld and Nicolson, 1986), 189. According to Shuckburgh (Eden's private secretary), "we are getting very near having cheated the Americans on this question of starting talks on SEA security. Dennis told Harold and me at lunch today that when Dulles was in London, A.E. *did* indicate that we should be willing to start such talks at once, provided we were not committed to any action in Indochina. The American record showed that but ours was obscure on the point and A.E. has always denied it."; Neff, *Warriors*, 146–47; JFD Press Conf., 13 April 1954, box 79, JFDP; JFD to Under Secretary Smith, 12 May 1954, box 7, CS. Bowie and Robertson, heads respectively of State's Planning and Far Eastern divisions, agreed with Dulles. See Bowie OHI, pp. 25–26; Robertson OHI, p. 60, JFDOH. Lord Home later recalled that Dulles had taken a very practical view of the UK's stand on Vietnam and seemed almost resigned. This squares perfectly with Dulles' statement on 11 May that he had not even discussed joint military intervention with the British. See JFD Press Conf., 11 May 1954, DSPR #4, box 82, JFDP; Lord Home OHI by author, 23 July 1986.

39. Paul Ely, *Mémoires: L'Indochine dans la tourmente* (Paris: Plon, 1964), 88–89; Jebb to FO, 23 April 1954; Eden to U.K. Embassy, Paris, 25 April 1954 (6:25 P.M.); Eden to FO, 26 April and 2 May 1954; Memo of 10 Downing Street Meeting, 25 April 1954 (4:00 P.M.), PREM 11/645; Eden to Makins, 12 June 1954, PREM 11/649, PRO.

40. Eden to Churchill, 16 May 1954, PREM 11/666; Makins to FO, 3 April 1954, PREM 11/645; DDE to Churchill, 5 April 1954; Memo on British Discussions with Dulles, 13 April 1954; Record of Churchill-Radford-Anderson-Colville Conv. at Chequers, 26 April 1954 (Radford making a direct connection between Vietnam and Egypt); Memo of 10 Downing Street Meeting, 25 April 1954 (4:00 P.M.); CAB 128/27 pt. 1, 13 April 1954 (Eden linking Egypt with Indochina); Draft of a message from Churchill to DDE, 22 December 1953 ("Dismiss from your mind the idea that we shall be deterred from supporting you about China because you take sides against us in Egypt. It will only be a heavier task"), PREM 11/699; CAB 128/27 pt. 2, 7 July 1954; Eden to Makins, 18 March 1954, PREM 11/701, PRO. It is important to differentiate between what Dulles and Eisenhower called "united action" on the one hand (implying immediate military action, either aerial or ground) and, on the other, the creation of a defensive treaty organization with an eye more to the long haul. Of course, the British were properly fearful that any encouragement given the latter might be construed as moral support for the former even though the "treaty track" would require more time. See also Ely, *L'Indochine*, 88–89.

41. Jebb to FO, 23 April 1954; Eden to Churchill, 24 April 1954; Eden to FO, 24 April 1954 (7:34 P.M.); Jebb to FO, 24 April 1954; FO to Paris, 25 April 1954 (6:25 P.M.); CC (54) 155, Record of Cabinet Meeting, 27 April 1954; Eden to FO, 26 April 1954; Colville to Eden, 27 April 1954, PREM 11/645, PRO. On atomic bombs, see Bidault, *Resistance*, 196; Fall, *Hell*, 299, 306–7, 475n; Drummond and Coblentz, *Duel*, 121–22; Ambrose, *Ike's Spies*, 258; Twining OHI, p. 29, JFDOH; Ely, *L'Indochine*, 90; J. R. Tournoux, *Secrets d'Etat* (Paris: Plon, 1960), 48, 54; Radford Memo on Meeting with Ely, 29 March 1954, microfilm LM 71, roll 11, RG 59, NA (Radford told General Ely of France on 29 March that "Americans were growing very impatient with France over its lack of action on EDC"). Nixon erred in *No More Vietnams* when he said that atomic bombs were never seriously considered. He also confuses Operation Vulture (which was a plan for conventional bombing to relieve the garrison at Dien Bien Phu) with plans for the use of atomic weapons. See *No More Vietnams*, 30. It is virtually certain that in lieu of the airstrike that Dulles succeeded in blocking, Eisenhower offered the French two or three atomic bombs for use in Vietnam. The French military, along with at least one member of the cabinet, had considered the use of such weapons; France's minister of the interior was on record as having asked Premier Laniel to obtain the bombs; and the U.S. offer is mentioned in the diaries and memoirs of General Ely, Foreign Minister Bidault, and Jean Chauvel, permanent head of the Quai d'Orsay (see Laurent Césari and Jacques de Folin, "Military Necessity, Political Impossibility: The French Viewpoint on Operation Vautour," in Kaplan et al., eds., *Dien Bien Phu*, 113–14. For Dulles' insistence on French support for SEATO in return for large-scale military aid in Vietnam, see ibid., 111–12.

42. Bidault, *Resistance*, 199; Ambrose, *Ike's Spies*, 258; Eden to FO, 26 April 1954; Private Secretary to Prime Minister, 26 April 1954, PREM 11/645, PRO. Denise Artaud, who has examined all pertinent documents on the French side, concludes that Laniel was somewhat cynical ("not completely honest") in dealing with Dulles, most likely seeing French approval of EDC as unlikely, if not impossible, *with or without* an American air strike at Dien Bien Phu. According to Artaud, he tried to "blackmail" the Americans on a grand scale, and Dulles called his bluff. See Artaud, "Conclusion," in Kaplan et al., eds., *Dien Bien Phu*, 270–71. She also sees Laniel as having been willing to make a trade-off with Moscow: defeat of EDC in return for Soviet support in Vietnam (ibid., 262).

43. Johnson, *Right Hand*, 221; Eden to FO, 17 May 1954, PREM 11/649; Record of White House Meeting, 26 June 1954, PREM 11/702; CC (54) 47, 7 July 1954; CC (54) 55, 28 July 1954; CAB 128/27 pt. 2; Stark to Browne, 13 August 1954, PREM 11/651, PRO.

44. JFD-DDE Conv., 19 May 1954, box 1, WHMS; Roberts, "Air Strike," 4; Notes on Legislative Leaders Meetings, 3 May, 23 and 28 June 1954, Russell Papers, UG.

45. Roberts, "Air Strike," 4; Ambrose, *Ike's Spies*, 259; Admiral Felix Stump OHI by RDC, 29 October 1964, p. 65, JFDOH; JFD to Eden, 2 May 1954; Memo given by R. C. to DDE, 3 May 1954, box 8, SS; JFD Memo, 30 April 1954, box 2, DH; Eden to FO, 3 May 1954; Eden to FO, 7 May 1954; FO to U.K. High Commissioners, 19 May 1954; Makins to FO, 21 May 1954; Eden to FO, 22 May 1954; Eden Memo, 23 May 1954; Eden to FO, 25 May 1954, PREM 11/649, PRO; Gurtov, *Vietnam*, 148, 151. The staff talks began on 3 June.

46. Geoffrey Warner, "From Geneva to Manila," in Kaplan et al., eds., *Dien Bien*

Phu, 163–64 (on Churchill's later reaction); Goold-Adams, *Dulles,* 147–49; DDE, *Mandate,* 368; Cabinet Conclusions Minute 4, 30 September 1952, PREM 11/818; Eden to FO, 1 and 12 May 1954; CC (54) 43 Conclusions, Minute 2, 22 June 1954, PREM 11/649; Record of JFD-Eden Meeting, 27 June 1954, PREM 11/650; CC (54) 52, Confidential Annex, 23 July 1954, CAB 128/27, pt. 2, PRO. In considering possible terms for an Austrian peace treaty, London and Paris were willing to allow the permanent stationing of Soviet troops in Austria while Washington was not. See U.K. Embassy, Berlin, to FO, 5 February 1954, PREM 11/818, PRO.

47. DDE to Churchill, 12 July 1954 (JFD draft); JFD to Mendès-France, 10 July 1954, box 3, DH; Johnson, *Right Hand,* 221–23, 225; Gerson, *Dulles,* 183–85; Ely, *L'Indochine,* 199–200.

48. Hagerty Diary, 18 July 1954, in Ferrell, ed., *Hagerty,* 93; Drummond and Coblentz, *Duel,* 123; JFD-DDE Conv., 19 July 1954, box 1, WHMS.

49. Tyler Memo, 5 June 1954, FR (1952–54), 5:967; Ely, *L'Indochine,* 175–76; Eden to FO, 17 May 1954, PREM 11/649, PRO; Johnson, *Right Hand,* 224–25. General Navarre is one of the few French leaders who characterized the American position as one of "bluff" which did more harm than good. See Navarre, *Indochine,* 245n.

50. Gurtov, *Vietnam,* 152. For the rise of Diem in Vietnam, see Anthony T. Bouscaren, *The Last of the Mandarins: Diem of Vietnam* (Pittsburgh: Duquesne University Press, 1965); Colby, *Honorable Men,* 144–45, 157–58.

51. Howard Schonberger, "Peacemaking in Asia: The United States, Great Britain, and the Japanese Decision to Recognize Nationalist China, 1951–52," *Diplomatic History* 10 (Winter 1986): 61–62 (re: "placating modifications"); Sebald, *With MacArthur,* 256; Koo-JFD Conv., 28 June 1951, box 184, WKP; JFD to MacArthur, 10 February and 2 March 1951, boxes 19, 88, RG 5, MacArthur Papers, Norfolk, Virginia.

52. Macmillan, *Storm,* 513; Edward L. Freers OHI by PAC, 21 May 1966, p. 22; Hagerty OHI, p. 27, JFDOH; DDE Press Conf., 21 August 1957, box 116, JFDP; JFD-Eban Conv., 28 February 1957, box 7, SS; Goodpaster Memo, 16 and 24 July 1958, box 35, DDE Diary, AWF; *Time,* 8 April 1957, p. 25; 6 May 1957, p. 35.

53. DDE, *Waging Peace,* 340–42; JFD Remarks to Congressional Leaders Meeting, 5 January 1959, box 138, JFDP; Goodpaster Memo, 16 July 1958, box 35, DDE Diary, AWF; Hagerty Diary, 12 January 1955, box 1, Hagerty Diary, EL.

54. Drummond and Coblentz, *Duel,* 91–92; Javits OHI, p. 16, JFDOH; Lloyd on BBC, 24 May 1959, box 83, Allen Dulles Papers, PU; Garvey Minute on Makins to FO, 13 October 1953, FO 371/103523, PRO.

CHAPTER 4

1. According to Stang, Dulles was merely posing as an anti-Communist and deserves blame for America's failure to roll back the Communist menace in Korea, Vietnam, Hungry, Cuba, and the Tachens. See Alan Stang, *The Actor: The True Story of John Foster Dulles, Secretary of State, 1953–1959* (Boston: Western Islands, 1968); also Krock OHI, p. 6, JFDOH; Adenauer, *Mémoires: 1953–1956,* 417–19, 462. Chinese Foreign Minister Yeh was alarmed to hear Dulles speculate on the possibility of evolutionary change within the USSR. See George K. C. Yeh OHI by Spencer Davis, 23 September 1964, JFDOH. For other perceptions of JFD as "soft"

on communism, see Leverett Saltonstall OHI by PAC, 12 March 1966, p. 17, JFDOH; *New York Times*, 8 January 1985, p. B6 (Robert Welch, Jr., head of the John Birch Society, accused Dulles of being a member of the Communist underground and Eisenhower of being "a dedicated conscious agent"). Senators William Jenner of Indiana, Pat McCarran of Nevada, and Everett McKinley Dirksen of Illinois attacked Dulles for his work on the Japanese Peace Treaty, claiming that it was too lenient where Soviet interests were concerned (confirming the Yalta arrangements on South Sakhalin and the Kurile Islands). See Edward Bryce Reynolds, "The Japanese Peace Treaty, A Study in Cold War Diplomacy," (M.A. Thesis, Central Missouri State University, 1976), 63, 67, 94. See also Bly, "Dulles," 42. For scholarly opinions of Dulles as rigid, simplistic, and obsessed, as well as overly legalistic and moralistic, see Dooner, "Dulles," 35; John Stoessinger, *Crusaders and Pragmatists* (New York: Norton, 1979), 97–106; Challener and Fenton, "Dulles," 13; Hoopes, *Dulles*, 403, 490–91; Ulam, *Rivals*, 132, 147, 231; Ambrose, *EP*, 445; Toulouse, *Dulles*, 8, 13, 157, 160, 162, 199–200, 238, 250 (Dulles is twice referred to as an "uncompromising zealot"), 251–53; Mulder, "Moral World," 182; Ole R. Holsti, "Will the Real Dulles Please Stand Up?" *International Journal* 30 (Winter 1974–75): 37–42, 44; Goold-Adams, *Dulles*, 13–14; John Lukacs, *A New History of the Cold War* (Garden City: Doubleday, 1966), 106–7. For the "seachange" theory, see Toulouse, *Dulles*; and Keim, "Dulles," 89.

2. W. Macomber OHI, p. 40; Nixon OHI, pp. 10, 16; Spender OHI, p. 18, JFDOH; Makins to Eden, 4 July 1953, FO 371/103495, PRO. See especially the documentation in note 85.

3. Hoopes, *Dulles*, 68; Leonard Mosley, *Dulles: A Biography of Eleanor, Allen, and John Foster Dulles and Their Family Network* (New York: Dial Press, 1978), 167, 195–96, 198–99; Spaak, *Memoirs*, 131; JFD Interview by William D. Clark, 23 October 1958; JFD, "Can We Guarantee a Free Europe?" *Colliers* (12 June 1948 clipping); JFD Statement to Mr. Angelopoulos, 30 December 1949; idem, "A Policy of Boldness," *Life*, 19 May 1952; *Christian Science Monitor*, 7 July 1948, sec. 2, p. 1 (clipping), boxes 127, 284–86, 398, JFDP; Dooner, "Dulles," 5; JFD Speech Draft, 29 January 1947, box 2, Vandenberg Papers, MHCBHL; *Time*, 8 July 1957, p. 9.

4. JFD, *War, Peace, and Change* (New York: Harper, 1939), 155–56; Edward Corsi OHI by RDC, 2 April 1965, pp. 1–3; Couve de Murville OHI, p. 29, JFDOH; Alphand, *Journal*, 288; JFD Press Conf., 17 November 1953, FO 371/111688, PRO. Needless to say, Dulles did not approve of *the way* in which recognition had been granted in 1933.

5. Toulouse, *Dulles*, 247 (re: Kennan); Adams, *Firsthand Report*, 456; Allison OHI, pp. 3–4; Henderson OHI, p. 29; W. Walton Butterworth OHI by RDC, 8 September 1965, p. 16; John Sherman Cooper OHI by RDC, 11 May 1966, pp. 21–22; W. Macomber OHI, p. 46; Reston OHI, pp. 20–21, JFDOH; Beam, *Multiple Exposure*, 131 ("colossal vanity"); Vandenberg Diary, 23 June 1945, Vandenberg Papers, MHCBHL (on Dulles' good nature); Heeney, *Memoirs*, 139, 158; *Daily Telegraph of London*, 25 May 1959 (clipping), box 83, Allen Dulles Papers, PU (re: JFD's bequest of land to Canada).

6. Pineau, *Suez*, 195; Alphand, *Journal*, 291. See also Hoopes, *Dulles*, 381; Elliott V. Bell OHI by RDC, 7 July 1964, p. 3, JFDOH; JFD-DDE Conv., 3 December 1956, box 4, WHMS; Heeney, *Memoirs*, 139.

7. JFD, *War or Peace*, 77, 124; Horace G. Torbert, Jr. OHI by PAC, 2 November 1965, p. 3; Twining OHI, p. 4; Aiichiro Fujiyama OHI by Spencer Davis, 23 October 1964, pp. 11–12, 15; Louis W. Jefferson, Jr. OHI by PAC, 15 January 1966, p. 35; W. Macomber OHI, p. 10; Merchant OHI, pp. 47–50 (on JFD's evident liking for Eden), JFDOH; JFD to Smith, 20 May 1954, box 7, CS; Lloyd, *Suez*, 152; Dean Acheson, *Present at the Creation* (New York: Norton, 1969), 605; Clarissa Eden to JFD, 9 June 1953, box 68, JFDP (JFD sent Eden flowers when he was ill in Massachusetts); NSC Meeting, 6 October 1954, FR (1952–54), 5:1382; JFD to Eden, 5 February 1953, FO 371/103510, PRO (extremely cordial, even warm in tone). According to Robertson, Eden was "the weakest sister and the most difficult foreign minister in the world"—his words were obscure and meant nothing. See JFD and the Far East (Radford and Robertson) OHI by PAC and RDC, 17 July 1964, pp. 73–74, JFDOH. By comparison with Dulles' behavior toward Eden, which was unfailingly courteous and correct, Eden did a number of things widely regarded as hostile: (1) he failed to meet the secretary of state when the latter arrived in England early in 1953 and sent, as his representative, an official of subcabinet rank—this was interpreted, even in the UK, as a snub; (2) when Eden addressed the House of Commons on 24 June 1954, he made no reference to Dulles although the subject was American foreign policy (of which he was critical); he also proposed a non-aggression pact for Southeast Asia without prior consultation with Dulles (according to the British ambassador in Washington, this was taken by Americans as a "deliberate slight" and journalists were left in no doubt as to whether or not Dulles was angry); (3) Eden declined to attend the charter meetings of SEATO (1954). See *Daily Express*, 6 February 1953 (clipping), FO 371/103510; Makins to FO, 27 June 1954; Scott to FO, 28 August and 4 September 1954, FO 371/109101, PRO.

8. Pineau, *Suez*, 46 (for Eden's opinion of Dulles). In his private life, Dulles was extraordinarily devoted to his wife, Janet, and she to him. Eden, on the other hand, was divorced and remarried after a union which had lasted twenty-seven years and yielded two sons. As the first British prime minister to be divorced, he selected for his cabinet three other divorcés; Neff, *Warriors*, 185; *Time*, 6 May 1957, p. 35. Eden was also well known for holding personal grudges and for being openly vindictive (as when he vowed to destroy Nasser). See Harvey to Emrys Evans, 31 August 1956, #58235, Emrys Evans Papers, British Library; Henderson Chronology Notes for 2 November 1956, box 6, Loy Henderson Papers, Library of Congress; Cooper, *Lion's Last Roar*, 86. At the same time, he tended to be markedly pro-Arab, which is another way in which he differed from the more detached and dispassionate Dulles. See Neff, *Warriors*, 206; Harvey to Emrys Evans, 31 August 1956, #58235, Emrys Evans Papers, British Library. For Britain and the Japanese Peace Treaty, see Schonberger, "Peacemaking," 62–65, 67, 69–71; Reynolds, "Peace Treaty," 80–82; Morrison, *Autobiography*, 280. Public release of the Yoshida letter soon after Eden's return to England was another point of criticism seized upon by Eden, who charged that "its publication so soon after my visit to Washington was embarrassing and could give the impression that I had agreed to its contents" (as he clearly had). See Schonberger, "Peacemaking," 70. For further evidence of a gentlemen's agreement between Dulles and Eden which the latter violated, see Smith Memo, 11 January 1952, box 107, Alexander Smith Papers, PU; JFD-Koo Conv., 2, 19, 21, 28 June 1951, box 184, WKP (the British cabinet and British periodicals such as *New Statesman* saw quite clearly what was meant by the Dulles-Morrison formula

and Dulles came out openly in expressing his "expectation" that Tokyo would recognize Taipei rather than Peking).

9. Carlton, *Eden*, 337. For Ike's use of barrack room language in a phone conversation with Eden, see Thomas, *Suez*, 134. For Eden's denial, see Aldrich OHI, pp. 30–31, JFDOH. According to Eden, Ike never used harsh language on the phone; neither did he phone at all until after Britain had accepted the cease-fire. American records are well laundered and reveal only fragments of one phone call from Eisenhower to Eden on 6 November (12:55 P.M.). The tone appears friendly, with Ike expressing pleasure that Eden has decided to accept the cease-fire. Lloyd, however, mentions another call that came from the White House the same day at 1:43 P.M. (British time presumably) and it would appear to be either this call, the text of which is unavailable, or one placed on the previous day (for which, once again, there is no readily available text) that is the phone call in question. Eisenhower's secretary, Bernard M. Shanley, referred to it as "quite a phone call." See Lloyd, *Suez*, 209; DDE-Eden Phone Conv., 6 November 1956 (12:55 P.M.), box 19, DDE Series, AWF; Shanley OHI, p. 46, JFDOH.

10. Pineau, *Suez*, 33, 35; Drummond and Coblentz, *Duel*, 72–77, 179; Dulles, *War, Peace, and Change*, 35, 58, 109–12; Pineau, *Khrouchtchev*, 186; JFD, "Challenge and Response," pp. 25–26; Yeh OHI, p. 13; Jefferson OHI, p. 35; Bell OHI, pp. 18–19, JFDOH (on Dulles' complete lack of dogmatism regarding free enterprise capitalism); JFD News Conf., 21 July 1956, box 101, JFDP; JFD to Krock, n.d., box 8, WHMS.

11. Judd OHI, p. 113, JFDOH; Gerson, *Dulles*, 193–94; Reinhold Niebuhr, "The Moral World of Foster Dulles," *New Republic* 139 (December 1958): 8; Clutterbuck to Swinton, 29 May 1953, FO 371/106857, PRO.

12. Heller and Heller, *Dulles*, 240; Berding, *Dulles*, 117; Kaufman, *Trade*, 69–70; Henry Luce OHI by RDC, 28 July 1965, p. 39; Hollister OHI, p. 56; Riddleberger OHI, pp. 30–31; Harold Stassen OHI by RDC, 3 June 1965, p. 52; Robert H. Thayer OHI by PAC, 7 September 1965, p. 23, JFDOH; JFD Statement Before House Foreign Affairs Committee, 5 April 1954; JFD TV interview, 23 June 1958; *Freedom and Union* 10 (June 1955): 15–16 (clipping); JFD Statement to Mr. Angelopoulos, 30 December 1949; JFD, "Policy of Boldness," boxes 79, 98, 126, 285–86, JFDP; NSC Meeting, 23 December 1953, box 5, NSC; JFD to DDE, 16 March 1956, box 5, DH (for Dulles' generous views on Sukarno's Indonesia); Greenstein, *Hidden-Hand*, 130; Notes on Legislative Leaders Meeting, 28 June 1955, Russell Papers, UG; Adenauer, *Mémoires: 1953–1956*, 434; Eden to DDE, 28 May 1955, FO 371/115052, PRO (for Nehru's claim that Peking was releasing four American prisoners at his personal request). Britain's high commissioner to India observed that Dulles had made a tactful press statement on arrival in India, followed by a "graceful broadcast" and a short press conference which was "reported with more friendliness than was expected." While the secretary still had his critics, he gave the unexpected impression of being "a kindly, frank, and friendly man who had come . . . in all sincerity to find things out for himself and to get to know the leaders of the Asian countries." See Clutterbuck to Swinton, 29 May 1953, FO 371/106857, PRO.

13. Young, *Chinese*, 223; Heikal, *Cairo Documents*, 298–99; Pineau OHI, p. 5, JFDOH; *Freedom and Union* 10 (June 1955): 20 (clipping) in box 98, JFDP; U.S. Ambassador to Turkey to JFD, 3 June 1958, box 8, DH; Robertson OHI #121,

p. 29, EL; Professor Revilo P. Oliver, Address to 8th Annual Congress of Freedom, 9 April 1959, Russell Papers, UG.

14. Eleanor Dulles OHI, p. 141, JFDOH; Livy Merchant, "Recollections of the Summit Conference, Geneva 1955," p. 34; JFD News Conf., 21 June 1956; JFD Address to U.S. and Japanese Chambers of Commerce, 14 December 1951, boxes 92, 101, 107, JFDP; JFD-DDE Conv., 27 February 1956, box 4, WHMS; NSC Meeting, 18 February 1953, box 4, NSC; Stephen G. Rabe, "The Johnson (Eisenhower?) Doctrine for Latin America," *Diplomatic History* 9 (Winter 1985): 99.

15. Heikal, *Cairo Documents*, 138–40, 261; JFD Manuscript, 21 April 1956, box 287, JFDP; Kissinger, "Reflections," 44; Sadat, *Autobiography*, 127; Cronin, *Austria*, 151.

16. Drummond and Coblentz, *Duel*, 150–51; John C. Dreier OHI by PAC, 24 May 1965, p. 10, JFDOH; JFD to DDE, 7 November 1955, box 5, DH; C. B. Luce OHI #220, p. 56, EL (Dulles' trip to the Vatican), CUOHC.

17. Macmillan, *Storm*, 637; DDE, *Waging Peace*, 337; Drummond and Coblentz, *Duel*, 152, 154, 201–6; Eleanor Dulles OHI, pp. 90–91, JFDOH; Allen Dulles' Address to Business Advisory Council, 11 March 1959, box 85, Allen Dulles Papers, PU; JFD News Conf., 26 November 1958; JFD-McInnis TV Interview, 23 June 1958; JFD Statement to Mr. Angelopoulos, 30 December 1949; JFD, "Policy of Boldness," boxes 126, 285, 286, JFDP; Sir Kenneth Grubb Manuscript on Dulles, 3 March 1959, box 1, DAP; Wiggins, "Notes," 18 November 1958, box 2, DAP; Roberts, *Rough Draft*, 141–42 (on meeting with Rusk); Adenauer, *Mémoires: 1953–1956*, 417–19, 462. Dulles' sister, Eleanor, who headed the Berlin desk at State, felt as concerned as Adenauer did about her brother's liberal leanings. The upshot of negotiations on Berlin was that East German officials were permitted to inspect, but not to stamp, Western transit passes.

18. JFD, *War or Peace*, 157; Goodpaster OHI, p. 7; Kennan OHI, p. 51, JFDOH; JFD News Conf., 23 April and 27 August 1957 (re: Dulles' doubt "that Communist China is a satellite country in the same sense or the same degree, that the Western European satellites are"); JFD Address, 28 June 1957; JFD Press Conf., 10 September 1957, boxes 114 and 119, JFDP; Adenauer, *Mémoires: 1953–1956*, 245; JFD to DDE, 12 November 1954; DDE to Churchill, 14 December 1954, FR (1952–54), 5:1471, 1499; Makins to FO, 7 February 1955, FO 371/115033, PRO (Dulles told the British ambassador that the ultimate aim of his Asian policy was to foster genuine independence on the part of Peking and thus to produce a Sino-Soviet balance of power pending Japanese recovery which would in turn allow the United States to step back somewhat).

19. Mayers, "Containment," 66–67; JFD, *War or Peace*, 157; JFD Press Conf., 10 September 1957, box 119, JFDP; Bipartisan Legislative Leaders Meeting, 22 March 1956, Russell Papers, UG; British Embassy to FO, 16 January 1954, FO 371/109100; Scott to FO, 21 August 1954, FO 371/109101, PRO (on membership in the Communist party).

20. Berding, *Dulles*, 33; JFD, "Challenge and Response," 28; JFD to Avery Dulles, 3 March 1949, "Thirteen Letters from John Foster Dulles to Avery Dulles," DAP-AM 19456 (on Soviet evolution); Yeh OHI, p. 27; Hanes OHI, p. 164; James J. Wadsworth OHI by PAC, 21 June 1965, p. 19, JFDOH; JFD, "Advice to the United States from John Foster Dulles," *U.S. News and World Report*, 27 April 1959, pp. 42–43; JFD Statement, 21 December 1954; JFD Press Backgrounder, 15

May 1955; JFD Statement (draft), 13 August 1955; JFD Speech to American Society of International Law, 25 April 1956; JFD Press Conf., 2 July 1957; JFD Speech to National Press Club, 16 January 1958; JFD Interview for Independent TV, 23 October 1958; JFD, "Thoughts on Soviet Foreign Policy and What to Do About It," *Life*, 10 June 1946; idem, "The Christian Citizen in a Changing World" (pamphlet prepared for the First Assembly of the World Council of Churches, 22 August 1948), pp. 7–8, 33, boxes 79, 83, 91, 104, 127, 284, JFDP; *Central Daily News*, 30 October 1958 (clipping), Foreign Relations File #721–13, HCKMT; JFD Address to Council on American Foreign Relations, 12 January 1954, in Norman Graebner, ed., *Ideas and American Diplomacy* (New York: Oxford University Press, 1964), 809–10 (on Soviet evolution).

21. JFD, *War or Peace*, 111, 165–66; Eleanor Lansing Dulles OHI by author, 11 September 1984; Bell OHI, pp. 12, 18–19; Wilson OHI, p. 9, JFDOH; JFD, "Christian Citizen," 24, box 284, JFDP; DDE Address at Princeton, 15 May 1962, *Princeton University Library Chronicle* 23 (Summer 1962): 154; Sir William Hayter, *Russia and the World* (London: Secker and Warburg, 1970), 118.

22. JFD Speech (draft) to Chicago 4-H Clubs, 22 November 1954, box 62, Allen Dulles Papers, PU.

23. U. Alexis Johnson OHI by PAC, 28 May 1966, p. 33, JFDOH; JFD-DDE Conv., 20 June 1955, box 3, WHMS; JFD to Vandenberg, 25 July 1950, box 3, Vandenberg Papers, MHCBHL; U.S. Del/33 (PR/20), 10 June 1954, box 192, WKP; Eden to U.K. High Commissioner in India, 29 April 1955, PREM 11/879, PRO.

24. JFD Press Conf., 9 November 1953, box 68, JFDP; Reynolds, "Peace Treaty," 30; Rankin Press Conf., 2 March 1957, box 29, Karl Rankin Papers, PU; JFD-DDE Conv., 17 August 1954, box 1, WHMS; JFD-Nixon Phone Conv., 2 July 1954, box 8, CS; JFD to Hoover, 25 February 1955, box 3, DH; Cohen, *Rusk*, 85; JFD to Vandenberg, 25 July 1950, box 3, Vandenberg Papers, MHCBHL; Yeh-JFD-Koo-Robertson Conv., 21 January 1955; JFD-Koo Conv., 2 August 1951; Koo Diary, 19 July 1954, boxes 184, 195, 220, WKP; CC (54) 69, 22 October 1954, CAB 128/27, pt. 2; Makins to FO, 21 January 1955, FO 371/115024; Makins to FO, 7 February 1955, FO 371/115033, PRO.

25. Young, *Chinese*, 84–85; U.S. Del/39 (PR/26); Koo-Robertson Conv., 1 March 1956; Koo-Sebald Conv., 13 March 1956; Koo-Knowland Conv., 15 March 1956, boxes 192, 200, WKP. The American consul in Hong Kong estimated that there were at least seven hundred cases of Chinese having obtained American citizenship under false pretenses. Truman, during the Korean War, had barred Chinese nationals with certain types of technical and scientific skills from leaving the United States, and Dulles used these cases as leverage to strike his deal with Chou. On 3 April 1945, the *New York Times* reported that seventy-six Chinese students, hitherto refused permission to go home, were now "free to depart." See Makins to FO, 3 April 1955, FO 371/115164, PRO.

26. Adams, *Firsthand Report*, 388; Crowe OHI, pp. 2–3, JFDOH; JFD Remarks, Tokyo, 19 March 1956; JFD Press Backgrounder, 11 July 1958, boxes 104, 126, JFDP; Harkness, "Notes," 12 February 1955; Wiggins, "Notes," 12 February 1955, boxes 1 and 2, DAP; JFD Meeting with Aides, 28 March 1955; Position Paper on Offshore Islands, 26 March 1955; Memo of Conv. Between Delegation Chiefs, Bermuda, 7 December 1953, box 1, SS; JFD-DDE Conv., 24 October 1958, boxes 2 and 7, WHMS; NSC Meeting, 4 June 1953, box 4, NSC; Koo-Robertson Conv., 9

January 1956, box 200, WKP; Minute on Makins to Eden, 23 February 1954, FO 371/109099; FO Meeting, 17 September 1954, PREM 11/867; Steel to FO, 8 May 1955, PREM 11/893; CM (55)z, 12 April 1955, CAB 128/29; Allen Memo on Formosa Straits, 18 February 1955; Gage to FO, 13 March 1955, FO 371/115042; Makins to Macmillan, 14 April 1955, FO 371/115048; Trevelyan to FO, 26 February 1955, FO 371/115040, PRO; Canadian UN Delegation to DEA, 16 February 1955, vol. 32, MG26N1, Pearson Papers, PAC; Dulles Draft of Taiwan Policy, 7 April 1955, box 2, WHMS.

27. Drummond and Coblentz, *Duel*, 25; Drummond OHI, p. 7, JFDOH; JFD-Bowie et al. Meeting, 28 March 1955, box 2, WHMS; JFD Draft of Taiwan Policy, 7 April 1955; DDE Draft of Taiwan Policy, 5 April 1955; Combined Draft, 8 April 1955; White House Memo, 5 April 1955, box 2, WHMS (it is interesting to compare Dulles with Eisenhower and then to examine Dulles' draft combining the views of both men); DDE-JFD Conv., 7 and 11 March 1955, box 3, WHMS; Yeh-JFD et al. Conv., 21 January 1955, box 195, WKP; FO Meeting, 17 September 1954, PREM 11/867, PRO (on Dulles' original silence/reluctance to defend Matsu). On prior American commitment to the Tachens, see Rankin to Robertson, 13 March 1955; Memo on National Intelligence Estimate 100, 1 April 1955, box 26, Rankin Papers, PU; DDE-JFD Conv., 22 May 1954, box 1, WHMS. For military opinion on the defensibility of the offshore islands, see JFD and the Far East (Radford and Robertson) OHI, pp. 3, 23; Radford OHI, p. 41, JFDOH; Koo Diary, 14 September 1954, box 220, WKP (the military at the Pentagon, as opposed to the civilian heads, took a positive stand on defensibility, according to Koo); FO Meeting, 17 September 1954, PREM 11/867, PRO (Dulles told Eden and Lloyd that the Joint Chiefs and most military men wanted Washington to aid in the defense of Quemoy and the Tachens).

28. Barrett to Rankin, 21 April 1954; Rankin to McConaughy, 13 September 1954; JFD-Chiang Conv., 9 September 1954; Rankin Memo, 12 September 1954, 15 November 1955; Rankin to Radford, 8 October 1956, boxes 23, 26, 29, Rankin Papers, PU; JFD-DDE Conv., 18 October 1954, box 1, WHMS; JFD to Hoover, 25 February 1955; JFD to DDE, 19 March 1956, boxes 3 and 5, DH; File B-13-1C; Notes on General Chiang Ching-kuo Press Conf., 9 October 1953; Koo Diary, 6 November 1954; Koo-Allen-JFD-Chiang Conv., 1 October 1953; Koo-McConaughy Conv., 16 June 1955, boxes 145, 187, 195, 220, WKP.

29. Hagerty Diary, 2 December 1954, in Ferrell, ed., *Hagerty*, 122; JFD-DDE Conv., 22 May 1954, box 1, WHMS (on Dulles' preference for ambiguity); Yeh-JFD et al. Conv., 19 January 1955 (top secret), 21 January 1955, files B.13.1d and c; Yeh-JFD-Koo Conv., 19 January 1955; Yeh-JFD-Koo-Robertson Conv., 21 and 22 January 1955; State Department Memo (top secret), 21 January 1955, boxes 145, 195, WKP.

30. DDE, *Mandate*, 469; Yeh-Koo-Robertson Conv., 27 January 1955; Yeh-Koo-JFD Conv., 28 January 1955; Koo-Robertson Conv., 29 January 1955; Top Secret Report, 31 January 1955; McConaughy to Wang (top secret text), 31 January 1955; Yeh-Robertson Conv., 3 February 1955; Yeh-Koo-Hoover-Murphy-Robertson Conv., 4 February 1955; Koo Diary, 28 January 1955, boxes 195, 220, WKP.

31. DDE, *Mandate*, 470; JFD Far East (Radford and Robertson) OHI, p. 21; Radford OHI, p. 38, JFDOH; JFD Press Conf., 15 March 1955; *Sunday Star* (D.C.), 6 March 1955 (clipping), boxes 93, 95, JFDP; Wiggins, "Notes," 12 February 1955, box 2, DAP; Randall, "Journal," 16 March 1955, Clarence B. Randall Papers, PU; JFD-Green Conv., 12 October 1958, box 1, GCMS; JFD-George Conv., 7 March

1955, box 5, SS; *Time*, 15 April 1957, p. 32; JFD New York Address, 16 February, 1955, FO 371/115039, PRO.

32. Hagerty Diary, 2 December 1954 and 12 January 1955, in Ferrell, ed., *Hagerty*, 122, 159; Gerson, *Dulles*, 204; JFD-DDE Conv., 22 May 1954, box 1, WHMS; Vandenberg to JFD, 2 May 1949, box 3, Vandenberg Papers, MHCBHL; JFD-Koo Conv., 19 March 1953, box 187, WKP. Interestingly enough, Ambassador Rankin at Taipei urged ambiguity as early as 13 September 1954. See Rankin to Robertson, 13 September 1954, box 23, Rankin Papers, PU. Even before this, at a press conference on 28 August 1954, Dulles was using such a formula to define America's commitment to the ROC islands. See Scott to FO, 28 August 1954, FO 371/109101, PRO.

33. Chiang OHI, p. 19, JFDOH; JFD Press Conf., 4 September 1958, box 127, JFDP; White House Meeting, 11 March 1955, box 2, WHMS; Hagerty Diary, 24 May 1954, box 1, EL; Legislative Leaders Meetings, 7 and 22 May 1954; Bipartisan Legislative Leaders Meeting, 30 March 1954, Russell Papers, UG; Yeh-JFD et al. Conv., 19 January 1955; Ku to Koo, 31 March 1955, file B.13.1c; Yeh-Koo-Richards Conv., 9 February 1955 (on the tenor of congressional debate), boxes 145 and 195, WKP; Makins to FO, 19, 20, 21 January 1955, PREM 11/867; CC (55) 6, 24 January 1955; CC (55) 7, 27 January 1955; CC (55) 13, 15 February 1955, CAB 128/28; Makins to FO, 21 January 1955, FO 371/115024, PRO.

34. DDE, *Mandate*, 482; Rankin Memo, 29 April and 4 May 1955, box 26, Rankin Papers, PU; JFD to DDE, 18 May 1955, box 4, DH; FO to U.K. Embassy, Washington, 8 February 1955, FO 371/115033; Canadian Permanent UN Delegate to Canadian High Commissioner, 16 February 1955; Makins to FO, 16 March 1955, FO 371/115042; Makins to FO, 17 February 1955; Dixon to FO, 17 and 18 February 1955, FO 371/115038; Makins to Macmillan, 14 April 1955, FO 371/115048; Trevelyan to FO, 26 February 1955, FO 371/115040; Pearson Diary, 8 February 1955, vol. 19, Pearson Papers, MG26N1, PAC. Among the things Chiang was offered during this period in return for his evacuation of Matsu and Quemoy was an American naval patrol of the Chinese coast along with interception of contraband and the introduction of U.S. ground and air units on Taiwan proper. See Rankin Memo, 29 April 1955, box 26, Rankin Papers, PU; Whitman Memo, 3 May 1955, box 4, Whitman Diary, AWF.

35. Young, *Chinese*, 139–40; JFD Press Conf., 1 July 1958, box 127, JFDP; Goodpaster Notes on Intelligence Briefing, 1 August 1958, DDE Diary, AWF; Beam, *Multiple Exposure*, 118.

36. Young, *Chinese*, 144, 182, 188–89, 216; Mayers, "Containment," 75–76; DDE, *Waging Peace*, 297; Ambrose, *EP*, 483; Beam, *Multiple Exposure*, 134; Dulles, *Dulles*, 178. On 31 August, *Pravda* declared that a threat to China would be regarded as a threat to the Soviet Union and that Peking would not lack the requisite moral and material assistance. See Young, *Chinese*, 145.

37. DDE, *Waging Peace*, 295; Mayers, "Containment," 83. For Dulles' commitment to the defense of Quemoy as compared with the approach favored by Ike, see White House Memo, 5 April 1955; JFD-DDE Conv., 12 August, 11 and 23 September 1958, boxes 2 and 7, WHMS; Gray Memo, 12 September 1958, box 3, WHOSANSA.

38. Beatrice Bishop Berle and Travis Beal Jacobs, eds., *Navigating the Rapids, 1918–1971: From the Papers of Adolf A. Berle* (New York: Harcourt Brace Jovanovich,

1973), 689; Richard Nixon tribute to Dulles in *Life*, 8 June 1959 (clipping), p. 36, box 81, Allen Dulles Papers, PU; Stump OHI, p. 2; JFD Far East (Radford and Robertson) OHI, p. 11; Nixon OHI, p. 33, JFDOH; DDE, *Waging Peace*, 300; JFD Press Conf., 9, 30 September, 14 October 1958, box 127, JFDP; JFD-Green Conv., 12 October 1958, GCMS (on private support from Tokyo); JFD to DDE, 10 October 1958, box 8, DH; Gerson, *Dulles*, 201, 205–6; Dulles, *Dulles*, 179; JFD-DDE Conv., 11 March 1955, box 3, WHMS (for Bowie's opposition as head of State's planning division in 1955). Mail, even in 1955, had been running on the negative side. See State Department Correspondence, 11–15 April 1955, box 95, JFDP; Robertson-Koo Conv., 5 May 1955, box 195, WKP. The notice to Senator Green came in the form of a letter under Eisenhower's name. See DDE to Green, 2 October 1958, in Branyan and Larsen, eds., *Eisenhower*, vol. 2, 757–58.

39. Young, *Chinese*, 186; DDE; *Waging Peace*, 303; JFD Press Backgrounder, 17 September 1958, box 127, JFDP; Crowe, "Reflections," p. 84, box 2, DAP; JFD-DDE Conv., 30 October 1958, WHMS; Beam, *Multiple Exposure*, 133–34. For an excellent discussion of American diplomacy during the Quemoy crisis, see Gordon, "Taiwan Strait." It should be noted that the ROC declaration (technically the Dulles-Chiang communiqué of 23 October 1958), which states that "under the present conditions, the defense of Quemoy together with the Matsus is closely related to the defense of Taiwan and Penghu [the Pescadores]" renounced the use of force only as a "principal means" of reconquest. It was further diluted when Foreign Minister Yeh stated on 27 October that his country had not foresworn force as one possible means of reclaiming the Mainland. See Yeh Speech, 27 October 1958, file #556–122, HCKMT.

40. DDE, *Waging Peace*, 340; Burke OHI, pp. 49–50, JFDOH; JFD-Couve de Murville Conv., 7 February 1959, box 1, GCMS; JFD to DDE, 8 February 1959, box 8, DH; Ambrose, *EP*, 503–4; *China Post*, 11 November 1954, p. 1; 1 December 1954, p. 1; 2 December 1954, p. 1; 14 January 1955, p. 1; Makins to FO, 4 December 1954, FO 371/109101, PRO. Eisenhower's choice for secretary of state drew considerable criticism from abroad, especially Britain, where Dulles was perceived as something of a fire-breathing chauvinist. However, British observers soon changed their minds. By early 1954, the U.K. ambassador had credited Dulles with a "relaxation" in Soviet-American relations, and by 1955, he was applauding the secretary for the increasingly nonconfrontational tone of U.S. policy. Of course, East bloc publications such as *Pravda* went right on singling Dulles out as a person who delighted in whipping up "an atmosphere of hysteria." See Garvey Minute on Makins to FO, 13 October 1953, FO 371/103523; Makins to Eden, 1 March 1955, FO 371/114349; Makins to Eden, 23 February 1954, FO 371/109099; British Embassy Chancery in D.C. to FO, 2 April 1954, FO 371/109114, PRO; Gerson, *Dulles*, 92–93.

41. Makins to Eden, 21 and 28 February 1953, FO 371/103495, PRO.

42. Hagerty Diary, 5 February 1955, in Ferrell, ed., *Hagerty*, 186; *China Post*, 6 February 1955, p. 1; Notes on Legislative Leaders Meeting, 28 June 1955, Russell Papers, UG; Mackenzie Minute on Scott to FO, 11 September 1954; Makins to FO, 13 November 1954, FO 371/109101; Makins to FO, 12 February, 14 May, 25 June 1955, FO 371/114350; Makins to Eden, 14 March 1953, FO 371/103495; Dixon to FO, 7 September 1954, FO 371/111688, PRO.

43. JFD, "Challenge and Response," p. 25; Phillip G. Henderson, "Advice and Decision: The Eisenhower National Security Council Reappraised," in R. Gordon

Hoxie, ed., *The Presidency and National Security Policy* (New York: Center for the Study of the Presidency, 1984), 168; Bell OHI, p. 17, JFDOH; Wiggins, "Notes," 29 December 1956, box 2, DAP; Gerson, *Dulles*, 340–41n (on "Mr. Fixit"); *Time*, 21 January 1957, p. 12; DDE to Churchill, 14 December 1954, FR (1952–54), 5:1499.

44. Beal, *Dulles*, 312, 314; JFD Interview on "Face the Nation," 21 October 1956; DDE Address, 31 October 1956, in Branyan and Larsen, eds., *Eisenhower*, 1:666–69; 2:696–97; JFD, *War or Peace*, 247; Wiggins, "Notes," 30 October 1956, box 2, DAP.

45. DDE, *Waging Peace*, 199–200; Macmillan, *Storm*, 277–85; Hoopes, *Dulles*, 412–14; Eban, *Autobiography*, 261; DDE-JFD-Macmillan-Lloyd Conv., 25 October 1957; JFD-Norstad Conv., 28 October 1957, box 1, GCMS; Mohamed Heikal, *The Sphinx and the Commissar: The Rise and Fall of Soviet Influence in the Middle East* (New York: Harper and Row, 1978), 76–77; Sadat, *Autobiography*, 149. On 6 August, Syria's defense minister, a former ambassador to Moscow, signed a wide-ranging economic and technical agreement with the USSR. On 17 August, Syria's army chief was replaced by a suspected Communist sympathizer (according to Heikal a "known Communist") who purged the service of senior officers in favor of closer ties with Iraq and Jordan. On the following day, the *New York Times* pronounced Syria a "Soviet satellite." See Heikal, *Sphinx*, 76–77; Seale, *Syria*, 291–92.

46. DDE, *Waging Peace*, 519; JFD Remarks to AFL-CIO Executive Council, 19 August 1958, box 132, JFDP; JFD-DDE Conv., 21 July 1958, WHMS; JFD to U.S. Embassy, Beirut, 13 May 1958, box 16, CS; JFD-DDE Phone Conv., 15, 16 July 1958; Goodpaster Intelligence Briefing, 19 July 1958, box 34, DDE Series, AWF; Margaret M. Bodron, "U.S. Intervention in Lebanon—1958," *Military Review* 56 (February 1976): 73–74; Dulles, *Dulles*, 160.

47. Khrushchev, *Khrushchev Remembers I*, 398; idem, *Testament*, 362–64; DDE-Macmillan Phone Conv., 14 July 1958; Goodpaster Intelligence Briefings, 19 and 23 July 1958, box 34, DDE Diaries, AWF; U.S. Position Papers on Bermuda Conference, 21–23 March 1957, box 9, Confidential File, Subject Series, White House Central Files, EL.

48. Robert Murphy, *Diplomat Among Warriors* (Garden City: Doubleday, 1964), 399–400; Hughes, *Ordeal of Power*, 263; Lodge, *As It Was*, 111; Hoxie, "Eisenhower," 599; DDE Message to U.S. Armed Forces in Lebanon, 19 July 1958; DDE Address to UN General Assembly, 13 August 1958, in Branyan and Larsen, eds., *Eisenhower*, 2:733; Chamoun OHI, pp. 13–14, JFDOH; Bodron, "Lebanon," 73–75.

49. De Gaulle, *Renewal*, 11; Hoopes, *Dulles*, 334; Murphy, *Diplomat*, 382, 391; Dilks, ed., *Cadogan*, 799; Arthur M. Johnson, *Winthrop W. Aldrich: Lawyer, Banker, Diplomat* (Boston: Harvard University Press, 1968), 402–3; Lord Home OHI by author, 23 July 1986 (for a candid admission of British mishandling of the Suez expedition); Cooper, *Lion's Last Roar*, 106, 204, 207, 209, 271.

50. See, for example, Fred J. Cooke, *The Nightmare Decade* (New York: Random House, 1971), 7 (Dulles "cringed" and the result was "a creeping demoralization at the highest levels of government"). See also ibid., 404–5, 407, 549, 551; Lately Thomas [R.V.P. Steele], *When Even Angels Wept* (New York: Morrow, 1973), 287–89 (hereafter Thomas, *Angels*).

51. Gerson, *Dulles*, 108.

52. Vincent's dismissal was especially galling to liberals because Dulles had shown an initial willingness to stand up for him (Cook, *Nightmare*, 407).

53. Robert Griffith, *The Politics of Fear* (Lexington: University of Kentucky Press, 1970), 216; Cooke, *Nightmare*, 421. According to the State Department, about eighteen authors and three hundred titles were banned (compared with the *New York Times'* estimate of forty authors—see Thomas, *Angels*, 327).

54. Griffith, *Fear*, 204. A joint communiqué issued by McCarthy and Dulles stated that although foreign relations was "in the exclusive jurisdiction of the chief executive," McCarthy's action had nevertheless been "in the national interest" (Thomas, *Angels*, 301).

55. Roberta Strauss Feuerlicht, *McCarthyism: The Hate That Haunts America* (New York: McGraw Hill, 1972), 101. Eisenhower's executive order #10450 on security, dated 27 April 1953, required all applicants for government jobs to be screened and all who had been investigated by Truman's review boards to be reinvestigated. Persons, moreover, with adverse information filed against them had to undergo a full field investigation, and any evidence indicating that they might be a security risk was cause for immediate suspension (Cook, *Nightmare*, 440–41). For Truman, see Griffith, *Fear*, 59. Interestingly enough, the refusal to hand over executive files and order employees to testify was criticized by Arthur Schlesinger in his volume, *The Imperial Presidency* (for reference to Schlesinger, see Ambrose, *EP*, 619).

56. Griffith, *Fear*, 190. Although both Dulles and Ike agreed that McCarthy was a problem, they were reluctant to challenge him head-on. Eisenhower, thinking aloud at a National Security Council meeting, wondered if the threat could not be dealt with by means of "covert radio"; but this is as far as it went. See minutes of NSC meeting, 9 July 1953, box 4, NSC.

57. Greenstein, *Hidden-Hand*, 169–72.

58. In Green Bay, Eisenhower declared that subversion was an issue to be dealt with by the executive, not Congress, and while agreeing with McCarthy's aims, he said he could not sanction his methods. By one account, the senator, who was seated on the dais beside Ike, "shook his head vigorously and frowned in disagreement and disapproval" (Griffith, *Fear*, 191–93). Ike, as noted above, had taken a stand in defense of Marshall while speaking in Denver two weeks earlier (ibid.). See also Cook, *Nightmare*, 383–84.

59. It should perhaps be noted that Eisenhower was already on record as having criticized McCarthy's tactics while president of Columbia University (Griffith, *Fear*, 103).

60. McCarthy attacked Dulles for having "summarily" overridden security chief Scott McLeod in granting Bohlen security clearance. He also accused him of lying and demanded that he appear under oath before the Senate Foreign Relations Committee (Griffith, *Fear*, 202). Nevertheless, when the vote was taken, Dulles triumphed by a whopping 74–13 (Thomas, *Angels*, 294–96). As regards strategy, Dulles suggested to Ike that instead of McLeod testifying on the contents of Bohlen's security file, it would be better to have two senators, Taft and Sparkman, and this turned out to be decisive (Greenstein, *Hidden-Hand*, 166). On Nitze, see Gerson, *Dulles*, 112. Bohlen was described by one foreign envoy as "hectoring," "indiscrete," and "drinking heavily" on occasion. See Ward to Caccia, 11 November 1954, FO 371/109114, PRO.

61. By this time, two Harvard professors who had earlier invoked the Fifth Amendment were admitting former membership in the Communist party (Thomas, *Angels*, 293, 399).

62. Griffith, *Fear*, 200–201.

63. Makins to Eden, 2 May 1953, FO 371/103495, PRO (outlining the new review procedure). William F. Buckley, Jr. and L. Brent Bozell claim that Dulles reversed the finding of Truman's review board (on Vincent) "without authority and in clear violation of the regulations of the federal loyalty program." See Buckley and Bozell, *McCarthy and His Enemies* (Chicago: Regnery, 1954), 199–200. Vincent's name had been on McCarthy's famous list of suspects in part because Louis Budenz, former editor of the Communist *Daily Worker* and a witness whose reliability had been repeatedly tested under oath, said that he had known Vincent to be a Communist (ibid.). See also Thomas, *Angels*, 291. On Davies, see Cook, *Nightmare*, 550.

64. Griffith, *Fear*, 203.

65. Thomas, *Angels*, 638.

66. According to the rule introduced by Dulles, books could be banned only if deemed deleterious to the national interest (Cook, *Nightmare*, 422–23).

67. In the clash with McCarthy over unauthorized contact with Greek shipowners, it was really Ike, more than Dulles, who struck a conciliatory note by suggesting that Harold Stassen's initial criticism had been harsh and exaggerated (Thomas, *Angels*, 302; Griffith, *Fear*, 204). According to Thomas, McCarthy "expected to be praised for a patriotic action daringly performed. Instead he ran into a storm of denunciation" (Thomas, *Angels*, 299). See also ibid., 301; Greenstein, *Hidden-Hand*, 167–68; Eleanor Lansing Dulles, "Footnote to History: A Day in the Life of Senator Joe McCarthy," *World Affairs* 143 (Fall 1980): 158–61 (Dulles "wanted results, not banner headlines. And that is what he got"—his approach was quiet, dignified, and firm); *New York Herald Tribune*, 1 March 1954 (on Allied trade).

68. See UP dispatch, 2 December 1954, box 78, JFDP.

69. Walter Judd OHI, pp. 19–25; Saltonstall OHI, p. 17, JFDOH.

70. See, for example, Griffith, *Fear*, 232–33, 247 (re: the army); Thomas, *Angels*, 301 (re: Greek shipowners), 384. See also Cook, *Nightmare*, 413–17, 459, 470–71 (on Johnson's management of the IIA as well as the conduct of army secretary Robert T. Stevens); Feuerlicht, *Hate*, 116 (on Stevens); Thomas, *Angels*, 335 (on Allen Dulles). For Nixon's involvement with Stevens, see Thomas, *Angels*, 436.

71. Griffith, *Fear*, 200; and Cook, *Nightmare*, 459 (on the opinion of Vice President Nixon and General Persons, as opposed to C. D. Jackson). See also Griffith, *Fear*, 190 and 198 (in Griffith's words, Ike faced "the difficult task of soothing the feelings of the disgruntled party conservatives" knowing that effective political power on the Hill was exercised by those who had opposed his nomination. At the same time, he had to entrust his legislative program to Taft and it was "this particular relationship between president and majority leader" that "insured McCarthy his privileged position").

72. Thomas, *Angels*, 369–71. No sooner had Truman denied seeing the FBI file than former Secretary of State James F. Byrnes in effect accused him of lying. According to Byrnes, Truman had received the report on White and discussed it. Subsequently, Truman claimed that federal agents had approved his action (on White), which in turn was denied by FBI director J. Edgar Hoover.

73. Gerson, *Dulles*, 111. Eventually, Eisenhower let several thousand federal

employees go, about four hundred of whom were fired on charges relating to "subversion" (Cook, *Nightmare*, 548).

74. Henry M. Wriston OHI, p. 30, JFDOH.

75. Buckley and Bozell, *McCarthy*, 29n; Cook, *Nightmare*, 66 (270 were dismissed by Truman, of whom 69 were later reinstated).

76. Cook, *Nightmare*, 62–63, 177.

77. Ibid., 333; Feuerlicht, *Hate*, 68.

78. Feuerlicht, *Hate*, 47–49. Two years before McCarthy made national headlines, Americans for Democratic Action (ADA) invoked guilt by association in trying to prove that Henry Wallace's Progressive party was Communist-dominated (ibid., 49).

79. Cook cites a questionnaire sent to mission heads in forty-three countries, but it is unclear when it was sent and how the questions were formulated. Even the whereabouts of the documentation appears in doubt. As further evidence, Cook reports that the State Department instituted a freeze on hiring and that its payroll shrank. This, however, does not necessarily prove that there was a crisis in morale; nor does it indicate, assuming such to have existed, that it was the fault of Dulles' strategy in regard to McCarthy. Cook adds that in 1960 "a State Department official" told Professor Tillet of Princeton University that it had been eight years since any mission chief had forwarded a report to State with which said mission chief disagreed. One is not sure, however, whether subordinates were cowed by their mission chiefs or whether the chiefs were cowed by Washington (assuming one or the other to have been true). Nor is any of this certain evidence of declining morale since we do not know the name of the official who testified and whether or not he or she was properly understood by Tillet. See Cook, *Nightmare*, 551, 612n.

80. Loy Henderson OHI, p. 51, JFDOH.

81. Ibid., 51–52; Sherman Adams OHI, pp. 36 and 38; Herman Phleger OHI, p. 11, JFDOH.

82. Henderson OHI, p. 51, JFDOH.

83. Berding, *Dulles*, 172–74; Dean Rusk OHI, p. 11, JFDOH (according to Rusk, by the time Dulles left State, his relationship with the career foreign service was as good as that of any other secretary).

84. John W. Hanes, Jr. OHI, p. 17, EL (CUOHC).

85. According to Robert Murphy, Dulles had "more sessions with different working groups than any secretary I know of." See Robert D. Murphy OHI, p. 30; James Bryant Conant OHI, p. 19 (he was quick to learn from younger men such as Livingston Merchant and Douglas MacArthur); William Rountree OHI, pp. 7–8 (he delegated responsibility, consulting Rountree three or four times daily); Ambassador Joseph C. Satterthwaite OHI, p. 11 (he did not generally shove things down the throats of his senior advisers); Joseph J. Sisco OHI, pp. 4, 23–24 (he consulted often with subordinates and called on some very young men, including Sisco, for advice); Gerard Smith OHI, p. 33 (he did not carry the department around in his hat; he had an open ear); Robert H. Thayer OHI, p. 22 ("you never sent a cable to Foster that you didn't get a personal answer"); George V. Allen OHI, p. 35 (he was ready to listen and take advice; he was no more remote than any other secretary); Loy Henderson OHI, p. 33 (he consulted more than any other secretary from Hughes to Herter), JFDOH; Loy Henderson OHI, p. 34 (he was completely open to criticism in daily staff meetings with a group of fifteen senior officers); Walter Robertson OHI, pp. 47–48 (he thrived on frank, open discussion; every day he met with his assistant

secretaries, legal counselor, and under secretaries; and thrice a week, the group was enlarged to include desk officers), EL (CUOHC).

CHAPTER 5

1. Stalin wrote in 1934 that the Bolshevik revolution would never be safe in one country until it gained a foothold in others (*Problems in Leninism*, 19, 26).

2. Achilles OHI, pp. 1–3, JFDOH; War Trade Board Manuscript, 30 November 1918, ED; JFD, "Notes on the Situation in Europe," 7 October 1944; idem, "America's Role in the Peace," *Christianity in Crisis* 4 (22 January 1945): 3–4 (clipping); Radio Monitors Conference Transcript, 29 April 1947, boxes 283, 398, JFDP; Gerson, *Dulles*, 40–41.

3. Memo (n.d.) in JFD to Vandenberg, 5 December 1949; Vandenberg Diary, 4, 5, 7, 8, 20, 23 June 1945, boxes 3 and 6, Vandenberg Papers, MHCBHL; Bly, "Peace Treaty," 400, 413; Sebald, *With MacArthur*, 283. See also Gross OHI, pp. 6, 8–10, JFDOH.

4. *Christian Science Monitor*, 7 July 1948, sec. 2, p. 1; Liang, *Essays*, 204; Hoopes, *Dulles*, 96–97; Paik OHI, p. 2, JFDOH; JFD, "To Save Humanity from the Deep Abyss," *New York Times Magazine*, 30 July 1950 (clipping), box 285, JFDP; JFD to Vandenberg, 29 January 1947; JFD Speech Draft, 29 January 1947, box 2, Vandenberg Papers, MHCBHL; Sebald, *With MacArthur*, 184–86 (MacArthur spoke of "writing off" Korea); JFD-Koo Conv., 12 June and 27 December 1950, boxes 180, 184, WKP; Dulles and Allison to Acheson and Rusk, 25 June 1950, RG 9, MacArthur Papers, MacArthur Memorial Archives, Norfolk, Virginia; Margaret Truman, *Harry S. Truman* (New York: Morrow, 1973), 466–67. Dulles told the Koreans, "You are not alone."

5. Goold-Adams, *Dulles*, 276; DDE, *Waging Peace*, 204n; Drummond and Coblentz, *Duel*, 12; JFD, *War or Peace*, 6, 229; Berding, *Dulles*, 121; Radio Moscow Excerpts, box 73, Allen Dulles Papers, PU; *Reporter*, 15 June 1946 (clipping); JFD, "What I've Learned About the Russians," *Colliers*, 12 March 1949 (clipping); Vishinsky Speech, 1950, boxes 284, 285, 399, JFDP; M. Harvey Memo, 29 January 1953, box 11, SS; U.K. Embassy, D.C., to FO, 2 April 1954, FO 371/109114, PRO.

6. Hoopes, *Dulles*, 64; Luce OHI, p. 5; Carl W. McCardle OHI by PAC, 2–4 December 1964, p. 109; Thompson OHI, p. 19, JFDOH; JFD Press Conf., 11 February 1958, box 125, JFDP. The full-page ad appeared in the *New York Times* on 3 June 1946.

7. Thompson OHI, p. 14, JFDOH; JFD-Koo Conv., 19 December 1950, 20 March 1951, boxes 180, 184, WKP.

8. Richard M. Nixon, *Six Crises* (Garden City: Doubleday, 1962), 239; DDE, *Waging Peace*, 353, 404; JFD Statement, 4 February 1954, box 78, JFDP.

9. Bohlen, *Witness*, 362 (re: lip-reader); Merchant OHI, p. 102, JFDOH; *Washington Daily News*, 25 May 1959 (clipping), box 83, Allen Dulles Papers, PU; Merchant, "Recollections," p. 34, box 92, JFDP; Bernard Bromage, *Molotov: The Story of an Era* (London: P. Owen, 1956), 231.

10. JFD Statement at Berlin Conf., 26 January 1954, DSPR #38, box 78, JFDP.

11. Draft of JFD Statement on German Unification, box 78, JFDP. These may or may not have been Dulles' actual spoken words.

12. JFD Statement, 28 January 1954, DSPR #47, box 78, JFDP.

13. Ibid.

14. JFD Statement, 28 January 1954, DSPR #47; JFD Statement, 28 January 1954, to Fourth Plenary Session of the Berlin Conference; JFD Statement, 2 February 1954, DSPR #50; Draft of JFD Speech, February 1954; JFD Speech, 5 February 1954, box 78, JFDP.

15. See, for example, JFD Statements, 14 and 16 February 1954, box 78, JFDP.

16. Drummond and Coblentz, *Duel*, 144–45; Weintal OHI, p. 6, JFDOH; JFD Address to Kiwanis International, 21 June 1956, box 69, Allen Dulles Papers.

17. Berding, *Dulles*, 52, 164; Love, *Suez*, 405; JFD, *War or Peace*, 27–28, 170; W. Park Armstrong, Jr. OHI by RDC, 10 September 1965, p. 13; Bell OHI, p. 13; Lindley OHI, p. 25; Gray OHI, p. 16; Merchant OHI, p. 61; Wadsworth OHI, p. 25, JFDOH; JFD Remarks to Congressional Leaders Meeting, 5 January 1959, box 138, JFDP; CC (54) 178 Note by Secretary of State for Foreign Affairs, 28 May 1954, PREM 11/649, PRO (on Molotov-Smith talks); Pearson Diary, 11 October 1955, vol. 68, Pearson Papers, MG26N1, PAC.

18. JFD, *War or Peace*, 3; Wadsworth OHI, pp. 19, 21; Goodpaster OHI, p. 20, JFDOH; JFD Address, 4 May 1948, in Van Dusen, ed., *Spiritual Legacy*, 152; JFD, "Advice to the United States," *U.S. News and World Report*, 27 April 1959, p. 42; idem, "The Christian Citizen in a Changing World" (22 August 1948), pp. 7–8; *Christian Science Monitor*, 7 July 1948, sec. 2, p. 1 (clipping), boxes 284 and 398, JFDP; JFD to DDE, 7 November 1955, box 5, DH; JFD, "Not War, Not Peace" (Address to Foreign Policy Association of New York; 17 January 1948, privately printed), p. 2.

19. JFD Address to National War College, 16 June 1953, in Van Dusen, ed., *Spiritual Legacy*, 83; Nixon OHI, pp. 42–43, JFDOH; JFD to Adenauer, 30 June 1958; JFD News Conf., 3 April 1953, boxes 67, 125, JFDP; Wiggins, "Notes," 4 April 1958, box 2, DAP; JFD, "What I've Learned"; JFD Address to UN Association in Japan, 23 April 1951, box 107, Smith Papers, PU; DDE Dictation, 15 July 1958, box 34, DDE Diaries, AWF; *Christian Science Monitor*, 26 February 1985, p. 17; JFD Press Conf., 10 January and 10 June 1958, boxes 125, 127, JFDP.

20. U.S. Delegation at NATO Meeting to State, 17 December 1954, FR (1952–54), 5:552; John Sparkman OHI by PAC, 19 March 1966, p. 11, JFDOH; JFD Press Conf., 9 November 1953; JFD Statement, 21 December 1954, boxes 68, 79, JFDP; *Time*, 8 April 1957, p. 25; 22 April 1957, p. 40. Prior to the signing of the Japanese Peace Treaty, there was talk in the Soviet Union of bombing Japan from Soviet bases on Sakhalin Island as well as overthrowing the Japanese government by repatriating thousands of indoctrinated war prisoners. At the same time, Moscow offered, in return for diplomatic cooperation, cheap raw materials and vast markets. As soon as the treaty was signed, however, such talk was heard no more. Honeyed words took the place of threats, and the Soviet mission in Tokyo, which had been predominantly military in personnel, was altered to reflect more of a civilian tone. See JFD Addresses at Des Moines, 16 February 1952, and Paris, 5 May 1952, box 107, JFDP.

21. JFD Remarks to AFL-CIO Executive Council, 19 August 1958, box 132, JFDP; JFD Remarks to Princeton Alumni Dinner, 22 February 1952, box 107, Smith Papers, PU; JFD Longhand Notes, box 8, SS; Memo of Conv. between U.K. and U.S. officials, 11 June 1958, box 21, International Series, AWF (hereafter IS); Ambrose, *EP*, 132.

22. JFD "Advice to the U.S.," *U.S. News and World Report*, 27 April 1959,

pp. 42–43; JFD Address, 28 June 1957; JFD, "Thoughts on Soviet Foreign Policy and What To Do About It," *Life*, 3 and 10 June 1946 (clipping); JFD Manuscript, 21 April 1956; JFD News Conf., 18 October 1955 and 16 July 1957, boxes 92, 114, 119, 284, 287, JFDP. When Eisenhower suggested an exchange of visits with the USSR (10 January 1956), Dulles objected that it would put third world countries under pressure to do the same. When Ike proposed that American educational institutions host five thousand Soviet students, Dulles expressed doubt as to the probability of its "acceptance." It may well be that the president's enthusiasm for people-to-people programs and educational exchange stemmed from the wishes of his brother, Milton. In any case, the United States did negotiate an exchange program with Soviet leaders in December 1957. By this time, France had opened its door with an exchange between Moscow University and the Sorbonne. The Comédie Française took its production of *Tartuffe* to Russia and a French photographer was given wide latitude to travel within the Soviet Union. See DDE, *Waging Peace*, 410–11; JFD Press Conf., 13 March 1958, box 128, JFDP; JFD-DDE Conv., 10 January 1956, box 4, WHMS; DDE to JFD, 21 March 1958, box 7, DH; Bromage, *Molotov*, 233.

23. Bell OHI, pp. 12, 18–19; Beale OHI, p. 3, JFDOH; Wiggins, "Notes," 4 April 1958, box 2, DAP; Cyrus L. Sulzberger, *The Last of the Giants* (New York: Macmillan, 1970), 578; DDE Address at PU, 15 May 1962, *Princeton University Library Chronicle* 23 (Summer 1962): 154. See also Allen Dulles Manuscript (n.d.), box 206, JFDP.

24. Graebner, ed., *Ideas and Diplomacy*, 809–10.

25. Hagerty Diary, 5 January 1954, in Ferrell, ed., *Hagerty*, 3; DDE State of the Union Message, 2 February 1953, in Branyan and Larsen, eds., *Eisenhower*, 1:91. For Dulles' speeches in 1950–51, along with his article in *Life* (19 April 1952), see boxes 95 and 286, JFDP; also box 107, Alexander Smith Papers, PU.

26. For "massive retaliation" as a bluff, see Michael Howard, "Nuclear Danger and Nuclear History," *International Security* 14 (Summer 1989): 179; Richard Immerman, "Confessions of an Eisenhower Revisionist: An Agonizing Reappraisal," *Diplomatic History* 14 (Summer 1990): 326.

27. See, for example, Dulles' press conference of 16 March 1954 (Gerson, *Dulles*, 149). For recognition of Eisenhower's flexibility in recent historiography, see Divine, *Eisenhower and the Cold War*, 65–66.

28. Sulzberger Diary, May 1952, in Sulzberger, *Candles*, 747.

29. Gerson, *Dulles*, 77; unidentified manuscript in box 287, JFDP.

30. DDE, *Mandate*, 361.

31. JFD Address to American Association for the United Nations, 29 December 1950, box 107, Alexander Smith Papers, PU. See also JFD Speeches, 2 February and 27 November 1951, box 95, JFDP.

32. DDE, *Waging Peace*, 204. For Dulles' belief that the threat of massive retaliation would keep Red China out of Vietnam, see Gerson, *Dulles*, 77. On privileged sanctuaries, see DDE, *Mandate*, 454, 464.

33. DDE, *Mandate*, 453 (on the defense of Europe and first use of nuclear weaponry). The American advantage over Moscow in terms of nuclear superiority during Dulles' tenure has been estimated at about 5 or 6 to 1.

34. Britain's defense minister, Duncan Sandys, expressed concern in 1957 that if the United States did not plan massive retaliatory action in case of a Soviet attack

on Europe and let Moscow know of its plans, the Soviets might initiate minor probing operations. See JFD-Sandys Conv., 17 December 1957, box 1, GCMS. For French reaction, see Gerson, *Dulles*, 145.

35. See outline of JFD Speech, 14 June 1957, box 115, JFDP. Dulles began speaking in 1957 of the use of tactical nuclear weapons and then in 1958 of "flexible response." For 1958, see NSC Meeting, 1 May 1958, box 10, NSC.

36. DDE, *Waging Peace*, 291.

37. Minutes of JFD Meeting with Aides, 28 March 1955, box 2, WHMS (on Dulles' enunciation of "2X" theory).

38. Harkness Notes, 17 August 1953, box 1, DAP (re: "greater sanctions").

39. Lippmann, *Cold War*, 14, 19–20, 29.

40. JFD Address to CFR, 12 January 1954, in Graebner, ed., *Ideas and Diplomacy*, 809 (on Dulles).

41. DDE, *Mandate*, 131.

42. JFD Address to the American people, 7 July 1954, box 192, WKP; JFD, "Road to Peace" speech, 10 October 1952, box 107, Alexander Smith Papers, PU; idem, "Policy of Boldness," *Life*, 19 April 1952, box 286, JFDP.

43. For the opinion of Generals Twining and White that America continued to have a strong capability for limited warfare even though the fact was not widely advertised, see Minutes of NSC Meeting, 1 May 1958, box 10, NSC.

44. For Britain, see *Time*, 15 April 1957, p. 36; Woodhouse, *Dulles*, 84. For the USSR, see Khrushchev, *Khrushchev Remembers I*, 392–93, 515–16.

45. For Immerman, see note 26 above. Immerman's piece followed the publication of an article by another writer of similar mind: Howard, "Nuclear Danger," 179.

46. See, for example, Richard K. Betts, *Nuclear Blackmail and Nuclear Balance* (Washington, D.C.: The Brookings Institution, 1987); David Rosenberg, "Reality and Responsibility: Power and Process in the Making of United States Nuclear Strategy, 1945–68," *The Journal of Strategic Studies* 9 (March 1986); Marc Trachtenberg, "A 'Wasting Asset': American Strategy and the Shifting Nuclear Balance, 1949–1954," *International Security* 13 (Winter 1988–89).

47. For his apparent denial of any intent to go nuclear, see Ambrose, *EP*, 184; Betts, *Nuclear Blackmail*, 53. For statements on the other side of the ledger, see ibid., 38–41, 67–68; Lawrence Freedman, *The Evolution of Nuclear Strategy* (New York: St. Martin's Press, 1983), 78, 82; Trachtenberg, "Nuclear Balance," 7, 37–40.

48. Betts, *Nuclear Blackmail*, 38–41.

49. Ibid., 67–68.

50. Samuel Wells, "The Origins of Massive Retaliation," *Political Science Quarterly* 96 (Spring 1981): 38.

51. JFD, "Policy for Peace and Security," *Foreign Affairs* 32 (April 1954); JFD Address to Council on Foreign Relations, 12 January 1954, in Graebner, ed., *Ideas and Diplomacy*, 810.

52. For assurances to Taiwan, see Koo-Nixon Conv., 15 July 1954; JFD-Robertson-Phleger-McConaughy-Yeh-Koo Conv., 2 November 1954, boxes 191–92, WKP. For assurances to Britain and France, see Memo of Conv. between Chiefs of Delegations, Bermuda Conference, 7 December 1953, box 1, SS.

53. Sulzberger Diary, May 1952, in Sulzberger, *Candles*, 747; DDE, *Mandate*, 354; idem, *Waging Peace*, 295, 339.

54. Hagerty Diary, 5 January 1954, in Ferrell, ed., *Hagerty*, 3.

55. Ambrose, *EP*, 658–59 (Ike urging a more vigorous prosecution of the war and the danger of appearing to put limits on American retaliatory action).

56. JFD manuscript, 21 April 1956, box 287, JFDP.

57. Bidault, *D'Une résistance a l'autre* (Paris: Les Presses du Siècle, 1965), 200 ("Foster Dulles *à défini un jour sa politique comme celle du risque calculé! Dans l'affaire, il y avait alors beaucoup de calculs et beaucoup de circonlocutions, mais pas de risques*").

58. JFD Speech to UN General Assembly, 19 September 1957; JFD-McInnis TV Interview, 23 June 1958; JFD Remarks at Princeton Alumni Dinner, 22 February 1952; JFD Statement before the UN First Committee on the Chinese Interim Committee Item, 21 November, 1950, boxes 107, 119, 126, JFDP; JFD Memo for DDE, 15 May 1954, box 8, WHMS; JFD Handwritten Notes on Dien Bien Phu, box 8, SS; JFD, "Security in the Pacific," *Foreign Affairs* 30 (January 1952): 187; Holmes to Department of External Affairs, 28 March 1956, box 219, U-15, vol. 6, St. Laurent Papers, MG26L, PAC.

59. Department of State Statement, 14 July 1960, in Ruhl J. Bartlett, ed., *The Record of American Diplomacy* (New York: Knopf, 1964), 861; JFD TV and Radio Address, 30 June 1954; DSPR #357; JFD Speech, 9 June 1956, boxes 81 and 102, JFDP; JFD Address, 30 June 1954, in Branyan and Larsen, eds., *Eisenhower*, 1:313–14; Richardson, *Eisenhower*, 178–79; Ambrose, *EP*, 193; JFD Speech Draft, 29 January 1947, box 2, Vandenberg Papers, MHCBHL; JFD Speech, 7 May 1954, box 192, WKP; Makins to FO, 3 July 1954, FO 371/109101, PRO; Willard L. Beaulac, *A Diplomat Looks at Aid to Latin America* (Carbondale: Southern Illinois Press, 1970), 16–17.

60. For samples of American historiography that follow the Arbenz line, see David Atlee Phillips, *The Night Watch* (New York: Atheneum, 1977); Schlesinger and Kinzer, *Bitter Fruit*; Immerman, *CIA*; Sharon I. Meers, "The British Connection: How the United States Covered Its Tracks in the 1954 Coup in Guatemala," *Diplomatic History* 16 (Summer 1992): 421. According to Schlesinger and Kinzer, the United States was the "secret creator" of the rebel movement—Americans were in "full control." Furthermore, the interests of United Fruit (UFC) were the controlling factor in Eisenhower's decision to intervene since (1) Communist threats in other countries such as Brazil, Chile, and Costa Rica had not provoked a similar reaction, and (2) U.S. "national security considerations were never compelling." According to Immerman, communism was no threat; the United States "cried wolf"; and the "overriding concern" of the Eisenhower administration was "to advance the capitalist system." Criticizing Dulles for upholding "the sanctity" of the Monroe Doctrine and stressing the various links between UFC and Washington, Immerman claims that the only opposition to Arbenz was among the "large landholders" and he quotes Deputy Assistant Secretary of State Roy Rubottom as saying that the Caracas Conference was the low point in U.S. relations with Latin America under Eisenhower. Finally, he views American support for Castillo Armas as a blunder of the first magnitude leading to Castro's take-over of Cuba. See Schlesinger and Kinzer, *Bitter Fruit*, 13, 22, 106–7; Immerman, *CIA*, 7, 10, 124–25, 148–49, 184, 187, 198–200, and chap. 5.

61. Schlesinger and Kinzer, *Bitter Fruit*, 17, 111, 113, 174, 191–92, 205; Immerman, *CIA*, 3–4, 85, 161–62, 164, 166–68, 174–75, 186; Rabe, *Eisenhower*, 56; Ambrose, *EP*, 194–96. For inconsistencies in the revisionist literature, see Frederick

W. Marks III, "The CIA and Castillo Armas in Guatemala, 1954: New Clues to an Old Puzzle," *Diplomatic History* 14 (Winter 1990): 69n.2.

62. Luis Alberto Hurtado Aguilar, *Así se gestó la liberación* (Guatemala City: Secretaria de Divulgacion, Cultura y Turismo de la Republica, 1956), 184; Guillermo Putzeys Rojas, *Así se hizo la liberación: decade de la lucha cívica, 1944–1954* (Guatemala City: Tipografía Nacional, 1976), 51; Virgilio Pacheco interview with author, 1 January 1988 (Esquipulas). Putzeys Rojas's account of the Liberation is an updated version of Hurtado Aguilar's *Así se gestó.* Both versions are several hundred pages long with detailed maps of individual battles and an impressive array of statistics, and neither has been challenged by Arbenzistas (such as César Augusto Silva Girón, who published a military history in 1977) for its basic veracity.

63. Eight American tourists said that rebel contingents had government troops "on the run" and one reporter, also an American, testified to seeing about four hundred wounded being returned for medical care to Guatemala City on trucks. Armed convoys from Guatemala City to Zacapa and from Zacapa to Puerto Barrios were intercepted and destroyed, and even before Castillo Armas entered Guatemala, guerrilla bands operating under his aegis were engaged in train hijacking and bridge-blowing, tearing up rails and ripping down telegraph and telephone lines. See *New York Times*, 5 July 1954, p. 3; *New York Herald Tribune*, 26 June 1954, p. 2; Comision Permanente del Primer Congreso Contra La Intervencion Sovietica en America Latina, *El libro negro del comunismo en Guatemala* (Mexico City, 1954), 6–7 (hereafter *Libro negro*); Pacheco OHI; Thomas and Marjorie Melville, *Guatemala—Another Vietnam?* (New York: Free Press, 1971), 105; Amy Elizabeth Jensen, *Guatemala* (New York: Exposition Press, 1955), 219; Gregorio Selser, *El Guatemalazo: la primera guerra sucia* (Buenos Aires: Ediciones Iguazú, 1961), 102–3; Hurtado Aguilar, *Así se gestó*, 184, 192; Putzeys Rojas, *Así se hizo*, 39, 54, 184, 199, 213; Schlesinger and Kinzer, *Bitter Fruit*, 16; DDE, *Mandate*, 425; *El Espectador* (Guatemala City), 24 June 1954, p. 1; *Tribuna Popular* (Guatemala City), 21 June 1954, p. 1; Peurifoy to Dulles, 19 June 1954 (12:00 P.M.), 25 June (8:00 P.M.), boxes 3244A and B, file 714.00, RG 59, NA.

64. *New York Times*, 5 July 1954, p. 3; *New York Herald Tribune*, 21 June 1954, pp. 1, 4; Peurifoy to Dulles, 16, 18 (9:00 P.M.), 19 (12:00 P.M.), 23 (6:00 P.M.), 24 June 1954: Leddy to U.S. delegation to the UN, 22 June, box 3244A, file 714.00, RG 59, NA.

65. The taking of Esquipulas, which required five hours and claimed the lives of several Arbenzistas, forced the withdrawal of an estimated fifty government troops. For the subsequent broad advance of the insurgents and a listing of the towns they seized, see Marks, *CIA*, 71n.

66. Before overrunning the main government position, it was necessary to seize two of the surrounding hills in triple formation involving about 450 men, and seventy-four soldiers were needed to capture one of these hills. In Chiquimula, the Loyalist commander of an artillery battalion fled and government soldiers fired on one another in complete confusion before retreating to Zacapa. Six hundred hand-picked rebels stormed the plaza, and Chiquimula, with its fabulous cache of arms, was theirs at an estimated cost of between seventeen and twenty lives (counting losses on both sides). A provisional government was formed and it is from Chiquimula that Castillo Armas issued his formal order for the arrest of Arbenz. Incredibly enough, elements of the Liberation Army then proceeded to occupy the strategic mountain pass, La

Vuelta del Tuño, which overlooks the approach to Zacapa. It is interesting to note that one of the published accounts devotes a full thirty pages to a detailed description of how Vado Hondo was won. See *El Espectador*, 9 July 1954, p. 4; Hurtado Aguilar, *Así se gestó*, 185, 195; Silva Girón, *Gualán*, 114; Pacheco OHI; *Libro negro*, 202–3; *New York Times*, 5 July 1954, p. 3; *New York Herald Tribune*, 26 June 1954, p. 1; Putzeys Rojas, *Así se hizo*, 87, 185–214, 274, 296; Jensen, *Guatemala*, 229–30; *Prensa Libre*, 26 June 1954, p. 7; Peurifoy to Dulles, 25 June (8:00 P.M.) 1954, box 3244B, file 714.00, RG59, NA. Other campaigns, while not fought on the same scale or with quite the same intensity, perhaps, were far from insignificant. One hundred eighty men attacked Ipala in standard triple column formation, and the crucial battle for Gualán has been the subject of book-length treatment by Silva Girón, the Arbenzista commander who organized its defense. Typically, Silva Girón is missing from the current bibliographies. Other strategic points taken with the aid of heavy military hardware include: Octopeque with twenty-nine muleloads of equipment including two 20 mm cannon and three antiaircraft guns; El Florido with heavy artillery, forty-seven mortars, and an attack culminating in a violent assault lasting fifteen minutes. Determined resistance by a small group of Arbenz forces was reported at St. Estéban, while much fighting was required to occupy key posts at Shup and Comotán (where a large number of Communist leaders were captured). See *El Espectator*, 9 July 1954, p. 4; Putzeys Rojas, *Así se hizo*, 61–64, 83, 172, 182, 219, 226; César Augusto Silva Girón, *La batalla de Gualán* (Guatemala City: Impreso en Imprenta Eros, 1977), 110, 114. There were eight hundred government troops stationed at Ipala (Putzeys Rojas, *Así se hizo*, 291).

67. When Chiquimula was visited by the Red Cross, it was found to be functioning normally and in no need of relief. See Peurifoy to JFD, 27 June 1954, FR (1952–54), 4:1189; Jensen, *Guatemala*, 223, 229; *New York Times*, 5 July 1954, p. 3; *New York Herald Tribune*, 4 July 1954, p. 2; Hurtado Aguilar, *Así se gestó*, 185, 195; Putzeys Rojas, *Así se hizo*, 292–93; *El Imparcial*, 8 July 1954, p. 1; 10 July 1954, p. 6; 14 July 1954, p. 6; *El Espectador*, 27 June 1954, p. 4; 6 July 1954, p. 6; 9 July 1954, p. 4. Indicative of the Liberation's success on the battlefield is the fact that when the military junta that succeeded Arbenz refused to deal with Castillo Armas, Ambassador Peurifoy pointed out that they had no choice since the rebel commander had "inflicted severe punishment on government troops." No one contradicted him. See Peurifoy to Dulles, 28 (5:00 P.M.) 1954, box 3244B, file 714.00, RG 59, NA. The armory located at Zacapa was the nation's largest, containing most of its artillery (Putzeys Rojas, *Así se hizo*, 293). What is remarkable about the sources that throw the most light on the military history of the Liberation is that, with the exception of government propaganda, they are in virtually complete agreement. Oral histories, official histories, diplomatic dispatches (available at the National Archives), and leading newspapers in both Guatemala and the United States (during, as well as after, the Liberation), not to mention the memoirs of participants such as Silva Girón, jibe perfectly when it comes to the broad outline of the story. For an explanation of why Arbenz lost control of the air, see Marks, *CIA*, 73.

68. Marks, *CIA*, 74–75.

69. Ibid. See also Kreug to Department of State, 10 May 1954, box 3244A, file 714.00 RG 59, NA (on use of torture).

70. Marks, *CIA*, 75–76.

71. Ibid., 76–77.

72. Ibid., 77.

73. One of the best analyses along this line is a thirteen-page, single-spaced briefing paper entitled "Soviet Communism in Guatemala" in box 3244A, file 714.00, RG 59, NA.

74. Ibid., 77–78.

75. The link between Guatemala City and Moscow could hardly have been closer judging from the volume of traffic between the two capitals. Guatemala had, of course, been the only country in Latin America to oppose both the Rio and Caracas declarations and, on Stalin's death, it again distinguished itself when its congress reacted to the news by voting a minute of silence (ibid., 78–79). See also McClintock to Leddy, 30 April 1954 (on the number 32); briefing paper, "Soviet Communism in Guatemala," thirteen pages, mimeographed copy (on minute of silence), box 3244A, file 714.00, RG 59, NA.

76. Castillo Armas capitalized on the widespread fear of communism by launching a clever public relations campaign involving numerous committees, publications, and carefully graduated stages of intensity, not to mention a wide range of overseas activity. A ton of literature, along with collapsible machine guns, was smuggled into Guatemala disguised as consignments of coal and oranges (Marks, *CIA*, 79).

77. Ibid., 80–81. Canadian diplomats, who were hardly beholden to Washington in their private correspondence, concluded that Castillo Armas had forged his own victory with "the assistance, support, and money of the Guatemalan people." Richard Allen, the British envoy in Guatemala, observed similarly that "the funds for the rebellion were mostly contributed by wealthy Guatemalans. . . . There is no evidence that the insurgents received important material help from the United States apart from some aircraft and a few arms." Allen added that the depth and breadth of "potential opposition to the regime" were "revealed by the fact that all classes of Guatemalans listened eagerly" to the clandestine antigovernment radio station (ibid.). It may be added that Arbenz alienated important segments of the army when he insisted in a desperate, last-minute gamble that they distribute arms to left-wing civilian groups. Such a move would surely have been regarded as subversive, unprofessional, and unjust from a military point of view. The colonels insisted on a clean sweep of all Communists, and several days later, when they delivered their refusal to arm the civilian populace, they also submitted a list of twenty questions on the subject of communism. Meanwhile, Arbenz tried to arm the civilian sector himself, and his foreign minister, in desperation, appealed to the United Nations Security Council to help disarm the rebels and intern them. Two days later, the military chiefs called for Arbenz's resignation, whereupon he took refuge in the Mexican embassy and army chief Diaz took over (ibid., 81–82). For the role of the United Fruit Company, see ibid., 84–86.

78. DDE, *Mandate*, 161; Report from U.S. Embassy, Teheran, 6 July 1953, FO 371/104568, PRO; Mohammed Reza Shah Pahlavi, *Answer to History*, trans. Michael Joseph (New York: Stein and Day, 1980), 84–85; U.S. Embassy, Teheran, to JFD, 22 August 1953, box 4111, file 788.00, RG 59, NA.

79. Pahlavi, *Answer*, 86–88; *Times* of India (Delhi), 16 and 18 September 1953; *Statesman* (Delhi), 17 September 1953 (clippings), FO 371/104568, PRO; Mattison to JFD, 17 August 1953, box 4111, file 788.00, RG 59, NA.

80. DDE, *Mandate*, 162; Far Eastern Division Memo, 13 March 1953; Far Eastern Division Political Summaries for December 1952 through January 1953, March

through April 1953, May 1953, FO 371/104574; *Statesman,* 17 September 1953 (clipping); Rothnie Minutes, 30 June and 8 July 1953; Report from American Embassy, Teheran, 6 July 1953, FO 371/104568, PRO; JFD to U.S. Embassy, Teheran, 17 July 1953; Aldrich to JFD, 24 August 1953, box 4111, file 788.00, RG 59, NA.

81. DDE, *Mandate,* 163; *Statesman,* 17 September 1953 (clipping), FO 371/104568, PRO; U.S. Embassy, Teheran to JFD, 19 August 1953, box 4111, file 788.00, RG 59, NA.

82. Pahlavi, *Answer,* 91; Kermit Roosevelt, *Countercoup: The Struggle for the Control of Iran* (New York: Macmillan, 1979), 120–22, 190; Ambrose, *Ike's Spies,* 204; *Times* of India, 16 September 1953, and *Statesman,* 17 September 1953 (clippings), FO 371/104568, PRO.

83. Roosevelt, *Countercoup,* 210; British Embassy, Baghdad, to Marquis of Salisbury, 26 August 1953, FO 371/104658; Makins to FO, 16 January 1953; Helm to FO, 19 August 1953; Gandy Memo, 4 September 1953, FO 371/104573, PRO.

CHAPTER 6

1. JFD Remarks at PU, 22 February 1952, box 107, Smith Papers, PU.

2. JFD, "The American People Need to be Imbued with a Righteous Faith," in JFD et al., *A Righteous Faith for a Just and Durable Peace* (Federal Council of Churches, 1942), 7; idem, "The United Nations: Its Challenge to America" (remarks on receiving an honorary degree at Princeton University, 22 February 1946); London *Observer,* 23 July 1942 (manuscript of article by JFD), box 282, JFDP; JFD, "The Church and World Affairs," *The Presbyterian Tribune* 63 (October 1947): 11; JFD to Krock, n.d., box 8, WHMS; Gerson, *Dulles,* 7–8. In an address at Watertown in 1952, Dulles remarked that "today American history is often taught as a doctor would report his post-mortem examination of a diseased corpse. Historians today seem to take pride in trying to find defects in our great national figures, and to show hypocrisy in our national conduct. Of course, our nation has not been perfect, and its leaders have not been perfect, no human beings ever are. But our national history is a great record, and the acts and utterances of the Americans who made it can be an inspiration and help to each new generation." For George Kennan's concern about moral decadence in America, similar in some respects to that of JFD, see *New York Times Magazine,* 12 September 1954 (clipping), box 4, Kennan Papers, PU.

3. Van Dusen, ed., *Dulles,* 95, 164–65, 173; JFD, "Challenge and Response," 42; idem, *War or Peace,* 258; JFD Speech to NATO Ministerial Meeting, December 1953; JFD Speech at National War College, 16 June 1953; JFD Speech to National Press Club, 22 December 1953; JFD Radio Broadcast (CBS), 1 January 1952, boxes 73, 75, 107, JFDP; JFD Address at Gatlinburg, Tennessee, 1 October 1951, box 19, RG5, MacArthur Papers, MacArthur Memorial Archives, Norfolk, Virginia; JFD, "The United Nations," box 1, DAP. For JFD's carbon copies of the Washington Farewell Address and his essay on Washington and Lincoln, see boxes 397 and 279, respectively, JFDP.

4. JFD, *War or Peace,* 243–44; JFD Speech to UN General Assembly, 17 September 1953; *Christian Science Monitor,* sec. 2, p. 1 (clipping), boxes 71, 398, JFDP; Heller and Heller, *Dulles,* 117.

5. JFD Remarks at PU, 22 February 1952, box 107, Smith Papers, PU (for the figure of water striking stone).

6. JFD, *War or Peace*, 229; Prince Krommun Naradhip Bongsprabandh Wan Waitthayakon OHI by Spencer Davis, 16 September 1964, JFDOH; JFD Press Conf., 7 February 1956, box 106, JFDP; DDE to Elson, 31 July 1958, box 34, DDE Series, AWF.

7. The four copies are in box 397, JFDP.

8. *Life*, 2 February 1948 (clipping), box 398, JFDP; Konrad Adenauer, *Mémoires: 1956–1963*, trans. Jacques Peltier and Pierre Frédèrix (Paris: Hachette, 1969), 182.

9. JFD, *War or Peace*, 255, 260; JFD Speech at National War College, 16 June 1953; JFD Interview by Martin Agronsky, 15 September 1957, boxes 75, 114, JFDP; JFD Speech at Geneva, 28 April 1954, box 192, WKP.

10. JFD to Kennan, 29 October 1952, quoted in Kennan OHI, p. 17, JFDOH; JFD Address to American Legion, 10 October 1955, box 92, JFDP; JFD-Scott Conv., 17 September 1955, box 1, GCMS; JFD, "As Seen by a Layman," *Religion in National Life* 7 (Winter 1938): 39–42; Think Piece, 19 July 1954, box 7, SS; JFD, "The United States and the World of Nations" (Address to the Federal Council of Churches National Study Conference on the Churches and the International Situation), 27 February 1940 (Federal Council of Churches, 1940?), 14; idem, "Moral Force in World Affairs," *Presbyterian Life*, 10 April 1948, box 284, JFDP; JFD to Krock, n.d., box 8, WHMS.

11. Lansing Secret War Diary, September 1916, file 2, John W. F. Dulles Papers, University of Texas, Austin: Van Dusen, ed., *Dulles*, 95, 126; Bell OHI, p. 8, JFDOH; JFD, "Long Range Objectives," 18 September 1941, box 282, JFDP; *China Post*, 13 January 1955, p. 1.

12. Allison, *Ambassador*, 292; DDE First Inaugural Address, 20 January 1953; DDE State of the Union Message, 6 January 1955; DDE to Green, 2 October 1958, in Branyan and Larsen, eds., *Eisenhower*, 1:29–30, 449; 2:757–58; Chiang OHI, p. 33; Hanes OHI, p. 208; Malik OHI, p. 41; Chung Il Kwon OHI by Spencer Davis, 29 September 1964, p. 40; Ikazaki OHI, p. 29; Paik OHI, p. 21; Pyun OHI, p. 21; Romulo OHI, p. 47; Yoshida OHI, p. 31, JFDOH; JFD Address to American Legion, 10 October 1955; JFD Speech to VFW, 18 August 1958, boxes 92, 128, JFDP. It is interesting that when news of the Dewey defeat reached him in Paris at a dinner hosted by Filipinos, although he was greatly disappointed (as he had expected to be named the next secretary of state), he told his hosts that someday, when he did become secretary, he would accept a Philippine invitation before any other. Later, when the time came to make good on his promise, he did so despite the demands of protocol (Romulo OHI, p. 47, JFDOH).

13. JFD, *War or Peace*, 168–69; Harkness, "Notes," 12 February 1955, box 1, DAP.

14. JFD Far East OHI (Robertson-Radford), p. 63, JFDOH; Rhee to DDE, 8 April 1954, box 2, DH.

15. JFD et al., *Righteous Faith*, 8; Eban, *Autobiography*, 175; Avery Dulles to JFD, 22 February 1956; JFD Interview by Martin Agronsky, 15 September 1957, NBC TV ("not peace but a sword"); JFD Address to National Council of Churches, November 1958, boxes 102, 114, 126, JFDP; JFD, "The Christian Citizen in a Changing World" (World Council of Churches pamphlet of forty-two pages prepared for the WCC Study Department Commission at the First Assembly of the World Council, 22 August 1948), 1; JFD Address at Chicago, 28 May 1941, file 18, John W. F. Dulles Papers, University of Texas; Dulles, *Dulles*, 197–99. For scholarly

criticism of Dulles along this line, see Toulouse, *Dulles*, 175, 202; Niebuhr, "Moral World," 8.

16. Beal, *Dulles*, 28, 49; Eleanor Lansing Dulles OHI, pp. 4–5; Samuel McCrea Cavert OHI by RDC, 29 July 1963, p. 37; Edwards OHI, p. 15, JFDOH. Grandfather Foster could sound ardently religious, even censorious, while at the same time being a man of the world. See John Watson Foster, *Diplomatic Memoirs*, 2 vols. (Boston: Houghton Mifflin, 1909), 1:129–30, 161–62, 187, 237–38, 300, 316–28, 330; 2:257–58, 265. According to his sister, Eleanor, and also Andrew Berding, JFD had frequent recourse to these volumes. See Dulles, *Chances*, 380; Berding, *Dulles*, 13. JFD's mother taught religion to Auburn girls as well as to Spanish youngsters (in Spanish while living in Madrid). She also radiated happiness and faith even as an invalid (in her old age). See Edith Foster Dulles, "The Story of My Life" (unpublished manuscript, 1934); also "A Memorial for Mrs. Edith Dulles Read at the Fortnightly on 29 October 1941," box 397, JFDP; Edwards OHI, p. 22, JFDOH. At the close of her "Story," she remarks, "So, as we go fearlessly on our way through life, enjoying the world round about us, appreciating the great thoughts of the world's wise ones, exploring our own selves, we come to know 'Another' who reveals Himself in the beauty of nature, in the thoughts of the great writers, in the depths of our own souls, and we are never alone. Life, death, and the great Forever are His, and we are His (If this sounds like a sermon, remember I lived with a preacher for over forty years)." There has been an idea, traceable perhaps to Thomas Dewey and retailed by such writers as Townsend Hoopes, that Dulles spent some time as an atheist during the early part of his life as an attorney. But this is denied by Mark Toulouse who has made the most thorough study of the subject to date. See Toulouse, *Dulles*, chap. 1 (especially pp. 16–17); Hoopes, *Dulles*, 35; also Dulles, *Dulles*, 129.

17. Dreier OHI, p. 2 (Dulles had a Bible prominently displayed on the desk of his small UN office after the war); Lillias Dulles Hinshaw OHI by PAC, 29 May 1966, pp. 20, 24 (Dulles did not attend church regularly at Cold Spring Harbor, but he carried a pocket-size New Testament with him through life); Hollister OHI, p. 68 (Dulles "never said anything mean about anybody"); Gerard Lambert OHI by PAC, 14 May 1964, p. 18; P. B. Macomber OHI, p. 30; Roderic L. O'Connor OHI by PAC, 2 April 1966, p. 152; Avery Dulles OHI by PAC, 30 July 1966, p. 26; Raymond B. Fosdick OHI by RDC, 7 July 1965, p. 3; Lisagor OHI, p. 31; Seligman OHI, p. 15; Sisco OHI, p. 9; Thomas E. Stephens OHI by RDC, 7 December 1965, pp. 28, 31; Harkness OHI, p. 6; Eleanor Dulles OHI, p. 43, JFDOH; *Central Daily News*, 26 May 1959 (clipping), file 721–65, HCKMT; JFD Press Conf., 19 January 1954, box 78, JFDP (re: *Deo volente*); Gerson, *Dulles*, xi (re: St. Paul's); Monnet, *Memoirs*, 105; Cutler, *No Time for Rest*, 334; Nixon, *Memoirs*, 205 (calls Dulles "the most conscientious public man I have ever known"); JFD Interview by Martin Agronsky, 15 September 1957, box 114, JFDP; JFD to Avery, 30 March 1954, "Thirteen Letters," DAP ("I do not doubt that those Masses and the prayers help me to carry my responsibilities. Surely, they are more heavy than could be carried by anyone without spiritual sustenance").

18. Beal, *Dulles*, 127–28; Richard M. Fagley OHI by RDC, 3 December 1964, p. 19; Hall OHI, p. 6; McCardle OHI, pp. 45–47, 50; Sebald OHI, p. 94; Torbert OHI, p. 23, JFDOH; *Evening Star*, 25 April 1959, p. A8 (clipping), box 83, Allen Dulles Papers, PU; JFD to Krekeler, 29 January 1954; JFD Manuscript, 21 April 1956, boxes 78, 287, JFDP (it should be noted that the manuscript dated 21 April

which deals with indissolubility is mislabeled as an article for *U.S. News*); JFD, "The Panama Canal Controversy Between Great Britain and the United States" (privately printed pamphlet, 1913), p.14, JFDP. Divorce and remarriage were relatively uncommon during the 1950s, especially for public officials. Notable, among the exceptions, were Eden and Batista.

19. Cooper, *Lion's Last Roar*, 95–96; Eban, *Autobiography*, 204; Macmillan, *Tides*, 658; Aldrich OHI, pp. 8–9; Black OHI, pp. 9–10; Humphrey OHI, pp. 28, 33; W. B. Macomber OHI, pp. 53–54; Allen OHI, p. 42 (the offer of December 1955 was conditional upon the signing of a final document, something which never happened); Sparkman OHI, pp. 35–36 (makes light of cotton as a factor), JFDOH; *Evening Standard* (London), 1 April 1957 (clipping), box 113, JFDP (Randolph Churchill's opinion); Henderson Chronology Notes for 9 February 1956, box 6, Henderson Papers, LC. According to Eisenhower, he made a mistake in not making public his initial rejection of Egypt's terms (which amounted to a withdrawal of the American offer). See Bipartisan Legislative Leaders Meeting, 9 November 1956, Russell Papers, UG. For additional documentation on the Anderson mission, see DDE Diary, 11 January and 8 March 1956, in Ferrell, ed., *Eisenhower*, 308, 318–19; Hoopes, *Dulles*, 332; Heikal, *Cairo Documents*, 55–56; Ewald, *Eisenhower*, 196; Francis H. Russell OHI by PAC, 6 April 1966, pp. 15–16, JFDOH.

20. Mosley, *Dulles*, 385; Beaufré, *Suez*, 24; James E. Dougherty, "The Aswan Decision in Perspective," *Political Science Quarterly* 74 (March 1959): 24–25; Aldrich OHI, pp. 9–10; Allen OHI, p. 33; Henderson OHI, pp. 23–24; Humphrey OHI, pp. 26–27, 32–33; Richards OHI, p. 26, JFDOH; JFD Press Conf., 2 April 1957; JFD Manuscript, 21 April 1956, boxes 123, 287, JFDP; JFD Memo for DDE, 28 March 1956, box 5, SS; Henderson OH #191, p. 45, EL (CUOHC); Thomas, *Suez*, 23–24; Cooper, *Lion's Last Roar*, 96.

21. Eban, *Autobiography*, 205; Lloyd, *Suez*, 71; Roberts, *Rough Draft*, 138; Thomas, *Suez*, 25 (according to Thomas, Dulles played into Nasser's hands); Home, *Autobiography*, 138–39.

22. Heikal, *Cairo Documents*, 64–65; Nutting, *No End*, 44; Dougherty, "Aswan," 38; Brian Urquhart, *Hammarskjold: The Years of Decision* (New York: Knopf, 1972), 154n, 155; Aldrich OHI, pp. 9–11; Allen OHI #1, pp. 39, 41; Anderson OHI, p. 36; W. Macomber OHI, pp. 55–56; Russell OHI, pp. 11–12, 19; Lord Sherfield (Roger Makins) OHI by PAC, 5 June 1964, p. 7; Wiggins OHI, p. 10, JFDOH; JFD Press Conf., 2 April 1957, box 123, JFDP; Wiggins, "Notes," 2 July 1957, box 2, DAP; Thomas, *Suez*, 23; Gerson, *Dulles*, 281; Lloyd, *Suez*, 69.

23. JFD Press Conf., 2 April 1957, box 123, JFDP. Nasser's attack came only six weeks after the last British troops had withdrawn (Beaufré, *Suez*, 24). For Marroquín and Panama, see Frederick W. Marks III, *Velvet on Iron: The Diplomacy of Theodore Roosevelt* (Lincoln: University of Nebraska Press, 1979), 96–105.

24. Van Dusen, ed., *Dulles*, 178; Avery Dulles OHI, p. 19, JFDOH; JFD Speech, Williamstown, 6 October 1956; JFD Interview by Martin Agronsky, 15 September 1957; JFD, "Peace Without Platitudes," *Fortune* 25 (January 1942—clipping), boxes 106, 114, 282 JFDP; Dulles, *Dulles*, 186.

25. Macmillan, *Storm*, 483, 559; JFD, *War or Peace*, 2: JFD to Barnes, 7 October 1937; JFD Economic Club Speech, 22 March 1939; JFD Press Conf., 16 October 1957; JFD Williamstown Speech, 6 October 1956; JFD Interview by McInnis, 23 June 1958; JFD, "Road to Peace," *Atlantic Quarterly* 156 (October 1935): 499 (clipping), boxes 16, 18, 106, 126, 281, JFDP; Humphrey OHI, p. 21; Nixon OHI, p. 28,

JFDOH; Kaufman, *Trade*, 60–63; Memo for Conv. between Delegation Chiefs, Bermuda, 7 December 1953, box 1, SS; NSC Meetings, 4 June 1953 and 11 March 1954, boxes 4 and 5, NSC; Beam, *Multiple Exposure*, 80.

26. Berding, *Dulles*, 155; JFD Williamstown Speech, 6 October 1956; JFD Remarks to AFL-CIO Executive Council, 19 August 1958, boxes 106 and 132, JFDP; Harkness, "Notes," 21 July 1958, box 1, DAP; JFD-Green Conv., 12 October 1958, box 1, GCMS; JFD to DDE, 14 April 1958, box 8, DH; Ambrose, *EP*, 615; *Time*, 14 January 1957, p. 16; Koo-Robertson Conv., 6 April 1956, box 200, WKP; Holmes to DEA, 28 March 1956, box 219, U-15, vol. 6, St. Laurent Papers, MG26L, PAC; Memo on Tange Discussions with Ottawa officials, 10 March 1955, vol. 32, Pearson Papers, MG26N1, PAC; Dulles, *Dulles*, 170.

27. JFD, "Church," 11; idem, *War or Peace*, 45–46; Gross OHI, pp. 13–14; Sisco OHI, p. 11; Wainhouse OHI, pp. 6–10, JFDOH; Memo of Conv. at Bermuda, 24 March 1957; JFD UN Speech, 18 September 1958; JFD Speech to New York Bar Association, 31 January 1959; JFD Paper on Rogers Lamont, 14 September 1948, boxes 113, 127, 138, 284, JFDP; JFD-DDE Conv., 21 July 1958; JFD Memo for DDE, 15 May 1954, boxes 7 and 8, WHMS; JFD Memo for McCardle, 22 July 1954, box 8, CS; JFD to DDE, 6 February 1959, box 8, DH; Gerson, *Dulles*, 42; Makins to FO, 29 August 1953, FO 371/103496; Tripartite Meeting, Quai d'Orsay, 25 April 1953, PREM 11/429, PRO.

28. For Kashmir, see *Time*, 28 January 1957, p. 33.

29. Murphy, *Diplomat*, 434–35; Khrushchev, *Testament*, 411; Macmillan, *Storm*, 464–65, 476; Van Dusen, ed., *Dulles*, 175–77; Bowie OHI, p. 19, JFDOH; JFD Speech to American Society of International Law, 25 April 1956; JFD to Adenauer, 30 June 1958; JFD Address at Durham, N.H., 2 May 1958, boxes 104, 125, 126, JFDP; Wiggins, "Notes," 4 April 1958, box 2, DAP; JFD, "Church," 10; JFD-Gruenther Conv., 19 February 1958, box 1, GCMS; JFD to DDE, 14 October 1958, box 8, DH; Ambrose, *EP*, 403–4; Gerson, *Dulles*, 308; *Time*, 20 May 1957, p. 32. For an excellent discussion of arms control from the viewpoint of Dulles and Eisenhower, see H. W. Brands, Jr., *Cold Warriors* (New York: Columbia University Press, 1988), 142–43, 145–47, 149.

30. Macmillan, *Storm*, 290; DDE, OHI, p. 43, JFDOH; JFD Press Conf., 10 January 1958; JFD Press Backgrounder, 11 July 1958, boxes 125, 126, JFDP; *Time*, 28 January 1957, p. 20; Beam, *Multiple Exposure*, 94–95. Dulles spent an enormous amount of time on inspection proposals without achieving anything concrete. Only when Washington appeared to be drawing even technologically did Moscow subscribe to the convention on outer space. See Berding, *Dulles*, 92; Smith OHI, p. 13, JFDOH; JFD to Adenauer, 30 June 1958, box 125, JFDP. One scholar has called Eisenhower's "Atoms for Peace" proposal "the most generous and the most serious offer on controlling the arms race ever made by an American president" because it was not "loaded" against the Russians (the United States proposed a 5–1 ratio of donation). Even with such a favorable ratio, however, the Russians may well have felt at a disadvantage, as indeed the same author is prepared to admit (Ambrose, *EP*, 149). Eisenhower first proposed "Atoms for Peace" on 8 December 1953 at the United Nations. Initially, the Soviet Union condemned the plan, saying that what was important was *complete* elimination of existing stocks. But by 1957, the International Atomic Energy Agency had become a reality with Soviet participation. Donations were modest, and the arms balance remained virtually unaffected, but

like "Open Skies,"which never won acceptance, Eisenhower scored in the area of propaganda; in addition, many free world nations benefited from America's willingness to share its advanced technology. See Adams, *Firsthand Report*, 111; DDE Address, 8 December 1953, in Branyan and Larsen, eds., *Eisenhower*, 1:199, 201.

31. Berding, *Dulles*, 24; Neff, *Warriors*, 170 (re: *Suaviter in modo, fortiter in re*); JFD UN Speech, 18 September 1958, box 127, JFDP; Krock Memo, 7 April 1960, bk. 2, box 1, Krock Papers, PU.

32. JFD, *War or Peace*, 249; *U.S. News*, 16 May 1958, p. 71; *Christian Science Monitor*, 7 July 1948, sec. 2, p. 1; JFD Notes aboard *S.S. Helena*, 11 December 1952, box 8, SS.

33. Beal, *Dulles*, 131–32; Young, *Chinese*, 144–45; DDE, *Waging Peace*, 297, 340; Gunther, *Eisenhower*, 120; Berding, *Dulles*, 31, 128–29; Bohlen, *Witness*, 428–29, 433; JFD Statement, 4 September 1958; DDE Message to Congress, 24 January 1955, in Branyan and Larsen, eds., *Eisenhower*, 2:750–51, 756; JFD Testimony Before Senate Foreign Relations Committee, March–April 1954, pp. 21, 25; JFD, *War or Peace*, 99; JFD Address to Republican Woman's Centennial Conf., 7 April 1955; JFD Address to American Legion, 10 October 1955; JFD Press Conf., 16 October 1957, boxes 79, 92, 116, JFDP; Wiggins, "Notes," 29 December 1956, box 2, DAP; JFD Cabinet Remark, 13 January 1953; Hughes Diary Notes of Meetings, box 1, Emmet Hughes Papers, PU; JFD-DDE Conv., 22 January 1958, box 6, WHMS; JFD Speech to American Legion, 2 September 1953, box 8, SS; Gallman, *Iraq*, 185; Radford, *Memoirs*, 420–21, 442 (on ambivalence in Vietnam); *Time*, 21 January 1957, p. 12; 25 February 1957, p. 22; Koo-McConaughy Conv., 16 June 1955, box 195, WKP (on JFD's use of India's Menon as an intermediary); JFD-Hagerty Conv., 31 March 1954, box 10, Tel. Conv., EL (on Dulles' intent to use the term "united action" ambiguously).

34. JFD Press Conf., 31 January 1954, box 78, JFDP; Goodpaster OHI #37 and #477, EL; JFD Speech to National War College, 16 June 1953, box 75, JFDP; Milton Eisenhower, *President*, 364–65; JFD Notes aboard the *S.S. Helena*, 11 December 1952, box 8, SS.

35. DDE, *Waging Peace*, 510; Berding, *Dulles*, 146; JFD Memo for DDE, 18 June 1955, box 91, JFDP; Ambrose, *EP*, 626; Johnson, *Right Hand*, 165; *China Post*, 16 January 1955, p. 1; Makins to FO, 4 December 1954, FO 371/109101, PRO.

36. Beal, *Dulles*, 127; Hoopes, *Dulles*, 332; Bar-Zohar, *Ben-Gurion*, 192; Nixon, *Memoirs*, 129; JFD Press Conf., 30 September 1958, box 127, JFDP; Robertson OHI #121, pp. 62, 66, EL; *China Post*, 23 December 1954, p. 1; Nixon OHI, p. 18, Russell Papers, UG.

37. DDE, *Mandate*, 416; Walter Hallstein OHI by Gordon A. Craig, 29 July 1964, p. 5; Lucet OHI, p. 4; Thompson OHI, pp. 8–9, JFDOH; Thomas, *Suez*, 134; Ely, *Suez*, 70; Kirkpatrick, *Inner Circle*, 260.

38. Goold-Adams, *Dulles*, 51; Heller and Heller, *Dulles*, 116–17; JFD, *War or Peace*, 256; *Christian Science Monitor*, 7 July 1948, sec. 2, p. 1; Henderson, "Advice," 168.

39. Lodge OHI, p. 2, JFDOH; JFD to Vandenberg, 17 November 1951, box 3, Vandenberg Papers, MHCBHL; Adenauer, *Mémoires: 1953–1956*, 242.

40. DDE Diary, 30 June 1950, in Ferrell, ed., *Eisenhower*, 175; DDE, *Waging Peace*, 355; Mayers, "Containment," 63–64, 72; Pineau, *Suez*, 34–35, 93–94; JFD Speech to NATO Council, 23 April 1954, FR (1952–54), 5:514; O'Connor OHI,

p. 101, JFDOH; JFD San Francisco Address, 4 December 1958; JFD, "The Meaning of the Crisis" in letter to Van Kirk, 18 December 1950, boxes 127, 286, JFDP; Memo of Conv. between Delegation Chiefs, 7 December 1953, box 1, SS; Ambrose, *EP*, 638; Gerson, *Dulles*, 331n; Carlton, *Eden*, 367 (re: Ike on appeasement).

41. DDE, *Mandate*, 414–15; idem, *Waging Peace*, 194; JFD Statement, 4 September 1958, in Branyan and Larsen, eds., *Eisenhower*, 2:756; JFD Address to American Legion, 10 October 1955, box 92, JFDP; Memo of DDE-JFD Conv., 14 October 1953, box 1, WHMS; Goodpaster Memo, 16 July 1958, box 35; DDE Diary, AWF; Vandenberg Diary, 7 June, box 6, Vandenberg Papers, MHCBHL. Greek Prime Minister Karamanlis told Eisenhower that removal of the Sixth Fleet from the Mediterranean would mean the loss of the entire region to communism (Eisenhower, *Waging Peace*, 506).

42. Urquhart, *Hammarskjold*, 115, 129–31; Nixon OHI, p. 40, JFDOH; JFD Press Backgrounder, 20 July 1955; JFD Report to the Nation, 18 November 1955, box 92, JFDP; Harkness, "Notes," 17 August 1953, box 1, DAP; Ambrose, *EP*, 261.

43. JFD Address to the Economic Club, 22 March 1939, box 18, JFDP; JFD, "Notes on the Situation in Europe," 7 October 1944, box 283, JFDP; *Time*, 25 February 1957, p. 21. For an example of scholarship that charges Dulles with bluffing as a general practice, see Holsti, "Real Dulles," 38.

44. Schonberger, "Peacemaking," 65 (on the Japanese Peace Treaty).

45. Walters, *Silent Missions*, 299; Hagerty OHI, p. 41; Nixon OHI, p. 12; Riddleberger OHI, pp. 24–25, JFDOH; JFD Essay on Washington and Lincoln, n.d., box 279, JFDP; JFD to Krock, n.d., box 8, WHMS (on Woodrow Wilson). Dulles deliberately chose a career foreign service officer to serve as ambassador to Yugoslavia confident that his man would not be swayed by domestic politics. Girard, who was with American troops on maneuvers in Japan, had been given a machine gun and told to cover for his men. Japanese nationals would often pilfer the brass casings of exploded shells in order to sell them. Girard fired at one interloper and missed. He then fired again at a woman, and this time the shot proved lethal. His superiors claimed that because the incident was an "on duty" case, he was entitled to an American trial. Japanese leaders saw it differently. Because they had "voluntarily" yielded to American justice in 97 percent of the "off-duty" cases (14,000 crimes all told between 1953 and 1957), they were adamant about treating this as another "off-duty" incident in order to save face. Dulles, by acceding to their wishes in the matter, took a definite risk in terms of his standing at home. For the Girard case, see Heller and Heller, *Dulles*, 269–70; DDE, *Waging Peace*, 141–43; Branyan and Larsen, eds., *Eisenhower*, 2:1157–60; Becker OHI, pp. 6–8; Nobusuke Kishi OHI by Spencer Davis, 2 October 1964, p. 8, JFDOH; JFD Backgrounder, 28 June 1957, box 118, JFDP; Goodpaster Memo on Conf. with DDE, 15 September 1958, box 36, DDE; Robertson OHI #121, pp. 141–44, EL (CUOHC).

46. Hagerty Diary, 1 February 1954, in Ferrell, ed., *Hagerty*, 13; JFD, Testimony Before Senate Foreign Relations Committee, March–April 1954, p. 9; Riddleberger OHI, pp. 30–31, JFDOH; Duane A. Tannanbaum, "The Bricker Amendment Controversy: Its Origins and Eisenhower's Role," *Diplomatic History* 9 (Winter 1985): 73–93; Kennedy, "Foreign Policy," 56; JFD-Dean Conv., 18 March 1954, box 2, Tel. Conv., EL.

47. Dillon Anderson OHI #165 by John Luter, 30–31 December 1969, p. 39, EL (CUOHC); Richardson, *Eisenhower*, 180; Ambrose, *EP*, 135; Makins to FO, 10 July

1954, FO 371/109101, PRO. What Eisenhower did was to appoint a Civilian Board of Consultants headed by the wily old David K. E. Bruce and composed of persons eminent enough to inspire confidence while at the same time protecting confidentiality. See DDE Diary, 24 January 1956, in Ferrell, ed., *Eisenhower*, 312; Paul Johnson, *Modern Times* (New York: Harper, 1983), 463.

48. Hoopes, *Dulles*, 435; Adams, *Firsthand Report*, 291; Harkness, "Notes," 21 July 1958, box 1, DAP; Goodpaster Memo on Legislative Leaders Conf., 16 July 1958, box 35, DDE Diary, AWF; Ambrose, *EP*, 471.

49. JFD Statement Before Joint Session of Senate Foreign Relations and Armed Services Committees, 14 January 1957, box 116, JFDP; *Time*, 28 January 1957, p. 20; 4 February 1957, p. 13.

50. *Time*, 4 February 1957, pp. 13–14; 11 February 1957, p. 15; 18 February 1957, p. 16; 25 February 1957, p. 17.

51. JFD-DDE Conv., 13 May 1958, box 6, WHMS.

CHAPTER 7

1. Dulles drew six rounds of laughter at a National Press Club appearance on 25 March 1958 (box 129, JFDP). As regards physical ailments, he also suffered from chronic back problems, mumps, diverticulitis, and astigmatism; he was struck by lightning, thrown from a carriage, and knocked unconscious. Even before his birth, events seemed to conspire against him. His mother's home was gutted by fire the night before her wedding, and later, in the process of giving birth to her first son, she contracted a nearly fatal case of puerperal fever and was bedridden for months (Edith Dulles, "Story," box 397, JFDP). See also Dulles, *Chances*, 274; Eleanor Dulles OHI, pp. 136–37; Leonard D. Heaton OHI by PAC, 19 August 1966, p. 17; Hinshaw OHI, p. 60; Arthur C. Peckham OHI by PAC, 7 July 1965, pp. 1–2, 15; Paul Sheldon OHI by RDC, 14 February 1966, p. 1; Riddleberger OHI, p. 61 (early in 1959, Dulles appeared quite vigorous), JFDOH; JFD Speech to National Council of Churches, November 1958, *New York Herald Tribune*, 27 July 1959 (clipping); JFD Diary, 3–9 February 1919 (on mumps); "Man with a Mission" article from *Reader's Digest* (November 1951—clipping) in boxes 126, 139, 278, 399, JFDP; Jackson log, 11 January 1958, box 57, C. D. Jackson Papers, EL; Ambrose, *EP*, 443; File 721–13, HCKMT; Fish to DDE, 26 September 1958, International General File, Russell Papers, UG; Dulles, *Dulles*, 27–28, 54–55, 197. For a marvelous account of JFD's final days at State, see Dulles, *Dulles*.

2. JFD Press Conf., 10 January 1958, box 125, JFDP (see also box 134); Nixon OHI, p. 42, Russell Papers, UG.

3. Spaak, *Memoirs*, 132; Drummond and Coblentz, *Duel*, 208; Nolting OHI, p. 12; Smith OHI, p. 44, JFDOH; JFD News Conf., 13 January 1959; JFD Day Book 1958, boxes 139, 382, JFDP. For his first two and a half years in office, Dulles claimed never to have left the State Department for more than two weeks (JFD News Conf., 30 August 1955, box 93, JFDP).

4. Drummond and Coblentz, *Duel*, 211–13; Heaton OHI, pp. 5–6, JFDOH; *Life*, 8 June 1959, p. 36 (tribute by Nixon—clipping), box 81, JFDP; Couve de Murville, *Politique*, 165–66; *Time*, 1 June 1959, p. 13.

5. Drummond and Coblentz, *Duel*, 228; Dulles, *Chances*, 275; Heaton OHI, pp. 8–10, JFDOH; *Newsweek*, 30 March 1959, p. 60; *New York Herald Tribune*

(undated clipping), JFD Day Book, 1959, boxes 139, 382, JFDP; *Time*, 1 June 1959, p. 12.

6. By 1979, the year CENTO was formally disbanded, Pakistan, Iran, and Turkey had defected and the pact was moribund. Only four SEATO members fought in Vietnam: Australia, New Zealand, Thailand, and the United States. During the 1960s, France and Pakistan opposed America's role in the Vietnam War even as Britain began withdrawing its forces from Asia. In 1972, Pakistan withdrew from SEATO. Three years later, the ministerial council decided to phase out the treaty organization, and when it was dissolved on 30 June 1977, only the treaty itself remained in effect. Nonmilitary programs continued on a bilateral basis. It is interesting to note, though, that even Dulles' most severe critics do not hold him responsible for the Vietnam War. See, for example, Holsti, "Real Dulles," 43.

7. Castillo Armas was assassinated in July 1957, and in 1973, Arthur Schlesinger published *The Imperial Presidency*.

8. Henry A. Kissinger, *White House Years* (Boston: Little, Brown, 1979), 122, 126–29, 131–33, 537 (for the Nixon years); Samuel Pisar, "Let's Put Détente Back on the Rails," *New York Times Magazine*, 25 September 1977, 116 (on Aswan).

9. Young, *Chinese*, 15, 237–44; Heeney, *Memoirs*, 115, 176–78. Rusk spoke over NBC radio in 1963.

10. Robert H. Ferrell, *American Diplomacy* (New York: Norton, 1969), 846; Kissinger, *White House Years*, 116. Forty naval vessels participated in LBJ's Dominican intervention which won the support of the OAS and cost an estimated $150 million.

11. Eisenhower, *Wine*, 224; DDE, *Waging Peace*, 538; Spaak, *Memoirs*, 457; Macmillan, *Storm*, 645; Krock Memo, 9 March 1960, box 1, Krock Papers, PU; Alphand, *Journal*, 317, 321; Heeney, *Memoirs*, 163, 177. Relations with France ended on a recriminatory note with open disagreement on Congo policy (Alphand, *Journal*, 340–41). For assassination plots against Trujillo, see Rabe, *Eisenhower*.

12. DDE, *Waging Peace*, 613; Beaulac, *Latin America*, 16; Lukacs, *Cold War*, 233–34; Eisenhower, *Wine*, 265–66; Jules Dubois, *Fidel Castro* (Indianapolis: Bobbs Merrill, 1959), 364; Ambrose, *EP*, 545, 583; Hill OHI, p. 94, CUOH; William Benton, *The Voice of Latin America* (New York: Harper, 1965), 96. Eisenhower severed diplomatic relations with Cuba within forty-eight hours of Castro's order. Needless to say, the Cuban dictator had ample reason to clamp down on Americans. Ike was maturing plans for an invasion, and Herter was prepared to manufacture a suitable pretext (Ambrose, *EP*, 609).

13. DDE, *Waging Peace*, 404, 406–7; Harold Macmillan, *Pointing the Way, 1959–1961* (London: Macmillan, 1972), 78–79; Young, *Chinese*, 15, 134, 217, 227; Goodpaster OHI #37, pp. 101–3, EL; Nixon, *No More Vietnams*, 49; Beam, *Multiple Exposure*, 135, 138. Dulles' method had been to dictate a memo after all important meetings with Eisenhower. He would then read it back to the president over the phone as an added precaution (DDE, *Waging Peace*, 407).

14. Hughes, *Ordeal of Power*, 303, 306–7 (on Japan and the U-2).

15. George S. Franklin, Jr. OHI by RDC, 12 March 1965, p. 29, JFDOH; JFD Speech to CIO, 18 November 1953 (on Vietnam); JFD Press Backgrounder, 3 April 1958, boxes 75, 89, 133, JFDP; Harkness, "Notes," (1958?), box 1, DAP. Long before Castillo Armas encountered problems as president of Guatemala, Dulles had spoken of his "demonstrated lack" of "ability to govern." See JFD to U.S. Embassy, Guatemala City, 31 August 1954, FR (1952–54), 4:1224.

16. De Gaulle, *Revival*, 203; W.T.R. Fox, "The Military and United States Foreign Policy," *International Journal* 38 (Winter 1982–83): 39–58; JFD Address to Atlantic Treaty Association, 27 September 1958, box 127, JFDP; Alphand, *Journal*, 295, 298.

17. Wiley OHI, p. 7, JFDOH; Makins to FO, 16 January 1954, FO 371/109100, PRO; Heeney, *Memoirs*, 164 ("there has never been an administration in Washington which knew more about Canada and Canadian affairs or tried harder to meet Canadian wishes"); DEA Report on the Americas, 1958; Press Opinion Summary, 26 August 1958; House of Commons Debate, 10–11 February 1960 (remarks by Messers Smith of Calgary and Green), file #1415–40 (vols. 6 and 7), RG 25, DEA; *Daily Telegraph* (of London), 25 May 1959 clipping, box 83, Allen Dulles Papers, PU (on the expectation that Main Duck Island would go to Canada).

18. Eisenhower, *President*, 351; John M. Cabot OHI by PAC, 15 November 1965, p. 5, JFDOH; JFD to DDE, 10 September 1954; Herter to DDE, 19 August 1958; Hill to JFD, 22 July 1958, boxes 3 and 8, DH; Rabe, *Eisenhower*, 77–83; DDE, *Waging Peace*, 532; Nixon, *Six Crises*, 185.

19. Ellis Briggs, *Farewell to Foggy Bottom* (New York: David McKay and Company, 1964), 125, 127, 142–49; Cabot OHI, p. 4, JFDOH.

20. When Eisenhower visited Argentina in 1960, he was welcomed by a crowd numbering approximately one million. Even Communist banners declaimed not against him but rather against President Frondizi. In Chile, he got along famously with President Jorge Alessandri in what proved to be the warmest of all receptions on a triumphal tour—seven hundred thousand people, 10 percent of Chile's population, turned out to wave, applaud, and cheer. In Brazil, hundreds of thousands threw confetti and yelled "Viva Eke!" while in Uruguay, he received the most impressive reception ever accorded a foreigner. There were scattered protests, to be sure, but the tone was reassuringly positive almost everywhere he went. Fifty Uruguayan students who displayed hostile banners were nearly torn to pieces. See Nixon, *Six Crises*, 187–88, 192, 195–206, 208–9, 227; Smith, *President's Odyssey*, 148–52, 164, 176, 187; Eisenhower, *Wine*, 190, 202, 217, 240, 248; DDE, *Mandate*, 426; idem, *Waging Peace*, 527–31; Cutler, *No Time for Rest*, 280–81; U.S. Embassy, Taipei, to State, 31 May 1957; Rankin to Smith, 13 June 1957; Rankin to Nash, 17 June 1957, box 29, Rankin Papers, PU (the "Black Friday" riots of 24 May 1957, the worst anti-American demonstrations of all time in Taipei, "almost completely destroyed the contents of the American Embassy and the U.S. Information Service buildings." Ambassador Rankin's safe was thrown out of the window onto his Cadillac; and his marine guard, along with several of his employees, were stoned and beaten. Chiang, calling out 33,000 troops, placed Taiwan under marshal law); Schlesinger and Kinzer, *Bitter Fruit*, 188–89 (on Latin reaction to American intervention in Guatemala); U.K. Annual Report on Mexico, 1954, FO 371/114259, PRO; Confidential Department of State biographical information (on Ruiz of Mexico), box 219, U-15, vol. 6, St. Laurent Papers, MG26L, PAC; Beaulac, *Diplomat*, 14; *Time*, 20 May 1957, p. 39; 3 June 1957, p. 19. On "Bloody May Day" 1952, three days after Japan regained her independence, there were anti-American demonstrations more violent than the 1960 riots (themselves the greatest mass uprisings in Japan since the rice riots of 1918). Fourteen hundred persons were injured, including several Americans, and a number of U.S. military vehicles were overturned and set aflame. The alleged reason for the violence was Prime Minister Yoshida's effort to pass an antisubversive activities law, but it backfired with unanticipated results; all thirty-

five Communists in the lower house of Japan's parliament were defeated in their bid for reelection two years later (Packard, *Tokyo*, 25, 91). Eight years later, in 1960, the American embassy in Tokyo was stoned and Eisenhower's press secretary was so endangered by mobs threatening to overturn his limousine that he had to be evacuated by helicopter (Smith, *President's Odyssey*, 211). One should not forget, along somewhat similar lines, the violent anti-Americanism confronting Vice President Wallace when he visited Mexico City in 1940, not to mention Secretary Marshall's encounter in Bogotá in 1948 (mentioned in chap. 1). For the Wallace debacle, see Frederick W. Marks III, *Wind over Sand: The Diplomacy of Franklin Roosevelt* (Athens: University of Georgia Press, 1988), 224.

21. John C. Dreier, *The Organization of American States and the Hemisphere Crisis* (New York: Harper, 1962), 60–61; Berle and Jacobs, eds., *Berle*, 635, 640–41; Smith to Merriam, 27 December 1960, in Branyan and Larsen, eds., *Eisenhower*, 2:1338; JFD Speech to Council on Foreign Relations, 7 June 1957, box 122, JFDP; *China Post*, 12 January 1955, p. 1; 13 January 1955, pp. 1, 3; 14 January 1955, pp. 1, 3; 17 January 1955, p. 3; 18 January 1955, p. 3; 19 January 1955, p. 3; 1 February 1955, p. 3; Robert J. Alexander, *Rómulo Betancourt and the Transformation of Venezuela* (New Brunswick: Transaction Books, 1982), 360; Third Progress Report on NSC 144/1, 25 May 1954, FR (1952–54), 4:47–48; *New York Times*, 11 March 1954 (clipping), FO 371/108739; Annual Review for Costa Rica (1954), FO 371/114300; Annual Review for Nicaragua (1954), FO 371/114278; Annual Review for Peru (1954), FO 371/114158, PRO.

22. Lodge, *As It Was*, 103; Eisenhower, *President*, 285; Smith to Merriam, 27 December 1960; DDE State of the Union Message, 12 January 1961, in Branyan and Larsen, eds., *Eisenhower*, 2:1343–45, 1949.

23. Larson, *Eisenhower*, 100–101; JFD Press Conf., 20 May 1958, box 128, JFDP; DDE, *Mandate*, 241; Milton Eisenhower OHI #345, pp. 13, 16, 31–33, EL; *Time*, 18 February 1957, p. 36. Milton Eisenhower studied in the Soviet Union in 1959, 1970, and 1971 (OHI, p. 16).

24. Willard L. Beaulac, *The Fractured Continent* (Palo Alto: The Hoover Institution Press, 1980), 162; Zoumaris, "Castro," 162; Eisenhower, *Wine*, 212. Ellis Briggs, American ambassador to Uruguay, Peru, and Brazil, sized Milton up as well-meaning but "profoundly ignorant." According to Briggs, "Milton's views were almost entirely worthless" and his book, *The Wine is Bitter*, had been characterized by a competent Latin American critic as "perhaps the worst book on Latin American affairs written during the century"; Briggs OHI #172 by Douglas Scott, 19 June 1970, pp. 117–18, EL (CUOHC).

25. JFD Radio and TV Speech, 27 January 1953; *Christian Science Monitor*, 7 July 1948, sec. 2, p. 1 (clipping), boxes 75, 398, JFDP; JFD Remarks at NSC Meeting, 31 March 1953, box 8, WHMS; JFD Memo for DDE, 3 September 1953, box 6, SS; JFD Speech, Bloomfield, N.J., 10 October 1952, box 107, Smith Papers, PU (re: "courteous attentions").

26. Cecil B. Lyon OHI by PAC, 18 December 1965, p. 12, JFDOH; JFD Press Conf., 26 March 1957; JFD Press Conf., 20 May 1958; JFD Address, Rio, 6 August 1958, boxes 113, 128, 131, JFDP; JFD Memo for DDE, 22 September 1958, box 8, DH; Smith Memo, 20 November 1953; Peurifoy to State, 7 July 1954, FR (1952–54), 4:29, 1206. Canada was as reluctant to accept the tripartite arrangements as Mexico was eager (Heeney to DEA, 3 February 1956, U-15, vol. 6, St. Laurent

Papers, MG26L, PAC); JFD to DDE, 20 July 1954, in Branyan and Larsen, eds., *Eisenhower*, 1:317–18.

27. DDE, *Mandate*, 420; Nixon OHI, p. 50, JFDOH; DDE to JFD, 14 June 1955, box 4, DH; DDE to Macmillan, 3 April 1958, box 21, IS; Milton Eisenhower OHI #292, pp. 17–18; Henderson OHI #191, pp. 36–38, 57, EL (CUOHC); Third Progress Report on NSC 144/1, 25 May 1954, FR (1952–54), 4:49; Annual Review for Peru (1954), FO 371/114158, PRO. For denial of neglect, see JFD Statement Before House Appropriations Committee, 8 February 1955; JFD Press Conf., 26 March 1957, boxes 95, 113, JFDP. For the more liberal line, see Thomas C. Mann OHI by PAC, 24 May 1966, p. 2, JFDOH; NSC Meeting, 1 May 1958, box 10, NSC.

28. Dulles viewed Cuba's government as corrupt. At the same time, he was not anxious to support Castro. According to Loy Henderson, "a good example of the difference in the views of the Secretary and Milton was their attitude toward Castro," whom Dulles regarded "from the beginning as a Communist or at least a tool of the Communists," whereas "Milton, on the other hand, was inclined to give support to Castro. [Ultimately], the Secretary remained silent while Milton's policy was followed. . . . During many of the staff meetings under the Secretary's chairmanship, both Tom Mann, at the time Assistant Secretary for Economic affairs, and I warned that if Castro would gain control over Cuba, he would lead it down the Communist road. Tom Mann was an expert on Latin America; he had spent most of his career in that area and had been ambassador to several Latin American countries. . . . No one who did not know Dulles well could understand how much he grieved over his helplessness in this matter." See Henderson OHI #191, pp. 37–39, 55, EL (CUOHC). See also Hollister OHI, p. 70; Clarence Dillon OHI, p. 3, JFDOH; Goodpaster OHI #37, p. 60, EL; Earl E. T. Smith, *The Fourth Floor: An Account of the Castro Communist Revolution* (New York: Random House, 1962), 7.

29. Rabe, *Eisenhower*, 166; Krock, *Memoirs*, 275–76; Fulgencio Batista, *The Growth and Decline of the Cuban Republic* (New York: Devin-Adair, 1964), 48, 103, 268–69, 276, 292; DDE, *Waging Peace*, 521; Twining OHI, pp. 41–42, JFDOH (the Joint Chiefs' warnings to Herter were ignored); Krock Notes on White House Dinner, 28 July 1959, bk. 2, box 1, Krock Papers, PU; Smith, *Fourth Floor*, 98, 225, 233–34. Robert Hill claims that his warnings to Dulles (on Castro) went unheeded. See Hill OHI, pp. 35, 58, 101, JFDOH. Cuba was the world's number one producer of cobalt, second in the production of nickel, eighth in chrome, and eleventh in copper. See Batista, *Growth and Decline*, 292. Allen Dulles told the NSC on 23 December 1958 that "Communists and other extreme radicals appear to have penetrated the Castro movement," but Herter could report, as late as March 1960: "Our own latest National Intelligence Estimate does not find Cuba to be under Communist control or domination." See Ambrose, *EP*, 505, 555. When JFD told reporters on 5 November 1957 that "we do not take a grave view of the situation" in Cuba, it was doubtless indicative of the intelligence gap. See *New York Times*, 6 November 1957, p. 14 (Dulles is misquoted in Braden, *Diplomats and Demagogues*, 301).

30. Dubois, *Castro*, 173; Fulgencio Batista, *Cuba Betrayed* (New York: Vantage Press, 1962), 94n; Braden, *Diplomats*, 300; DDE, *Waging Peace*, 520; Twining OHI, p. 41, JFDOH; Smith, *Fourth Floor*, 12, 20–21, 24, 28, 60, 64–65, 116–30, 171, 225–27, 229 (see also 32–33, 36).

31. One can argue that American losses in Cuba were offset by the success of the

Liberation Army in Guatemala coupled with the fact that the states of the hemisphere voted overwhelmingly to reinforce and multilateralize Monroe's dictum against an alien ideology (the Caracas Declaration, which Nixon regarded as a great help in combatting communism). Still, the events that transpired in Havana during Dulles' tenure at State and immediately thereafter are bound to affect one's estimate of his overall performance.

32. DDE, *Waging Peace*, 493, 495, 497–98; Gallman, *Iraq*, 58, 184–94, 198.

33. Eban, *Autobiography*, 257–58; *Time*, 15 April 1957, p. 39; 22 April 1957, p. 28.

34. Lord Home interview with author; Hayter interview with author; Lucet OHI, p. 8; Woods OHI, p. 18, JFDOH; Ambrose, *EP*, 539. Pineau, writing in 1965, called Suez "an American success" (*Khrouchtchev*, 151). And while General Beaufré may have been right in concluding that French failure at Suez led to a decline in European prestige, along with the fall of the Fourth French Republic and the loss of Algeria, much of this may also have been inevitable or, if not inevitable, then for the best. See Beaufré, *Suez*, 14, 145. Hayter was Britain's ambassador to the Soviet Union at the time.

35. Kilmuir, *Memoirs*, 279; Bowie, *Suez*, 111; Love, *Suez*, 671–72; Sadat, *Autobiography*, 148; *Time*, 25 February 1957, p. 17; 18 March 1957, p. 21; 6 May 1957, pp. 32, 35; 27 May 1957, p. 29; 24 June 1957, p. 33.

36. Bromberger and Bromberger, *Secrets*, 18–19; Heikal, *Cairo Documents*, 115–16, 148; *Time*, 25 February 1957, p. 27; Kissinger, *White House Years*, 360.

37. Lodge Statement, 30 October 1956, in Branyan and Larsen, eds., *Eisenhower*, 2:693; DDE, *Waging Peace*, 288–89; Lukacs, *Cold War*, 144. Mikes argues that the Kremlin opted for massive intervention on 30 October even though elements of the Soviet army continued to leave Hungary on the 31st (as other elements were entering) and even though 30 October was the day that Russia offered to withdraw *all* of its troops from Hungary and announced a new era of noninterference and equality as between socialist regimes. The Russians may have made their liberal move merely for show—to stiffen American resistance to the Anglo-French aerial attack and Israel's lightning drive to capture Soviet arms. Kennett Love sets the date for Russian reentry as 1 November. But Adenauer, in support of Mikes, reports that German intelligence traced Soviet troop reinforcements on their way to Hungary as early as 30 October. See Love, *Suez*, 581; George Mikes, *The Hungarian Revolution* (London: André Deutsch, 1957), 140–41; Adenauer, *Mémoires: 1956–1963*, 67.

38. Seale, *Syria*, 289; *Time*, 22 April 1957, p. 28; 13 May 1957, p. 23; 17 June 1957, p. 23; 24 June 1957, pp. 33–34; 15 July 1957, p. 39; Lord Home interview with author. For Dulles as the originator of the Eisenhower Doctrine, see *Time*, 18 March 1957, p. 20.

39. Dougherty, "Aswan," 44; Heikal, *Cairo Documents*, 138, 146, 149–50, 153; Seale, *Syria*, 316–24; JFD-DDE Conv., 1 October 1957, box 5, WHMS; Wiggins, "Notes," 29 December 1956, box 2, DAP; Heikal, *Sphinx*, 86–87, 101–2. Syria had been the first Arab country to elect a Communist deputy and, by February 1955 it was fairly clear that the Soviets had taken Damascus under their wing. Syria's Communist party, with legal recognition, became the strongest in the Arab world. See Seale, *Syria*, 4; Heikal, *Sphinx*, 86.

40. Heikal, *Sphinx*, 101–2, 109, 114; DDE, *Waging Peace*, 290; Heikal, *Cairo Documents*, 138–40, 150, 153; Sadat, *Autobiography*, 153–54.

41. From 1945 to 1952, American secretaries of state made nineteen trips overseas, but there were no official visits to the Far East. As early as 1949, Dulles told the Senate that the United States would have to foster a NATO equivalent in Asia or risk giving the wrong impression. See JFD Manuscript, 21 April 1956, box 287, JFDP; JFD Buffalo Speech, 27 August 1952, box 107, Smith Papers, PU.

42. Allison OHI, pp. 39–41, JFDOH; DDE, *Waging Peace*, 607–12; Johnson, *Right Hand*, 296–303. As in the case of Cuba, Dulles may not have had his hand firmly on the tiller where Laos was concerned, particularly toward the latter part of the decade (even though he had made it clear in late 1956 and early 1957 that he was adamantly opposed to coalition government). See JFD-Nehru Conv., 16 December 1956, box 1, GCMS; *Time*, 6 May 1957, p. 22.

43. DDE, *Mandate*, 181 (on passing word to Peking through India as well as through the Formosa Straits area and Panmunjom); Keefer, "Eisenhower," 277, 280 (on Nehru's role as an intermediary); Adams, *Firsthand Report*, 48 (atomic missiles were shipped to Okinawa in the spring of 1953); David Rees, *Korea, the Limited War* (Baltimore: Penguin, 1970), 381–82, 417–18; Larson, *Eisenhower*, 86 (Ike told Larson that word had been discreetly passed to the Russians, Chinese, and North Koreans that the use of atomic bombs would not be ruled out if Washington found itself involved in a larger war); JFD Address to Republican Women, 7 April 1954, box 79, JFDP (Red China was threatened with the loss of some of her most vital industrial assets north of the Yalu River); Hughes Cabinet Notes, 5 June 1953, box 1, Diary Notes of Meetings, Hughes Papers, PU (quoting Dulles as saying, "I impressed on Nehru that truce failure would mean bigger war—we've alternatives"); Memo of Conv. between Chiefs of Delegations, Bermuda, 7 December 1953, box 1, SS (Ike ensured that the means of delivering atomic weapons to the Korean battlefield were in place in the Far East theater prior to achieving his armistice and, as Dulles put it, "this became known to the Chinese Communists through their good intelligence sources—in fact we were not unwilling that they should find out"); Bernstein, "Foreign Policy," 20 (on the dikes); Makins to Eden, 21 March 1953, FO 371/103495, PRO; JFD-Wiley-George Tel. Conv., 4 June 1953, box 1, Tel. Convs., EL (JFD told Senator George that he felt his conversations with Nehru had definitely been instrumental in bringing the armistice talks to term). By Rees' account, when Eisenhower began bombing the dikes in early May 1953, his strikes achieved "spectacular tactical success" at a time when armistice talks at Panmunjom "seemed bogged down"—two dams out of five that had been targeted (and out of a total of twenty) were hit, causing the air force to feel that it had found a "possibly decisive target system." See Rees, *Korea*, 381–82. According to James Shepley, Dulles made it clear that it was India's Panakar, rather than Menon, who conveyed the American message to Peking. See Shepley OHI, p. 27, JFDOH.

44. Rees, *Korea*, 408–9, 411–14; Wheeler-Bennett, ed., *Action This Day*, 131; Adenauer, *Memoirs, 1945–53*, 434; NSC Meeting, 4 March 1953, box 4, NSC; Makins to Eden, 7 March 1954 (Representative Mendel Rivers thought Stalin's death might well be "more dangerous to world peace than Stalin's dictatorship"); Makins to Eden, 14 March 1953 (on the shooting down of two Allied aircraft in Germany and the harassing of a third after Stalin's death); Makins to Eden, 21 March 1953 (on the downing of an American weather reconnaissance aircraft off the Siberian coast); Makins to Eden, 18 July 1953 (on Communist renewal of an all-out offensive in Korea and news broadcasts reporting an admission by Pentagon officials that the United

States might have recourse to atomic weapons—the secretary of the army had apparently spoken off-the-record of guns that were capable of firing atomic weapons being available in the battle area); Makins to FO, 3 August 1953, FO 371/103495, PRO (the Korean truce was followed by the shooting down of an American bomber over the Sea of Japan); DDE, *Mandate*, 181; Kennan, *Russia*, 17–20; Maxwell D. Taylor OHI by RDC, 11 May 1960, p. 6, JFDOH.

45. Briggs, *Farewell*, 242–43; *Pravda*, 21 June 1954 (clipping), box 64, Allen Dulles Papers, PU; JFD Speech, 16 February 1955, DSPR #86, box 98, JFDP; NSC Meetings, 31 March, 8 April, 6 May 1953, box 4, NSC; Fall, *Hell*, 294–95; Gurtov, *Vietnam*, 46–47; Tournoux, *Secrets*, 29; Henry Kissinger, "Military Policy and Defense of the Gray Areas," *Foreign Affairs* 33 (April 1955): 425–26. Other critics of the "half-loaf" solution included Senators Taft and Knowland. See Hoopes, *Dulles*, 187.

46. Rees, *Korea*, 420; Lodge, *As It Was*, 33–34; Drummond and Coblentz, *Duel*, 114; JFD Statement, 26 July 1953; DSPR #397, 26 July 1953, boxes 68, 71, JFDP; Koo Diary, 2 September 1954, box 220, WKP. See also FO 371/115178, PRO. North Korea was forced to yield an area of approximately 1500 square miles.

47. Sulzberger, *Giants*, 135; JFD, *War or Peace*, 230; Bissell OHI, p. 11; JFD Far East (Robertson-Radford) OHI, pp. 62–63; Judd OHI, p. 90; Hanes OHI, p. 171; Stump OHI, pp. 10–11, JFDOH; JFD Statement Before House Appropriations Committee, 8 February 1955; JFD Speech, Bangkok, 23 February 1955; JFD Remarks, 6 September 1957, DSPR #500; JFD Manuscript, 21 April 1956, boxes 95, 98, 114, 287, JFDP; JFD to DDE, 1 March 1955, box 4, DH; Packard, *Tokyo*, 33–34; Johnson, *Right Hand*, 227; Alexander to Prime Minister, 20 September 1954, PREM 11/647 (on American reluctance to commit ground forces to SEATO); Starke to Browne, 13 August 1954, PREM 11/651 PRO (on the British origin of SEATO's name and American objection to the fact that it sounded too much like another NATO with large ground forces). Needless to say, any influence that SEATO may have had on the situation in Malaya depended on the success of the brilliant U.K.-Malayan counterinsurgency campaign.

48. Lyndon Baines Johnson, *The Vantage Point* (New York: Holt, Rinehart and Winston, 1971), 356–58; SEATO Council Communiqué, 13 March 1958, box 134, JFDP; JFD to DDE, 14 April 1958; JFD to DDE, 11 March 1958, boxes 7 and 8, DH.

49. SEATO Council Communiqué, 13 March 1958, box 134, JFDP; JFD to DDE, 11 March, 14 April 1958, boxes 7 and 8, DH.

50. Edwin Hooper, Dean C. Allard, and Oscar P. Fitzgerald, *The United States Navy and the Vietnam Conflict* (Washington, D.C.: Department of the Navy, 1976), 359–61; *Sunday Star*, 6 March 1955 (clipping), box 95, JFDP.

51. Hughes, *Ordeal of Power*, 163, 177; Murphy, *Diplomat*, 422–26 (on Trieste); JFD to DDE, 20 July 1954, in Branyan and Larsen, eds., *Eisenhower*, 1:317–18; Dillon to State, 20 September 1953; Luce to State, 17 December 1953, 4 May 1954, FR (1952–54), 5:809, 870, 953–54; Riddleberger OHI, pp. 55–57, 59 (on Cyprus); Barbour OHI, p. 5 (on Trieste), JFDOH; Gordon Home, *Cyprus, Then and Now* (London: J. M. Dent and Sons, 1960), 200–201; R. R. Denktash, *The Cyprus Triangle* (London: George Allen and Unwin, 1982), 21–25; Hal Kosut, ed., *Cyprus, 1946–48* (New York: Facts on File, 1970), 25–26, 53, 71, 79, 133; Ely, *Suez*, 229–33; Minutes on Mallet to FO, 15 March 1954, FO 371/113165, PRO. The Trieste settlement came

on 5 October 1954. Cyprus obtained its independence in 1960, but it did not prove lasting. Several years later, responding to the recrudescence of ethnic warfare, a UN peace-keeping force arrived to police a mile-long buffer zone. Still later, Greek Cypriot attempts to unite the country with Athens caused Turkey to occupy the northern portion of the island and, as of this writing, they are still there.

52. Nixon, *No More Vietnams*, 31; Alphand, *Journal*, 290; *Time*, 4 February 1957, p. 14.

53. JFD, *War or Peace*, 79–81, 142–43, 159; idem, "Long Range Peace Objectives," 18 September 1941, box 20, JFDP; JFD Press Conf., 21 June 1956, 2 July 1957, boxes 101, 114, JFDP; Grubb Manuscript (on Dulles), box 1, DAP; JFD-DDE Conv., 3 December 1956, box 4, WHMS; Alphand, *Journal*, 291.

54. Nixon, *Six Crises*, 241; Krock, *Memoirs*, 299; DDE, *Waging Peace*, 483–84; Berding, *Dulles*, 45, 51; Smith to Merriam, 27 December 1960, in Branyan and Larsen, eds., *Eisenhower*, 2:1340; Woodhouse, *British Foreign Policy*, 25 (the Cominform was disbanded in the mid–1950s); Robert A. Divine, *Blowing on the Wind: The Nuclear Test Ban Debate, 1954–1960* (New York: Oxford University Press, 1978), 318; JFD Press Conf., 13 March 1958, box 128, JFDP; Nixon OHI, p. 42, Russell Papers, UG; Bromage, *Molotov*, 239–40. The Antarctica Treaty, signed in December 1959 by twelve countries and providing for an unlimited right of inspection, was first proposed by the United States in May 1958, and the test ban proposal (which became the basis for the Kennedy treaty of 1963) came in April 1959. The International Atomic Energy Agency grew out of "Atoms for Peace," under which agreements for aid in nuclear power research were signed with dozens of nations. Hundreds of foreign students and doctors were trained in the United States. $500 million worth of uranium "235" was allocated for sale or lease to other governments. Washington also committed itself to the support of an Asian nuclear center in Manila along with a training center in Puerto Rico. See Ambrose, *EP*, 149; Smith to Merriam, 27 December 1960, in Branyan and Larsen, eds., *Eisenhower*, 2:1340. One might add that Soviet-American cultural exchange was nothing new. It began under Truman during the honeymoon years immediately following World War II and was soon discontinued. See Department of State Policy Information Statement, 28 March 1955, FO 371/116665, PRO.

55. Pineau, *Khrouchtchev*, 126 (on Port Arthur); Lukacs, *Cold War*, 343; Young, *Chinese*, 14, 216; Mayers, "Containment," 83; Love, *Suez*, 245 (on Tito and the Balkan Pact); JFD Press Conf., 1 July 1958, box 127, JFDP; JFD to Bruce, 31 August 1954, box 2, GCMS; Couve de Murville, *Politique*, 181 (the first public manifestation of the Sino-Soviet split came in June 1959 when Moscow repudiated its accords with Peking on atomic energy cooperation); Cooper, *Lion's Last Roar*, 91; Churchill to DDE, 21 June 1954, PREM 11/649, PRO; Sulzberger, *Long Row*, 867, 938 (on Tito). Tito's pact with Greece and Turkey related only to attacks that might come from Bulgaria.

56. Allen Dulles Speech to Business Advisory Group, 11 March 1959, box 86, Allen Dulles Papers, PU; JFD, "Our Cause Will Prevail," *Life* 23 (December 1957— clipping); Eleanor Dulles Manuscript, 22 May 1957; JFD Address, 4 December 1958, boxes 113, 115, 127, JFDP; *China Post*, 17 December 1954, p. 1; *Time*, 25 February 1957, p. 21.

57. Love, *Suez*, 236 (on Turkey), 258 (Porkkala); Lukacs, *Cold War*, 127–28 (Porkkala), 132–34, 138–39 ("The Polish October led to important modifications of Com-

munist rule, to a restriction of police intervention, to a wide leeway given to intellectual liberty, to an almost complete lifting of the iron curtain to the West, and most significantly, to the curtailment of Russian military authority within Poland. . . . Cardinal Wyszynski, released from prison, helped Gomulka in his efforts to establish national unity"); JFD Speech, 9 June 1953; Nixon Speech, 9 June 1957, boxes 102, 120, JFDP; Hayter, *Double Life*, 140–41; Henderson Chronology Notes, 19 July 1953, box 6, Henderson Papers, LC; Bromage, *Molotov*, 235–36, 239–40. Spanish base negotiations wound up in 1956 after a long period of stalling.

58. Goodpaster OHI, p. 20; Javits OHI, p. 15, JFDOH. The description of Dulles as "moving" America "away from confrontational politics" was Javits' own. The secretary's aim, according to Goodpaster, was to bring his countrymen "through a period of transition to a new relationship with the Soviet Union."

Select Bibliography

PRIMARY SOURCES

Unpublished Official Records

CANADA
Department of External Affairs, Ottawa, Record Group 25.

GREAT BRITAIN
Public Record Office, Kew, Record Groups CAB 128; FO 371; PREM 11.

UNITED STATES
National Archives, Record Groups, 43, 59, 218.

Published Official Records

FRANCE
Ministère des Affaires Étrangères, *Documents diplomatiques français* (July 1954–)
Paris, 1987– .

UNITED STATES
Congress. Senate Committee on Foreign Relations. *Statements of Secretary of State
John Foster Dulles and Admiral Arthur Radford* (Hearings). 83rd Cong., 2nd
sess., 19 March, 14 April 1954.
Department of State. *Berlin Discussions, January 25–February 18, 1954.* Washing-
ton, D.C., 1954.
———. *Foreign Relations of the United States* (1952–1960). Washington, D.C., 1979–
86.
———. *The Geneva Conference of Heads of Government, 18–23 July 1955.* Wash-
ington, D.C., 1955.

———. *The Geneva Meeting of Foreign Ministers, 27 October–16 November 1955.* Washington, D.C., 1955.

Manuscript Collections

Archives Nationales (Paris)
  Georges Bidault Papers

Bentley Historical Library, Ann Arbor, Michigan
  Arthur H. Vandenberg Papers

Birmingham University Library (England)
  Anthony Eden (Lord Avon) Papers

Bodleian Library, Oxford, England
  R. A. Butler Papers

British Library (British Museum)
  P. V. Emrys Evans Papers

Churchill College, Cambridge, England
  Viscount Chandos (Oliver Lyttelton) Papers

Columbia University
  Oral History Collection
  Wellington Koo Papers

Dartmouth College Library
  Sherman Adams Papers

Eisenhower Library, Abilene, Kansas
  Eleanor Lansing Dulles Papers
  Dwight D. Eisenhower Papers
  James C. Hagerty Diary
  John W. Hanes, Jr. Papers
  C. D. Jackson Papers
  Carl McCardle Papers

Franklin Delano Roosevelt Library, Hyde Park, N.Y.
  Adolf Berle Papers

Harvard University Business School
  Winthrop Aldrich Papers

Historical Commission of the Kuomintang (KMT) at Yangmingshan, ROC
  Chiang Kai-shek Papers

Institute Pierre Mendès-France (Paris)
  Pierre Mendès-France Papers

Library of Congress, Washington, D.C.
  Loy Henderson Papers
  G. Bromley Oxnam Papers

MacArthur Archives and Museum, Norfolk, Virginia
  Douglas MacArthur Papers

Princeton University
  Allen Dulles Papers
  John Foster Dulles Papers
  Emmet Hughes Papers
  George F. Kennan Papers
  Arthur Krock Papers
  Livingston Merchant Papers
  Herman Phleger Papers
  Clarence B. Randall Papers
  Carl Lott Rankin Papers
  Alexander Smith Papers

Public Archives of Canada, Ottawa
  Arnold Danford Patrick Heeney Papers
  Lester D. Pearson Papers
  Louis S. St. Laurent Papers

United States Army Military History Institute, Carlisle Barracks, Pennsylvania
  Matthew B. Ridgway Papers

United States Historical Center, Washington Navy Yard, Washington, D.C.
  Arleigh Burke Papers
  Arthur W. Radford Papers

University of Georgia
  Richard B. Russell Papers

University of Texas, Austin
  Nettie Lee Benson Latin American Collection
  John W. F. Dulles Papers

Western Reserve Historical Society, Cleveland, Ohio
  George M. Humphrey Papers

Periodicals

Antigua (Guatemala)

China Post (Taipei)

Christian Science Monitor

Ecos del Sur (Guatemala)

El Espectator (Guatemala)

La Hora (Guatemala)

El Imparcial (Guatemala)

Life

Nuestro Diario (Guatemala)

Newsweek

New York Herald Tribune

New York Times

Prensa Libre (Guatemala)

Tiempo Nuevo (Guatemala)

Time

Tribuna Popular (Guatemala)

La Pulga (Guatemala)

El Rebelde (Guatemala)

U.S. News and World Report

Collected Works

Berle, Beatrice Bishop, and Travis Beal Jacobs, eds. *Navigating the Rapids, 1918–1971: The Papers of Adolf A. Berle.* New York: Harcourt Brace Jovanovich, 1973.

Branyan, Robert L., and Lawrence H. Larsen, eds. *The Eisenhower Administration, 1953–1961: A Documentary History,* 2 vols. New York: Random House, 1971.

Cohen, Warren I., ed. *New Frontiers in American-East Asian Relations.* New York: Columbia University Press, 1983.

Dilks, David, ed. *The Diaries of Sir Alexander Cadogan.* New York: Putnam's, 1972.

Ferrell, Robert H., ed. *The Diary of James C. Hagerty: Eisenhower in Mid-Course, 1954–1955.* Bloomington: Indiana University Press, 1983.

———. *The Eisenhower Diaries.* New York: Norton, 1981.

Immerman, Richard H., ed. *John Foster Dulles and the Diplomacy of the Cold War,* Princeton: Princeton University Press, 1989.

Kaplan, Lawrence S., Denise Artaud, and Mark Rubin, eds. *Dien Bien Phu and the Crisis of Franco-American Relations, 1954–1955.* Wilmington: Scholarly Resources Press, 1990.

Melanson, Richard A., and David Mayers, eds. *Reevaluating the Eisenhower Presidency in the 1950s.* Urbana: University of Illinois Press, 1987.

Sheenan, Neil, Hendrick Smith, E. W. Kenworthy, and Fox Butterfield, eds. *The Pentagon Papers.* New York: Bantam, 1971.

Van Dusen, Henry P., ed. *The Spiritual Legacy of John Foster Dulles.* Philadelphia: Westminster Press, 1960.

Wheeler-Bennett, Sir John, ed. *Action This Day: Working with Churchill.* New York: St. Martin's, 1968.

Memoirs and Other Works by Contemporaries

Acheson, Dean. "The Illusion of Disengagement." *Foreign Affairs* 36 (April 1958): 371–82.

———. *Present at the Creation.* New York: Norton, 1969.

Adams, Sherman. *Firsthand Report.* New York: Harper, 1961.

Adenauer, Konrad. *Erinnerungen.* 4 vols. Stuttgart: Deutsche Verlags-Anstalt, 1965–68.

———. *Memoirs, 1945–53.* Translated by Beate Rum von Oppen. Chicago: Regnery, 1965.

———. *Mémoires: 1953–1956.* Translated by Geneviève Teissèdre and Georgette Chatenet. Paris: Hachette, 1967.

———. *Mémoires: 1956–1963.* Translated by Jacques Peltier and Pierre Frédèrix. Paris: Hachette, 1969.

Adolfo Rey, Julio. "Revolution and Liberation: A Review of Recent Literature on the Guatemalan Situation." *Hispanic American Historical Review* 38 (May 1958): 239–55.

Aldrich, Winthrop. "The Suez Crisis: A Footnote to History." *Foreign Affairs* 45 (April 1967): 541–52.

Allison, John M. *Ambassador from the Prairie, or, Allison Wonderland.* Boston: Houghton Mifflin, 1973.

Alphand, Hervé. *L'Etonnement d'être: journal, 1939–1973.* Paris: Fayard, 1977.

Arévalo, Juan José. *Anti-Kommunism in Latin America.* Translated by Carleton Beals. New York: L. Stuart, 1963.

———. *Guatemala, la democracia y el imperio.* Montevideo: Marcha, 1960.

———. *The Shark and the Sardines.* Translated by June Cobb and Raúl Osegueda. New York: L. Stuart, 1961.

Batista, Fulgencio. *Cuba Betrayed.* New York: Vantage Press, 1973.

———. *The Growth and Decline of the Cuban Republic.* New York: Devin-Adair, 1964.

Beam, Jacob D. *Multiple Exposure: An American Ambassador's Unique Perspective on East-West Issues.* New York: Norton, 1978.

Beaufré, Andre. *The Suez Expedition.* New York: Praeger, 1969.

Beaulac, Willard L. *A Diplomat Looks at Aid to Latin America.* Carbondale: Southern Illinois Press, 1970.

———. "The Communist Effort in Guatemala." Department of State *Bulletin,* vol. 31, #790 (August 1954): 235–37.

———. *The Fractured Continent.* Palo Alto: The Hoover Institution Press, 1980.

Ben Gurion, David. *Ben Gurion Looks Back: In Talks with Moshe Pearlman.* New York: Simon and Schuster, 1965.

Benson, Ezra Taft. *Cross Fire: The Eight Years with Eisenhower.* Garden City: Doubleday, 1962.

Benton, William. *The Voice of Latin America.* Revised Edition. New York: Harper, 1965.

Berding, Andrew H. *Dulles on Diplomacy.* Princeton: Van Nostrand, 1965.

Bergson, Henri. *The Two Sources of Morality and Religion.* Translated by R. Ashley Audra and Cloudesley Brereton. New York: Holt, 1935.

Bidault, Georges. *D'Une résistance a l'autre.* Paris: Les Presses du Siècle, 1965.

———. *Resistance: The Political Autobiography of Georges Bidault.* Translated by Marianne Sinclair. New York: Praeger, 1967.

Bohlen, Charles E. *The Transformation of American Foreign Policy.* New York: Norton, 1969.

———. *Witness to History, 1929–1969.* New York: Norton, 1973.

Bowie, Robert Richardson. *Shaping the Future: Foreign Policy in an Age of Transition.* New York: Columbia University Press, 1964.

———. *Suez, 1956.* London: Oxford University Press, 1974.

Braden, Spruille. *Diplomats and Demagogues.* New Rochelle: Arlington House, 1971.

Briggs, Ellis. *Farewell to Foggy Bottom.* New York: David McKay and Company, 1964.

Butcher, Harry C. *My Three Years with Eisenhower.* New York: Simon and Schuster, 1946.

Butler, Richard Austen, Baron. *The Art of the Possible: The Memoirs of Lord Butler.* London: Hamish Hamilton, 1971.

Castillo Armas, Carlos. "How Guatemala Got Rid of the Communists." *American Mercury* 80 (January 1955); 137–42.

Chauvel, Jean. *Commentaire: de Berne à Paris, 1952–1962.* Paris: Fayard, 1971.

Colby, William, and Peter Forbath. *Honorable Men: My Life in the CIA.* New York: Simon and Schuster, 1978.

Collins, Joseph Lawton. *Lightning Joe: An Autobiography.* Baton Rouge: Louisiana State University Press, 1979.

———. *War in Peacetime: The History and Lessons of Korea.* New York: Houghton Mifflin, 1969.

Conant, James Bryant. *The Federal Republic of Germany: Our New Ally.* Minneapolis: University of Minnesota Press, 1957.

———. *Germany and Freedom: A Personal Appraisal.* Cambridge: Harvard University Press, 1958.

Couve de Murville, Maurice. *Une politique étrangère, 1958–1969.* Paris: Plon, 1971.

Cutler, Robert. *No Time for Rest.* Boston: Little, Brown, 1966.

Dayan, Major General Moshe. *Diary of the Sinai Campaign.* London: Weidenfeld and Nicolson, 1966.

———. *Story of My Life.* Jerusalem and Tel Aviv: Steimatzky's Agency Ltd., 1976.

Debré, Michael. *Français choisissons l'espoir.* Paris: A. Michel, 1979.

———. *Trois républiques pour une France: Mémoires.* Paris: A. Michel, 1984.

De Gaulle, Charles. *Discours et Messages: Mai 1958—Juillet 1962.* Paris: Plon, 1962.

———. *Memoirs of Hope: Renewal and Endeavor.* New York: Simon and Schuster, 1971.

Dreier, John C. *The Organization of American States and the Hemisphere Crisis.* New York: Harper, 1962.

Dulles, Allen. *The Craft of Intelligence.* New York: Harper, 1963.

Dulles, Edith Foster. "The Story of My Life." Unpublished manuscript, 14 February 1934 (box 397, JFDP).

Dulles, Eleanor Lansing. *Chances of a Lifetime.* Englewood Cliffs: Prentice Hall, 1980.

———. "Footnote to History: A Day in the Life of Senator Joe McCarthy." *World Affairs* 143 (Fall 1980): 156–62.

———. "The Historian as Gossip." *The American Spectator* 11 (June–July 1978): 19–21.

———. *John Foster Dulles: The Last Year.* New York: Harcourt Brace, 1963.

Dulles, John Foster. "As Seen by a Layman." *Religion in National Life* 7 (Winter 1938): 36–44 (box 281, JFDP).

————. "Challenge and Response in United States Policy." *Foreign Affairs* 36 (October 1957): 25–43.

————. "The Christian Citizen in a Changing World." World Council of Churches pamphlet, 22 August 1948 (box 284, JFDP).

————. "The Church and World Affairs." *The Presbyterian Tribune* 63 (October 1947) (box 284, JFDP).

————. "Moral Force in World Affairs." *Presbyterian Life*, 10 April 1948 (box 284, JFDP).

————. "Not War, Not Peace." Address published by the Foreign Policy Association of New York, 17 January 1948.

————. "The Panama Canal Controversy Between Great Britain and the United States." Privately printed pamphlet, 1913.

————. "Peace Without Platitudes." *Fortune* 25 (January 1942): 42–43, 87–88, 90.

————. "Policy for Security and Peace." *Foreign Affairs* 32 (April 1954): 353–64.

————. "A Policy of Boldness." *Life*, 19 May 1952 (box 286, JFDP).

————. *A Righteous Faith for a Just and Durable Peace.* Federal Council of Churches, 1942.

————. "The Road to Peace." *Atlantic Quarterly* 156 (October 1935): 492–99 (box 281, JFDP).

————. "Security in the Pacific." *Foreign Affairs* 30 (January 1952): 175–87.

————. "A Study of the Conditions Which Produce Totalitarian Wars." Privately printed pamphlet, Forrestal Library, Princeton University.

————. "Thoughts on Soviet Foreign Policy and What to Do About It." *Life*, 3 and 10 June 1946 (box 284, JFDP).

————. "The United States and the World of Nations." National Council of Churches pamphlet, 27 February 1940 (date of Dulles' address).

————. *War or Peace.* New York: Macmillan, 1950.

————. *War, Peace, and Change.* New York: Harper, 1939.

————. "What I've Learned About the Russians." *Colliers*, 12 March 1949 (box 285, JFDP).

Eban, Abba Solomon. *Abba Eban: An Autobiography.* New York: Random House, 1977.

Eden, Anthony. *Full Circle: The Memoirs of Anthony Eden.* Boston: Houghton Mifflin, 1960.

Eisenhower, Dwight D. *At Ease.* Garden City: Doubleday, 1967.

————. *Crusade in Europe.* Garden City: Doubleday, 1948.

————. *Letters to Mamie.* Edited by John S. D. Eisenhower. Garden City: Doubleday, 1977.

————. *Mandate for Change, 1953–1956.* Garden City: Doubleday, 1963.

————. *Waging Peace, 1956–1961.* Garden City: Doubleday, 1965.

Eisenhower, John S. D. *Strictly Personal.* Garden City: Doubleday, 1974.

Eisenhower, Milton. *The President is Calling.* Garden City: Doubleday, 1974.

————. *The Wine is Bitter.* Garden City: Doubleday, 1963.

Ely, Paul. *Mémoires: L'Indochine dans la tourmente.* Paris: Plon, 1964.

————. *Mémoires: Suez . . . le 13 Mai.* Paris: Plon, 1969.

Eveland, Wilbur Crane. *Ropes of Sand: America's Failure in the Middle East.* New York: Norton, 1980.

Faure, Edgar. *Prévoir le présent.* Paris: Gallimard, 1966.

————. *Mémoires: Avoir toujours raison c'est un grand tort*. Paris: Plon, 1982.

Foster, John Watson. *Diplomatic Memoirs*. 2 vols. Boston: Houghton Mifflin, 1909.

Gallman, Waldemar J. *Iraq Under General Nuri*. Baltimore: Johns Hopkins University Press, 1964.

Glubb, Lieutenant General Sir John Bagot. *Britain and the Arabs*. London: Hodder and Stoughton, 1959.

————. *A Soldier With the Arabs*. London: Hodder and Stoughton, 1957.

Gromyko, Andrei. *Memoirs*. New York: Doubleday, 1989.

Hayter, Sir William. *A Double Life*. London: Hamilton, 1974.

————. *The Kremlin and the Embassy*. London: Hodder and Stoughton, 1966.

————. *Russia and the World*. London: Secker and Warburg, 1970.

Heeney, Arnold. *The Things That Are Caesar's: Memoirs of a Canadian Public Servant*. Toronto: University of Toronto Press, 1972.

————. "Washington Under Two Presidents: 1953–57; 1959–62." *International Journal* 22 (Summer 1967): 500–511.

Heikal, Mohamed Hassanein. *The Cairo Documents*. Garden City: Doubleday, 1973.

————. *The Sphinx and the Commissar: The Rise and Fall of Soviet Influence in the Middle East*. New York: Harper and Row, 1978.

Hillsman, Roger. *To Move A Nation*. New York: Delta, 1967.

Lord Home of the Hirsel. *Letters to a Grandson*. London: Collins, 1983.

————. *The Way the Wind Blows: An Autobiography*. New York: Quadrangle, 1976.

Hughes, John Emmet. *The Ordeal of Power*. New York: Atheneum, 1963.

Hussein, King of Jordan. *Uneasy Lies the Head*. New York: B. Geis, 1962.

Jackson, Elmore. *Middle East Mission*. New York: Norton, 1983.

Johnson, Lyndon Baines. *The Vantage Point*. New York: Holt, Rinehart and Winston, 1971.

Johnson, U. Alexis. *The Right Hand of Power*. Englewood Cliffs: Prentice Hall, 1984.

Joyaux, Francois. *La Chine et le règlement du premier conflit d'Indochine: Genève, 1954*. Paris: University of Paris Press, 1979.

Kennan, George F. "Disengagement Revisited." *Foreign Affairs* 37 (January 1959): 187–210.

————. *Realities of American Foreign Policy*. Princeton: Princeton University Press, 1954.

————. *Russia, the Atom and the West*. New York: Harper, 1957.

Kennedy, John F. "A Democrat Looks at Foreign Policy." *Foreign Affairs* 36 (October 1957): 44–59.

Khrushchev, Nikita. *Khrushchev Remembers I*. Boston: Little, Brown, 1970.

————. *Khrushchev Remembers: The Last Testament*. Translated by Strobe Talbot. Boston: Little, Brown, 1974.

————. "On Peaceful Coexistence." *Foreign Affairs* 38 (October 1959): 1–18.

Killian, James Rhyne. *Sputnik Scientists and Eisenhower: A Memoir of the First Special Assistant to the President for Science and Technology*. Cambridge: MIT Press, 1977.

Earl of Kilmuir. *Political Adventure: The Memoirs of the Earl of Kilmuir*. London: Weidenfeld and Nicolson, 1964.

Kirkpatrick, Ivone. *The Inner Circle*. London: Macmillan, 1959.

Krock, Arthur. *Memoirs: Sixty Years on the Firing Line*. New York: Funk and Wagnalls, 1968.

Laniel, Joseph. *Le drame Indochinois: De Dien-Bien-Phu au pari de Genève*. Paris: Plon, 1957.

———. *Jours de gloire et jours cruels*. Paris: Presses de la cité, 1971.

Lansing, Robert. *The Big Four and Others of the Peace Conference*. Boston: Houghton Mifflin, 1921.

———. *The Peace Negotiations: A Personal Narrative*. Boston: Houghton Mifflin, 1921.

Larson, Arthur. *Eisenhower: The President Nobody Knew*. New York: Scribner's, 1968.

Lippman, Walter. *The Cold War*. New York: Harper, 1947.

Lloyd, Selwyn. *Suez 1956: A Personal Account*. London: Jonathan Cape, 1978.

Lodge, Henry Cabot, Jr. *As It Was*. New York: Norton, 1976.

———. *The Storm Has Many Eyes*. New York: Norton, 1973.

Macmillan, Harold. *Pointing the Way, 1959–1961*. London: Macmillan, 1972.

———. *Riding the Storm, 1956–1959*. London: Macmillan, 1971.

———. *Tides of Fortune, 1945–1955*. New York: Harper, 1969.

Marroquín Rojas, Clemente. *La derrota de una batalla*. Guatemala City: n.p. (1956?).

Massigli, René. *Une comédie des erreurs, 1943–1956*. Paris: Plon, 1978.

Meir, Golda. *My Life*. New York: Putnam's Sons, 1975.

Mendès-France, Pierre. *Gouverner c'est choisir: Recueils de textes, 1953–1958*. 2 vols. Paris: Julliard, 1953–55.

Menzies, Sir Robert G. *Afternoon Light: Some Memoirs of Men and Events*. New York: Coward-McCann and Geoghegan, 1967.

Monnet, Jean. *Memoirs*. Translated by Richard Mayne. London: Collins, 1978.

Monzón, Elfego. *Diálogos con el Coronel Monzón: historia viva de la Revolución Guatemalteca, 1944–1954*. Edited by Tomas Sierra Roldan. Guatemala City: Editorial San Antonio, 1958.

Lord Moran. *Churchill: Taken From the Diaries of Lord Moran, 1940–1965*. Boston: Houghton Mifflin, 1965.

Morrison, Herbert. *Herbert Morrison: An Autobiography*. London: Odham's Press, 1960.

Murphy, Robert. *Diplomat Among Warriors*. Garden City: Doubleday, 1964.

Nájera Farfán, Mario Efrain. *Cuando el árbol cae . . . (un presidente que murió para vivit)*. Guatemala City: n.p., 1958.

———. *Los estafadores de la democracia*. Buenos Aires: Editorial Glem, 1956.

Navarre, Henri. *Agonie de L'Indochine (1953–1954)*. Paris: Plon, 1956.

Niebuhr, Reinhold. "The Moral World of Foster Dulles." *New Republic* 139 (1 December 1958): 8.

Nixon, Richard M. *Leaders*. New York: Warner, 1982.

———. *Memoirs of Richard Nixon*. New York: Grosset and Dunlap, 1978.

———. *No More Vietnams*. New York: Arbor House, 1985.

———. *Real Peace*. Boston: Little, Brown, 1983.

———. *Six Crises*. Garden City: Doubleday, 1962.

Nutting, Anthony. *I Saw for Myself: The Aftermath of Suez*. Garden City: Doubleday, 1958.

———. *No End of a Lesson: The Story of Suez*. New York: Clarkson N. Potter, 1967.

Osegueda, Raúl. *Operación Guatemala $$OK$$*. Mexico City: América Nueva, 1957.

Pahlavi, Mohammad Reza Shah. *Answer to History*. Translated by Michael Joseph. New York: Stein and Day, 1980.

Pearson, Lester B. *Memoirs*. 2 vols. Edited by John A. Munro and Alex I. Inglis. Toronto: University of Toronto Press, 1973.

Peurifoy, John E. "The Communist Conspiracy in Guatemala." Department of State *Bulletin*, vol. 31, #802 (8 November 1954): 690–97.

Phillips, David Atlee. *The Night Watch*. New York: Atheneum, 1977.

Pineau, Christian. *Nikita Serguéevitch Khrouchtchev*. Paris: Perrin, 1965.

———. *1956/Suez*. Paris: R. Laffont, 1976.

Putzeys Rojas, Guillermo. *Así se hizo la liberación: década de la lucha cívica, 1944–1954*. Guatemala City: Tipografía Nacional, 1976.

Radford, Arthur W. *From Pearl Harbor to Vietnam: The Memoirs of Admiral Arthur W. Radford*. Edited by Stephen Jurika, Jr. Stanford: Stanford University Press, 1980.

Randall, Clarence Belden. *Adventures in Friendship*. Boston: Little, Brown, 1965.

Rankin, Karl Lott. *China Assignment*. Seattle: University of Washington Press, 1964.

Ridgway, Matthew B. *Soldier: The Memoirs of Matthew B. Ridgway*. New York: Harper, 1956.

Roberts, Chalmers. "The Day We Didn't Go To War." *The Reporter* 11 (14 September 1954): 31–35.

———. *First Rough Draft: A Journalist's Journal of Our Times*. New York: Praeger, 1973.

———. "United States Twice Proposed Indochina Air Strike." *Washington Post and Times Herald*, 7 June 1954, pp. 1, 4.

Roosevelt, Kermit. *Countercoup: The Struggle for the Control of Iran*. New York: McGraw Hill, 1979.

Sadat, Anwar. *In Search of Identity: An Autobiography*. New York: Harper Colophon Books, 1978.

Samayoa Chinchilla, Carlos. *El quetzal no es rojo*. Mexico City: Anana Hermanos, 1955.

Sebald, William. *With MacArthur in Japan: A Personal History of the Occupation*. New York: Norton, 1965.

Shen, James C. "The U.S.A.–R.O.C. Defense Treaty, 1954–1979." *Tamkang Journal of American Studies* 1 (Spring 1985): 15–23.

Shepley, James. "How Dulles Averted War." *Life*, 16 January 1956, pp. 70–80.

Shuckburgh, Evelyn. *Descent to Suez: Diaries, 1951–1956*. London: Weidenfeld and Nicolson, 1986.

Sihanouk, Norodom Sihanouk Varman, King of Cambodia. *My War With the CIA: The Memoirs of Prince Norodom Sihanouk*. New York: Pantheon, 1973.

Silva Giron, César Augusto. *La batalla de Gualán*. Guatemala City: Impreso en Imprenta Eros, 1977.

Smith, Earl E. T. *The Fourth Floor: An Account of the Castro Communist Revolution*. New York: Random House, 1962.

Spaak, Paul-Henri. *The Continuing Battle: Memoirs of a European, 1936–1966*. Translated by Henry Fox. London: Weidenfeld and Nicolson, 1971.

Stalin, Joseph. *Problems in Leninism*. New York: International Publishers, 1934.

Sulzberger, Cyrus L. *The Last of the Giants*. New York: Macmillan, 1970.

————. *A Long Row of Candles: Memoirs and Diaries*. New York: Macmillan, 1969.

Taylor, Maxwell. *The Uncertain Trumpet*. New York: Harper, 1960.

Toriello Garrido, Guillermo. *La batalla de Guatemala*. Mexico City: Editorial Cultura, 1955.

Trevelyan, Humphrey. *The Middle East in Revolution*. London: Macmillan, 1970.

————. *Public and Private*. London: Hamilton, 1980.

Truman, Margaret. *Harry S. Truman*. New York: Morrow, 1973.

Walters, Vernon A. *Silent Missions*. Garden City: Doubleday, 1978.

Wriston, Henry. "Young Men and the Foreign Service." *Foreign Affairs* 33 (October 1954): 28–42.

Ydígoras Fuentes, Miguel. *My War With Communism, As Told to Mario Rosenthal*. Englewood Cliffs: Prentice Hall, 1963.

Yoshida, Shigeru. *The Yoshida Memoirs*. London: Heineman, 1961.

Personal Interviews

Bernau, Phyllis (Mrs. William B. Macomber, Jr.), 5 June 1985, New York City.

Dulles, Fr. Avery, S.J., 3 August 1984, Washington, D.C.

Dulles, Eleanor Lansing, 11 September 1984, Washington, D.C.

Dulles, Professor John W. F., 25 July 1985, San Antonio, Texas.

Gómez, Vitalino, 31 December 1987, Chiquimula, Guatemala.

Hayter, Sir William, 21 July 1986, Oxford, England.

Hébert, Brother Robert, 1 January 1988, Esquipulas, Guatemala.

Lord Home of the Hirsel, 23 July 1988, House of Lords, London.

Macomber, William B., Jr., 5 June 1985, New York City.

Pacheco, Virgilio, 1 January 1988, Esquipulas, Guatemala.

Quezada Toruño, Bishop Rodolfo (of Zacapa), 1 January 1988, Esquipulas, Guatemala.

Simon Waguespack, Gerardo, 31 December 1987–1 January 1988, Esquipulas, Guatemala.

SECONDARY WORKS

University Dissertations and Theses

Bly, John J. "The Diplomacy of John Foster Dulles in Negotiating the Japanese Peace Treaty." M. A. Thesis, East Texas State University, 1979.

Dooner, Janice Patricia. "John Foster Dulles, Anti-communism, and the Suez Canal Crisis of 1956–57." Senior Thesis, Princeton University, 1981.

Petersen, John Holger. "The Political Role of University Students in Guatemala, 1944–1969." Ph.D. Dissertation, University of Pittsburgh, 1969.

Reynolds, Edward Bryce. "The Japanese Peace Treaty, A Study in Cold War Diplomacy." M. A. Thesis, Central Missouri State University, 1976.

Articles

Accinelli, Robert. "Eisenhower, Congress, and the 1954–55 Offshore Island Crisis." *Presidential Studies Quarterly* 20 (Spring 1990): 329–48.

Adelman, Kenneth. "Summitry: The Historical Perspective."*Presidential Studies Quarterly* 16 (Summer 1986): 435–41.

Anderson, David L. "Eisenhower, Dienbienphu, and the Origins of United States Military Intervention in Vietnam." *Mid-America* 71 (April–July 1989): 101–17.

———. "J. Lawton Collins, John Foster Dulles, and the Eisenhower Administration's 'Point of No Return' in Vietnam." *Diplomatic History* 12 (Spring 1988): 127–47.

Barnes,Trevor. "The Secret Cold War: The C.I.A. and American Foreign Policy in Europe, 1946–1956." *The Historical Journal* 24 (June 1981): 399–416 (part 1); 25 (September 1982): 649–70 (part 2).

Bernstein, Barton. "Foreign Policy in the Eisenhower Administration." *Foreign Service Journal* 50 (May 1973): 17–20, 29–30, 38.

Bishku, Michael B. "The United States, Lebanon, and the Middle East During 1958." *American-Arab Affairs* (Winter 1989–90): 106–19.

Bodron, Margaret M. "U.S. Intervention in Lebanon—1958." *Military Review* 56 (February 1976): 66–76.

Brands, H. W., Jr. "The Age of Vulnerability: Eisenhower and the National Insecurity State." *American Historical Review* 94 (October 1989): 963–89.

———. "Testing Massive Retaliation: Credibility and Crisis Management in the Taiwan Strait." *International Security* 12 (Spring 1988): 124–51.

Challener, Richard D. "John Foster Dulles: The Princeton Connection." *Princeton University Library Chronicle* 50 (1988–89): 7–29.

Challener, Richard D., and John Fenton. "Which Way America? Dulles Always Knew." *American Heritage* 22 (June 1971): 13, 84–93.

Chang, Gordon H. "To the Nuclear Brink: Eisenhower, Dulles, and the Quemoy-Matsu Crisis." *International Security* 12 (Spring 1988): 96–123.

Dingman, Roger. "The Anglo-American Origins of the Yoshida Letter, 1951–52." In David J. Lu, ed., *Perspectives on Japan's External Relations*, pp. 26–107. Lewisburg: Center for Japanese Studies, Bucknell University, 1982.

———. "Atomic Diplomacy During the Korean War." *International Security* 13 (Winter 1988–89): 50–91.

———. "John Foster Dulles and the Creation of the South-East Asia Treaty Organization in 1954." *International History Review* 11 (August 1989): 457–77.

Dougherty, James E. "The Aswan Decision in Perspective." *Political Science Quarterly* 74 (March 1959): 21–45.

Fish, M. Steven. "After Stalin's Death: The Anglo-American Debate Over a New Cold War." *Diplomatic History* 10 (Fall 1986): 333–55.

Foot, Rosemary J. "Nuclear Coercion and the Ending of the Korean Conflict." *International Security* 13 (Winter 1988/89): 92–112.

Fox, W.T.R. "The Military and United States Foreign Policy." *International Journal* 38 (Winter 1982–83): 39–58.

Gordon, Bernard K. "The Third Indochina Conflict." *Foreign Affairs* 65 (Fall 1986): 66–85.

Gordon, Leonard H. D. "United States Opposition to the Use of Force in the Taiwan Strait, 1954–1962." *Journal of American History* 72 (December 1985): 637–60.

Greenstein, Fred I. "Eisenhower as an Activist President: A Look at New Evidence." *Political Science Quarterly* 94 (Winter 1979–80): 575–99.

Hahn, Peter L. "Containment and Egyptian Nationalism: The Unsuccessful Effort to Establish the Middle East Command, 1950–53." *Diplomatic History* 11 (Winter 1987): 23–40.

Handy, Jim. " 'The Most Precious Fruit of the Revolution': The Guatemalan Agrarian Reform, 1952–54." *Hispanic American Historical Review* 68 (November 1988): 675–705.

Herring, George C., and Richard H. Immerman. "Eisenhower, Dulles, and Dienbienphu: 'The Day We Didn't Go to War' Revisited." *Journal of American History* 71 (September 1984): 343–63.

Holsti, Ole. "The 'Operational Code' Approach to the Study of Political Leaders: John Foster Dulles' Philosophical and Instrumental Beliefs." *Canadian Journal of Political Science* 3 (March 1970): 123–57.

———. "Will the Real Dulles Please Stand Up?" *International Journal* 30 (Winter 1974–75): 34–44.

Hoxie, R. Gordon. "Eisenhower and Presidential Leadership." *Presidential Studies Quarterly* 13 (Fall 1983): 589–612.

Immerman, Richard H. "Diplomatic Dialings: The John Foster Dulles Telephone Transcripts." Society for Historians of American Foreign Relations *Newsletter* 14 (March 1983): 1–15.

———. "Eisenhower and Dulles: Who Made the Decisions?" *Political Psychology* 1 (Autumn 1979): 21–38.

———. "The United States and the Geneva Conference of 1954: A New Look." *Diplomatic History* 14 (Winter 1990): 43–66.

Keefer, Edward C. "President Dwight D. Eisenhower and the End of the Korean War." *Diplomatic History* 10 (Summer 1986): 267–89.

Keim, Albert N. "John Foster Dulles and the Protestant World Order Movement on the Eve of World War II."*Journal of Church and State* 21 (Winter 1979): 73–89.

McMahon, Robert J. "Eisenhower and Third World Nationalism: A Critique of the Revisionists." *Political Science Quarterly* 101 (Fall 1986): 453–73.

———. "United States Cold War Strategy in South Asia: Making a Military Commitment to Pakistan, 1947–1954." *Journal of American History* 75 (December 1988): 812–40.

Marks, Frederick W., III. "The CIA and Castillo Armas in Guatemala, 1954: New Clues to an Old Puzzle." *Diplomatic History* 14 (Winter 1990): 67–86.

———. "John Foster Dulles: The Man and the Myth, With Particular Reference to Taiwan." *Tamkang Journal of American Studies* 6 (Fall 1989): 5–24.

———. "The Real Hawk at Dienbienphu: Dulles or Eisenhower?" *Pacific Historical Review* 59 (August 1990): 297–321.

Mayers, David. "Eisenhower's Containment Policy and the Major Communist Powers, 1953–1956." *International History Review* 5 (February 1983): 59–83.

Meers, Sharon I. "The British Connection: How the United States Covered Its Tracks in the 1954 Coup in Guatemala." *Diplomatic History* 16 (Summer 1992): 409–28.

Metzler, John. "The Hungarian Revolution of 1956 and the United Nations: Taipei's and Peking's Roles." *Issues and Studies* 22 (October 1986): 47–66.

Morgenthau, Hans. "John Foster Dulles." In Norman Graebner, ed., *An Uncertain Tradition: American Secretaries of State in the Twentieth Century*, pp. 289–308. New York: McGraw Hill, 1961.

Mulder, John M. "The Moral World of John Foster Dulles." *Journal of Presbyterian History* 49 (Summer 1971): 157–82.

Nelson, Anna Kasten. "John Foster Dulles and the Bipartisan Congress." *Political Science Quarterly* 102 (Spring 1987): 43–64.

Pemberton, Gregory James. "Australia, the United States, and the Indochina Crisis of 1954." *Diplomatic History* 13 (Winter 1989): 45–66.

Rabe, Stephen G. "The Johnson (Eisenhower?) Doctrine for Latin America." *Diplomatic History* 9 (Winter 1985): 95–100.

Reichard, Gary W. "Divisions and Dissent: Democrats and Foreign Policy, 1952–1956." *Political Science Quarterly* 93 (Spring 1978): 51–72.

———. "Eisenhower as President: The Changing View." *South Atlantic Quarterly* 77 (Summer 1978): 266–81.

Rovere, Richard H. "Eisenhower Revisited—A Political Genius? A Brilliant Man?" *New York Times Magazine*, 7 February 1971, pp. 14, 54, 58–59, 62.

Rubin, Barry. "America and the Egyptian Revolution, 1950–1957." *Political Science Quarterly* 97 (Spring 1982): 73–104.

Rushkoff, Bennett C. "Eisenhower, Dulles and the Quemoy-Matsu Crisis, 1954–55." *Political Science Quarterly* 96 (Fall 1981): 465–80.

Saunders, Richard M. "Military Force in the Foreign Policy of the Eisenhower Presidency." *Political Science Quarterly* 100 (Spring 1985): 97–116.

Schonberger, Howard. "Peacemaking in Asia: The United States, Great Britain, and the Japanese Decision to Recognize Nationalist China, 1951–52." *Diplomatic History* 10 (Winter 1986): 59–73.

Smolansky, O. M. "Moscow and the Suez Crisis, 1956: A Reappraisal." *Political Science Quarterly* 80 (December 1965): 581–605.

Snyder, William P. "Dean Rusk to John Foster Dulles, May–June 1953: The Office, the First 100 Days, and Red China." *Diplomatic History* 7 (Winter 1983): 79–86.

Tananbaum, Duane A. "The Bricker Amendment Controversy: Its Origins and Eisenhower's Role." *Diplomatic History* 9 (Winter 1985): 73–93.

Warner, Geoffrey. "The Anglo-American Special Relationship." *Diplomatic History* 13 (Fall 1989): 479–99.

Zoumaras, Thomas. "Containing Castro: Promoting Homeownership in Peru, 1956–61." *Diplomatic History* 10 (Spring 1986): 161–81.

Books

Alexander, Charles C. *Holding the Line: The Eisenhower Era, 1952–1961*. Bloomington: Indiana University Press, 1976.

Alexander, Robert J. *Biographical Dictionary of Latin American and Caribbean Political Leaders*. New York: Greenwood, 1988.

———. *Rómulo Betancourt and the Transformation of Venezuela*. New Brunswick: Transaction Books, 1982.

Ambrose, Stephen E. *Eisenhower the President*. New York: Simon and Schuster, 1984.

————. *Ike's Spies*. Garden City: Doubleday, 1981.

————. *Nixon: The Education of a Politician*. New York: Simon and Schuster, 1987.

Arend, Anthony Clark. *Pursuing a Just and Durable Peace: John Foster Dulles and International Organization*. New York: Greenwood, 1988.

Aybar de Soto, José M. *Dependency and Intervention: The Case of Guatemala in 1954*. Boulder: Westview Press, 1978.

Bar-Zohar, Michael. *Ben-Gurion*. Translated by Len Ortzen. Englewood Cliffs: Prentice Hall, 1966.

Beal, John Robinson. *John Foster Dulles: A Biography*. New York: Harper, 1957.

Billings-Yun, Melanie. *Decision Against War: Eisenhower and Dien Bien Phu, 1954*. New York: Columbia University Press, 1988.

Bouscaren, Anthony Trawick. *The Last of the Mandarins: Diem of Vietnam*. Pittsburgh: Duquesne University Press, 1965.

Brands, H. W., Jr. *Cold Warriors: Eisenhower's Generation and American Foreign Policy*. New York: Columbia University Press, 1988.

————. *The Specter of Neutralism: The United States and the Emergence of the Third World, 1947–1960*. New York: Oxford University Press, 1989.

Bromage, Bernard. *Molotov: The Story of an Era*. London: P. Owen, 1956.

Bromberger, Merry and Serge. *The Secrets of Suez*. London: Pan Books, Ltd., 1957.

Buckley, William F., Jr., and L. Brent Bozell. *McCarthy and His Enemies*. Chicago: Regnery, 1954.

Calderón Salazar, José. *Letras de Liberación; Homenaje al Horimiento de Liberación Nacional, en el I Anniversario de Aquella Cruzada*. Guatemala: Tipografía Nacional, 1955.

Cardoza y Aragon, Luis, *La Revolución Guatemalteca*. Mexico City: Ediciones Cuadernos Americanos, 1955.

Carlton, David. *Anthony Eden*. London: Allen Lane, 1981.

Charno, Steven M. *Latin American Newspapers in United States Libraries*. Austin: University of Texas, 1968.

Cohen, Warren. *Dean Rusk*. Totowa: Cooper Square Publishers, 1980.

Comfort, Mildred Houghton. *John Foster Dulles: Peacemaker*. Minneapolis: T. S. Denison and Co., 1960.

Comision Permanente del Primero Congreso Contra la Intervencion Sovietica en America Latina. *El libro negro del Comunismo en Guatemala*. Mexico: Secretaria General, 1954.

Cook, Fred J. *The Nightmare Decade*. New York: Random House, 1971.

Cooper, Chester. *The Lion's Last Roar: Suez 1956*. New York: Harper, 1978.

Cronin, Audrey Kurth. *Great Power Politics and the Struggle over Austria, 1945–1955*. Ithaca: Cornell University Press, 1986.

Davis, Kenneth. *Soldier of Democracy: A Biography of Dwight D. Eisenhower*. Garden City: Doubleday, 1945.

De Gaury, Gerald. *Faisal*. New York: Praeger, 1967.

Del Valle Matheu, Jorge. *La verdad sobre el caso de Guatemala*. N.p. (1956?).

Denktash, R. R. *The Cyprus Triangle*. London: George Allen and Unwin, 1982.

Devine, Michael J. *John W. Foster: Politics and Diplomacy in the Imperial Era, 1873–1917*. Columbus: Ohio State University Press, 1981.

Divine, Robert A. *Blowing on the Wind: The Nuclear Test Ban Debate, 1954–1960*. New York: Oxford University Press, 1978.

————. *Eisenhower and the Cold War*. New York: Oxford University Press, 1981.

————. *Foreign Policy and U.S. Presidential Elections, 1952–1960*. New York: New Viewpoints, 1974.

Donovan, Robert J. *Eisenhower, The Inside Story*. New York: Harper, 1956.

Drummond, Roscoe, and Gaston Coblentz. *Duel at the Brink: John Foster Dulles' Command of American Power*. Garden City: Doubleday, 1960.

Dubois, Jules. *Fidel Castro*. Indianapolis: Bobbs Merrill, 1959.

Duroselle, Jean-Baptiste. *Le conflit de Trieste, 1943–1954*. Brussels: Institut de Sociologie de l'Universite libre de Bruxelles, 1966.

Elgey, Georgette. *La République des contradictions, 1951–1954*. Paris: Fayard, 1968.

Engler, Robert. *The Politics of Oil: A Study of Private Power and Democratic Directions*. New York: Macmillan, 1961.

Ewald, William Bragg, Jr. *Eisenhower the President: Crucial Days, 1951–1960*. Englewood Cliffs: Prentice Hall, 1981.

Fall, Bernard B. *Hell in a Very Small Place: The Siege of Dien Bien Phu*. New York: Vantage, 1967. Paperback.

Ferrell, Robert H. *American Diplomacy*. New York: Norton, 1969.

Feuerlicht, Roberta Strauss. *McCarthyism: The Hate That Haunts America*. New York: McGraw Hill, 1972.

Finer, Herman. *Dulles over Suez*. Chicago: Quadrangle, 1964.

Finke, Blythe Foote. *John Foster Dulles: Master of Brinkmanship and Diplomacy*. Charlottesville, N.Y.: SamHar Press, 1971.

Foot, Rosemary. *A Substitute for Victory: The Politics of Peacemaking at the Korean Armistice Talks*. Ithaca: Cornell University Press, 1990.

Gaddis, John L. *The United States and the Origins of the Cold War*. New York: Columbia University Press, 1972.

Galich, Manuel. *Por qué lucha Guatemala, Arévalo y Arbenz: dos hombres contra un imperio*. Buenos Aires: Elmer Editor, 1956.

Gardner, Lloyd C. *Approaching Vietnam: From World War II Through Dienbienphu, 1941–1954*. New York: Norton, 1988.

Geiger, Theodore. *Communism Versus Progress in Guatemala*. Washington, D.C.: National Planning Association, Pamphlet #85, 1953.

Gelber, Lionel. *America in Britain's Place*. New York: Praeger, 1961.

Gerson, Louis L. *John Foster Dulles*. New York: Cooper Square, 1967.

Gibbons, William Conrad. *The United States Government and the Vietnam War: Executive and Legislative Roles and Relations, pt. 1: 1945–60*. Princeton: Princeton University Press, 1986.

Gott, Richard. *Guerrilla Movements in Latin America*. Garden City: Doubleday, 1971.

Goold-Adams, Richard. *The Time of Power: A Reappraisal of John Foster Dulles*. London: Weidenfeld and Nicolson, 1962.

Greenstein, Fred I. *The Hidden-Hand Presidency: Eisenhower as Leader*. New York: Basic Books, 1982.

Griffith, Robert. *The Politics of Fear*. Lexington: University of Kentucky Press, 1970.

Guhin, Michael A. *John Foster Dulles: A Statesman and His Times*. New York: Columbia University Press, 1972.

Gunther, John. *Eisenhower: The Man and the Symbol*. New York: Harper, 1951.

Gurtov, Melvin. *The First Vietnam Crisis: Chinese Communist Strategy and United States Involvement, 1953–1954*. New York: Columbia University Press, 1967.

Halle, Louis J. *The Cold War as History*. New York: Harper, 1967.

Hartness-Kane, Ann. *Revolution and Counterrevolution in Guatemala, 1944–1963: An Annotated Bibliography of Materials in the Benson Latin American Collection*. Austin: University of Texas Press, 1984.

Heller, David, and Deane Heller. *John Foster Dulles: Soldier for Peace*. New York: Harcourt Brace, 1960.

Herring, George C. *America's Longest War*. New York: Wiley, 1979.

Higgins, Marguerite. *Our Vietnam Nightmare*. New York: Harper, 1965.

Home, Gordon. *Cyprus, Then and Now*. London: J. M. Dent and Sons, 1965.

Hooper, Edwin, Dean C. Allard, and Oscar P. Fitzgerald. *The United States Navy and the Vietnam Conflict: The Setting of the Stage to 1959*. Washington, D.C.: Department of the Navy, 1976.

Hoopes, Townsend. *The Devil and John Foster Dulles*. Boston: Little, Brown, 1973.

Horne, Alistair. *Macmillan*. London: Macmillan, 1988–89.

Hurtado Aguílar, Luis Alberto. *Así se gestó la Liberación*. Guatemala City: Secretaría de Divulgación, Cultura y Turismo, 1956.

Immerman, Richard H. *The CIA in Guatemala: The Foreign Policy of Intervention*. Austin: University of Texas Press, 1982.

James, Daniel. *Cuba: The First Satellite in the Americas*. New York: Avon Books, 1961.

———. *Red Design for the Americas: Guatemalan Prelude*. New York: John Day, 1954.

James, Robert Rhodes. *Anthony Eden*. New York: McGraw Hill, 1987.

Jensen, Amy Elizabeth. *Guatemala*. New York: Exposition Press, 1955.

Johnson, Arthur Menzies. *Winthrop W. Aldrich: Lawyer, Banker, Diplomat*. Boston: Harvard Business School, 1968.

Johnson, Paul. *Modern Times*. New York: Harper, 1983.

Kaufman, Burton I. *Trade and Aid: Eisenhower's Foreign Economic Policy, 1953–1961*. Baltimore: Johns Hopkins University Press, 1982.

Kissinger, Henry A. *The Necessity for Choice*. New York: Harper, 1960.

———. *Nuclear Weapons and Foreign Policy*. New York: Harper, 1969. Paperback.

———. *The Troubled Partnership: A Reappraisal of the Atlantic Alliance*. New York: McGraw Hill, 1965.

———. *White House Years*. Boston: Little, Brown, 1979.

Kosut, Hal, ed. *Cyprus, 1946–68*. New York: Facts on File, 1970.

Lacouture, Jean. *Pierre Mendès France*. Paris: Seuil, 1981.

Liang, Chin-tung. *Essays on Sino-American Relations*. Taipei: Lien-Jing Publishing Company, 1982.

Lisagor, Nancy, and Frank Lipsius. *A Law Unto Itself: The Untold Story of Sullivan and Cromwell*. New York: William Morrow, 1988.

Love, Kennett. *Suez: The Twice-Fought War*. New York: McGraw Hill, 1969.

Lukacs, John. *A New History of the Cold War*. Garden City: Doubleday, 1966. Paperback.

Martz, John D. *Communist Infiltration in Guatemala*. New York: Vantage, 1956.

Mayers, David. *Cracking the Monolith: U.S. Policy Against the Sino-Soviet Alliance, 1949–1955*. Baton Rouge: Louisiana State University Press, 1986.

Mélandri, Pierre. *Les Etats-Unis face à l'unification de l'Europe, 1945–1954*. Paris: A. Pedone, 1980.

Melville, Thomas and Marjorie. *Guatemala—Another Vietnam?* New York: Free Press, 1971.

———. *Guatemala: The Politics of Land Ownership*. New York: Free Press, 1971.

Mikes, George. *The Hungarian Revolution*. London: André Deutsch, 1957.

Mosley, Leonard. *Dulles: A Biography of Eleanor, Allen, and John Foster Dulles and Their Family Network*. New York: Dial Press, 1978.

Neff, Donald. *Warriors at Suez: Eisenhower Takes America into the Middle East*. New York: Linden/Simon and Schuster, 1981.

North American Congress on Latin America. *Guatemala*. Edited by Susanne Jones and David Tobin. Berkeley: Waller Press, 1974.

Oshinsky, David M. *A Conspiracy So Immense: The World of Joe McCarthy*. New York: Free Press, 1983.

Packard, George R., III. *Protest in Tokyo: The Security Treaty Crisis of 1960*. Princeton: Princeton University Press, 1960.

Parmet, Herbert, S. *Eisenhower and the American Crusades*. New York: Macmillan, 1972.

Peeters, Paul. *Massive Retaliation: The Policy and Its Critics*. Chicago: Regnery, 1959.

Ponomaryov, B., A. Gromyko, and V. Khvostov. *History of Soviet Foreign Policy, 1945–1970*. Translated by David Skvirsky. Moscow: Progress Publishers, 1974.

Prados, John. *Presidents' Secret Wars: CIA and Pentagon Covert Operations Since World War II*. New York: Morrow, 1986.

———. *The Sky Would Fall: Operation Vulture: The U.S. Bombing Mission in Indochina, 1954*. New York: Dial, 1983.

Pruessen, Ronald W. *John Foster Dulles: The Road to Power*. New York: Free Press, 1982.

Pusey, Merlo J. *Eisenhower the President*. New York: Macmillan, 1956.

Rabe, Stephen G. *Eisenhower and Latin America: The Foreign Policy of Anticommunism*. Chapel Hill: University of North Carolina Press, 1988.

Rabel, Roberto G. *Between East and West: Trieste, the United States, and the Cold War, 1941–1954*. Durham: Duke University Press, 1988.

Randle, Robert F. *Geneva 1954: The Settlement of the Indochinese War*. Princeton: Princeton University Press, 1969.

Rees, David. *Korea, The Limited War*. Baltimore: Penguin, 1970.

Revel, Jean-Francois. *How Democracies Perish*. Garden City: Doubleday, 1984.

Richardson, Elmo. *The Presidency of Dwight D. Eisenhower*. Lawrence: University of Kansas Press, 1979.

Robertson, Terence. *Crisis: The Inside Story of the Suez Conspiracy*. New York: Atheneum, 1965.

Rosenthal, Mario. *Guatemala: The Story of an Emergent Latin American Democracy*. New York: Twayne, 1962.

Roy, Jules. *La bataille de Dien Bien Phu*. Paris: Julliard, 1963.

Ruddy, T. Michael. *The Cautious Diplomat: Charles E. Bohlen and the Soviet Union, 1929–1969*. Kent: Kent State University Press, 1987.

St. John, Robert. *Ben-Gurion: The Biography of an Extraordinary Man*. Garden City: Doubleday, 1959.

Schick, Jack M. *The Berlin Crisis, 1958–1962*. Philadelphia: University of Pennsylvania Press, 1971.

Schlesinger, Stephen, and Stephen Kinzer. *Bitter Fruit: The Untold Story of the American Coup in Guatemala*. Garden City: Doubleday, 1982.

Schneider, Ronald. *Communism in Guatemala: 1944–1954*. New York: Praeger, 1959.

Seale, Patrick. *The Struggle for Syria: A Study of Post-War Arab Politics, 1945–1958*. London: Oxford University Press, 1965.

Selser, Gregorio. *El Guatemalazo: la primera guerra sucia*. Buenos Aires: Ediciones Iguazú, 1961.

Shadegg, Stephen C. *Clare Boothe Luce: A Biography*. New York: Simon and Schuster, 1970.

Short, Anthony. *Origins of the Vietnam War*. London: Longman, 1989.

Smith, Merriman. *A President's Odyssey*. New York: Harper, 1961.

Smith, Richard Norton. *Thomas E. Dewey and His Times*. New York: Simon and Schuster, 1982.

Smith, Wayne S. *The Closest of Enemies: A Personal and Diplomatic History of the Castro Years*. New York: Norton, 1987.

Spector, Ronald H. *Advice and Support: The Early Years of the United States Army in Vietnam*. London: Collier's Macmillan, 1985.

Speier, Hans. *Divided Berlin: The Anatomy of Soviet Blackmail*. New York: Praeger, 1961.

———. *The Soviet Threat to Berlin*. Santa Monica: Rand Corporation, 1960.

Stang, Alan. *The Actor: The True Story of John Foster Dulles, Secretary of State, 1953–1959*. Boston: Western Islands, 1968.

Stassen, Harold, and Marshall Houts. *Eisenhower: Turning the World Toward Peace*. St. Paul: Merrill/Magnus, 1990.

Steele, R.V.P. [Lately, Thomas]. *When Even Angels Slept*. New York: Morrow, 1973.

Stoessinger, John. *Crusaders and Pragmatists*. New York: Norton, 1979.

Thomas, Hugh. *Suez*. New York: Harper, 1966.

Toulouse, Mark G. *The Transformation of John Foster Dulles*. Macon: Mercer University Press, 1985.

Tournoux, J. R. *Secrets d'Etat*. Paris: Plon, 1960.

Tsou, Tang. *The Embroilment Over Quemoy: Mao, Chiang, and Dulles*. Salt Lake City: University of Utah, 1959.

Ulam, Adam. *The Rivals: America and Russia Since World War II*. New York: Viking, 1971.

Urquhart, Brian. *Hammarskjold: The Years of Decision*. New York: Knopf, 1972.

Watson, Robert J. *The Joint Chiefs of Staff and National Policy, 1953–1954*. Washington, D.C.: Historical Division, Joint Chiefs of Staff, 1986.

Welch, Richard E., Jr. *Response to Revolution: The United States and the Cuban Revolution, 1959–1961*. Chapel Hill: University of North Carolina Press, 1985.

Weymar, Paul. *Adenauer, His Authorized Biography*. Translated by Peter de Mendelsohn. New York: Dutton, 1957.

Wise, David, and Thomas B. Ross. *The U-2 Affair*. New York: Random House, 1962.

Woodhouse, C. M. *British Foreign Policy Since the Second World War*. New York: Praeger, 1962.

Yoshitsu, Michael M. *Japan and the San Francisco Peace Settlement*. New York: Columbia University Press, 1983.

Young, Kenneth T. *Negotiating With the Chinese Communists: The United States Experience, 1953–1967*. New York: McGraw Hill, 1968.

Index

Moscow prior to 1953, x, 98;
overseas reputation of, x, 4–7, 66,
68–69, 72, 74, 77, 81, 91, 103, 109,
122, 124, 141–42, 153, 170, 201 n.12;
and "pactomania," 5, 13; personality
of, 3–4; power of, as secretary, 3;
protection of Eisenhower, 40; public
image of, 6–8; rapport with the
American people, 45–46; refusal to
bluff, 135–36; relationship with
Congress, 43–45; relationship with
the press, 40–43; resignation of, 40;
role in shaping the United Nations,
9–10, 98, 128–29; and "rollback"
theory, 12–13, 52, 89, 136; and self-
abnegation, 58–62, 73, 132, 194
n.30; and sense of humor, 24, 41,
226 n.1; setbacks of, 2; and Soviet-
American détente, xi, 103–4, 145,
161–63, 206 n.40, 235 n.58; tact,
face-saving, and restraint, 61, 68, 71–
72, 86–91, 132; and tailoring ends to
means, 51; use of ambiguity and
studied vagueness, 83–84, 131; use of
Congress and allies to influence the
White House, 25–26, 31, 36, 178
n.9; use of the United Nations, 68,
81, 98, 128–29, 149, 162; and verdict
of history, 143–45; views on:
American decadence, 119–20;
arbitration, 129; arms control, 129–
30; atmospherics, 135; balance of
power, 133–34; big stick diplomacy,
130–33; causes of World Wars I and
II, 107, 125, 127, 131, 135; danger of
misunderstanding, 131; decisiveness
in the use of force, 91, 134–35;
executive leadership of public
opinion, 40–46, 80–88, 105, 136–39,
225 n.45; executive prerogative, 136–
37, 139, 226 n.47; foreign aid as an
instrument of peace, 127;
international communism, 75, 77–81,
100; international friendship, 122;
international law, 129–30;
isolationism, 133–34; Korean
armistice, 26; neutralism, 75–77,
134, 136; "New Look" thinking, 27;

preparedness, 131–32, 134;
propaganda, 131; public opinion, 40–
46, 80–88, 105; religion, 4, 24–25,
119–25, 221 nn.16–17; Sino-Soviet
split, 28, 134, 202 n.18; Soviet-
American cultural exchange, 28;
Soviet Union, xii, 24, 78–79, 103–6,
120, 198 n.1; summit conferences,
25–26, 28, 47–50, 52–53, 62, 135,
142; teaching of American history,
219 n.2; trade as a political weapon,
127–28; trade with Communist
nations, 81, 127–28; use of the CIA,
131; value of secrecy, 132–33, 137;
world government, 129; world
opinion, 128, 130; and willingness to
negotiate: with the German
Democratic Republic, 28; with the
People's Republic of China, 28, 78–
81, 123, 137
Dulles' differences with Eisenhower
on: control of the Republic of China's
military forces, 29; defense of
Quemoy, 28, 85–86; demilitarized
European buffer zone, 28; dumping
of American cotton surpluses, 39;
intervention at Dien Bien Phu, 32–
38; intervention: in Lebanon, 28; in
Korea, 26; in Latin America, 150,
230 n.28; McCarthyism, 27;
negotiation with and recognition of
Peking, 28; negotiation with East
German authorities, 28; "New Look"
thinking, 27; "rollback" of
Communism, 89; State Department
personnel, 125; Suez crisis, 26–27,
29–32, 222 n.19; summitry, 25–26;
use of military force, 28
Dumbarton Oaks Conference, 9

Eastern Europe, Dulles' support for, x
East Germany. *See* Germany
Eban, Abba, 124, 126
Ecuador, 149
Eden, Anthony (Lord Avon), 6, 26, 36–
37, 58–62, 65–66, 74, 200 nn.7, 8;
breach of agreement with Dulles, 62,
73, 196 n.38; duplicity of, 62, 73–74,

ABOUT THE AUTHOR

FREDERICK W. MARKS III has taught at Purdue and St. John's Universities. In addition to lecturing widely on the subject of diplomatic history, he has published over a dozen articles in scholarly journals both at home and abroad. He is the author of three previous books: *Independence on Trial: Foreign Affairs and the Making of the Constitution*, *Velvet on Iron: The Diplomacy of Theodore Roosevelt*, and *Wind over Sand: The Diplomacy of Franklin Roosevelt*. Widely traveled, he has tapped archives in France, Germany, Britain, Canada, and Taiwan, not to mention Central and North American repositories in Guatemala and throughout the United States.